Communication Programming for Persons with Severe Handicaps

Communication Programming for Persons with Severe Handicaps
Vocal and Augmentative Strategies

Second Edition of
Communication Programming for the Severely Handicapped:
Vocal and Non-vocal Strategies

Caroline Ramsey Musselwhite, Ed.D., C.C.C.-SPL
Irene Wortham Center
Asheville, North Carolina

and

Karen Waterman St. Louis, M.S., C.C.C.-SPL
Monongalia County Board of Education
Morgantown, West Virginia

A College-Hill Publication
Little, Brown and Company
Boston   Toronto

Cover Artwork by Carol Goossens', Ph.D.

College-Hill Press
A Division of
Little, Brown and Company (Inc.)
34 Beacon Street
Boston, Massachusetts 02108

© 1988 by Little, Brown and Company (Inc.)

Second Printing

Library of Congress Cataloging in Publication Data
Main entry under title:

Musselwhite, Caroline Ramsey.
    Communication programming for persons with severe handicaps: vocal and augmentative strategies / Caroline R. Musselwhite and Karen W. St. Louis. — 2nd ed.
        p.   cm.
    Rev. ed. of: Communication programming for the severely handicapped. c1982.
    "A College-Hill publication."
    Bibliography.
    Includes index.
    1. Communicative disorders.   2. Handicapped — Language.   I. St. Louis, Karen W., 1947–   II. Musselwhite, Caroline Ramsey, 1951– Communication programming for the severely handicapped.   III. Title.
RC423.M76 1988
616.85′5—dc19   CIP 87-36890

ISBN 0-316-59216-1

Printed in the United States of America

Contents

Dedication

This book is dedicated to women who are pursuing their professional goals while juggling families, homes, jobs, continuing education, and other personal responsibilities.

Acknowledgments

As in the initial version, this project began and ended without institutional support! However, the miracle of microcomputers allowed this book to become a reality (Caroline zapped two computers before it was all over!). The revision mushroomed far beyond the cutting and pasting that was originally suggested. Both the field of augmentative and alternative communication, and our own experiences in that field, have greatly expanded since our first book was published in 1982. This revision is an attempt to make this book more closely mirror existing knowledge and to provide more clinical support than in the first edition. We would like to acknowledge and thank the many people who provided the support that made this revision possible.

First, our immediate and extended families again gave a wide range of support. Our children, Matt, Katie, and Melinda, now in elementary and middle school, continued to learn new skills ("Isn't Worldsign new, Mom?") and remained patient of the interruptions of their routines. Our mothers, Julia and Louise, and mother-in-law, Sallie, magically invited our children to visit just days before crucial deadlines. Our fathers, Gene and Ed, were also very supportive.

More than 20 professionals from the United States, Canada, Europe, and Australia filled out a questionnaire regarding changes that enhance the book. In this way, we were able to obtain feedback from university teachers, direct service providers, students, and consumers. All of the suggestions were helpful, especially the ideas from Arlene Kraat.

Numerous professionals also took time to review various sections of the book, including: the staff at the Blissymbolics Communication International (Blissymbolics); Harry Bornstein (Signed English); Faith Carlson (PICSYMS); Gerilee Gustason (Signing Exact English); Roxanne Johnson (Picture Communication Symbols); David Orcutt (Worldsign); Lyle Lloyd (Sigsymbols); Dick Sobsey (Chapter 2); and Louise Kaczmarek (updated resources for Chapter 6).

Blissymbolics used herein are derived from the symbols described in *Semantography,* original copyright C. K. Bliss, 1949, Blissymbolics Communication International (a division of the Easter Seal Communication Institute, exclusive licensee, 1982).

Coworkers and administrative staff at the Irene Wortham Center offered considerable direct and indirect support. The Director, Bruce Fitchett, was most supportive and the following individuals reviewed sections or provided information: Arianne Piercy, Susan Royster, Stacy Small, and Sandy Showalter. The IWC children and their parents also provided inspiration and moral support. Inspiration was also provided by the students at North Elementary School in Morgantown, West Virginia.

Many members of the North Carolina Augmentative Communication Association (population 160+ and growing!) gave specific support in the form of reviewing sections, providing information, and taking over Caroline's newsletter duties, especially Karen Casey, Jean Sandhofer, Ken Whitley, and Gracie Williams.

Several individuals were available by phone each time a trauma occurred, including Barry Romich and Carol Goossens'. On the home front, friends provided the support needed to survive this project. Notable among them are Beverly Bieniek, Mary Lou Hutchinson, Maggie Lauterer, Kathy McGuire, and Phyllis Stiles.

Preface

The closest simile as to how people treat nonspeech people is how they treat pet dogs . . . think about that for a minute. How much difference is there? People take good care of pet dogs. They give them love, food, warm homes, attention when they are not busy. And people don't expect much out of their pet dogs. Just affection and obedience. This is the sad part. People just don't expect much from nonspeech people.

— Personal communication via voice synthesizer,
Rick Creech, *paravocal communicator*

Focus

This book covers both vocal and nonvocal, or augmentative communication strategies, as well as related topics such as preliminary skills and support systems. We chose not to limit the scope of this book strictly to augmentative strategies because we believe strongly that vocal communication, being the primary and normative mode, must always be considered. Including vocal language programming in conjunction with a more in-depth coverage of augmentative programming will, we hope, help keep these communication modes in perspective. Throughout this book we will stress the potential usefulness of augmentative modes to facilitate or supplement vocal language. Observation of proficient augmented communicators has shown that use of multiple modes (e.g., vocalizations, gestures, and symbols) can greatly enhance success of communicative interactions. Therefore, we will stress use of a combination of modes, rather than selection of a single mode. Still, it is important to recognize that for some individuals augmentative modes will serve as an alternative to speech, at least for a portion of their lives.

The emphasis in the various chapters of this book reflects our varied purposes in covering different topics. Chapters in Part I are designed to acquaint the reader with background information and considerations that apply to all modes of communication programming. Therefore, these chapters explore important topics and provide directions and resources for further study. Part II presents an overview of selected vocal language programs and issues in vocal language training. Because of the large number of available programs, this is not intended to be a comprehensive literature review. Its purpose is to provide the reader with a basis for comparing various programs in relation to specific issues about developing communication strategies. Part III receives the greatest emphasis, as information concerning augmentative communication is less available and less integrated. In addition, this part covers a wide variety of communication systems rather than focusing only on specific programs. We think it is important to provide sufficiently detailed descriptions of each system to allow the communication specialist to make informed decisions. The four appendices are designed to supplement, through various types of resources, the information presented in this text.

Overview of Chapters

Chapter 1 presents a decision-process model that can be used for structuring the increasingly detailed decisions that must be made regarding communication programming. Recent theoretical approaches to selecting communication modes for primary emphasis in training are described, and a visual continuum is presented as a means of following a client's progress.

Chapter 2 presents selected issues that relate to general communication programming. These issues, such as methodology selection, the content to be trained, and the context in which the training will take place, are described and then presented in later chapters as they relate to each communication mode (vocal, aided, or unaided).

Chapter 3 presents preliminary training strategies for skills usually considered prerequisites to language training. We have stressed the idea and trend apparent in recent literature that these preliminary skills, such as attending, can often be taught concurrently with communication oriented tasks.

Support services are described in Chapter 4. The need for a team of professionals, including occupational, physical, and speech–language pathologists, along with the classroom personnel and parents, is emphasized in planning and implementing communication programming. Sources of funding at the local, state, and national levels are discussed.

Vocal communication strategies are presented in Chapter 5. Several communication programs are reviewed as they relate to the general issues in communication programming raised in Chapter 2. Both general and prescriptive assessment strategies are presented. Involvement of parents in their child's programming is also discussed.

Chapters 6, 7, 8, and 9 deal with augmentative communication strategies. Chapter 6 describes the functions of augmentative systems and the implications for their use. Factors to consider in exploring the potential applications of aided and unaided modes are briefly discussed. Chapters 7 and 8 deal specifically with unaided and aided modes, respectively. An in-depth description of the communication systems that can be utilized with each of these modes is presented. Chapter 9 introduces the concept of using technology to increase interaction opportunities for people with severe communication impairments.

Populations for Whom This Book is Intended

This book is intended for a wide variety of client populations. These people may be divided into categories according to the basic impairment that influences the communication disorder. Table A lists these categories and indicates client populations that may fall within each. This table does not include all possible client populations. Also, the categories are not mutually exclusive; clients often have more than one impairment contributing to the communication disorder. For example, mental retardation may accompany autism or cerebral palsy. Our opinion is that considering the impairment leading to the communication disorder will often be more helpful than looking at population labels. The wide range of capabilities and limitations existing within a client population requires that decisions ultimately be made on a case-by-case basis.

This book is also intended for a wide range of people involved in working with those with communication handicaps. It is primarily intended for professionals designing and implementing communication programs. The major professional groups involved in these activities are speech–language pathologists and special educators. Physical therapists, occupational therapists, and developmental psychologists may also find this information useful in their overall program planning. Portions of this book could serve as background information for others working with people with communication problems, such as social workers and rehabilitation specialists. Augmented communicators themselves, and their families, should also find portions of the book useful, particulary the appendices.

Terminology

Terminology selection is often a controversial issue. Publications in the field of augmentative communication frequently print articles or letters concerning terminology, especially as it relates to labeling individuals or populations. The International Society for Augmentative and Alternative Communication (ISAAC) is currently working to standardize terminology across a diverse range of professionals and countries. The definitions in Appendix A are from a preliminary set of terms proposed by Lloyd (1985) in an ISAAC publication, and Vanderheiden and Yoder (1986) in an ASHA publication.

There are many terms to choose from in describing people who do not communicate through oral language (e.g., *nonspeaking, nonoral, nonverbal, nonvocal*). Each of these terms focuses on what the individual does *not* do, while the terms *augmented speaker* or *augmented communicator* focus on how the person *does* communicate. Therefore, we have chosen to use these posi-

TABLE A

Categories of Impairment Frequently Accompanied by Severe Communication Disorder

Cognitive Impairment	Sensory Impairment	Neurological Impairment	Emotional Impairment	Structural Impairment	Other
Developmental disabilities	Deafness	Cerebral palsy	Elective mutism	Glossectomy	Autism
Mental retardation	Deaf-blind	Aphasia	Childhood psychosis	Laryngectomy	Attention deficit disorders
		Apraxia			
		Dysarthria			
		Progressive disorders (e.g., myasthenia gravis, multiple sclerosis, amyotropic lateral sclerosis)			
		Dysphonia (e.g., head trauma)			

tive labels. To the extent that labels shape the way we think about people, it is possible that use of positive terms may increase listener expectations.

The term *nonspeaker* will refer to people who are not yet using augmentative strategies. We have selected the term *instructor,* rather than the limiting title of "teacher" or the sterile title of "trainer," to refer to the person providing direct instruction across different environments. It is our view that a variety of professionals and other caregivers will serve as instructors.

We feel strongly that naturally occurring communication opportunities are the most powerful learning situations. However, several factors may reduce the effectiveness of this type of learning:

- Insufficient number of naturally occurring opportunities
- A pattern of passivity or noninteraction on the part of the nonspeaker
- Failure to capitalize on opportunities due to logistic constraints (e.g., instructor occupied by another student).

Therefore, structured opportunities must be planned to supplement situations that occur naturally. A distinction can be made between *naturally structured techniques* — focusing on events that are, or at least appear to be naturally occurring — and *artificially structured techniques* — using rote instruction apart from context. Clearly, naturally structured training events should have the added advantages of context and intention. Musselwhite (1986a) presented numerous examples for adapting tasks from artificially to naturally structured.

As to our opening quote from Rick Creech, it is our hope that this revised edition will help professionals to better serve the needs of augmented speakers so that we may expect more from them, and they may experience greater self-fulfillment in the future. It must also be a goal of professionals and augmentative system users alike to educate the public to recognize the communication capabilities of people with severe handicaps, even though they may not be expressed through traditional modes.

Part I: Preliminary Issues

Chapter 1

The Decision Process

Developing and implementing a communication program for individuals with severe communication impairments involves making a series of decisions. The initial decision to introduce communication augmentation leads to a number of related, increasingly fine decisions. Even if very little time and thought go into the decision process, the resulting communication plan reflects a number of crucial decisions. It is critical that this process be brought to a high level of awareness so that decisions are based on the best information available about the individual, about persons with severe communication impairments generally, and about available augmentative systems and techniques.

Recent authors (Beukelman, Yorkston, & Dowden, 1985; Vanderheiden & Lloyd, 1986) have pointed out that decisions can best be based on the needs of individuals with severe communication impairment. This need-based matching of users with communication systems promotes individualization and ensures that decisions are based on the individual and his or her environment, rather than on preconceived ideas of systems that are "right" for specific populations. The diversity of needs for a single individual dictates that a single technique (for example, pointing to pictures) or aid will not be sufficient for meeting all of the communication needs of that individual. Vanderheiden and Lloyd (1986) speak of the need for a multi-component communication system, which includes "not only provision of the techniques (and any specific symbols and aids needed to implement them), but also the development of the skills in the individual and the teaching of strategies that promote effective use of aids and techniques in varying situations and environments" (p. 52).

The concept of a "multi-component system" is reminiscent of "total communication" for hearing-impaired persons. However, in common usage, the total communication (TC) concept may be inappropriately restricted to only unaided modes. For example, Wilbur (1987) described TC as "loosely, the simultaneous use of signs and speechreading." The introduction of the multi-component system concept allows for the use of a wider variety of techniques, aids, skills, and strategies. For example, Shirley, an adult with severely dysarthric speech might quickly specify the following communication needs, for which a multi-component system would be required: (1) conversing with her adult, literate children; (2) communicating with her pre-reading grandchildren; (3) preparing messages for use in public ordering (restaurants, stores); (4) writing letters to her sister in another town; and (5) sending emergency messages via the telephone. Structured use of a needs assessment form, such as that developed by Beukelman, Yorkston, and Dowden (1985, pp. 209–211, and summarized in Chapter 6 of this book), can assist a communication team in determining the array of needs that a multi-component system must address. Vanderheiden and Lloyd (1986) have developed a checklist of needs that should be met by an overall multi-component communication system. That checklist, reprinted as Figure 1-1, covers general needs, with specific needs further defined for individual users. As the authors stressed, a combination of components will be required to enable a given individual to achieve all of his or her communication goals.

A three-stage decision process model is presented as a framework for making the major decisions. Figure 1-2 illustrates this model, which is referred to throughout this book. The first stage involves determining candidacy for an augmentative communication system. The second stage involves symbol system selection decisions for choosing aided systems (such as Blissymbolics) and unaided systems (such as Signed English). The third stage considers implementation features such as content, access, method of training, and developing environmental support. A previous model (Musselwhite & St. Louis, 1982) included an additional stage for choosing between aided and unaided modes, with the caution that individuals will often need both modes. The present three-stage model reflects current thinking that a multi-component system, including multiple modes, will typically be required. To avoid promoting an either/or approach, the aided/unaided stage has been omitted.

Stage I: Candidacy for an Augmentative System

This stage of the decision process involves determining both who is a candidate for augmentative communication, and when augmentative intervention should begin.

Checklist for Client's System	
Yes	No

A. PROVIDES FULL RANGE OF COMMUNICATIVE FUNCTIONS
— Communication of basic needs
— Conversation
— Writing and messaging
— Drawing
— Computer access (electronic communication, learning, & information systems)

B. COMPATIBLE WITH OTHER ASPECTS OF INDIVIDUAL'S LIFE
— Seating system & *all* other positions
— Mobility
— Environmental controls
— Other devices, teaching approaches, etc., in the environment

C. DOES NOT RESTRICT COMMUNICATION PARTNERS
— Totally obvious yes/no for strangers (from 3-5 feet away) — Promotes face-to-face communication
— Useable with peers/community
— Useable with groups

D. USEABLE IN ALL ENVIRONMENTS AND PHYSICAL POSITIONS
— Always with the person (always working)
— Functions in noisy environments
— Withstands physically hostile environments (sandbox, beach, travel, classroom)

E. DOES NOT RESTRICT TOPIC OR SCOPE OF COMMUNICATION
— Any topic, word, idea can be expressed
— Open vocabulary
— User definable vocabulary

F. EFFECTIVE
— Maximum possible rate (for both Quicktalk & Exacttalk)
— Very quick method for key messages (phatic, emergency, control)
— Yes/no communicable from a distance

— Basic needs communicable from a distance
— Ability to interrupt
— Ability to secure and maintain speaking turn (e.g., override interruptions)
— Ability to control message content (e.g., not be interpreted)
— Ability to overlay emphasis or emotion on top of message
— Low fatigue
— Special superefficient techniques for those close to individuals

G. ALLOWS AND FOSTERS GROWTH
— Appropriate to individual's current skills
— Allows growth in vocabulary, topic, grammar, uses
— New vocabulary, aspects, easily learned

H. ACCEPTABLE AND MOTIVATING TO USER AND OTHERS
— Individual
— Family
— Peers/friends
— Education or employment environment

I. AFFORDABLE
— Purchase
— Maintenance

Figure 1-1

A checklist of the requirements of an overall multi-component communication system. A multi-component system is one of different symbols, techniques (with aids as required), and strategies that are used together to meet an individual's overall needs and constraints. This checklist is useful in evaluating the systems of individual clients. Remember that the questions apply to the overall system of symbols, techniques, and strategies, not just to a single symbol or technique. From Vanderheiden, G., and Lloyd, L. (1986). Communication systems and their components. In S. Blackstone (Ed.), *Augmentative communication: An introduction.* Rockville, MD: American Speech-Language-Hearing Association. Reprinted with permission.

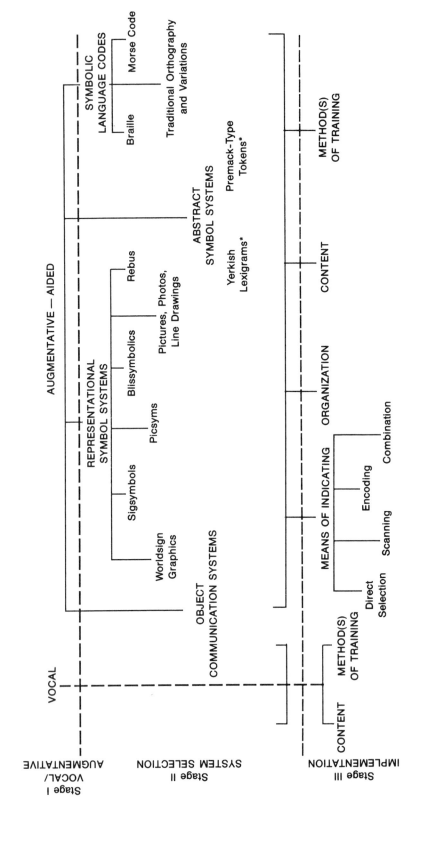

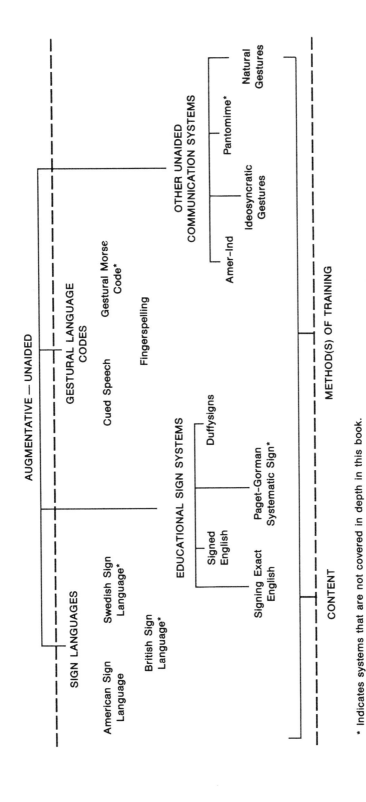

Figure 1-2

The decision process model.

* Indicates systems that are not covered in depth in this book.

The Vocal/Augmentative Continuum

It should be noted that pure examples of either vocal or augmentative modes are rare. For example, an individual with a severe physical disability may receive messages primarily through the vocal mode, but may send messages primarily through an aided mode, such as an electronic device using printed words. Obviously, natural speakers transmit much of their messages through modes other than speech, including facial expressions, gestures, and vocal inflections. Likewise, augmented communicators often support their messages by vocal expressions such as laughter or grunts.

Selecting a communication mode may be viewed as a continuum, with augmented communication at one end and vocal communication at the other, as illustrated:

Augmented ——————————————————————————————— Vocal

The selection decision is then changed from an either/or issue to a question of how much augmentation is provided, to whom, and at what point in time.

It is generally agreed that vocal communication should be given priority, since it is the normative mode of communication. However, even primarily vocal individuals may need to learn augmentative techniques for use when there is a communication breakdown. For example, Chad, a 5-year-old child with severely dysarthric speech, is intelligible to classmates only when the context of his speech is known. Therefore, he uses a topic-setter notebook (see Chapter 8), incorporating Picture Communication Symbols and teacher-drawn symbols, to establish the context when necessary. Such an instance is visualized on the continuum as follows:

However, with some communication partners (e.g., his mother and kindergarten teacher), Chad rarely needs to augment his speech. Communication with those partners would be visualized as follows:

The degree of augmentation needed may also be situation-specific. For example, Juan, an individual who has had a laryngectomy, uses esophageal speech as his primary mode of communication. In some situations (e.g., a noisy environment, when he has a cold, or is very tired), he typically uses augmentation in the form of an electrolarynx. These two situations would be visualized as follows:

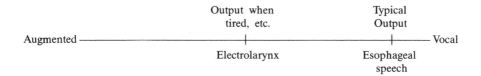

For some persons, it may be desirable, at least initially, to place equal emphasis on vocal and augmentative components. In this case, the word to be communicated by the individual would be spoken simultaneously with a symbol or sign for the word, as a combined input method. The individual may also use simultaneous production, such as signed speech, Cued Speech, or Blissymbols plus speech, for output. For example, Sharon, an adult with dysarthric speech, uses an initial letter cueing board (Beukelman & Yorkston, 1977) to indicate the first letter of each word as it is spoken. This would be represented on the continuum as follows:

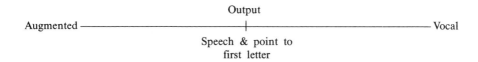

In many cases this equal emphasis would change as the individual progressed, moving toward the vocal end of the continuum. To continue the previous example, Sharon could begin pointing to the first letter for only those words not understood by the listener. A similar approach was taken by Schaeffer (1980) with an unaided system used with four autistic individuals; gradually, signs were faded from both input and output so that they ultimately listened to and produced spoken utterances.

Some individuals will need an initial augmentative emphasis. For example, a child who demonstrates persistent abnormal oral reflexes, such as biting or rooting, may be considered a poor candidate for early development of functional oral speech. An augmentative system such as a Blissymbol board plus natural gestures might serve the child's immediate communication needs, while therapy would focus on inhibiting abnormal reflexes, therefore developing functional speech. Useful vocalizations such as laughter and vocal feedback would also be encouraged. This system can be represented on the continuum as seen below:

Output

Augmented ———————|———————————————————————————— Vocal

Bliss board &
natural gestures &
vocalization

The input to the individual may also emphasize vocal or augmentative approaches. Partners will typically provide input that is primarily vocal, or a combination of vocal and augmentative (e.g., speech plus signs). Primary emphasis on augmentative modes is less common for input than for output, with the exception of some individuals who are deaf or deaf-blind. A variety of possible input modes may be represented on the continuum:

Input	Input	Input	Input
Signs/symbols without speech	Total communication, or cued speech, or speech & symbols	Speech & exaggerated gestures, facial expressions, etc.	Normal speech

Augmented ———×————————————×——————————×————————×——— Vocal

Both input and output can be represented on the same line. Below is an example of a continuum for an individual who receives natural speech as input and produces signs plus vocalizations as output:

Output   Input

Augmented ———|————————————————————————————×——— Vocal

Signs &   Normal
vocalizations   speech

Charting the degree of augmentation of input and output on a continuum can be useful for several reasons. First, and most important, such a visual device can help bring the decision to a higher level of consciousness and possibly result in greater individualization. Second, it helps indicate the individual's present distance from normalization in the form of oral speech. A rule of thumb is that the closer the input and output marks are toward the vocal end of the continuum, the more normalized the individual's communication is. Finally, this visual aid can be used to follow progress across time, with the sketch redrawn each time the degree of augmentation is changed (e.g., when signs are faded from either input or output). Hopefully, this would visually document progress toward the vocal end. Change toward the augmentative end may also be noted across time, especially in individuals with progressive disorders. For example, a person with Parkinson's disease might initially use primarily vocal output, but at a slower rate; gradually it might be necessary to introduce a communication display for establishing context and, finally, to use communication displays as the primary mode, accompanied by vocalization. Dates of charting would be noted as followes:

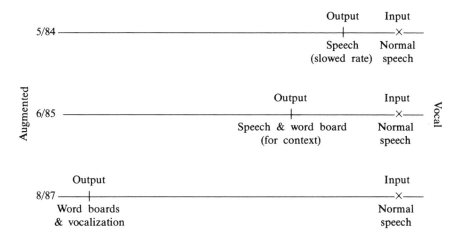

In summary, this continuum emphasizes the normalization part of the vocal/augmentative decision, and provides a method of visualizing that decision.

Making Decisions About Output Mode

Obviously, several factors other than normalization must influence the initial selection decision. Several authors (e.g., Chapman & Miller, 1980; Nietupski & Hamre–Nietupski, 1979; Owens & House, 1984; Shane & Bashir, 1980) have suggested decision models for determining candidacy for an augmentative system. Shane and Bashir (1980) made this process operational by developing a branching decision matrix intended for individuals with congenital disorders. This matrix includes 10 categories (see Figure 1–3). Answers to questions in each of the 10 categories lead to decisions to elect, delay, or reject augmentative communication. The authors discuss each of the categories, and provide several case examples demonstrating use of the decision matrix.

A formalized process such as Shane and Bashir's has several advantages. First, it is comprehensive, structuring the consideration of important factors into 10 clusters. Thus, use of the matrix helps ensure that decisions will not be based on limited information. Second, the matrix process is efficient because branching allows the decision-making team(s) to eliminate some clusters for specific individuals. For example, evidence of oral system persistent reflexes interfering with control of the oral mechanism yields a

LEVEL I COGNITIVE FACTORS

At least Stage V sensori-motor intelligence?
At least 18 months mental age; or ability to recognize at least at photograph level?

YES — Go to II
NO — Delay

LEVEL II ORAL REFLEX FACTOR

Persistent (1) Rooting; (2) Gag; (3) Bite; (4) Suckle/Swallow; or (5) Jaw Extension Reflex?

YES — ELECT — Got to X
NO — Continue to III

LEVEL III LANGUAGE AND MOTOR SPEECH PRODUCTION FACTORS

A. Is there a discrepancy between receptive and expressive skills?

YES — Go to III B
NO — Go to V

B. Is the discrepancy explained predominantly on the basis of a motor speech disorder?

YES — Go to V
NO — Go to III C
UNCERTAIN — Go to IV

C. Is the discrepancy explained predominantly on the basis of an expressive language disorder?

YES — Go to VII
NO — Go to VI
UNCERTAIN — Go to V

LEVEL IV MOTOR SPEECH — SOME CONTRIBUTING FACTORS

Presence of neuromuscular involvement affecting postural tone and/or postural stability?
Presence of parxic disturbance?
Vocal production consists primarily of vowel production?
Vocal production consists primarily of undifferentiated sounds?
History of eating problems? Excessive drooling?

YES — Evidence to support motor speech involvement (Go to V)
NO — Evidence against motor speech involvement (Go to V)

LEVEL V PRODUCTION — SOME CONTRIBUTING FACTORS

Speech unintelligible except to family and immediate friends?
Predominant mode of communication is through pointing, gesture, facial-body affect?
Predominance of single word utterances?
Frustration associated with inability to speak?

YES — (Evidence to ELECT) Go to VII
NO — (Evidence to DELAY or REJECT) Go to VII

LEVEL VI EMOTIONAL FACTORS

A. History of precipitous loss of expressive speech?

YES — Go to VIII
NO — Go to VI B

B. Speaks to selected persons or refuses to speak?

YES — Go to VIII
NO — Go to V

LEVEL VII CHRONOLOGICAL AGE FACTORS

A. Chronological age less than 3 years?

YES — Go to VIII A

B. Chronological age between 3 and 5 years?

YES — Go to VIII A

B. Chronological age greater than 5 years?

YES — Go to VIII A

LEVEL VIII PREVIOUS THERAPY FACTORS

A. Has had previous therapy?

YES — Go to VIII B
NO — Go to IX, weigh evidence (DELAY with Trail Therapy or ELECT) Go to X

B. Previous therapy appropriate?

YES — Go to VIII C
NO — DELAY with Trail Therapy

C. Therapy progress too slow to enable effective communication?

YES — ELECT — Go to X
NO — DELAY — continue therapy

D. Therapy appropriately withheld?

YES — ELECT — Go to X
NO — DELAY with trial therapy

LEVEL IX PREVIOUS THERAPY — SOME CONTRIBUTING FACTORS

Able to imitate (with accuracy) speech sounds or words; gross motor or oral motor movements?

YES — (Evidence to DELAY) Go to VIII
NO — (Evidence to ELECT) Go to VIII

LEVEL X IMPLEMENTATION FACTORS — ENVIRONMENT

Family willing to implement (use, allow to be introduced) Augmentative Communication System recommendation?

YES — IMPLEMENT
NO — COUNSEL

Figure 1-3

The election decision matrix. From Shane, H., and Bashir, A. (1980). Election criteria for the adoption of an augmentative communication system: Preliminary considerations. *Journal of Speech and Hearing Disorders.* Reprinted with permission.

decision to elect an augmentative approach without requiring completion of the entire decision matrix. Third, the matrix process provides documentation of the path taken to arrive at this important decision, an increasingly important matter in this "age of accountability." In addition, the matrix may be helpful in supporting an intuitive clinical decision, and in helping to demonstrate to parents, teachers, administrators, and system users the rationale behind the election decision. Finally, using a decision matrix may help evaluators and instructors avoid employing augmentative systems as a panacea for all new severely speech-impaired individuals.

For some individuals, results of the decision matrix in Stage I will point clearly toward either a vocal or an augmentative output approach. For individuals in the vocal track, content and method of training will be determined next in Stage III of the decision process model. For those in the augmentative track, the next decision will involve selecting augmentative system(s) to be introduced, as discussed in Stage II.

For many persons, however, even this clearly delineated decision matrix may not yield a definitive choice. Failure to clearly "reject" or "elect" an augmentative approach could be due to one of two reasons.

First, the team might be forced to wait because of either the lack of cognitive readiness in the client, or inadequate therapy. Individuals who are very young and/or severely delayed in cognitive development will "fail" Level I of the decision matrix; that is, they will not demonstrate at least Stage 5 sensorimotor intelligence, 18 months mental age, or the ability to recognize at least at the photograph level. However, recent evidence suggests that this delay may be unnecessary. For example, research conducted by Reichle and Yoder (1985) demonstrated that learners at the Stage 4 level of sensorimotor development were able to learn rudimentary communication board skills, including requesting desired items. Wilbur (1987) summarized research demonstrating that in hearing children of deaf parents, the child's first sign may emerge several months before the same child's first spoken words. In addition, a vocabulary of approximately 20 signs (for hearing-impaired children) has been reported at 10 months of age, the age at which a hearing child typically produces the first spoken word. It has been suggested that this earlier emergence and growth of signs can be attributed to greater control of the muscles of the hand, as compared to the oral musculature. Thus, the previously established levels for chronological age (e.g., 18 months to 5 years, depending on the decision rules) or cognitive development (e.g., Stage 5 or 6 sensorimotor development) would appear to be too restrictive. Further, rather than stopping at Level I in Shane and Bashir's decision matrix, we have found it helpful to proceed as far as possible through the matrix in order to identify individuals likely to have severe difficulty in learning to produce speech. McDonald (1980) addressed this issue of the child who is "at risk for speech development," recommending early identification through studying the child's history, developmental lags, and evaluation findings. Most areas of concern noted by McDonald are covered in Shane and Bashir's decision matrix. For example, they noted that "persistent oral reflexes suggest an extremely poor prognosis for oral speech development. We view these factors as an early predictor of failure to develop speech and one which leads to election of an augmentative communication system" (1980).

Clustering of factors included in Level IV of the matrix (such as neuromuscular status, eating skills, and vocal repertoire) may also help identify high-risk individuals. Thus, although the person may not presently have the cognitive skills necessary to use an augmentative system, the team can identify a poor prognosis for early development of speech. The instructor can use this additional evidence in designing a presymbolic program for the individual. For example, focus might be on skills such as head control, tracking, scanning, and motor imitation, if necessary, to prepare the individual for later learning of an augmentative output mode (see Chapter 3 for a review of preliminary skills). This seems to be a safe approach which in no way rules out the eventual development of vocal language. Chapter 5 in this book includes further discussion of prognostic factors related to vocal language development.

There is a second reason why Shane and Bashir's matrix may not yield a definitive decision regarding candidacy. For some individuals, answers to several of the questions within the 10 levels may not be a clear *yes* or *no*. In this case the team may find it difficult to make the final decision. Shane and Bashir note that "intuitive good sense" will be a part of this process. When neither a vocal nor an augmentative mode is clearly "right," the most appropriate choice is likely to be a combination of output modes falling more toward the center of the vocal/augmentative continuum presented earlier.

Another major decision point has been a significant lag in production skills, as compared to comprehension. For example, Chapman and Miller (1980) compared development in four dimensions with chronological age in determining candidacy. They asserted that "when development is equal across these four dimensions — cognitive development, comprehension, production, and communication function (and the speech production mechanism is normal) — the child is not a candidate for nonvocal systems" (p. 183). As Reichle and Karlan (1985) have pointed out, "Several investigations demonstrate the effect of gestures upon the establishment of language comprehension skills among learners with disabilities" (p. 153). Thus, a candidacy selection protocol that requires a major comprehension/production gap or several years of "appropriate" therapy (directed toward oral communication) fails to take into account the facilitative possibilities of augmentative communication. Silverman (1980) reviewed a number of published and unpublished reports to determine the impact of speech of nonvocal output modes. He concluded that "intervention with nonspeech communication modes can be rationalized for the purpose of speech facilitation as well as improving message transmission" (p. 45). Silverman's reports covered both children and adults having a wide variety of diagnoses and using a range of augmentative approaches. This supports facilitative use of an augmentative mode, possibly on a trial-therapy basis, at least for those individuals for whom the election decision is not obvious. Table 1-1 presents a list of advantages and disadvantages of augmentative output modes compared to vocal output. For the individual who could potentially use either mode, this list may assist in deciding which mode should receive primary emphasis.

Making Decisions About Input

The evaluation team must also follow a thorough decision process in determining the appropriate input mode for an individual. The relevant considerations may be quite different from those involved in the decision regarding the output mode. Sensory deficiencies, especially those involving vision and hearing, assume greater importance, while motor impairments, such as cerebral palsy, will be of less concern. Cognitive and emotional status of the individual should also be considered. Numerous researchers have been successful in using various augmentative systems as primary or supplemental input modes, as discussed in Chapters 7 and 8. As illustrated earlier, input can extend on the augmentative/vocal continuum from natural speech to a combination (such as speech plus sign or symbols) to primarily augmented input (such as sign or symbols alone).

Current decision models for determining candidacy are intended for use with persons having developmental impairments. Guidelines are less clear concerning adults with acquired impairments (e.g., aphasia, amyotrophic lateral sclerosis). Since such an individual has had access to communication in the form of speech, issues of normalization will often be more crucial. While some of the factors in existing guidelines (e.g., Levels III, IV, and V in Shane and Bashir's matrix) may be helpful, overall sets of decision rules are not available. Development of clear and useable guidelines for decision-making with persons having acquired impairments is a major need in the area of augmentative communication.

To summarize, the either/or stance that has traditionally been assumed in determining candidacy appears to be unnecessary and inappropriate. Rather than deciding who can use vocal communication and who can not, the focus should be on identifying candidates for whom communication augmentation may help, and determining the functions (e.g., facilitation, interim system) and degree of augmentation needed. Thus, given that augmentative systems have not been found inherently harmful, and may have

TABLE 1-1
Advantages and Disadvantages of Augmentative Communication Systems as Compared to Vocal Communication Systems

Disadvantages

1. Augmentative systems are not typical systems of communication and may not be as readily reinforced by natural speakers.
2. Persons in the environment may be hesitant to accept use of an augmentative system, as they may feel it represents giving up on vocal language.
3. Persons in the environment may be unable to receive the message (e.g., may not understand the sign or symbol system).
4. Persons in the environment may not be willing to take the time necessary to receive messages or converse.
5. Augmentative systems may be more expensive due to the need to buy equipment and/or to train persons to teach and receive messages.

Advantages

1. Augmentative systems may provide two simultaneous inputs (typically auditory and visual).
2. Augmentative systems have not been found to inhibit development of vocal language; studies suggest that they may enhance speech and/or language development (see Silverman, 1980).
3. Augmentative systems may serve various purposes relative to vocal language:
   a. Interim communication system
   b. Speech and/or language facilitation
   c. Supplement to vocal language
   d. Primary communication system
4. Augmentative systems are typically more static; thus entries are available for a longer period of time, or can be slowed more than vocal language, with less distortion.
5. Augmentative systems are often more amenable to physical prompting (shaping sign configuration, pointing to symbols).

some preventative value regarding any future communication handicap (Reichle & Karlan, 1985), the election decision can be based on individual need.

Stage II: Selection of Augmentative System(s)

This stage includes guidelines for matching optimal augmentative communication system(s) to potential users. As recent authors (e.g., Kraat, 1985a; Reichle & Karlan, 1985) have stressed, communication must be multi-modal. This includes both verbal modes of communication (whether represented by speech, unaided, or aided symbols) and nonverbal modes (such as pointing and use of facial expressions). Thus, the optimal match for an individual will typically require intervention in several communication modes. The case studies by Beukelman, Yorkston, and Dowden (1985) are particularly useful in documenting selection of multi-modal, multi-component communication systems in attempts to meet the range of needs for an individual with severe communication impairment. Thus, in the interest of avoiding a Procrustean Bed approach in which all travelers are forced to fit a single size of bed ("Too short?? We can stretch her . . . . Too tall? Just lop her head off!!"), a needs approach should be used, with selection of the modes and systems optimal for achieving each need.

Traditionally, a diagnosis of severe cognitive delay has led to introduction of unaided systems, while a diagnosis of severe physical impairment dictated use of an aided symbol system (Kiernan, Reid, & Jones, 1979). These assumptions are now being challenged. For example, recall that this revised Decision Process Model has omitted the aided/unaided decision, with the rationale that it may be inappropriate as an early decision, or as an either/or choice. Increasingly, individuals with severe cognitive delay are being introduced to aided communication systems (e.g., Mirenda, 1985; Reichle & Yoder, 1985), and individuals with severe physical impairment are being taught at least a limited repertoire of functional gestures (e.g., Beukelman, Yorkston, & Dowden, 1985). Thus, the choice of an augmentative system based merely on etiology, or degree of impairment, will be inappropriate for many individuals.

If logistics require that a single primary communication system be selected, the potential choice can be reduced to two systems that can be systematically sampled. Reichle and Karlan (1985) observed that families are often open to the idea of sampling systems from aided and unaided modalities, since that allows the eventual decision to be an objective one, based on the performance of the individual system user. They cautioned that the instructors must ensure that "all instructional activities implemented during modality sampling have educational value, even if the learner eventually does not use the communicative mode with which the task was associated" (p. 154). Previous authors (e.g., Alpert, 1980) have suggested sequential sampling of augmentative systems to determine which of two systems is optimal for an individual. Indicators that can be used include (1) learning nonspeech responses taught for each augmentative system; (2) percentage of correct vocalizations produced during each training condition; (3) performance on probes (probes of production, comprehension, association, and cross-modal transfer); (4) measuring trials to criteria to determine efficiency of learning; (5) generalization to untrained items (e.g., Blissymbolics, with its use of strategies and basic elements, may reduce training time through learner generalization across symbols); (6) spontaneous use of entries in a system; and (7) reaction of others in the environment, as noted formally (e.g., number of times others attempt to use each system) or informally (through soliciting opinions). As Kiernan (1981) observed, less time may be required for decision-making when systems under comparison are implemented during separate but contiguous activities (rather than using a sequential training approach).

Another important general consideration with regard to system selection is the issue of building toward systems that have advantages such as efficiency and support of educational goals. For example, while the notion of a fixed hierarchy of pictorial systems in terms of complexity may be less clear than initially thought (Mirenda, 1985), some pictorial systems support efficiency of display preparation and communication. Thus, object displays or minimally symbolic pictures or photos, while an appropriate starting point for some individuals, are limiting relative to the logistics of preparing displays (meaning that change in displays may not keep pace with change in needs and concept development) and communicating a wide variety of functions. Several aided symbol systems can offer support to communication efficiency and learning. For example, Blissymbolics enhances efficiency and facilitates concept development through symbol strategies. Van Tatenhove (1986a) summarized the goals of system selection and transition through the aided system hierarchy as follows:

> Rationale for selection of a primary system and transition through systems is based on the communicative and cognitive potential of the student, his or her ability to use the system as it was intended, and the final communication goal. The question, "Am I using this system simply because Johnny can learn it or because it will increase his communication and interactive potential?" must be asked. (p. 29)

Stage III: Implementation of a Multi-component Communication System

A wide range of factors must be considered in implementation. Some of these factors (content, training methodology) are relevant to all communication symbol systems, while others (e.g., means of indicating) are specific to individual systems. In Chapter 8, Tables 8–6 and 8–7 present a framework for intervention planning in augmentative communication, developed by Kraat (1986). This framework points out the many areas that must be considered in developing a comprehensive intervention program for individuals with severe communication impairment. Specific factors within this framework will be considered in the remaining chapters.

Summary

This chapter has presented a process for making the decisions necessary in developing a communication plan for an individual with severe communication impairment. We stress that often an "either/or" choice will not be evident. Rather, a careful decision-making process may delineate the diversity of needs that must be met using a multi-component system and may identify primary goals for intervention. This decision process is not a one-time undertaking. The individual's needs and abilities must be frequently reassessed in order to achieve the optimal implementation of a multi-component system.

Chapter 2

Issues in Communication Training

Sometimes it is better to relearn information that is old but important than to learn information that is new but trivial.

— Ben Johnson

Several issues appear with considerable frequency in literature related to communication training with persons having severe communication impairment. These issues will be briefly introduced in this chapter, then related to specific types of communication modes (vocal, aided, unaided) in the appropriate chapters. These issues are important regardless of whether a vocal or an augmented communication mode is selected.

Models of Language Acquisition and Training

The two models used most often in language intervention with severely handicapped learners are the developmental and the remedial. The developmental model follows the sequence of normal language acquisition. Many authors (e.g., Bloom & Lahey, 1978; Johnson-Martin, Jens, & Attermeier, 1985; Miller, 1977) have accepted the developmental model in planning language intervention, thus assuming that the acquisition process should follow the same sequence for children with severe disabilities as for normally developing children. A number of sources of developmental data are available. Trantham and Pedersen (1976) collected data on eight children who acquired language normally. Bloom and Lahey (1978) presented plans for language development goals based on normal development. Cohen, Gross, and Haring (1976) compiled sets of "developmental pinpoints," or measurable behavior, in a variety of areas, including receptive and expressive language. Their pinpoints were drawn from studies of large numbers of normally developing subjects, screening batteries, and developmental checklists, covering ages from 0.1 months to 72 months. Ruder and Smith (1974) summarized the justification for using a developmental model in saying, "It might be that little is to be lost and perhaps a great deal is to be gained from structuring training programs on such developmental data" (p. 566).

It seems, however, that the primary reason for using data from normally developing children may be the availability of that information, compared to the lack of extensive and accurate information on language acquisition in various populations of severely handicapped persons. Bloom and Lahey (1978) noted that a typical objection to the developmental model is that this approach merely provides the learner with more of the same experience, while something different from the normal model may be required. They contend, moreover, that children with disordered or delayed language do not continue to receive simple language models. For individuals with severe disabilities, the language models may never have been "normal."

The remedial model follows sequences other than those of normal development, with a rationale that the normal sequence is not appropriate for these populations, or is no longer appropriate due to the individual's age (Hogg, 1975; Switsky, Rotator, Miller, Freagon, 1979). That is, the adolescent with a measured mental age of 18 months is unlikely to parallel the normal 18-month-old infant in terms of knowledge and abilities. The older learner may demonstrate behavior that is considerably below or above that of a normal 18-month-old infant.

Although the remedial model is typically discussed as a single entity, several types of remedial sequences exist. Remedial sequences may be data-based, using language acquisition data from children with learning problems similar to those of the target population, just as the developmental model uses normal acquisition data. The assumption in this case is that persons with the same problem tend to learn language in the same way.

Remedial sequences may also be instructor-devised, based on "adult intuition" and/or analysis of the learning environment. One example of an intuitive approach is an additive sequence in which the language segments taught increase in length as the learner progresses. An example of learning environment analysis is a task analysis of the target of generalized requesting, with training on all necessary skills, beginning with the first step not already in the individual's repertoire and adding steps until the goal is met. Both of these instructor-devised sequences share the assumption that effective steps can be programmed more logically than the "normal" sequences, and can yield more efficient learning. Bloom and Lahey (1978) cautioned that intervention programs using a remedial model based on adult intuition may result in "cliches." For example, such programs often teach labeling of objects first, followed by word combination. However, developmental data show that, even at the single-word level, children talk about relations between objects and events rather than merely labeling objects.

Reichle and Keogh (1985) have asserted that most current programs represent a "blending" of remedial and developmental approaches. For example, a program may make use of developmental data as a place to start, then modify the sequence based on information from learners with similar disabilities, or fill in gaps with intuitive or task-analyzed steps.

The use of ecologic⁻¹ inventories is another approach to developing remedial sequences. In this approach, the instructor identifies environments (school, home), subenvironments (classroom, computer lab), activities (group discussion, in-seat work), and functions (information-sharing, joking). Analysis is then made of behavior by nondisabled persons. This approach to developing instructional sequences is described in *Community-Based Curriculum* (Falvey, 1986).

Methodology of Language Intervention

Methodology in language intervention has undergone considerable change in the past decade. Riechle and Keogh (1985) have divided methodology into two general categories.

• *Less Intrusive Strategies:* These techniques include the systematic use of naturally occurring discriminative stimuli, varied adult prompts, and functional reinforcers. This is typically termed *incidental teaching,* with incidental teaching episodes initiated by the child (Hart & Risley, 1982). Hart (1985) identified four steps in the incidental teaching process, which can be described using an example: (1) When the child initiates (Nikki looks at the merry-go-round and grunts), the adult focuses full attention on the child, creating joint focus on the child-selected topic; (2) The instructor asks for a language elaboration ("Do you want to ride?"); (3) If the child does not provide the appropriate elaboration, and the instructor feels that he or she is able, a prompt is given for an appropriate response ("Do you want to ride?" as adult signs RIDE; (4) The instructor confirms the correctness of the child's language ("Right. You want to RIDE."), then provides reinforcement in the form of a natural consequence (a ride on the merry-go-round). Some modifications of this approach may be needed for learners with severe disabilities. For example, the Expectant Time Delay Strategy

(Snell & Gast, 1981) can be combined with incidental teaching. In this strategy, the controlling stimulus (a prompt) is paired with new stimuli (task request and materials) to which control is to be transferred. Thus, in the previous example, the instructor could cue Nikki that an elaborated response (a sign, instead of a grunt) is expected by techniques such as gesturing to the merry-go-round, holding his or her hands in a preparatory position for signing, and looking expectant. A predetermined delay time (for example, 15 seconds) is then presented, followed by prompting at the appropriate level if Nikki does not respond. At present, it is unclear of the role of natural prompts in incidental teaching, and of adaptations needed for persons with severe handicaps.

• *More Intrusive Strategies:* In these strategies, a predetermined schedule of instructor-instigated training opportunities is presented. Some programs (e.g., Guess, Sailor & Baer, 1978) are structured to the extent that verbal instructions, training environments, and training materials are clearly specified. Reichle and Keogh (1985) noted that a frequent criticism of highly intrusive programs is that generalization may not be promoted. In addition, such programs train learners to respond to trainer-initiated communication but fail to promote self-initiation.

As with many other issues, intervention strategy need not be an either/or choice. Reichle and Keogh (1985) observed that a combination of structured and less intrusive training formats may yield the most efficient and generalized results. One example is the use of an interrupted behavior chain (Goetz, Gee, & Sailor, 1985; Hunt, Goetz, Alwell, & Sailor, 1986). In this strategy, instruction occurs directly in the midst of ongoing, active behavior sequence (e.g., Helge is playing the *Catch the Cow*[1] computer program). The instructor interrupts the action at a predetermined step by removing necessary materials or physically stopping the student (e.g., moves the switch out of reach), then presents instructional procedures identical to those used in traditional sequence training (e.g., "What do you need?"). For this approach, reinforcement would consist of maintenance of an ongoing event (e.g., Helge gets the opportunity to complete the computer game), rather than gaining access to the event (e.g., indicating the symbol for "switch" before initiating the game). One suggestion is that continuation of an ongoing event is a more powerful motivational consequence than beginning the event, or engaging in massed trials (numerous trials of the same learning event). Clearly, issues of normalization will need to be considered when selecting procedures for interrupting the behavior chain.

Another issue in methodology involves the way in which the curriculum is organized. There has been a progression away from a strong separation of

---

[1] *Catch the Cow,* by Jana Birch, 2346 Wales Drive, Cardiff, CA 92007.

content areas (communication, mobility, self-help) toward an integration of skill training in terms of time and space. As Guess and Helmstetter (1986) pointed out, this training of isolated skills was conducted to allow concentration on small, task-analyzed steps within a particular skill area, and to accomodate massed-trial training. This individual skill instruction has gradually been abandoned in favor of concurrent training across content areas, with distributed rather than massed training trials. The current skill-cluster approach is termed the *Individualized Curriculum Sequencing* (ICS) model (Holvoet, Guess, Mulligan, & Brown, 1980). Guess and Helmstetter (1986) and Sailor and Guess (1983) have summarized the status of empirical support for this model, and have carefully described programmatic considerations in applying the model. This training model is felt to be consistent with the current trend toward functional skill training with methods that are similar to occurrences in the natural environment.

Content and Context

Two primary areas of concern in developing a communication program for individuals with severe disabilities are the content and context of that program. Holland (1975) defined *content* as the words focused on in therapy. Current thinking would provide a much broader definition, with the present focus on the pragmatic aspects of interactions between a "speaker" and a "listener" (Reichle & Keogh, 1986). For example, Keogh and Reichle (1985) have suggested that an appropriate early content would be teaching the listener to discriminate between the requesting, describing, and rejecting functions of communication. Such an approach considers the function of communication, with the specific content (e.g., the meaning "want") and form (e.g., expression through signing) being highly flexible, as depending on the needs of the communication partners, and the situation.

With the potential functions of communication clearly in mind, it may be necessary to select an initial core lexicon; a small, functional vocabulary that can be adapted to the needs of the individual (Holland, 1975; Lahey & Bloom, 1977). This may be particularly important for a user of an aided communication system, such as a symbol display. Table 2-1 lists considerations that should be made in selecting a core lexicon. Considerations specific to the various communication modes will be presented in appropriate chapters.

Ability to expand content, in terms of the specific vocabulary and the possible communication functions, will be an important consideration in selecting communication systems. Thus, a system that limits advanced functions, such as humor or sarcasm, or allows a restricted vocabulary set, will not meet the needs of many augmented communicators. These issues will be further discussed in appropriate chapters.

TABLE 2-1
Considerations in Selecting a Core Lexicon

Criteria	Exemplar	Non-Exemplar
Are of high interest to the individual	TAKE ME	TOILET
Have potential for frequent use	MORE	SHOE
Denote a range of semantic notions or pragmatic functions	SEE	WITH
Reflect "here and now" for ease of learning	BOOK	THINK
Potential for later multiword use	GET	THROW
Ease of production or interpretation*		

Adapted from Musselwhite and St. Louis, 1982; Goossens' and Crain, 1985b.
* Varies with speech, signs, symbols.

Holland (1975) defined *context* as the interrelated environmental conditions in which therapy exists. Warren (1985) asserted that "communicative context is more than the who, what, when, and where of a given situation" (p. 200). Thus, current thinking would extend the notion of context to all conditions in which communication exists, avoiding the separation between "therapy" and "real life." Increasingly, authors have stressed that communication intervention must be a part of the total environment, rather than being concentrated into therapy sessions with one instructor and one client (e.g., Hamre-Nietupski, Stoll, Holtz, Fullerton, Ryan-Flottum, & Brown, 1977; Kopchick & Lloyd, 1976; Reichle & Keogh, 1986). This focus on an environmental context also supports a greater role for parents as intervention agents (MacDonald, 1985; Manolson, 1984; Schumaker & Sherman, 1978).

Another issue with regard to context involves the grouping of learners. Traditionally, training has taken place in one-to-one instruction, with rigid training goals and materials, removed from normal context. Favell, Favell, and McGimsey (1978) reviewed two years of literature in journals relating to severely retarded individuals, finding that approximately 90 percent of the articles dealt with training carried out on a one-to-one basis. Given typical staff–student ratios, this arrangement is not realistic as the only mode of service delivery. Reid and Favell (1984) discussed the trend toward increased use of group instructional sessions through a critical review of the literature. They concluded that useful skills can be taught to individuals with severe disabilities using a group format. However, they noted unclear findings on factors such as the specific type of group intervention appropriate for various skill learning tasks, the range of skills that can be effectively taught through group instruction, and the instructional techniques that can enhance group training. Once again, a dichotomy should not be assumed; group instruction should not be deemed "more natural" and one-to-one instruction "unnatural." Hart (1985) pointed out that nearly all the literature on mother–infant interaction has focused on its one-to-one nature. Thus, a variety of instructional arrangements should be programmed into each day:

• *Free Activity Periods:* If integrated into the day, these allow the instructor to move from learner to learner engaging in brief one-to-one teaching episodes (Hart, 1985). Example: students are positioned with access to a variety of materials after lunch; the instructor helps Joanna practice activating her buzzer to get Tarshe's attention, after which Joanna uses her switch to send a finger puppet to Tarshe via a dump truck; the instructor then goes to Tarshe and helps her play with the finger puppet.

• *Small-Group Instruction:* Training is provided simultaneously for all students. Example: the signed song "Open Box" (Musselwhite 1985) is taught to the group, focusing on several functional signs, with the song related to an object identification task.

• *Clustered Individualized Instruction:* A group of four students watches while the instructor engages in individualized interactions with each student in turn (Brown, Nietupski, & Hamre-Nietupski, 1976). Example: each student is assisted in using symbols to make guesses about an upcoming event, with others providing feedback on each guess.

• *Adaptive Student Interactions:* Students engage in appropriate interchanges without direct instructor involvement, although instructors may suggest interactions or set up situations to increase the probability of interactions. Example: Set up two students with switches at the computer, and boot a switch program such as *Interactive Games.*[2]

Generalization

Guess, Sailor, and Baer (1977) asserted that "the issue of generalization is certainly the most current and pressing problem re: language training" (p. 363). A decade later this issue is still paramount. It is interesting to note that Warren and Rogers-Warren (1985) devoted approximately one-third of their book on functional language to this topic. Stremel-Campbell and Campbell (1985) have underlined the importance of generalization by stating that it is "an interactive process between the student, his language and communication skills, and the totality of the student's environment" (p. 253). Warren (1985) described two types of generalization. *Stimulus*

---

[2] *Interactive Games,* by Developmental Equipment, P.O. Box 369, Wauconda, IL 60084.

generalization refers to use of the trained response across persons, settings, objects, or time (traditionally referred to as "carryover"). *Response generalization* involves the display of different responses that are similar in function to a trained response. Thus, response generalization involves generalization of response classes (e.g., a morphological marker) across items and across modalites (e.g., comprehension and production).

The concept of a *zero inference strategy* (Brown, et al., 1976) has been suggested to account for a lack of generalization across cues, modalities, persons, and so forth. The implication is that some persons with severe disabilities (especially those with severe cognitive impairment) do not infer from one instance or one situation to another. Therefore, it would be necessary to teach directly *all* desired behaviors in *all* desired settings. Obviously, this would be an overwhelming task even for relatively discrete goals. A number of strategies, however, might be helpful in increasing the level of inference. One way to attack this problem is to train the learner in generalized learning strategies. Three examples are (1) training in generalized instruction-following (Streifel, Wetherby, & Karlan, 1976; Whitman, Zakaras, & Chardos, 1971), (2) generalized imitation skills (e.g., Baer, 1978), and (3) matrix training (e.g., Goldstein, 1985; Wetherby & Streifel, 1978). In each case, the individual is presumably "learning to learn," rather than merely learning a small set of responses. In generalized instruction-following, the individual learns to "do what I say," while in generalized imitation he or she learns to "do what I do." Either of these skills may enable the individual to learn incidentally rather than depending solely on direct teaching. In addition, generalized learning skills will increase the number of people from whom the individual can learn, even though these people may not realize that they are serving as models.

Stokes and Baer (1977) reviewed 200 studies involving generalization, and identified a set of tactics for promoting generalization. These strategies relate to both response generalization and stimulus generalization. Stremel-Campbell and Campbell (1985) have presented descriptions of five of the major techniques, plus guidelines for applying them. A summary of these techniques is provided in the following list.

• *Programming Multiple Exemplars:* This technique involves the selection and application of multiple examples of the desired behavior, persons, and/or settings. The purpose of this technique is to avoid rote response to specific stimulus conditions. Multiple behaviors may include: communication functions (request information, comment, request action); linguistic classes or vocabulary (e.g., agent-action can be represented by "baby sleep," "dog sleep," "dog eat"); and language response classes (e.g., vocal imitation of vowel sounds, plural markers, auxiliary verbs). In addition to the obvious meaning of "multiple exemplars" (e.g., teaching "book" by using a simple storybook, a pop-up book, and a textbook), two other components of training must be presented in multiple forms; the use of multiple trainers (teachers, bus driver, parents, peers) and multiple settings (classroom, playground, cafeteria, bank).

• *Programming Common Stimuli:* This technique involves programming salient stimuli or cues from the natural environment into training settings. These common stimuli can be programmed across the behavior being targeted (e.g., training nouns by means of the requesting function already taught). Use of common physical stimuli, such as a cup similar to the one the student uses, is another important feature of this technique. Peers can also be used as common stimuli, provided that specific techniques are used to promote peer interactions. Common settings should also be used, with training taking place in natural environments or simulating those environments.

• *Programming Natural Maintaining Consequences:* This technique involves reacting naturally to the intent of the communication through provision of tangible or social consequences. Thus, if Carmen indicates the symbol BABY while patting the doll, her comment should be confirmed ("Yes, that's your baby"). If she indicates the symbol BABY while the doll is on a shelf, she should be given the doll as the adult says "You want baby? Here she is." Tangible consequences unrelated to the student's behavior (e.g., giving a piece of apple following each labeling event) and non-normative consequences, such as responding "Good talking," would clearly violate this technique.

• *Programming "Loose" Training:* This technique allows for the systematic variation of the irrelevant stimuli. It does not imply a lack of structure or sloppy training, but suggests the need for carefully planned introduction of variations. This may need to be a gradual technique. Three types of "loose training" techniques are (1) concurrent training, in which responses are taught concurrently to ensure that they are controlled by relevant stimuli (e.g., teach "banana" and "cracker" concurrently to ensure that the student responds to the stimulus items, rather than to the consequence of eating); (2) varying verbal and nonverbal cues (e.g., training requesting in response to "What do you want?" or "Tell me what you'd like"); (3) accepting and reinforcing response variations (e.g., avoiding the robotic "I want _____ please" by targeting variations such as "I'd really like _____" or "Can I have _____?").

• *Programming Indiscriminable Contingencies:* For this technique, schedules of reinforcement are arranged so that the student may be unsure which stimuli are reinforced and which are not. Two types of indiscriminable techniques can be actively programmed. Delayed reinforcement, provides a natural delay between the response and the delivery of reinforcement, once acquisition has occurred. For example, Gannar requests a turn at the computer; he is told "Just a minute — let Carol finish this one game," then is given a turn. Intermittent reinforcement can reduce tangible or social reinforcement to levels more typical of the natural environment. For example, if Luke requests juice via buzzer and eye gaze, the adult might say "I have to get Pam's splint on — can you ask me again in a minute?" thus providing the reinforcement (juice) following two responses.

Williams and Fox (1977) developed an accountability procedure for determining when mastery of a skill has occurred. To achieve mastery, the individual must perform the skill in the "normal" manner, or a functional alternative, across functional tasks which frequently occur throughout the day, across people, across cues to response (verbal cues or the task itself cuing the behavior), across materials, and across time. A mastery assessment sheet (see Table 2-2) is provided to help the instructor ensure that all five conditions are met the minimum number of times for each skill.

Much support information is available on the issue of generalization of training. Stremel-Campbell and Campbell (1985) offer strategies and examples for using these five generalization techniques. A chapter by Horner, McDonnell, and Bellamy (1986) presents the teaching of generalized skills through the strategies of simulation and community settings.

Self-Initiation and Self-Regulation

Self-initiation and self-regulation are other crucial issues in training persons with severe disabilities. Several authors (Brown et al., 1976; Williams, Brown, & Certo, 1975) have noted that many persons with severe disabilities lack these skills. The problem, which is closely related to the generalization issue, must be considered relative to communication training, whether vocal or augmented. Williams et al. (1975) stated that those labeled severely handicapped are often referred to as externally controlled, relying on prompts and cues from caregivers. They noted that there are situations when it is appropriate to make a specific response to a specific cue ("What is your name?"), instances when a series of responses should be provided to a single cue ("Tell me about your family"), and still other situations when either one or a series of responses is required to nonspecific cues (individual is lost and must ask for help). In addition, it may be necessary to engage in a series of responses, evaluate their correctness, and correct them if necessary. All of this should be possible without direct cues from persons in authority. Thus, it is recommended that self-regulation training be included in a communication curriculum. Nietupski and Williams (1974) developed a training sequence for rudimentary self-regulation skills, consisting of the following steps:

1. Detecting or defining the task
2. Arriving at alternative ways to complete the task

TABLE 2-2
Mastery Assessment Score Sheet

TARGET MO *	School			Home			Other
	Functional Task 1	Functional Task 2	Functional Task 3	Functional Task 1	Functional Task 2	Functional Task 3	Functional Task 1
Gross Motor: supported sitting with head control	Head control while eating	Head control while sitting and playing W/busybox		Head control while washing after meal			
Response Cue	"head up"	No cue provided by teacher, self-initated		"Sit up"			
Person	Milly	Tutor — Ann		Mother			
How data obtained: a. Observed by evaluator	Yes	No		No			
b. Observed and reported to evaluator by	Tutor-Ann	Tutor-Ann Tutor-Carol		Mother and sister			
Date	9/10/76	10/20/76		11/1/76			

From Williams and Foxx (1977). Communication. In Williams and Foxx (Eds.), *Minimum objective system for pupils with severe handicaps: working draft number one.* Brighton, VT: University of Vermont. Reprinted with permission. * MO = minimum objective

3. Implementing an alternative
4. Assessing the outcome of the alternative
    a. if the task is not correctly completed, return to step 2
    b. if the task is correctly completed, end of task.

The first step covers self-initiation skills, while later steps cover abilities to make, implement, assess, and, if necessary, revise decisions regarding appropriate action. Application of such a self-regulation model could serve as the final step in generalization.

Imitation, Comprehension, and Production

Historically, reseachers have been interested in the relationships of imitation, comprehension, and production in language acquisition and training.

The role of imitation is a major issue, in terms of both language acquisition and language training. With regard to acquisition, Bloom and Lahey (1978) concluded that "there has not been a concensus in the literature as to whether imitation contributes to language learning" (p. 272). However, Hart (1985) asserted that "there is ample experimental evidence that language production improves when imitation is reinforced" (p. 81). Risley, Hart, and Doke (1972) suggested that "Whether or not imitation is crucial to the normal development of language, it is a crucial part of all procedures for remediating language deficits" (p. 110). While such a blanket assertion may be questionable, a casual review of both vocal and nonvocal language programs reveals that imitation is indeed widely used in training. This is perhaps not surprising in view of the potential increase in efficiency possible with imitative procedures, especially when the individual learns generalized imitation skills. However, several authors (Bloom & Lahey, 1978; Rees, 1975; Siegel & Spradlin, 1978) have expressed caution regarding extensive use of imitation as a training technique. First, imitation may be defined differently by various disciplines, or even by different workers within a single discipline. For example, in order for an instance of imitation to be counted, the following might be considered:

- Must the two behaviors be exactly alike? (If the instructor says "eat cookie" and the learner says "cookie," will an instance be counted?)
- Must the model and the response have a specific temporal relationship? (If the instructor says "eat cookie" and the learner says "eat cookie" in one second or one minute or one hour, would all be counted as instances of imitation?).

These examples may give a clue to why there is currently so much confusion over the issue of imitation.

A second concern regarding imitation relates to its functionality. Bloom and Lahey (1978) cautioned that imitation not supported by context or intention may not yield desired results. That is, if Judy does not see a cookie, and does not desire a cookie, her repetition of "eat cookie," whether verbal, gestural, or symbolic, may not be meaningful. Guess et al. (1978) also stressed the need for functional imitative responses. They defined imitative responses as ones that (1) produce an immediate consequence for the individual, (2) produce a consequence that is potentially reinforcing, (3) produce a consequence that is specific to the response, and (4) produce a response that is natural to the individual's interaction with the environment.

A theory expressed by Kuhn (1973) also has important implications for the use of imitation in language intervention. Kuhn suggested that children imitate only those behaviors already in their repertoires. Thus, Siegel and Spradlin (1978) questioned, "Is it possible that generalized imitation does not really involve imitation of novel behavior but simply the rearrangement of components already learned?" (p. 382). This component-recombination notion suggests that training should focus on recombinations of components already established. This is yet one more aspect to consider when using generalized imitation as a strategy.

Two major types of imitation are traditionally described; nonverbal and verbal (Harris, 1975). *Nonverbal imitation* may include gross and fine motor imitation, while *verbal imitation* may cover vocal imitation (imitation of nonmeaningful sounds and sequences) and imitation of words or larger linguistic units. Nonverbal imitation is often introduced first because researchers have reasoned that gross motor movements are topographically less difficult and can be physieally prompted more readily than verbal responses (Harris, 1976). However, as Harris (1975) noted, "the value of nonverbal imitation training has been more a clinical assumption than an empirical fact" (p. 566). Siegel and Spradlin (1978) asserted that if their theory of component recombinations is correct, there would be little reason to expect generalization from nonverbal to verbal imitation. Finally, Guess et al. (1978) suggested that the important factors regarding type of imitative response do not hinge on whether they are verbal or nonverbal, but on whether the response is in the individual's repertoire and how functional the response is to the individual.

Although the traditional view has been that comprehension precedes production in language acquisition, recent studies have indicated that this is not a fixed finding (Chapman & Miller, 1975; Keeney & Wolfe, 1972). Following an extensive literature review, Bloom and Lahey proposed the following hypothesis:

> [Comprehension and production] represent mutually dependent but different underlying processes [and] the developmental gap between comprehension and speaking probably varies among different children and at different times, and that the gap may be more apparent than real. (p. 238)

Many researchers have continued to use the traditional approach of training comprehension first, mainly because it appears to be a "safe" choice. For example, Schumaker and Sherman (1978), in an extensive literature review, found no studies in which receptive speech skills adversely affected production. Therefore, they concluded that "it seems safe to say that providing children with opportunities to discriminate differences in words and sentence forms can not hurt and, in some cases, may well foster productive language acquisition" (p. 248).

However, for learners with severe disabilities, withholding production training until comprehension training is completed may cause a delay before the individual is able to use language to control the environment. Thus, the sequence of training production *before* comprehension has been chosen by some researchers (Bloom & Lahey, 1978; Guess et al., 1978). Bloom and Lahey suggested that training production first would also facilitate comprehension, since content–form interactions are always presented in a context that represents the meaning relation being coded. For example, context would help define whether the word "milk" is intended as a comment ("You have milk") or a request ("May I have milk?"). Guess and associates (1978) noted that production skills allow an individual greater opportunity to manipulate and control the enviornment than do comprehension skills. The individual may thus receive natural reinforcement, possibly causing a reduction in passivity.

A third alternative is to train comprehension and production concurrently (Bloom & Lahey, 1978; Siegel & Spradlin, 1978; Reichle & Keogh, 1985). This is consistent with current practices of concurrent training, where appropriate, with the aim of avoiding long delays while waiting for the learning of prerequisites.

Reichle and Keogh (1985) also cautioned that the communication mode being trained (vocal, aided, unaided) may also influence the decision of whether to train comprehension or production first. For example, they pointed out that object name production using a direct selection communication display is almost the same as a nonidentical match-to-sample task.

Summary

This chapter has presented an introduction to a number of issues related to communication programming for persons with severe disabilities. The purpose of this brief overview was to stimulate consideraton of the numerous and complex issues that should be considered in planning communication intervention.

Two general multi-author texts summarize current thinking on most of the issues presented in this chapter: *Education of Learners with Severe Handicaps* (Horner, Meyer, & Fredericks, 1986), and *Teaching Functional Language* (Warren & Rogers-Warren, 1985).

Chapter 3

Preliminary Skills

The readiness is all.

— Shakespeare

During the evaluation and information gathering stage of planning an intervention program for an individual with a severe communication impairment, certain behavior (e.g., lack of cooperation during testing, limited motor control, poor attending) may indicate that the person needs to learn skills in addition to direct communication skills. These are often termed preliminary, prerequisite, precursory, or prelanguage skills. Throughout this chapter the term *preliminary skills* will be used in reference to initial training strategies that will facilitate learning of higher level communication skills. Although these preliminary behaviors have traditionally been taught prior to beginning a language training program (Horstmeier & MacDonald, 1978; Kent, 1974), the current trend advocates teaching them concurrently with communication training (Miller et al., 1980; Sapon, Kaczmarek, Welber, Rouzer, & Sapan-Shevin, 1976). The concurrent training approach may be described as a horizontally arranged training model in which, for example, tracking, scanning, and imitation skills are taught as a part of language training (Hamre-Nietupski et al., 1977). This contrasts with a vertically arranged training model, in which skills such as on-task behavior or imitation are taught prior to beginning direct language training (Kent, 1974; Makohon, & Fredericks, 1985).

Our view that communication is an integral part of every activity or interaction throughout the person's waking hours at home, school, and in other environments (shopping, traveling, visiting neighbors) will be evident throughout this chapter. Realistically, concurrent training in preliminary skills can quite naturally take place within communication training sessions and general daily activities. For example, when teaching attending skills, the instructor typically creates a situation in which attention is rewarded by an interesting consequence, such as allowing the student to play with a desired toy. Training should be organized in such a way that the student can simultaneously be introduced to skills, such as the functional use of an object, turn-taking, and associating a word label with the object, at the same time he or she learns the primary goal of attending to a task. Musselwhite (1986a, 1986b) provided numerous examples of telescoping activities within play tasks, to allow introduction of higher level communication skills, such as requesting, while working on preliminary skills, such as joint attention and turn-taking.

The preliminary skills to be discussed in this chapter are (1) improvement of positioning, (2) elimination of interfering behaviors (self-stimulating and self-injurious behaviors), (3) establishment of a desire to communicate, (4) improvement of attending, (5) enhancement of cognitive development, (6) stimulation of motor imitation, and (7) facilitation of oral-motor control. This is not intended to be an exhaustive review of these areas; such a review would be beyond the scope of this text. Our intention is to present an overview of the areas we consider to be especially crucial in training persons with severe disabilities, and to provide resources for assessment and intervention of these target areas.

Improving Handling and Positioning

For the individual with poor motor control, such as a child with cerebral palsy, proper positioning is crucial in allowing the maximum possible performance in any communication mode, as well as in performing the preliminary skills discussed in this chapter. It is widely recognized that positioning must be addressed by a team; each member of which will have imporant input. Such a team includes:

- *A Physical Therapist,* who often has primary responsibility for developing and monitoring appropriate positioning
- *An Occupational Therapist,* who may have special insights regarding stability of the shoulder girdle to enhance arm and hand control
- *A Communication Disorders Specialist,* who may provide input regarding specific communication needs (e.g., a raised ridge on the front of the laptray for insertion of eye-gaze frame)
- *An Educator,* who can suggest specific activities (e.g., playground, mealtime) for which positioning should be considered

- *The Parents,* who can give suggestions regarding the need for portability, flexibility, etc., based on lifestyle of family
- *The Client,* who can indicate comfort or discomfort, as well as reactions to features such as style and materials
- *A Rehabilitation Engineer,* who may be called in to help solve a difficult design problem
- *A Vendor,* who may assist in making needed modifications once a particular type of chair has been selected.

Doherty (1987) pointed out that improper handling of a child for activities such as play, feeding, and bathing can aggravate specific disabilities, such as spasticity. She provided specific suggestions for training staff and family members to improve their handling of the individual with severe physical disability. For example, problem-solving sessions and photographs of appropriate handling by familiar staff members may encourage caregivers to provide opportunities for counteracting abnormal muscle tone, reflexes, and movement through appropriate handling.

This issue is a complex one that involves positioning for a variety of activities, taking into account a myriad of physical problems. Changes that would appear to be rather slight can have a great impact —either positive or negative — on the individual with poor motor control. Several examples will demonstrate potential changes brought about through positioning.

- Penny is a 3-year-old child with Down syndrome, who is learning to sign. When seated in a traditional children's chair she has poor fine motor control due to balance problems (the curve in the chair seat causes her to slump, her feet do not touch the floor, the base of the seat is too long, causing her legs to extend slightly). When placed in a smaller chair with a flat seat, both her balance and her fine motor control improve noticeably.
- Jean-Luc sits in a wheelchair with foot rests that are too low for his feet. when the therapist raises the foot rest and straps his feet in securely, his teacher reports less hyperextension and improvement in his ability to activate a switch with his hand.
- Bruce has extremely poor head control during sitting, although his chair is equipped with H-shaped shoulder straps. When his chair is modified to include shoulder retraction pads and lateral trunk supports, he is able to begin training with an optical headpointer.

Doherty (1987) and Bachelor (1987, personal communication) pointed out several advantages of an upright position (e.g., seated in an adapted chair): (1) visual tracking can be enhanced to allow wide examination of the environment; (2) eye-hand coordination may progress as the person observes manual activity; (3) tactile stimulation may occur as the hands are brought together at midline, allowing manipulation of a wide range of objects; (4) interaction with a wide range of people and objects is facilitated; (5) the likelihood of deformity is decreased; (6) transportation can be accomplished with far greater ease; (7) feeding and self-feeding can be accomplished more effectively and with greater safety; and (8) with increased trunk and head control, the individual looks more normal, thus decreasing the likelihood that intellectual abilities will be underestimated.

Positioning is an ongoing process. As the individual grows, learns new skills, or begins to engage in new activities, positioning will need to be re-evaluated and modified. Each person who works with an individual needing handling, positioning, and adaptive equipment must be aware of strategies that can be used to optimize positioning, such as providing good foot support, positioning the pelvis such that the leg (thigh) is at a right angle with the back, remembering to use the laptray for arm stability, and positioning straps across the pelvis with the pelvis flat against the back of the chair, rather than around the waist, for maximum trunk stability and safety.

RESOURCES. Numerous chapters and books address positioning and related issues. Among them are "Approximating the norm through environmental child-centered prosthetics and adaptive equipment" (Campbell, Green, & Carlson, 1977); "Handling, positioning, and adaptive equipment" (Doherty, 1987); Handling the Young Cerebral Palsied Child at Home (Finnie, 1975); "Position and its effect on motor control" (Wright & Numura, 1985, Chapter 4); *Positioning the Handicapped Child for Function* (Ward, 1984); and *Positioning the Client with C.N.S. Deficits* (Bergen & Colangelo, 1982).

Reducing Interfering Behaviors

Some individuals with severe disabilities exhibit undesirable behaviors that can interfere to varying degrees with the ability to participate in expected daily activities and formal training programs. Two major types of interfering behaviors are discussed in this section:

- *Self-Stimulating Behavior,* such as body-rocking, hand-gazing, obsessions for particular objects (lights, water) and repetitious movements (hand-waving, clapping, foot-tapping) (Azrin, Kaplan, & Foxx, 1973; Dolan & Burton, 1976; Rincover, 1981)
- *Self-Injurious Behavior,* such as head-banging, hand-biting, and body-pinching (Favell & Greene, 1980; Gaylord–Ross, 1977).

These types of behavior may threaten the health of the individual, or may preoccupy the person so that learning new skills is difficult (Gaylord-

Ross, 1977). Therefore, it is necessary for the instructor to identify self-stimulating and self-injurious behavior and attempt to eliminate or control it.

The primary means of assessing interfering behavior is careful clinical observation by an instructor who observes the individual and documents any self-stimulating or self-injurious behavior. It is helpful to note during what types of situations this behavior occurs and the frequency of its occurrence. These observations should be made over a period of several days, at various times of the day, and during different activities. This baseline information can then be used to design procedures for reducing the interfering behavior.

Meyer and Evans (1986) have stressed the importance of identifying the function of an interfering behavior, as well as its form. Typical functions are social-communication (behaviors that indicate the need for attention, the desire to be left alone), self-regulatory (allowing selective attention to a particular activity), and play (behaviors that provide self-entertainment).

The instructor may use a variety of procedures to eliminate or reduce interfering behavior. One possible procedure is to normalize inappropriate behaviors by slightly modifying them or engaging in them at appropriate times or for reasons other than self-stimulation. Substituting an acceptable movement, such as rocking in a rocking chair for general body-rocking, is one approach toward reducing body-rocking in other situations; the individual gradually learns when rocking is acceptable.

Meyer and Evans (1986) have identified three broad categories of intervention for what they term "excess behavior."

- *Ecological:* This intervention requires rearrangement of the environment to prevent the behavior from occurring. For example, if Kevin is fascinated by lights and playing with water, a dark curtain may be used to screen out the light at various times, and the water table may be covered at most times. This may also be combined with teaching appropriate times for water play, and using a flashlight to make shapes on the wall to provide a more functional and normative interest in light. Physical intervention can also be used to restrict the individual's ability to engage in the behavior.
- *Curricular:* For this approach, the individual is taught an alternative positive behavior that can be used with equal effectiveness. For example, if Jenny engages in hand-biting as a means to express frustration with a task, she could be taught to push the materials toward an instructor instead, as a means of requesting help and expressing frustration.
- *Negative Consequence:* For this procedure, contingencies are rearranged so that negative stimuli are imposed as negative consequences contingent on the occurrence of the interfering behavior. For example, assume that

Margita engages in hand-chewing which serves no apparent function. A buzzer has been observed to be a negative stimuli for her; thus, a mercury switch is attached to her wrist so that the buzzer is activated each time she brings her hand to her mouth.

This section has presented several treatment approaches designed to eliminate or reduce self-stimulating or self-injurious behavior. Whatever the choice of procedure, eliminating interfering behavior will increase the person's attentiveness to other activities and enhance learning. In most cases, such training will be concurrent with other training goals, rather than isolated training.

RESOURCES. A variety of books is available on this topic. One series of how-to books is especially appropriate for use by paraprofessionals such as ward staff (see Appendix B): *How to Reduce Autistic and Severely Maladaptive Behaviors* (Luce & Christian, 1981); *How to Treat Self-injurious Behavior* (Favell & Greene, 1980); and *How to Use Sensory Extinction* (Rincover, 1981).

Establishing a Desire to Communicate

Kraat (1985a) asserted that "communication takes place through actions that a person makes in an effort to convey a particular intention to another person or persons, or through actions the person unconsciously makes that convey an intention" (p. 6). This section focuses on intentional, rather than unintentional, communication attempts.

An individual with a severe communication disability may be discouraged from communicating because of the great effort required (physically and/or cognitively), and because his or her needs may be anticipated by partners. Shea and Mount (1982) have addressed the issue of motivation and related skills through the procedure of manipulating the environment. They suggested that the desire to communicate is a special type of cause and effect understanding. Three environmental modifications that they suggested to enhance the desire to communicate are (1) providing materials and training to teach cause and effect (e.g., busy boxes, pop-up boxes, switch-activated battery devices), (2) having another person provide pleasurable stimulation, and (3) allowing time and opportunity for the student to become familiar with teachers and caregivers. The implication is that the student must understand that another person can make something happen, and that the student has the power to affect that other person's actions, through some form of communication. If communication involves considerable physical and cognitive energy, the motivation will need to be greater to overcome passivity. Thus, events and relationships must be highly reinforcing to the student. Porter and colleagues (1985) have suggested assessment procedures for determining preferences for individuals who do not demonstrate clear likes.

Thus, establishing the desire to communicate may be considered a prerequisite to successful communication training. The instructor must create an environment and relationship with the nonspeaker that demonstrates a caring, accepting atmosphere for the person to develop control over the environment through use of communication skills. Many programs that emphasize response only, in the absence of contextual support and communicative intent, may not elicit this desire. For example, asking "test questions" (e.g., "What's this," when it is clear that the learner knows what "this" is) is unlikely to stimulate the desire to communicate. Strategies suggested by Constable (1983) and Musselwhite (1986a), such as structuring events naturally (e.g., hiding objects, then labeling them as they are discovered) and withholding turns or objects by "accident" (e.g., "Let me know if you need anything"), provide the background support and communicative intent needed to develop a desire to communicate. Chapter 2 includes a summary of those strategies.

Siegel-Causey and Guess (in press) have developed a manual summarizing strategies for enhacing interactions between service providers and individuals who are severely multiply disabled. The five strategies presented for developing nonsymbolic communication can yield a greatly enhanced desire to communicate. Those strategies are briefly summarized in Table 3-1, with an example and a suggestion of how each strategy might support an enhanced desire to communicate.

Improving Attending

Attempting to teach a noncompliant, distractible, hyperactive, withdrawn, and/or uninterested child is a challenge to the evaluator or instructor. In developing attending skills in such a child, the instructor must not allow a power struggle to develop, which can happen if the training procedures involve tasks of little interest to the individual, and require unreasonable lengths of time (e.g., "the student must maintain eye contact with the instructor for 30 seconds"). Therefore, the instructor should consider the student's general level of physical and psychological development when determining specific training criteria. This section will focus on both physical attention and visual attention. This should not imply that these are totally separate behaviors; they may be taught concurrently in actual training.

TABLE 3-1
Strategies for Enhancing Early Communication Interaction

Strategy	Example	Rationale
Nurturance: Fostering an atmosphere of warmth and security, by providing sustenance and support	Singing to child while diapering	Builds sense of trust in service provider
Responsiveness: Perceiving and interpreting nonsymbolic behaviors in a sensitive fashion that is appropriate and satisfying to the recipient	Rachel whines; caregiver says "Oh, I hear Rachel" and goes to her	Child learns that her actions cause others to react to her
Structure: An organized framework is provided that establishes routines based on regularized formats, with events occuring in a similar manner using the same materials, same order, and same people	An activity, such as interactive games, can occur each day after lunch, using consistent cues, materials, and sequence of exchanges	Child develops a sense of anticipation, which can promote requesting
Need: Situations are set up to allow the person to feel a lack of something perceived as necessary	Expectant time delay can be used (see Chapter 2 in this book)	Child has an opportunity to communicate
Natural setting: Advantage is taken of spontaneous occurrences in settings, rather than imposing artificial structures or situations	Child hears a favorite song, looks and vocalizes, teacher shapes pointing request and complies	Training is directly applicable to daily life situations

Adapted from Siegel-Causey and Guess, in press.

Physical Attention

Physical attending includes establishing sitting, attending to instructor, and attending to a given task. Quiet sitting on the instructor's lap, or on a cushion on the floor, may be the first step in establishing independent chair sitting for more structured training sessions with some individuals. Comfortable positioning with good trunk and head control, and reduction of abnormal movement patterns will enhance training of attending. The section on positioning above provides several ideas and resources for achieving optimal positioning.

Bricker and Dennison (1978) suggested a three-phase attending program, including (1) sitting in a chair while playing with toys, (2) looking at the instructor as a prerequisite for later motor imitation training, and (3) working on-task to determine and increase the length of time a person can stay on-task. Woolman (1980) also divided physical attending into three phases: (1) sitting in a chair; (2) eliminating interfering behavior; and (3) sitting at a table. Each of Woolman's tasks has a mastery criterion of attending at the specified level for 30-second trials without participating in another activity. In addition, the individual was required to maintain a fixed position with back straight against the back of a chair, feet flat on floor, and knees together. Obviously, this stringent procedure might not be physically appropriate or realistic for many individuals — indeed, the non-normative nature of these tasks may be unrealistic even for most potential instructors!

It is crucial that the person have something to do while remaining relatively quiet and in the appropriate sitting position. The instructor must also become skilled in anticipating when the individual will tire of an activity, and must change the activity, or end the lesson, *before* the individual stops attending.

Musselwhite (1986a) discussed a more general form of attending and responding to the environment, termed *activation*. Activation implies a more active role for the learner than traditional attending tasks. Musselwhite suggested both assessment tools for determining activation level and sample strategies for enhancing activation.

Visual Attention

Visual attending skills covered in this section include visual fixation, visual tracking, and visual scanning skills. Most training programs for people with severe handicaps assume that the individual has adequate or corrected vision as a prerequisite for entering the program. Moreover, visual attending skills may be overlooked during initial training, when instructors are anxious to establish communication. However, for the person with a physical impairment, the development of visual skills may be the key to establishing a communication system, via eye gaze and scanning procedures. This becomes particularly important if an aided system is selected, such as a communication board or electronic device. This section will offer definitions of the terms *visual fixation, visual tracking,* and *visual scanning,* and will present sample training activities and resources for developing these skills.

Visual Fixation

Robinson and Robinson (1978) defined visual fixation as "regard of a stimulus which is held in a fixed position" (p. 115). Their criterion for establishing visual fixation is that the individual must look at an object within 1 to 10 seconds after its presentation, and must maintain eye contact with it for 10 to 15 seconds. They noted that if it is not clear whether the individual is visually fixating, the instructor may check for reflection of the stimulus in the person's pupil(s).

Several factors should be considered during assessment and training of visual attending skills:

• *Stimulus:* Developmentally, children respond first to light sources, and later to patterned stimuli such as faces (Fantz & Nevis, 1967); thus, "Look at me" may not be appropriate as an initial stimulus.

• *Distance:* The student should learn to attend to objects, people, and events that are out of reach as well as those within reach.

• *Latency:* It may be helpful to determine how long it takes the individual to respond to a visual stimulus, then to reduce this latency to allow attending to events of short duration (Robinson & Robinson, 1978).

• *Positioning:* Conjugate gaze, in which both eyes are focused on the same point, is most likely if there is sufficient support for the head to be stable and centered at the midline (Sternat, Messina, Nietupski, Lyon, & Brown, 1977).

• *Cues:* It may initially be necessary to supplement the visual stimulus with some type of cue, such as a verbalization ("Ashley, look!"), a vocalization ("ooooh"), a noise (using an animal noisemaker as the stimulus), or a gesture (moving the stimulus or pointing to it).

One or more of these factors may be systematically altered as needed to extend the individual's attending skills.

RESOURCES. *The Functional Vision Inventory for the Multiple and Severely Handicapped* (Langley, 1980) offers in-depth assessment and intervention strategies for skills such as awareness of visual stimuli, fixation, and convergence. Another program offering suggestions for teaching attending is *How to Arrange the Environment to Stimulate and Teach Pre-Language Skills in the Severely Handicapped* (Shea & Mount, 1982).

Visual Tracking

An operational training definition of visual tracking is following an object that is moved through a path, such as horizontal, vertical, or circular (Robinson & Robinson, 1978; Scheuerman, Baumgart, Sipsma, &

Brown, 1976). Visual tracking is vital to the development of other skills, such as object permanence (watching a bottle as it rolls under a blanket) and social interaction skills (playing computer games with a peer). Musselwhite (1986a) noted that individuals with disabilities may be at risk for developing good visual tracking skills due to motor or cognitive problems, or both. For example, poor head control may restrict head movements and limit visual field. However, visual tracking may be crucially important for a person whose movement is limited; it can enlarge the environment of that individual.

The *Functional Vision Inventory for the Multiple and Severely Handicapped* (Langley, 1980) presents items for assessing visual tracking skills on both the long and the short screening forms. When introducing a tracking task the instructor should stand or sit so that the individual does not become distracted by looking at the instructor when an item is presented for tracking. The individual may move just the eyes or, more commonly, move the head and eyes simultaneously to follow the object. Using a mirror to allow the individual to follow his own image may be a helpful technique. Rather than massed training trials, a variety of activities can be employed throughout the day to teach tracking skills. Examples of naturalized activities include:

- Rolling a ball to knock down a tower of blocks built during a fine motor task
- Dropping floating and nonfloating toys into water
- Pushing toy cars off a surface into a metal container
- Watching liquids being poured at mealtime.

Using barriers to partially or fully hide objects is a higher level task involving visual tracking, and leads to the concept of object permanence. For example, a cardboard tube can be used as a tunnel through which cars are sent from one student to another.

As noted previously, motor problems such as poor head control may interfere with visual tracking. For an individual who is motorically unable to accomplish the smooth oculomotor movements of tracking, an alternate response could be to shift the gaze from one object to another (Robinson & Robinson, 1978).

Several factors that should be considered in teaching tracking skills are listed in Table 3-2. These factors can be systematically manipulated during training to provide for optimal generalization, as suggested by the activities provided in the *Functional Vision Inventory*. Duckman (1987) presented some highly motivating oculomotor tasks arranged in a hierarchy from extremely simple (following a flashlight placed at one end of a tube, with the other end placed near the child's eyes) to quite

TABLE 3-2

Considerations in Assessing and Teaching Visual Tracking Skills

Consideration	Sample Adaptive Play Applications
Stimulus: Size, color, pattern, and complexity (e.g., presence of moving parts) may affect learning)	Use a wide variety of play materials rather than reusing a small set of toys. Include two or more exemplars of each characteristic listed (e.g., color)
Location: Distance may be within reach or out of reach	Manipulate objects within reach, letting child play with each after tracking it. After child watches event out of reach (children sliding), move child to event
The level relative to the child's eyes should be considered (above, below, and at eye level)	Provide opportunities for tracking at all levels: above (toy moving along string); at eye level (paper airplane flying); below (puppet marching across laptray)
Range: This can vary from a few degrees to 180 degrees. Crossing midline is difficult for some students	The trainer may need to manipulate the extent of range directly. When first crossing midline, choose slow-moving objects or events
Cue(s): Vocal / Verbal / Auditory / Gestural	Use rising pitch as toy goes up ("Oooo"). Should be relevant or fun: "There it goes!" Use a noisemaker (maraca) as the stimulus. Use nonlinguistic cues (point, open mouth)
Speed: A range is possible. Slow / Medium / Fast / Supersonic	Wind-up "walking feet". Battery-powered "attack" vehicle. Push-n-Go vehicles. Penny racers
Path: Potential paths include horizontal, vertical, diagnonal, circular, and random	Some battery-powered vehicles (Radio Shack Police Car) come with template to alter path movement
Barriers: Transparent / Translucent / Opaque	Roll marbles in box with vinyl lid. Walk animal behind filmy scarf "curtain". Roll ball into box with lid

From Musselwhite (1986a).

complex (following maze lines on a chalkboard). Hanson and Harris (1986) offer intervention ideas especially appropriate for use by parents.

RESOURCES: Several authors have presented programs or suggestions for teaching visual tracking to persons with severe handicaps (e.g., Dunst, 1981; Hanson & Harris, 1986; Johnson-Martin et al., 1985; Langley, 1980; Musselwhite, 1986; Scheuerman et al., 1976).

Visual Scanning

Visual scanning involves a visual search of parts of an object or the individual components of an array of objects (Scheuerman et al., 1976). Musselwhite (1986a) distinguished between general scanning skills, and those scanning skills used to gain access to aided augmentative communication displays. The general skill of scanning can assist an individual in identifying relevant features of items or events in the environment.

As with visual fixation and tracking, the instructor may need to provide cues initially, such as sounds (a noisemaker), gestures (indicating the target feature), movements (bringing the target item toward the individual), and verbalizations ("See the _____?").

Scanning can be used in augmentative communication as a means of indicating the target item. Chapters 8 and 9 provide summaries of scanning for nonelectronic and electronic displays.

One highly structured approach to teaching initial visual scanning and discrimination skills is the *Visual Symbol Communication Instruction Program* (Elder & Bergman, 1978). This procedure uses a Symbol Training Display,[1] an acrylic board with four pockets to hold objects or symbol cards. Initially, the person scans the pockets to determine which contains a card while the remaining three pockets are empty. The position of the card is then changed, eventually requiring scanning of all pockets. This procedure can be modified to introduce objects in the same manner. Langley (1980) offers a hierarchy of 10 steps in training scanning, using a variety of materials and tasks.

Scanning is often paired with decision-making, to allow the natural consequence of receiving a desired item. Porter and colleagues (1985) stressed the importance of visual scanning in the decision-making portion of their program for teaching prerequisites to augmentative communication.

Initial scanning instruction can be implemented during individual sessions (e.g., using adaptive switches with battery devices) or as part of other activities (e.g., during table preparation for a meal, the person

---

[1] Symbol Training Display available from Developmental Equipment, P.O. Box 639, Wauconda, IL 60084.

indicates which chair or utensils are missing). Scheuerman and associates (1976) suggested a variety of general scanning activities that can be practiced within the natural environment, such as having the individual indicate empty spaces of an egg carton, or purposely leaving crumbs on the table following a meal and having the individual indicate where to clean.

RESOURCES. Several programs offer suggestions for teaching general scanning (see Appendix B): Langley (1980); Porter et al. (1985); Scheuerman et al. (1976).

To summarize, although many of the programs designed for teaching physical and visual attending skills are artificially structured, they may be modified by using naturally structured activities, such as those suggested by Musselwhite (1986a; 1986b) and Scheuerman and associates (1976). Using naturally structured activities, natural settings, and a variety of trainers should ensure that newly learned attending skills are generalized, and that they serve to facilitate communication.

Increasing Cognitive Skills

Piaget's theory of intellectual development (Piaget, 1954; 1966), which delineates a series of invariant stages for normal cognitive development in children, has been borrowed by many disciplines in developing programming for individuals with a variety of handicapping conditions. Piaget's theory has been used as the basis for devising both assessment tools (Chappell & Johnson 1976; Miller, Chapman, Branston, & Reichle, 1980; Uzgiris & Hunt, 1975) and training programs (Robinson & Robinson, 1983).

Table 3-3 presents a visual overview of Piaget's stages of intellectual development. Robinson and Robinson (1983) provide a more thorough description for readers unfamiliar with Piaget's theory. The primary focus for cognitive development in individuals with severe handicaps is the sensorimotor and preconceptual preoperational stages. As illustrated in Table 3-3, the sensorimotor stage can be divided into six substages. The first three substages encompass the ages of birth to eight months, and concern unplanned or unintentional activities. Two examples of unintentional activities would be simple reflex activities like kicking, or repeating motions that accidentally cause an interesting event (randomly hitting a mobile). The second three substages involve the development of planned or intentional activities. An example of an intentional activity is deferred imitation, such as when a child sweeps with a broom when he or she has not recently seen someone sweeping.

TABLE 3-3
Piaget's Stages of Intellectual Development

Stage and Approximate Age	Characteristic Behavior
I. *Sensorimotor Operations*	
A. Reflexive (0–1 month)	Simple reflex activity. Example: kicking
B. Primary circular reactions (1–4.5 months)	Reflexive behavior becomes elaborated and coordinated. Example: eye follows hand movements
C. Secondary circular reactions (4.5–9 months)	Repeats chance actions to reproduce an interesting change or effect. Example: kicks crib, doll shakes, so kicks crib again
D. Coordination of secondary schema (8–12 months)	Acts become clearly intentional. Example: reaches behind cushion for ball
E. Tertiary circular reactions (12–18 months)	Discovers new ways to obtain desired goal. Example: pulls pillow nearer to get toy resting on it
F. Invention of new means through mental combinations (18–24 months)	Invents new ways and means. Example: uses stick to reach desired object
II. *Preoperational*	
A. Preconceptual (2–4 years)	Capable of verbal expression, but speech is repetitious; frequent egocentric monologues
B. Intuitive (4–7 years)	Speech becomes socialized; reasoning is egocentric, "to the right" has one meaning — to the child's right
III. *Concrete Operations* (7–11 years)	Mobile and systematic thought organizes and classifies information; is capable of concrete problem-solving
IV. *Formal Operations* (11 years and up)	Can think abstractly, formulate hypotheses, engage in deductive reasoning, and check solutions

Adapted from J. H. Favell. (1963).

Chapman and Miller (1980) discussed the "intentional sensorimotor child," encompassing sensorimotor substages D, E, and F. Following is a brief summary of behaviors seen in each of these stages. Further examples and discussion of these stages can be found in a variety of sources (Chapman & Miller, 1980; Ginsburg & Opper, 1969; Piaget & Inhelder, 1969; Robinson & Robinson, 1983).

• *Stage D* (8–12 months) — children at this stage can anticipate actions and imitate actions already in their repertoires. They also actively search for objects that vanish, indicating beginning development of the concept of object permanence. Although conventional language is not established, differentiated vocalizations and syllabic babbling are present.

• *Stage E* (12–18 months) — at this stage children learn new means to achieve familiar goals and become capable of systematic imitation of new models. Object permanence is more firmly established. Children begin to comprehend single words in context and produce performatives, in which a gesture accompanies a vocalization or word.

• *Stage F* (18–24 months) — children at this stage are beginning to demonstrate representational thought, as seen in understanding words when the referent is not present, and producing two word combinations.

This brief summary should help clarify general behavior characteristics to be expected at each stage. We will continue to refer to these three sensorimotor stages and the preoperational stage throughout the remainder of this book, without further definition.

Goossens' and Crain (1985a) have developed a chart describing behavioral observations of mentally retarded individuals demonstrating sensorimotor skills in various areas: operational causality; imitation; means for obtaining desired environmental events; visual pursuit/the permanence of objects; schemes for relating to objects; and construction of objects in space.

Functional Object Use and Symbolic Play

Many authors view the development of functional use of objects as a prerequisite skill for understanding the language employed to describe the use of the objects (Chappell & Johnson, 1976; Miller, Chapman, Branston, & Reichle, 1980). The exploratory action of young infants putting most objects into the mouth is gradually replaced by the discriminative use of objects as the child learns that an object can be manipulated in a variety of ways. Chappell and Johnson view such "sensorimotor exploration" as the first of three developmental levels of children's responses to objects. The latter phase of this level would involve using different action patterns based on the properties of each object (e.g., banging and waving rattles and squeezing soft or rubber toys). Level 2 involves self-utilization of items, which can be imitative or nonimitative. This stage is termed "functional object use" by some authors. Level 3 is labeled "primitive play application," whereby the child engages in symbolic play (e.g., pretending to give a doll a drink). The person who demonstrates primarily Level 1 exploration of objects may then be encouraged during training to imitate the instructor's use of objects. Concurrent communication training should be encouraged, with targets such as:

• *Vocal play and vocal imitation.* For example, sounds can be used to represent a variety of objects, and may perhaps be paired with music (e.g., /pppp/ can represent a motorboat [Musselwhite, 1985]).

• *Turn-taking with objects and with sounds.* This can include imitation of child-initiated actions on objects (MacDonald & Gillette, 1984).

• *Verbal, sign, or symbol representation of objects.* Early functions can be modeled. These include requesting (hold out hand and ask "baby?"), and labeling (lift up blanket, point, and sign BABY; and directing (point to doll crib, then to symbol of BABY).

For individuals at Levels 2 or 3, both the communicative functions and the language structures used to code those functions can be more advanced (e.g., "Have dolly call Daddy on the phone"). Chappell and Johnson (1976) and Westby (1980) have provided numerous examples for appropriate communicative skills for play levels.

RESOURCES. Numerous sources for assessment and intervention strategies for object interaction are provided in Musselwhite (1986a, Chapters 9 and 10). Additional resources are: The *Carolina Curriculum for Handicapped Infants and Infants at Risk* (Johnson-Martin et al., 1985); "Early communication: Development and training" (Bricker, 1983), and *Infant Learning: A Cognitive-Linguistic Intervention Strategy* (Dunst, 1981).

Object Permanence

Object permanence, or the awareness that an object still exists when it is not in sight, is an important cognitive concept developed during Piaget's sensorimotor stages. A number of authors have developed training programs to facilitate this skill (e.g., Johnson-Martin et al., 1985).

Object permanence is a crucial concept for a person who is nonspeaking and uses an aided communication system. For example, target items may be covered by the individual's arm or, in the case of a multipage display, may be located on another page. Object permanence skills will enable the individual to realize that the target item is still available.

Robinson and Robinson (1983) described a series of three object permanence tasks that increase in complexity:

1. *Prerequisite object permanence skills* — requiring the individual to visually follow an object to a place where it is partially hidden, and eventually to retrieve it, if the person is physically able to do so
2. *Simple object permanence problems* — requiring the individual to observe an object being completely hidden from view to then search for and retrieve it
3. *Complex object permanence problems* — requiring the person to search for and recover an object when its location is unknown.

During all these activities, the individual is learning to manipulate the environment physically.

As with other skills discussed in this chapter, object permanence should be presented as part of a concurrent communication training program, rather than in isolation. For example, when an item is located, the instructor can model a comment regarding the object ("Oooh! The whistle! You found it!").

RESOURCES. Goossens' and Crain (1985a) have prepared an in-depth series of behavioral observations for assessing sensorimotor skills. Strategies for accelerating object permanence can be found in Kahn (1978); Johnson-Martin and colleagues (1985); Hamre-Nietupski and colleagues (1977); and Robinson and Robinson (1983).

Other Early Cognitive Skills

Discriminating characteristics of objects through matching and sorting tasks may also be considered a helpful skill in later language learning. Being able to construct a whole from its pieces, as in puzzle manipulation, demonstrates the emergence of problem-solving skills. A variety of programs (e.g., Goossens' and Crain, 1985a; 1985b; Johnson-Martin et al., 1985) offer assessment devices and training strategies for introducing these skills.

Establishing Motor Imitation

Some prelanguage and language programs provide sequences for teaching motor imitation skills as preliminary skills. Typically, gross motor movements are taught initially and include such activities as clapping, waving "bye-bye," and touching body parts (Baer, 1978; Harris, 1975; Johnson–Martin, et al., 1985). Gradually, fine motor movements of the mouth may be taught (Harris, 1975) before presenting vocalizations for imitation.

Choosing the types of motor movements that should be taught, or are easiest to teach, will be covered in Chapter 7. Most authors suggest that motor tasks selected for initial imitation already be in the individual's repertoires. Once the student is able to imitate the instructor's imitation of a movement initiated by the student, the instructor may begin initiating familiar movements. Gradually, unfamiliar movements initiated by the instructor are presented for imitation.

Traditionally, the instructor is quite direct and indicates that the child should do as told. Goossens' and Crain (1985b) stressed that motor imitation training should take place in a playful, game-like format. MacDonald and Gillette (1986) also offer a procedure that focuses more on turntaking and allows each partner to initiate movements for imitation.

With regard to the functionality of the movement selected, Kent (1974) recommended teaching motor responses that will be used later in the training program (e.g., pointing to body parts and to objects on a table). St. Louis, Rejzer, and Cone (1980) suggested that it is useful to teach functional movements such as drinking from a cup, wiping hands with a towel, or some initial communicative gestures or signs (e.g., wave "bye-bye," sign MORE, rather than traditional motor tasks such as tapping a table or touching the head. Bricker and Dennison (1978) also recommended encouraging motor imitation in practical situations such as pushing elevator buttons, opening doors, and activating a light switch.

Once motor imitation is established, it may lead to developing vocal or verbal imitation, although there is little research to document this hypothesis. Kent (1974) suggested that motor imitation be used as a last attempt to accomplish vocal imitation if other techniques fail to elicit vocalizations. This procedure would have the client imitate a chain of events, beginning with motor movements and ending with a vocalization (e.g., tap table, stand up, say "Hi"). Gradually the motor movements should be faded and only the vocalization required. There is some controversy as to the role of motor imitation in the eventual establishment of verbal imitation (see Harris, 1975, for a review). However, with some individuals this chaining procedure may be useful.

The instructor should be aware of the individual's physical abilities and limitations before initiating motor imitation training. Consultation with the occupational and/or physical therapist should be sought to assist in program planning.

RESOURCES. Sample programs with sections for teaching gestural imitation are Goossens' and Crain (1985b), Johnson-Martin and colleagues (1985), and Struck (1977).

Facilitating Oral-Motor Control

Professionals working with individuals having neurological disorders, such as cerebral palsy and speech impairments related to aphasia (e.g., dysarthria, apraxia), will need to consider the individual's ability to control the oral mechanism to produce intelligible speech. The potential to improve oral-motor control is a vital consideration in electing to use vocal communication as the primary communication mode for an individual. Some researchers have investigated the relationship between feeding problems and speech performance in children with cerebral palsy (Love, Hagerman, & Taimi, 1980; Sheppard, 1964). They found a suggestive positive relationship between abnormal oral reflexes (e.g., rooting reflex, sucking reflex), or feeding problems, and speech proficiency. Alexander (1987) has developed a concise summary of prespeech and feeding development, followed by a summary of abnormal oral-motor and respiratory/phonatory functioning in persons with cerebral palsy. She described the relationship between low postural tone and the need to hold for stability, or to fix to attempt movement, resulting in compensatory movements (e.g., lip pursing, excessive tongue protrusion). Thus, intervention cannot focus simply on observed behaviors (the tongue protrusion), but must address underlying causes, such as difficulty in developing flexion against gravity. This section will present a brief overview of considerations in developing an individual's oral-motor control for eating, and possibly facilitating control for later speech production. The areas to be presented are inhibiting oral reflexes, oral sensory stimulation, inhibiting drooling, cup drinking, and spoon feeding.

Alexander (1987) cautioned that one cannot learn to assess and treat prespeech and feeding problems simply by reading about them. Rather, she recommended special training, followed by hands-on experience with experienced professionals. The suggestions offered in this section are exemplary of techniques used with persons having neurological dysfunction. The instructor should consult a communication disorders specialist and/or an occupational therapist, and should refer to the resources listed in this section, before initiating an intervention program for oral-motor skills.

Inhibiting Oral Reflexes

The persistence of primitive oral reflexes, such as the sucking, biting, and lip reflexes, can interfere with adequate feeding and speech articulation. Several assessment suggestions or tools are available for assessing oral reflex patterns (Goossens' and Crain, 1985a, p. 53; Radtka, 1978; Utley, Holvoet, & Barnes, 1977). Specific strategies for inhibiting persistent oral reflexes include proper handling, jaw control, and desensitization, described in a variety of resources (e.g., Finnie, 1975; Radtka, 1978; Utley et al., 1977).

Oral Sensory Stimulation

During normal motor development, a child places many objects in and around the mouth as one means of exploring the environment. Children with severe physical disabilities may be unable to bring things to their mouths, and therefore may be deprived of oral sensations. Alexander (1987) suggested that initial programming emphasize handling to stimulate more normal postural tone and movement; within this context, well graded tactile stimulation can be presented. Initial emphasis should be on the development of normal responses to tactile input on the body, before beginning the goal of modifying sensitivity to tactile stimulation in the oral area.

Liebman (1977) suggested that parents make oral stimulation part of their play time with the child. Bringing different textures to the cheeks and lips (e.g., rubbing a fuzzy stuffed toy on the child's cheek or allowing a rubber toy to touch the lips) will provide the child with tactile information, and may possibly help desensitize him or her to oral manipulation. Deep pressure oral tactile input should also be directed toward the gums, teeth, tongue, and hard palate using a small toothbrush. Alexander (1987) suggested that these stimulation activities should be incorporated into playtime with caregivers. She discussed a variety of factors that may influence the success of a program to modify oral tactile sensitivity.

- *Intensity of touch.* Light touch will initially be more difficult to tolerate
- *Type of touch.* A tickling style of touch will likely elicit more negative reactions than a firm rubbing or stroking motion
- *Speed of touch.* The hypersensitive child may initially respond more positively to a slow, graded touch, while the hyposensitive child may need a more rapid speed of well graded stimulation.

Inhibiting Drooling

Many individuals with cerebral palsy or other neuromuscular disorders may exhibit abnormal swallowing patterns (e.g., tongue thrust) and drooling. If a person has poor trunk or head control, drooling may occur. An individual whose mouth is habitually open, with the tongue carried forward in the mouth, may also drool. It is important to note that it is not advisable initially to verbally correct the person who drools. Obviously, once the saliva is out of the mouth, it is beyond the individual's control. Improving positioning, teaching correct mouth positioning, and developing a more normal swallowing pattern may reduce drooling (Crickmay,

1966). Reduction of drooling, even if vocal communication is not a realistic goal, helps the individual in general appearance, and may enhance his or her social interactions.

Drinking from a Cup

Drinking from a cup requires patience and practice for many individuals with severe physical disabilities. Taking liquid from a cup involves lip closure as well as control of the head and jaw. Starting with thickened liquids (e.g., fruit nectars, juice thickened with baby cereal or applesauce) in a plastic cup with a portion of the cup cut out for the nose will make the task of drinking easier (Liebman, 1977; Utley et al., 1977). Straw sucking is a difficult task and should not be introduced until cup drinking is well established and then only to increase lip mobility (Mueller, 1975).

Spoon Feeding

When introducing spoon feeding the instructor or parent should consider a number of factors that can influence success:

• *Positioning:* Both the student and the feeder should be positioned to promote optimal responses. For example, the feeder should be at, or slightly below student's eye level to avoid stimulating abnormal head and neck hyperextension (Alexander, 1987).

• *Food texture:* Thickened foods provide greater sensory information and are usually more easily controlled (Alexander, 1987).

• *Early introduction of solid foods* (5–6 months): This stimulates more normal oral tactile sensitivity and aids in the development of chewing and biting (Alexander, 1987). Sobsey (1983) systematically measured the effects of whole and pureed foods on feeding skills in an adolescent with severe oral-motor dysfunction, finding that chewing increased, spilling decreased, and gagging decreased when given whole food.

• *Feeding utensils:* The spoon should fit within the mouth without touching the side gums or teeth (Alexander, 1987). The bowl should be fairly flat, to allow success with minimal lip activity (Liebman, 1977).

• *Food presentation:* Utensils should be offered and removed at or slightly below the level of the student's mouth in a graded manner, to avoid eliciting abnormal activity due to the visual stimulation (Alexander, 1987).

RESOURCES. A number of resources are available to assist in development of prespeech and feeding skills: "Feeding reflexes and neural control" (Radtka, 1978); "Feeding therapy and speech: Some problems of oral motor control" (Liebman, 1977); "Handling, positioning, and feeding the physically handicapped" (Utley, Holvoet, & Barnes, 1977); "Prespeech and feeding development" (Alexander, 1987); *The Normal Acquisition of Oral Feeding Skills: Implications for Assessment and Treatment* (Morris, 1982a); *Pre-Speech Assessment Scale* (Morris, 1982b).

Summary

All of the preliminary skills discussed in this chapter are related to the eventual establishment of a means of communicating, regardless of communication mode. Most recent authors recommend teaching these skills concurrently with a communication program, as suggested throughout the chapter, and this book. We wish to stress that it is crucial not to wait for an individual to be "ready" for communication training. We believe that part of the roles of the educator, therapist (physical, occupational, and/or speech–language), and caregiver are to take the individual at whatever level he or she can function and create experiences that lead toward reaching his or her potential.

Chapter 4
Supportive Services

After the verb "to love," "to help" is the most beautiful verb in the world!
— Baroness von Suttner (1848–1914)

The development and utilization of support services are crucial to meeting the varied communication needs of persons with severe disabilities. Primary support systems include parents and other caregivers, professionals, paraprofessionals, and specialized service agencies or organizations.

The Team Approach

Team organization can be defined by three primary attributes (Golin & Ducanis, 1981):

• *Composition.* The membership of a team will depend on factors such as the disability of the individual and the goals of the team. For example, in developing an initial augmentative communication system for a cognitively intact 5-year-old with severe cerebral palsy, the services of specialists such as a rehabilitation engineer or computer programmer might be added to a core team consisting of a speech-language pathologist, occupational therapist, physical therapist, special educator and social worker. Development of a system for use by a cognitively delayed adult entering a job setting might require additional members such as a vocational specialist or a sign language instructor. The developmental approach (Krogman,

1979) may be followed, with professionals from various disciplines entering and leaving the team as appropriate to the needs of the individual. The core group of therapists may be supplemented as needed, thus keeping the number of team members at any one time to a minimum, and yielding a more realistic and manageable grouping. Roos (1977) asserted that every team, regardless of the model followed, should include the individual's parent(s) or spouse. Whenever feasible, the individual should also be a major contributor to the team's decisions.

• *Function.* This is determined by the organizations for which a team operates and the services it provides. In the past decade, augmentative communication evaluation teams have been formed in many countries, with the purpose of determining which individuals are candidates for an augmentative system, and matching that individual to an appropriate system. However, factors such as setting will affect team function; a school-based team will likely focus on implementation of systems within that setting only, while a hospital-based team may also see individuals in critical care settings, or individuals who have progressive disorders.

• *Task.* A team may have a limited and highly specified task, such as setting up a temporary system for a patient in an intensive care unit, or developing the initial match of system to user, with follow-up provided by another organization or by an individual.

Although there is almost uniform acknowledgement of the need to include members from various disciplines in working with persons with severe disabilities, several different models can be used for the team approach. Hart (1977) and Fewell and Cone (1983) described the following models:

1. The *multi-disciplinary approach,* based on the medical model, in which experts in diverse areas share information about each client
2. The *inter-disciplinary approach,* in which team members share information and attempt to unify their findings
3. The *transdisciplinary approach,* in which all team members make contributions to the initial diagnosis, but one team member assumes responsibility for carrying out recommendations.

Hart cautioned that the relative degree of importance attached to the information collected by various team members may be determined by several factors: (1) the setting (medical, psychotherapeutic, educational); (2) the person who collates the information; and (3) the manner in which the information is shared (staffing, report to teacher). She also warned that both the multi- and inter-disciplinary approaches "often lack an important step in their models: immediate and ongoing feedback with responsible follow-up of the recommendations" (p. 392). Therefore, she recommended using the transdisciplinary approach. Beck (1977) also observed that interdisciplinary team evaluations "have always included recommendations for intervention, but the resources for implementing them have been unavailable in most communities" (p. 397). It may be useful to use a multi- or interdisciplinary approach for the initial evaluation, then shift to a transdisciplinary approach for the intervention phase, to avoid as much as possible this lack of follow-up. Both Hart and Beck stressed that the person with primary responsibility (typically the parent or teacher) must have sufficient familiarity with each of the disciplines represented on the team to be able to ask appropriate questions, interpret data, and carry out specific intervention tasks.

The approach finally chosen, and the entire decision-making process that led to the choice, should be brought to a level of general awareness among the team members. In this way, the team can avoid selecting an inappropriate approach simply because that approach has been routinely used.

Goolsby and Porter (1984) identified support that must be provided by an organization wishing to establish an augmentative communication team. The following factors should be seen as the minimum support necessary.

- *Staff Time.* Time should be allotted for provision of client services, in-service training (both offering and attending such training), team meetings, and dissemination of information.
- *Resources.* It is crucial that the team have access to materials such as adaptive equipment (various equipment for positioning, switches), assessment instruments, and a supply of sample devices or materials (e.g., sample electronic hardware, materials for quickly developing a mock-up display).
- *Support Services.* For efficiency and effectiveness, the team must have secretarial assistance, development of funding sources, and integration into the clinic model.

In conclusion, there are several ways to approach the use of a team in serving persons with severe disabilities, and any of these approaches may be appropriate in certain situations. It is important that the team maintain a flexible attitude in order to best serve the individual's needs in a variety of different situations. Regardless of the team approach selected, group dynamics will be an important consideration. Several resources are available to help the team develop cohesiveness (Golin & Ducanis, 1981; Haynes, 1976; Holm & McCartin, 1978).

Parents and Other Primary Caregivers

There is general agreement about the need to actively involve parents in the intervention process for their children with severe disabilities. Recently, several authors have designed special communication programs to satisfy this need (MacDonald & Gillette, 1986; Manolson, 1984). This increased involvement of parents, requires that we reassess our roles in relation to parents, the parents' roles in relation to their children and the programs which serve those children.

Responsibilities of Professionals in Relation to Parents

Although professionals have many responsibilities to the parents of their clients with severe disabilities, the primary ones include sharing information with the parents, giving them emotional support, and directing their training.

Sharing Information

This goal traditionally includes explaining the nature of the child's problem(s), interpreting test results, and describing diagnostic and therapeutic procedures. However, parents should also be told how litigation (e.g., *Mills v. Board of Education,* 1972) and legislation (e.g., P.L. 94-142) affects their rights and responsibilities. Turnbull (1983) provided a framework for information-sharing from the parent's perspective using an extensive form offering parental suggestions for the IEP conference.

Information-sharing may also take the form of helping interested parents to pursue their own investigations. Parents can be informed of workshops or journal articles that might assist them in helping their children. This will allow parents to absord information directly, rather than having it constantly distilled through a professional. Parents should also be encouraged and helped to contact other local, regional, and national agencies and organizations which offer further information and support. For example, the International Society for Augmentative and Alternative Communication (ISAAC), described in Appendix D, offers a variety of publications and conferences.

The responsibility for information-sharing implies a two-way exchange in which a partnership develops between parent and professional. Roos (1977), of the National Association for Retarded Citizens, cautions that parents "sometimes feel that any suggestion made by a parent regarding his own child is categorically dismissed" (p. 73). One way that parents can share their views is by rating the importance of various services. Cansler, Martin, and Valand (1975) designed a form to rate areas such as training in classroom activities and teaching methods, counseling for family problems, and transportation services. Figure 4-1 presents a sample priority rating form for communciation-related services.

It is very important that family and staff work together as a cooperative team to help students at home and in school. This form will help us determine the best way to provide communication services to our students and their families.

Please check and add comments or suggestions:	Not Important	Of Some Importance	Very Important	Comments
Demonstration of classroom activities and training strategies				
Training to help develop materials such as symbol books				
Training in augmentative communication systems (e.g., signing)				
Exposure to electronic communication devices				
Training for brothers and sisters of child				
Parent meetings to share ideas on communication strategies				
Development of a reading library related to communication				
Suggestions for home communication activities for child				

What do you think would be the most helpful format for parent–staff contacts? Check one or more.

_____ Group meetings with information sharing (lecture/discussion on general areas)

_____ Small group discussion on parent-selected topics

_____ Periodic individual conferences between parents and staff members. How often?

_____ Visits to families' homes by staff member

_____ Classroom observation and participation by parents

_____ Demonstration sessions by staff members, with "hands-on" practice by parents

_____ Information-sharing via newsletter, with articles by staff and families

_____ All of the above, depending on need at the time

_____ I do not feel that parents should be involved in child's education program

Thanks so much for sharing!   Name _____

Figure 4-1

Sample priority rating form for communication-related services. Adapted from Cansler, Martin, and Valand (1975).

Support

Providing emotional support for parents of severely handicapped children may require more effort than that required for parents of less disabled children. Moving through the emotional adjustment process might be more prolonged and intense. Many local, regional, and national organizations offer parent support groups (see Appendix D for a listing of organizations). Professionals should be aware of these services so they can direct parents to them.

If a parent group is not available in the community, one can be established through various agencies such as public or private clinics and schools. Local chapters of organizations such as the Association for Retarded Citizens and United Cerebral Palsy can be extremely helpful, with considerable support provided by their national affiliations. Topics for meetings can be determined via parental rating scales such as the one reprinted in Turnbull (1983, p. 32).

Too often, parent support groups are not developed because of the perceived immensity of the task by professionals. Support groups can vary widely, from highly ambitious to relatively simple. For example, one easily replicable group[1] meets monthly at the developmental day center attended by the children. The simple covered dish lunch offers a relaxed atmosphere for sharing information and feelings. A topic is determined for each meeting, ranging from a short presentation from a professional ("Handling techniques," "How to make your communication more interactive"), to a project discussion ("How can we support the disability awareness program at the local science or health museum?"), to a sharing of information ("Respite care resources in the county," "Local physicians that seem to care about and understand the needs of our children"), or a discussion of feelings ("How can I use one-shot-learning to teach people to talk *to,* not *at* my child?"). This group has expanded to occasional night meetings to complete projects discussed in the day meetings. Resources for developing parent programs can be found in Arnold (1978), Bassin and Kreeb (1978), and Gallagher and Vietze (1986).

Support from parent groups should not replace personal support from the professional. As with information-sharing, support should be mutual, in which parents also demonstrate support for professionals. The professionals can encourage this support by including parents in the decision process and by providing sufficient data to back up program suggestions. Professionals should not overstep their limitations in providing support, but must take the initiative in referring parents to other specialists when the need arises.

---

[1] Mother-to-Mother is a support group at the Irene Wortham Center in Asheville, North Carolina.

Training Parents

Use of parents as primary or secondary instructors is widely recommended (MacDonald & Gillette, 1986; Schumaker & Sherman, 1978; Turnbull, 1983). Turnbull suggested a number of reasons why parents should be directly involved in teaching their children: (1) parents are powerful reinforcing agents; (2) parents know their children better than others and generally spend more time with their children than do professionals; (3) the effectiveness of intervention can be increased if parents follow up at home on the skills being taught at school; and (4) parents receive gratification from contributing to the development of their child.

Baker (1976) suggested that there is an especially strong rationale for parental involvement because communication development typically takes place during infancy and early childhood, and because communication is so basic to the development of other skills. Whether parents serve as primary or supportive instructors for their children, some training and supervision will likely be needed for all parents, if only to teach them to sustain communication skills learned by their child in the classroom. Some communication systems (e.g., most sign systems) may require considerable training merely to enable parents to interpret their child's communication attempts.

Turnbull (1983) identified three approaches to training parents to serve as instructors:

1. *Home Training.* This approach is often used in infant stimulation or preschool programs, typically in combination with an at-school program
2. *Group Training.* This model allows parents the opportunity to learn from each other. Turnbull discussed strategies for overcoming logistical problems inherent in group meetings, as well as rating systems for use in determining course content
3. *Classroom Helper.* In this approach the parent is able to observe firsthand training methods and interactions involving his or her child, and other students having similar or different disabilities and needs.

It may be possible to combine two of these approaches, to allow for maximum flexibility, while meeting the needs of a number of parents in an efficient manner. Baker (1976) stressed that any parent training program should include procedures for assessing its effectiveness. He asserted that "few families make a consistent and serious effort to carry out programs and still fail. Hence, encouraging participation becomes the paramount issue" (p. 717). Baker also described and reviewed several program incentives designed to increase family participation:

- *Social pressure and social support,* such as writing and signing specific performance contracts with the trainer
- *Money,* such as a "contract deposit" which is refunded contingent on completion of agreed-upon performance

- *Reinforcement by family members,* such as agreeing on special activities (e.g., a picnic) following specific gains in child performance
- *Contingent professional support,* such as cards for use in a toy-lending library or training time that is contingent on provision of data on child performance. (pp. 721–722)

Many of these strategies may be equally effective with siblings, who are often excellent sources of patient energy in carrying out simple repetitive programs (object-permanence games, functional object use, "Simon Says" with symbols, signed songs).

One approach to reinforcing learning by both parents and their children is use of a toy lending library. Although a toy lending library can have numerous goals and benefits, one exciting possibility is the chance for parents to practice their new skills (signing, using symbols interactively, matching their level of communication to that of their child) while playing with toys that allow their child to practice his or her newly learned skills. For example, a play dollhouse can be sent home with the Signed English storybook. *A Book About Me,* offering the parent a core of signs that can be used with the dollhouse. Specific goals for practice (by parents and children) can be listed on a sheet sent home with each toy. Musselwhite (1986a, Chapter 13) offered specific strategies for initiating a toy lending library.

The traditional roles of sharing information with, supporting, and training parents must be expanded to meet the greater needs of parents and to conform to the partnership concept deriving from changes in law and current thought. More specific suggestions for working with parents and other communication partners will be presented in the chapters dealing with specific communication systems.

Responsibilities of Parents

Like professionals, parents of children with severe disabilities may fulfill several roles. Turnbull (1983) asserted the need for parents to be parents, dealing with problems such as emotional adjustment and socialization. The role of parents as teachers of their children is widely recognized and accepted. Parents also have an important role as advocate, or agents of social change (Roos, 1977; Turnbull, 1978), working with or through organizations toward changes in law (such as lowering minimum age for reimbursed intervention within a state), policy (for example, local school policy on segregation of students with disabilities), and public attitudes in general. Each of these parental roles will require the professional to assume an appropriate role in response. The roles of parents and professionals are varied and interwoven, changing as the situation warrants. If professionals are to develop effective interactions with parents, they must be aware of and supportive of all these roles.

RESOURCES. *ECO System* (MacDonald & Gillette, 1986); *It Takes Two To Talk: A Hanen Early Language Parent Guide Book* (Manolson, 1984); "Parent-Professional Interactions" (Turnbull, 1983).

Environmental Support and Involvement

Several authors have noted that a major factor in the success of a communication program is the involvement of those in the individual's environment (Kopchick & Lloyd, 1976; Manolson, 1984). This may be of even greater importance with regard to augmentative communication modes, since the communication partner(s) typically must invest more time and effort in decoding the message. Learning a new system, such as signing or even the symbol strategies of Blissymbolics, may require more effort than some people in the environment are willing to make. In addition, unless the communication system has voice output or a hard copy printed message, the partner must pay full attention to the user. Lack of support from people in the environment may be a problem in initiating an augmentative communication system, or generalizing a system being learned by an individual.

Gaining Support for Initiating a System

The overall approach to gaining acceptance and support for introducing a system would seem to be advanced planning. That is, the instructor must anticipate potential objections or resistance and defuse them before significant opposition develops. The potential user, parents, and others in the environment should be involved as much as possible in the decision-making process, so that the suggestion of a new system will not come as a surprise. Thus, the first strategy for gaining support is *early involvement* by all who will be affected by such a major decision.

It is impossible for parents or users to make an informed decision without the proper background. Therefore, the second strategy is *providing information.* This should include general information (e.g., about augmentative systems in general) and specific information (e.g., about the system(s) identified as most appropriate for the individual). The information need not be highly technical, but should be sufficient to provide a basis for decision-making.

A number of concerns might be expressed by the people with whom the individual will communicate. In fact, it is a good idea to ask for a *discussion of concerns* if this does not happen spontaneously. Silverman (1980) identified several common concerns (e.g., "The clinician has given up on improving (or developing) the person's speech." p. 208). He suggested several ways for dealing with these attitudes, such as providing information to minimize the concern and giving reassurance. For example, a parent concerned that professionals have "given up" can be shown reviews of studies showing the impact of augmentative systems (Silverman, 1980, pp. 32–35, 40–44), and can be told exactly what intervention procedures will aim toward development of oral speech.

We recommend that professionals use additional methods for providing reassurance, such as giving *demonstrations of success* by individuals using comparable systems. This can be done through readings, films, or personal visits. Appendix 4–1 provides a listing of sample films in augmentative communication. The specific type of demonstration or information will depend on the system to be implemented and the interests of the potential user and family members. For example, numerous films and pamphlets about Blissymbolics are available through the Blissymbolics Communication International. Newsletters by various organizations often contain articles that are appropriate for this purpose. For example, *Communicating Together,* a publication of the organization, has articles written by consumers, family members, and professionals regarding many different aided and unaided systems. If use of a commerical electronic device is considered, information can also be obtained in advance. In addition to technical specifications regarding a device, many companies offer newsletters and other supportive information. For example, Phonic Ear has the following free information available concerning their VOIS devices (electronic voice output aids): brochures, a film entitled "Breaking Through the Wall," and a newsletter, *Echo On.* A personal visit with a user of the potential system or device can also be an excellent means of gaining support.

Finally, the *current and future uses of the proposed system(s)* should be discussed, focusing on the application to the individual client. For example, if the primary system under consideration is Signing Exact English, it could be helpful to explain that this system should provide a good foundation for future acquisition of reading skills needed by a mainstreamed student, as it parallels spoken and written English.

It may be necessary to gain support by having a trial period of implementation. The time span for this trial period would depend on considerations such as the amount of support provided by the environment and the individual's rate of learning. The intent of these strategies is not to railroad a user or a family into accepting a system that they find objectionable, but to ensure that any objections are based on reality, not misunderstandings or ignorance. As use of augmentative systems becomes more common, initial resistance to use of augmentative systems will hopefully continue to decline.

Gaining Support for Implementing a System

The preceding section was concerned primarily with augmentative communication systems. It is generally easier to gain support for initiating a vocal language program, simply because vocal language is more universally accepted. However, implementation of a vocal language program may pose problems as well, simply because it will require time from everyone involved with the individual.

Initially, at least, it may take less effort and time to anticipate needs rather than to wait for expression of those needs. Other potential demands on staff and family time by the individual who is developing communication skills are an increased demand for attention, the need for direct training, and the need for one-on-one attention during communication with many individuals using augmentative systems. All of these problems are compounded if staff and/or family members are indifferent to communication training programs. Areas in which support must be gained before a system can successfully be implemented include:

- Communicating effectively with the individual
- Assisting in interpreting messages for others or, hopefully, training others to receive messages and interact appropriately
- Training the individual (directly or indirectly)
- Setting up and monitoring a generalization program.

Since these areas are somewhat specific to the system used, they will be discussed in more detail where appropriate throughout the book. A summary of general strategies presented in the section on "Responsibilities to Parents" will be provided here.

First, the *group training sessions* suggested previously can be used for gaining support in implementation. Content can range from sign training (through music, games, and role-playing), to practice in drawing or creating symbols, to ideas for making early communication experiences fun and rewarding for users and partners.

Use of a *toy lending library* can enhance support of families for several reasons. First, the implementation of a new system or new skills can be more enjoyable when centered around play materials. Second, it offers a simple straightforward way of tailoring needs to individuals and to partners such as siblings. Third, it has been our experience that children ask for the toys, thus reminding parents to engage in practice sessions.

Another strategy previously suggested is the use of *sharing sessions.* Harris–Vanderheiden (1976) noted that idea exchange letters could also be used to share effective ways to meet the needs of an individual, a specific population, or a communication system.

Two additional strategies may be especially helpful for gaining support from busy staff members in school or residential settings. The first is to assign responsibility to one individual, who would serve as a *Communication Generalization Coordinator.* This practice follows the example of Foxx and Azrin (1973) in their toilet training program. Duties of this coordinator would be carefully specified, including record keeping and monitoring training and generalization programs.

It may be difficult to convince a staff member to serve as coordinator unless that person, in turn, is provided with support. A strategy to accomplish this is to *enlist the support of the administrator* (special education director, school principal), again as suggested by Foxx and Azrin. Some of the tactics suggested earlier relative to gaining initial support should be helpful. The communication specialist could ask the administrator for concrete support for the coordinator, such as a written declaration of support for the goals of the program, free time for staff to attend training sessions, relief from some duties and/or additional pay for the coordinator, or acknowledgment of program success in the form of memos. We realize that these suggestions may be somewhat idealistic. However, we believe that they are worth trying. We have found that, when given specific requests for support such as those described here, many administrators have been surprisingly helpful.

Funding

It is difficult to review the topic of funding for communication services to persons with severe disabilities. First, the resources change rapidly as new federal, state or province, and local funds become available and old sources of funding become unavailable. Changes in legislation or federal regulations, for example, allow different items and service to be eligible for funding at different times. In addition, many regulations may be interpreted differently by different regions or agencies, and some services are optional under the enabling legislation. An example would be prosthetic devices (including hearing aids) in state plans for Medicaid in the United States. Another important consideration is whether sources are sought for funding entire projects (an augmentative communication classroom, an array of switches for a team) or for individual communication devices, although some of the sources will be the same for both.

Montgomery (1979) listed a number of potential funding sources in the United States. A modification of that list follows:

• *Grants* (to set up centers or programs): Sources include governmental agencies such as the Department of Education, Bureau of Education for the Handicapped, and contract agreements with private colleges.

• *Public Agencies:* These include Children's Special Health Services, Department of Rehabilitation (for disabled adults with employment potential), Medicare, Medicaid, and P.L. 94-142 monies, use of which is determined by local agencies.

• *Private Agencies:* Sources include private insurance companies and foundations.

• *Local Service Organizations:* This includes advocacy groups such as the Association for Retarded Citizens, churches, Parent Teacher Associations, service organizations (Sertoma, Civitan, Telephone Pioneers of America), college fraternities or sororities that provide services to people with communication handicaps, and high school or college clubs.

• *Contributions:* These may come from private individuals and businesses (e.g., IBM provides matching funds for some equipment).

• *Rental or Leasing Agreements:* Many commercial firms allow clients to rent or lease products to determine if they are appropriate.

• *Used Equipment:* Although not a funding source, this option may substantially reduce costs. Sources of used equipment are manufacturers, and newsletters published by augmentative communication advocacy groups.

Several other authors have also developed lists of potential funding sources, including addresses (Hofmann, 1984; Johnson, 1987; Ruggles, 1979).

Manufacturers are typically quite knowledgeable regarding funding, and can offer further suggestions about sources. Hofmann (1984) developed a funding sources check list, reprinted in figure 4–2 that presents a summary of potential sources.

Some controversy exists concerning the use of local funding sources, such as service organizations and private contributors. As Enders (1983) observed, purchase of equipment should not have to depend on philanthropy. The main concern is that continued reliance on these sources may tend to cause agencies such as the local school systems, Medicare, and private insurance companies to ignore their responsibilities regarding funding. In addition, gaining funding haphazardly may give the impression that the projects funded are trivial (Judy Mongomery, personal communication). Professionals in the field of augmentative communication seem to have two possibly conflicting responsibilities: (1) we must ensure that our clients receive the best possible equipment with the shortest possible delay; but (2) we must pursue greater support of services for our clients, taking care not to set precedents that will misleadingly suggest to the public sector and private insurance companies that their assistance is not needed.

The application process involves several areas, outlined by the United Cerebral Palsy Association (UCP) of California (as reprinted in *The Many Faces of Funding* [Hofmann, 1984]):

1. *Reaching the Funding Source:* This refers to the consideration of both public and nonpublic sources. The UCP urged professionals to continue to apply even to agencies with a poor record for funding. As they stressed, "If claims are not filed, how else will these agencies become aware of the needs of the nonoral population?"

2. *Educating the Agency:* Several strategies for education of an agency are filing claims, submitting supportive documentation, and using appeal processes, thus building a record of requests with the agency.

FUNDING SOURCES CHECK LIST

Patient Name _____   Sex: M   F   Year Born _____

Address _____   Disability/Medical Diagnosis:

City _____ State _____ Zip _____   _____

Telephone _____

Patient status: ____ Mother   Time of onset: Birth _____
                ____ Father   If later, year _____
                ____ Son
                ____ Daughter
        _____ Other (specify)

FAMILY STATUS

	Employed?	If yes: Where? (name of co.)	Group Insurance	Name of Insurance Co.
Mother	Y N	Y N	_____	Y N	_____
Father	Y N	Y N	_____	Y N	_____
Other _____	Y N	Y N	_____	Y N	_____

Any family insurance? Y N   Anyone member of a labor union? Y N

If yes: (name of carrier) _____   If yes: Who? _____

                                               What union? _____

PATIENT EDUCATION

Attending school? Y N   If yes: Elementary _____   HS _____   College _____   Other _____

PATIENT EMPLOYMENT

	If yes: Where? (name of co.)	Dates Employed From	To	Group Insurance
Employed? Y N	_____	_____	_____	Y N
Ever Employed? Y N	_____	_____	_____	Y N

PUBLIC SERVICES PROVIDED TO DATE

_____ Medicare

_____ Medicaid

_____ Veterans Administration

_____ Education for Handicapped   PL 94-142/Section 504

_____ Vocational Rehabilitation

_____ Crippled Children's Services (CCS)

_____ Other (specify) _____

STEPS TOWARD SEEKING FUNDING

File applications with:

1. Public Services provided
2. Group insurance or private insurance
3. Labor union membership

If the foregoing do not provide funding, investigate non-public programs, i.e.:

• Corporate foundations: investigate local offices of large corporations
• Local businesses with benevolent funds for community programs
• Private foundations
• Volunteer agencies:

Kiwanis	Elks
Rotary	Knights of Columbus
Lion's International	Soroptimists
United Cerebral Palsy	Optimists
Sertoma	ALS
Bell Tele. Pioneers of America	Churches — especially patient's affiliation

• Advocacy groups for help/direction write for local representative name:
    Closer Look, Box 1492, Washington, DC 20013
    Pilot Parents, 3212 Dodge Street, Omaha, Nebraska 68131

Phonic Ear HandiVoice/VOIS

Printed in USA © 1984 Phonic Ear Inc.   823-4531-1-01 1084

Figure 4-2

Funding sources check list. From Hofmann, A. (1984). *The many faces of funding.* Mill Valley, CA: Phonic Ear, Inc.

DEFINITIONS

MEDICARE is designed to serve everyone over 65 years of age and disabled persons under 65 years of age who have been entitled to receive Social Security disability benefits for a total of 24 months.

The program is not based on income, but is available regardless of financial need.

Medicare program has two parts:
Part A: Hospital insurance at no cost
Part B: Voluntary medical insurance at a monthly premium

Phonic Mirror HandiVoice/Phonic Ear Vois claims are filed under Part B.

MEDICAID is a joint Federal/State program to provide physical and related health care services to persons with low income. Disabled persons may be eligible for Medicaid on the basis of their income.

Eligibility is determined by claimant's State program of public assistance. Generally, persons may be eligible for Medicaid if they are receiving welfare or other public assistance benefits or Supplemental Security Income or are blind or disabled.

VETERANS ADMINISTRATION The VA will fund any communication device prescribed for a person who has a "service connected" disability. Should the individual not have a "service connected" disability, funding may be obtained through the Prosthetics Evaluation Center in New York City for evaluation.

EDUCATION FOR HANDICAPPED Under the provisions of the Education for All Handicapped Children Act of 1975 (PL 94-142), your state and local school district must provide an appropriate elementary and secondary education for your disabled child from age six through 21. In those states mandating public education for children age three to five, PL 94-142 requires that disabled children of that age group be found and educated in the Least Restrictive Environment (LRE). This education must cost you no more than it costs parents of nonhandicapped children.

Final responsibility for implementing the Education for All Handicapped Children Act rests with the state education agency.

VOCATIONAL REHABILITATION All states have voc rehab agencies to help handicapped persons become employable, by providing a wide range of services, financial assistance, and training.

Expenses born by the program will vary widely from case to case and state to state. An individualized plan for rehab is worked out for every eligible handicapped individual, through meetings of that individual and the counselors, to determine the individual's potential existing skills, and other resources.

The Federal Government provides extensive support to the states for voc rehab services. However, the services themselves are very individualized, and information useful to the individual must be sought at the state and local, rather than the Federal level.

CRIPPLED CHILDREN'S SERVICES (CCS) is a joint Federal/state program to provide medical and related service to handicapped children from birth to age 21.

All states must provide medical diagnosis and evaluation free for all children. (No state residency period is required before such services are provided.) The range and cost of additional treatment or hospital care services vary from state to state. All programs accept third-party payments such as Medicaid, Blue Cross and Blue Shield and other medical insurance.

DEVELOPMENTALLY DISABLED The developmentally disabled (DD) program makes use of existing services in health, welfare, education, and rehabilitation to provide for the long-range needs of people with developmental disabilities. These disabilities are defined as severe, chronic disabilities attributable to mental or physical impairment, which are manifested before age 22, result in substantial functional limitations in several areas of life, and require services over an extended period.

Availability of services will vary in all communities. Each state has a designated agency to administer the developmental disabilities program. Also in each state is a protection and advocacy office where DD people or their parents can turn if they do not find help in their communities.

INSURANCE Whether the insurance carrier is Blue Cross/Blue Shield or one of the private insurance companies, coverage for a communication device by a carrier depends upon the terms of the policy and its interpretation. Each case stands on its own; precedence does not affect the determination of coverage.

When filing an application for insurance coverage, it is important to include a prescription by a physician. In addition, documentation from an SP, OT, or PT to show need and how technology can improve the environment of the physically impaired.

A claim with good documentation and supportive facts will provide the insurance carrier with better decision making tools.

Claims filed with unions deserve the same detailed information.

NON-PUBLIC PROGRAMS To reach the various types of funding sources listed requires some research at the library, the telephone book, or contacting your local Chamber of Commerce to determine what sources are available and where they can be reached.

If your patient or family members have any affiliation with some of these groups, find out from them who you might contact.

Don't forget your local newspapers, TV and radio — all of them have commitments to public service. Properly approached and presented, they may be willing to support your plans.

3. *Supporting Documentation:* Sample information might include letters from the potential user and family members, information on the device for which the funding is sought, and an assessment report (preferably, a team evaluation), demonstrating that the individual has the ability to use the device requested.

4. *Physician's Prescription:* The UCPA report lists six specific components that should be included, such as a pertinent diagnosis and estimate of the benefits expected from use of the communication equipment (attending school, employment, self-care activities, directing attendant care, freeing up family members to become employed, etc.).

Sample forms for each phase of the process can be found in Hofmann (1984) and the Prentke–Romich Funding Packet (1986). As Robison and Robison (1985) pointed out, keeping accurate records is crucial. They asserted that "the single most important factor to keep in mind is the accurate documentation of all reports and medical history pertinent to obtaining the equipment."

The UCPA report recognized that all funding agencies view clients from a particular perspective, such as enabling the individual to become a taxpayer (government agencies), or reducing therapy costs (insurance companies). In both general supportive documents and the physician's prescription, these goals should be emphasized, with a description of how those agency goals can be met through purchase of this particular device to meet the needs of this specific individual.

The appeal process is acknowledged as a step often required to finally receive funding. Several updates to *The Many Faces of Funding* (Hofmann, 1984) have presented general appeal strategies as well as strategies for appealing to specific agencies (August, 1984; January, 1985; July, 1985; November, 1985; May, 1986; November, 1986).

There are a number of guides to the funding maze. The primary resource is *The Many Faces of Funding* (Hofmann, 1984). This book, reviewed in Appendix B, provides extensive support to the general area of funding, plus monthly updates to meet changing needs. Several additional resources include chapters in various books (e.g., Cohen, 1986; Johnson, 1987), pamphlets (e.g., "Creative funding for services," Buzolich, 1987a; "Funding of non-vocal communication aids,' Ruggles, 1979), and newsletters (e.g., *Communication Outlook*) that issue frequent reports on funding. Organizations can also provide needed assistance. For example, The Foundation Center (see Appendix D) has many cooperating state collections that provide access to computer listings of funding sources appropriate for the needy.

For information on federal funding sources the *Catalog of Federal Domestic Assistance* (1986) is recommended (see Appendix B). It covers funding sources such as Children's Special Health Services, Medicare, and

Medicaid. The American Speech-Language-Hearing Association also provides informational packets on Medicare and Medicaid as they relate to speech–language pathology and audiology services. In addition, ASHA has initiated a quarterly publication, *Governmental Affairs Review*. It will cover areas such as developments in federal legislation (including funding components such as Medicare and P.L. 94-142), federal regulations (such as those concerning Medicare home health cost limits), and sources of further information.

Innovative approaches are occurring in the area of funding. For example, the Pennsylvania Bureau of Special Education has recently announced a program to fund long-term loans of devices to assist students with handicaps (Hofmann, 1986). In addition, many professionals report successes in achieving funding from sources that previously denied similar requests. The major keys to success appear to be knowledge (about the individual, the device, the agency) and perserverance.

Summary

Numerous sources of support are available to the family seeking augmentative communication services or the professional providing such services. This support ranges from that provided by team members, to support within the family, to support from the environment and the community. This support can take the form of information or services. This chapter has described several forms of support, and has provided suggestions for maximizing support and locating resources. The complexity of the challenge facing augmented communicators, their families, and the professionals who work with them demands that support systems be developed and tapped.

Appendix 4-1. Sample Videotapes in Augmentative Communication

Talk is Not a Four-Letter Word. Blackstone and Cassatt–Jones (1986); VHS, 16 minutes; Publications Department, American Speech-Language-Hearing Association, 10801 Rockville Pick, Rockville, MD 20852. (An overview of the area of augmentative communication, including an instructional guide.)

Now I Can Speak. Blissymbolics Communication International (1981); VHS/Beta, 20 minutes; Easter Seals Communication Institute, 24 Ferrand Drive, Toronto, Ontario, Canada M4C 3N2. (14 variations of Blissymbol use with children and adults.)

Amer-Ind Gestural Code. Skelly (1984); VHS/Beta, 60 minutes; Auditec of St. Louis, 330 Selma Avenue, St. Louis, MO 63119. (250 signals of the Amer-Ind Code in citation form, modeled by Dr. Madge Skelly.)

From Silence to Soloist. (1982); VHS, 27 minutes; Media Resource Center, Meyer Children's Rehabilitation Institute, 444 South 44th Street, Omaha, NE 68131. (Follows the development of oral and augmentative communication skills in a boy from age 4 to 11.)

To Be Like Anyone Else. Crippled Children's Hospital and South Dakota Department of Education (1984); VHS, 29 minutes; Speech Department, Crippled Children's Hospital and School, 2501 West 26th Street, Sioux Falls, SD 57105. (Demonstrates use of augmentative devices by children in a variety of real-life situations.)

A Voice Within. Montgomery and Dashiell (1987); VHS, 8 minutes; Lawren Productions, P.O. Box 666, Mendocino, CA 95460. (Samples of augmentative systems that can facilitate academics and interaction for nonspeakers from age 3 to 22.)

For a more extensive listing, refer to Brandenburg and Vanderheiden (1987a, b, c, Appendix B).

Part II: Vocal Communication Systems

Chapter 5
Vocal Communication Strategies

Speech is civilization itself. The word, even the most contradictory word, preserves contact — it is silence which isolates.

— Thomas Mann

This chapter provides an overview of 20 vocal language programs available to special educators and communication specialists working with people at the preverbal and early verbal stages of communication development. The general issues (the models, methodology, role of imitation, etc.) involved in examining a communication system, which were presented in Chapter 2, will be discussed in this chapter as they relate to vocal language programs and to the various stages or sequences which programs follow in developing vocal communication skills. The role of parents or other communication partners in a person's home environment will be discussed in terms of overall program planning and of establishing generalized language skills.

The decision-making process, as presented in Chapter 1, does not end with the selection of a mode of communication or a particular training program. The process must be ongoing, and the decision must be frequently assessed so that significant changes in the student's language abilities and living environment can be used to direct future programming. Moreover, the federally mandated requirement of developing an Individual Education Plan (I.E.P.) for each special needs student in the public schools stresses the individuality of each person. In many cases, a single vocal program will not meet the needs of a person with a severe communication handicap. The instructor should consider blending portions of several programs to meet the needs of each individual (Orelove & Sobsey, 1987).

Vocal Language Programs: An Overview

Once the decision is made to teach a person to use vocal communication as the primary system, the instructor must then design specific goals and tasks to teach the person appropriate vocal language skills. The instructor must utilize all the observational data, test results, and reported information gathered from the primary caregiver(s) during the assessment process to develop an I.E.P. for the student.

Many vocal language programs are available commercially. Twenty programs are listed in Table 5-1. For easy reference, they will be referred to throughout the rest of this chapter by the numbers assigned to them in Table 5-1. Each program is annotated in Appendix B.

Table 5-1 does not represent an exhaustive listing of vocal language programs. These 20 programs are included because of their general availability for use within public school and institutional settings. Most of the programs are relatively inexpensive, requiring only a manual for implementation. In these programs, the instructor typically supplies all of the stimulus materials which are readily found in most classrooms. The *Peabody Language Development Kits* (Table 5-1, item 4) provide materials such as pictures and puppets to accompany the lessons.

Ten of the language programs were developed as part of comprehensive skill training procedures for people with severe handicaps (Table 5-1, items 1, 2, 3, 10, 12, 15, 16, 17, 18, and 20). For example, *Volume II* of *Teaching the Moderately and Severely Handicapped* (Table 5, item 1) contains communication training plus socialization, safety, and leisure-time skills instruction. It is important to note that *Volumes I* and *III* (Bender & Valletutti, 1976; Bender, Valletutti, & Bender, 1985) are also available for use in other areas such as behavior, self-care, motor skills, and functional academics for people with mild to moderate handicaps. Since communication training is not contained in *Volumes I* and *III,* they are not included in Table 5-1.

The remaining ten programs (Table 5-1, items 4, 5, 6, 7, 8, 9, 11, 13, 14, and 19) were developed solely as language training procedures for people with mildly to severely disordered language abilities. Although the *Peabody Language Development Kits* were developed for students with mild communication handicaps, they are included in this overview because the materials and procedures they use are often used in language stimulation and generalization training for persons with severe handicaps.

TABLE 5-1
Vocal Language Programs

Program	Author(s)
1. *Teaching the Moderately and Severely Handicapped, Volume II*	Bender, Valletutti, & Bender (1985)
2. *Portage Guide to Early Education*	Bluma, Shearer, Frohman, & Hillard (1976)
3. *The Insite Model. Volume III: Communication*	Clark, Morgan, & Wilson-Vlotman (1984)
4. *Peabody Language Development Kits*	Dunn, Smith, Dunn, Horton, & Smith (1981)
5. *Infant Learning: A Cognitive-Linguistic Intervention Strategy*	Dunst (1981)
6. *Functional Speech and Language Training for the Severely Handicapped*	Guess, Sailor, & Baer (1978)
7. *Developmental Communication Curriculum (DCC)*	Hanna, Lippert, & Harris (1982)
8. *How to Use Incidental Teaching for Elaborating Language*	Hart & Risley (1982)
9. *Ready, Set, Go: Talk To Me*	Horstmeier & MacDonald (1978)
10. *The Carolina Curriculum for Handicapped Infants and Infants at Risk*	Johnson-Martin, Jens, & Attermeier (1986)
11. *Language Acquisition Program for the Retarded and Multiply Impaired*	Kent (1974)
12. *The Teaching Expressive and Receptive Language to Students with Moderate and Severe Handicaps*	Makohon & Fredericks (1985)
13. *It Takes Two To Talk*	Manolson (1984)
14. *Ecological Communication System (ECO)*	MacDonald et al., (1986)
15. *Program for the Acquisition of Language with the Severely Impaired (PALS)*	Owens (1982)
16. *A Prescriptive and Behavioral Checklist for the Severely and Profoundly Retarded*	Popovich (1977)
17. *WVS: Receptive Language Curriculum for the Moderately, Severely, and Profoundly Handicapped*	St. Louis, Mattingly, & Esposito (1986)
18. *WVS: Expressive Language Curriculum for the Moderately, Severely, and Profoundly Handicapped*	St. Louis & Rejzer (1986)
19. *Initial Communication Processes*	Schery & Wilcoxen (1982)
20. *Behavioral Characteristics Progression (BCP)*	Struck (1977)

See Appendix B for further details on these programs.

Prognostic Factors

The key to teaching any type of behavior is making sure that the person experiences success in his or her attempts to perform the required behavior. The instructor must carefully consider the person's present abilities and attempt to predict how successful he or she will be in establishing new behavior patterns. In establishing vocal language, at least 10 prognostic factors should be considered. Table 5-2 presents an outline of these factors.

One of the most important factors in teaching vocal language is the *person's physical ability to produce speech sounds*. Shane and Bashir (1978) asserted "that persistent oral reflexes suggest an extremely poor prognosis for oral speech development." They suggested that the person's eating patterns, drooling (if present), vocal repertoire, and neuromuscular status of the oral mechanism should be evaluated carefully. Love, Hagerman, and Taimi (1980) called for careful assessment of the neuromuscular status of the oral mechanism in cerebral palsied clients. They found the poor articulation and overall reduced speech proficiency occurred in subjects having fre-

TABLE 5-2
Prognostic Factors for Success with Vocal Language

1. Physical ability to produce speech sounds	(Guess, Sailor, & Baer, 1977; Love, Hagerman, & Taimi, 1980; Shane & Bashir, 1980)
2. Level of cognitive development	(Miller & Yoder, 1974)
3. Motivation and communication intent	(Miller & Yoder, 1974; McLean & Snyder-McLean, 1978; Bloom & Lahey, 1978; Siegel & Spradlin, 1978)
4. Age of less than five years at initiation of training	(Harris, 1975; Hayden & McGinness, 1977)
5. Ability to imitate words verbally	(Guess et al., 1977; Lovaas, 1981)
6. Ability to attend to trainer	(Kent, 1974)
7. Echolalia as observed in autism	(Harris, 1975)
8. Previous speaking as in selective mutism	(Harris, 1975)
9. Adequate hearing	(Guess et al., 1977)
10. Adequate vision	(Guess et al., 1977)

quent feeding problems caused by neuromuscular impairment, although the frequency of feeding problems was less than expected. A severely physically impaired person with cerebral palsy may not have sufficient control of the oral musculature to produce intelligible speech. A person with verbal or oral apraxia may be able to vocalize and produce selected sound patterns, but may be extremely frustrated by his or her inability to produce words correctly. For a systematic screening procedure to assess the oral mechanism, see St. Louis and Ruscello (1987).

The second factor, the *level of cognitive development*, implies that, given adequate physical ability to vocalize, the higher the person's level of cognitive development the more likely the development of vocal language. Miller and Yoder (1974) indicated that engaging in imaginative and representational play are foundations for cognitive development. A person who manipulates objects properly, and interacts with his or her environment, will likely understand the function of language and demonstrate a need to communicate with other people.

The third prognostic factor, *motivation,* relates closely to communicative intent. Current research interest in pragmatics related to language acquisition focuses on communicative interactions and the functional use of gestures or words to convey messages. Many authors (Constable, 1983; McLean and Snyder-McLean, 1978; Siegel & Spradlin, 1978) view communication intent as vital to language training. A person who has been unsuccessful in communicating his or her needs and desires may cease trying. In some situations the caregivers in the person's environment may anticipate the person's needs, or may quickly interpret gross movements or sounds without discriminating the actual intention of the person's communicative attempt. Misinterpretation of these attempts can be devastating to a nonspeaker or a speaker who is using limited vocalizations. Bigge and O'Donnell (1982) discussed a way to avoid or lessen "deadlock" situations, where the message giver and the message receiver find their attempts at communication are lost or misunderstood. Empathy conveyed in a statement like, "I don't understand what you mean. It sure makes me feel sad. Let's try again," may help the nonspeaker continue to try.

The fourth factor to be considered is the *age at which training is initiated.* Harris (1975) concluded from the studies she reviewed "that children who fail to develop speech by five years of age have a poorer prognosis than do those who have language by that time." Hayden and McGinness (1977) advocated early intervention with children at high risk for developmental disabilities. They asserted that "failure to provide a stimulating early environment leads not only to a continuation of the developmental status quo, but to actual atrophy of sensory abilities and to developmental regression" (p. 153). They stressed that there are critical periods for development of certain skills; early intervention may help bring these critical times to fruition. Carlson (1987) stressed the importance of intervening in infancy with high-risk children (e.g., those with cerebral palsy) rather than adopting a "wait and see attitude."

Educators agree that early intervention is best, but educators are frequently confronted with the challenge of training teenagers who still have little or no functional speech. Williams and Fox (1977) indicated that the instructor must consider how many years it may take to establish speech as the major communication mode. An augmentative means of communicating might then be the preferred choice of treatment (see Chapters 7, 8, and 9).

The next prognostic factor presented in Table 5-2 is the *ability to imitate words verbally.* Guess, Sailor, and Baer (1978) stated that verbal imitation is the most important factor for entrance into their functional language program (Table 5-1, item 6). During the field-test portion of their program development they found that about 30 to 40 percent of the children with severe handicaps participating in the training program failed to develop verbal imitation. A few nonimitative children did succeed in the language training sequences, but the authors noted that those children appeared to have "more of a motivational problem than a lack of imitative ability" (p. 365). Lovaas (1981) also noted that imitation was a key factor in predicting success in training speech. A more detailed discussion of the role of imitation in language development was presented in Chapter 2. For further discussion see the imitation section of this chapter.

Factor six indicates that the student needs to be able to *attend to the instructor and stimulus.* Many programs (Porter et al., 1985; Shea & Mount, 1982) and portions of curricula (e.g., Johnson-Martin et al., 1985; Kent, 1974; and Owens, 1982) address preverbal skills such as attending and eliminating interfering behaviors.

Factors seven and eight, *echolalia* and *previous speaking experience,* are presented in Harris' (1975) review of the literature as predictors for establishing speech with training. She indicated that researchers have found it easier to teach children who at some point have had speech than those who have not. Examples are autistic children who are echolalic, and persons who are selectively mute. If a client previously possessed speaking ability, he or she is more likely to have a foundation for communication interaction and a stronger desire to regain the ability to speak. Although the vocalizations may be extremely limited, some previous knowledge of language form and content can often be utilized to help teach speech again.

The final factors, *adequate hearing* and *adequate vision,* are listed as prerequiste skills for entrance into the Guess, Sailor, and Baer program (1978). Normal hearing and normal or corrected vision appear to be criteria for many vocal language programs. However, these criteria are often assumed rather than specifically stated as prerequisites. Some programs (e.g., Clark & Moores, 1984; Johnson-Martin et al., 1985; Kent, 1974) provide suggestions for adapting the programs for manual communication to accommodate the severely hearing impaired, as well as nonspeaking hearing clients. All of the vocal programs discussed in this chapter use visual stimuli in the form of objects, pictures, or other symbols as the focus for training. A person with blindness as his or her only handicapping condition could be expected to develop speech normally, although he or she might demonstrate problems in conceptual development. A person who is deaf or blind and severely physically impaired would require very specialized adapted training (see Chapters 7 and 8).

To summarize, the 10 prognostic factors presented in Table 5-2 should be considered carefully when designing a communication system for a specific client. Difficulty or impairment in one or more factors does not mean automatic rejection of vocal language training, but it does indicate that training procedures will need to be modified appropriately to meet the needs of the individual. If it is determined that the person has a very poor prognosis for developing functional speech, then the introduction of an augmentative approach to communication should be seriously considered.

Assessment

Part of the decision process described in Chapter 1 revolves around careful assessment of the person's current level of language functioning as well as evaluation of physical, mental, and emotional development. Each of the prognostic factors discussed in the previous section should be considered during assessment of vocal communication potential. The factors may be assessed formally and informally. For example, physical ability to produce speech sounds could be assessed directly, through an observation of speech sound production under spontaneous, imitative, and elicited conditions, or indirectly, through assessment of feeding ability, oral-motor movements, infantile oral reflexes, and so forth. Each of these subareas could also be assessed directly or indirectly. For example, the specific procedures described by Love and associates (1980) could be used in addition to informal observation and parental reports to assess feeding skills.

The use of formal standardized or criterion-referenced tests is usually recommended if reliable responses can be obtained. However, most of these tests are designed for a compliant, physically normal, auditorily and visually alert person. Most persons with severe handicaps have multiple handicapping conditions which may make it difficult to use many assessment tools exactly as they were intended. Wasson, Tynan, and Gardiner (1982) have presented many suggestions for adapting test instruments so that people with multiple handicaps can be evaluated using standardized tests. A skilled evaluator will use formal tests only as one reference point in the total assessment process. McDonald (1987) provided an extensive listing of psychological, occupational, language, and personality tests appropriate for evaluating people with cerebral palsy. However, adaptations for these tests were not provided although the need for adaptation was stated. Appendix B offers an overview of some available assessment devices. In the following section a general evaluation of vocal language assessment strategies will be presented. Part of this section will focus on prescriptive assessment procedures which accompany some of the specific language programs listed in Table 5-1.

General Assessment Strategies

Reichle and Yoder (1979) suggested using three general speech assessment strategies to evaluate the language abilities of a person with a language disorder. One strategy involves transcribing the person's emitted communication behavior (vocal as well as gestural) in a "free operating environment." This can be time-consuming if the person speaks or attempts to communicate infrequently within a given time period. Strategy two involves observing the individual in a variety of situations, noting communication interactions. This procedure can also be very time-consuming and may yield limited information. The third strategy is interviewing the caregivers (e.g., classroom personnel, ward staff, and parents). Reichle and Yoder have found in their review of literature pertaining to assessment strategies that interviewing can be as reliable as the first two strategies and, when used with transcribed samples and observational data, can supplement or support findings. Using all three strategies will obviously yield the most complete information for designing a comprehensive intervention program.

Most formal assessment devices require compliance to commands as part of the desired response. Huttenlocher (1974) indicated that until a developmental level of at least 12 months is reached, compliance may not be established and formal testing may be fruitless. Thus, for example, a teenager functioning at an estimated six to eight-month level will probably not be able to handle most formal test items regardless of adaptations. Smith (1972) found that pointing to pictures, a common test response mode, was not in the repertoire of normally developing children until the 18-month level. Chapman (1974) suggested that the use of a question-asking strategy, another common testing procedure, is not effective until at least the 24-month level.

Miller, Reichle, and Rettie (1977) found in their study of 15- to 20-month old normally developing children that, when asked to locate an object, these children made one of three responses: they either (1) ignored the stimulus, (2) looked at the object, or (3) pointed or vocalized. Thus, when evaluating low-functioning individuals, the evaluator should record not only the occurrence of the expected response, but an observational note as to what other type of response occurred (e.g., child turned head away from stimulus).

It is difficult to imagine a person who is totally unresponsive to his or her environment or who is totally uncommunicative. Therefore, the evaluator must be sensitive to subtle responses to the environment. Soltman and Reike (1977) presented suggestions for a systematic observation and recording procedure with an unresponsive child. Their procedure allows a communication specialist to carefully document antecedent events, client responses, client initiations, and staff responses to these initiations. They emphasized the need for a team approach (including parents) in the evaluation process. For example, understanding what annoys or frustrates the staff, parents, and client provides valuable information for program planning.

Prescriptive Assessment Devices

For the purpose of the following discussion, prescriptive assessment devices are defined as testing procedures, included in a specific language teaching program, which will help the instructor determine if the program is appropriate for the individual and, if so, at what point in the program training should begin. There are four ways in which the vocal language programs listed in Table 5-1 can be categorized regarding the use of prescriptive assessment devices.

1. Programs based on or coordinated with other separately published assessment devices
2. Programs that contain a detailed assessment device labeled as an inventory, checklist, or strand
3. Programs designed in very specific training steps, usually labeled as objectives, where each step or objective serves as its own pretest and posttest to determine movement through the program
4. Programs that do not provide or recommend specific assessment procedures.

Table 5-3 is a compilation of the 20 vocal language programs from Table 5-1 divided into these assessment categories.

Prescriptive assessment procedures, whether they are general inventories or involve specific objectives, may also be used as reassessment devices to chart progress and re-evaluate training priorities. Many of the programs are useful in generating I.E.P.s, using the general skill area targeted for treatment as long-term goals, and selecting specific objectives

TABLE 5-3

Vocal Language Programs Assessment Categories

Programs that Contain a Detailed Assessment Device	Programs Designed with Each Objective Serving as a Pre-test and Post-test	Programs that do not Provide Specific Assessment Procedures
2. Portage Guide for Early Intervention	1. Teaching the Moderately and Severely Handicapped: Vol. II	4. The Peabody Language Development Kits
3. Insite Model: Vol. III	5. Infant Learning: A Cognitive-Linguistic Intervention Strategy	8. How to Use Incidental Teaching to Elaborate Language
7. Developmental Communication Curriculum (DCC)	6. Functional Speech and Language Training	
9. Ready, Set, Go: Talk to Me	12. The Teaching Research Curriculum	
10. The Carolina Curriculum	17. WVS: Receptive Language Curriculum	
11. The Language Acquisition Program	18. WVS: Expressive Language Curriculum	
13. It Takes Two To Talk	20. Behavioral Characteristics Progression	
14. Ecological Communication System		
15. Program for the Acquisition of Language (PALS)		
16. A Prescriptive and Behavioral Checklist		
19. Initial Communication Processes		
20. Behavioral Characteristics Progression (BCP)		

All numbers correspond to the program listing in Table 5-1.

within that area as short-term goals (Table 5-1, items 1, 2, 3, 5, 6, 7, 10, 11, 12, 15, 16, 17, 18, 19, and 20).

In summary, preselection of a standardized assessment battery is not appropriate for the severely handicapped population. The communication specialist must utilize a variety of assessment tools and techniques as part of an ongoing decision process. These assessment procedures may be part of — or separate from — the vocal language program(s) being used.

Stages of Vocal Programs

Several authors (e.g., Garcia & DeHaven, 1974; Harris, 1975; Risley, Hart, & Doke, 1972) have noted that many language acquisition programs for people with severe handicaps utilize a series of stages, though not all programs include all stages. Harris (1975), in her review of language training for nonverbal children, identified four commonly used stages:

1. Attention
2. Nonverbal imitation — which may include imitation of body movements and vocal sounds but not meaningful words
3. Verbal imitation
4. Functional language.

Orelove and Sobsey (1987) reviewed these four stages with some reservations. They stated that "establishing attention is essential in all communication training" (p. 292). Their literature review suggested that "generalized imitation is not required to teach communication functions and its value as an intermediate step is questionable" (p. 292). However, use of verbal imitation may help production skills and facilitate development of spontaneous language. They presented several concerns about the use of structured programs:

1. Requiring steps that are too large for students with very severe handicaps
2. Lacking flexibility to respond individually to each learner
3. Encouraging the learners to respond to, rather than to initiate, conversation
4. Failing to generalize outside the lesson
5. Failing to teach the skills most functional for the individual. (p. 293)

Orelove and Sobsey also presented advantages of structured programs:

1. Providing a vastly increased number of learning trials, which reduces acquisition time
2. Structuring instruction to increase the probability of correct responses

3. Providing a turn-taking format that teaches a basic interaction pattern required for communication. (p. 293)

The instructor should take into consideration these advantages and disadvantages when using commercially available structured programs. A blending of structured and unstructured teaching techniques may best benefit the student.

Attending and Motor Imitation

Teaching an individual to attend, and establishing motor imitation, are often considered prerequisite skills to entering a language program. These stages were discussed in more detail in Chapter 3. Some of the vocal language programs reviewed in this chapter that present training sequences for establishing attention and motor imitation are items 1, 2, 7, 9, 10, 11, 12, 15, 16, 18, and 20 in Table 5-1. The main focus of this chapter will be on stage 3, verbal imitation, and stage 4, functional language.

Vocal and Verbal Imitation

Motor imitation, vocal imitation, and verbal imitation[1] are sometimes trained as successive skills. Rieke, Lynch, and Soltman (1977), in their presentation of language strategies, indicated that the goal of imitation training is for a person to imitate the action, sound, or word spontaneously, without prompting or reinforcement. They cautioned that over-reinforcing imitative acts once the person is producing them spontaneously may be detrimental because it may discourage further imitation of vocalizations.

Some authors suggest that motor and vocal imitation can be taught concurrently (Reichle & Yoder, 1979; Table 5-1, items 11, 12, and 18) rather than as consecutive skills. The use of a chaining procedure, by which the person is required to imitate a series of motor tasks ending with a vocalization, allows use of previously learned movements with a new skill of vocalizing (MacDonald, 1985).

A number of authors (e.g., Bloom & Lahey, 1978; Johnson-Martin et al., 1985; Reichle & Yoder, 1979; Schumaker & Sherman, 1978) have suggested strategies for training vocal imitation. The latter recommended beginning by increasing vocalizations such as "any sound a child makes with the vocal apparatus, excluding crying and reflexive coughing, sneezes and hiccups" (p. 291).

Reichle and Yoder (1979) discussed the training of "mutual imitation." The instructor imitates a sound or word made by the student, and the stu-

---

[1] "Vocal imitation" refers to imitation of sounds or nonmeaningful sound sequences, while "verbal imitation" refers to imitation of words.

dent is credited and reinforced if he or she then repeats the utterance again after the instructor. The goal is to bring sounds or words already in the student's repertoire under stimulus control. Once the client understands the turn-taking activity, unfamiliar stimuli can be introduced for imitation (MacDonald & Gillette, 1986). For a detailed teaching sequence for vocal imitation, the *Carolina Curriculum* (Johnson-Martin et al., 1985) includes 12 steps toward establishing vocal imitation.

Bricker, Dennison, and Bricker (1975) and Bricker and Dennison (1978) developed a training procedure whereby the instructor capitalizes on spontaneous utterances made by the client during natural interactions at play or other activities. One of their suggested procedures is to increase the amount of action play (such as swinging, tickling) that is physically stimulating to the child and may evoke vocalizations which can be imitated by the instructor and for which the child can be reinforced. MacDonald and Gillette (1986) have expanded this procedure in the *Ecological Communication System* (ECO).

In summary, many vocal language programs suggest that attending and motor imitation be established before or during the training of vocal or verbal skills. Of the 20 programs listed in Table 5-1, three programs assume that the client has some functional verbal language and that imitation skills are already established before the program is begun (Table 5-1, items 2, 6, and 8). Seventeen of the programs cited provide some sequences designed to train imitative skills (Table 5-1, items 1, 2, 3, 5, 7, 9, 10, 11, 12, 13, 14, 15, 16, 17, 18, 19, and 20).

Functional Language

Functional language, the fourth stage of many vocal language programs, will be discussed throughout the remainder of this chapter, relative to specific issues in language training. Pragmatics or communicative intent will be stressed as the overriding function of establishing expressive skills. Orelove and Sobsey (1987) presented the following communication functions to be considered with planning programs:

1. *Attention:* the communicator must get the attention of a partner before any communication can occur
2. *Requesting items and events:* which allows the person some control over the environment
3. *Rejection and protest:* also a means of controlling the environment
4. *Confirmation/negation:* very useful for individuals with good receptive skills, but limited expressive skills
5. *Reference and description:* more advanced functions, usually established by general match-to-sample (object-to-picture) strategy

6. *Questions:* an advanced function used to request more information about an object, event, or something previously said
7. *The interactive process:* the medium by which all other functions work.

MacDonald (1985) viewed this last function, the interactive process, as the most important aspect of communication training. These communicative functions will be addressed in the following sections.

Issues in Selecting a Vocal Program

The general issues involved in selecting a program were discussed in Chapter 2. Models, methodology, comprehension and production, content, context, and generalization will now be presented as they relate specifically to vocal communication training.

Models

Language programming seems to pivot on the assumption that expressive language (vocal or augmented) allows a person control over his or her environment. Two theoretical models based on developmental logic and remedial logic were discussed in Chapter 2. Most language programs are designed primarily from developmental data on normally developing children. Caution must be exercised in relying entirely on developmental norms because there is evidence of a large variation in normal development (Bloom & Lahey, 1978; Siegel & Spradlin, 1978; Stremel-Campbell, 1978).

Guess, Sailor, and Baer (1978) described the choice of a remedial model for their functional language program as an attempt to meet the immediate needs of the disabled individual. They attempt to teach the person to control his or her environment through expressive language as soon as possible, suggesting that such control will reinforce in itself, and thus will stimulate more language. However, it is not clear how the instructor should proceed once the individual progresses beyond the early stages of communicating. It appears that the choice of units taught in this program (persons, possession, and so forth) is influenced by normal developmental patterns and by data from severely handicapped learners who have completed the program. Siegel and Spradlin (1978) asserted that the two models (remedial and developmental) are not precise enough to allow a clear choice between them. Therefore, they suggested that both approaches should be blended to design an adequate individualized program for each person.

Methodology

The methods by which a language program is introduced may vary, depending upon the type of reinforcement employed and the setting in which the program is conducted. The two major methods used in the programs in Table 5-1 are based on the following:

1. *Artificially structured techniques:* primarily using operant technology and drill-type tasks in individual or small group sessions
2. *Naturally structured techniques:* primarily utilizing the natural language environment to stimulate language in group training sessions or during activities of daily living.

Artificially structured techniques employed by many programs are typically conducted in individual training sessions employing carefully controlled data collecting procedures. *The West Virginia System Curricula* (Table 5-1, items 17 and 18) employ a Universal Data Sheet for recording trial responses in order to access acquisition of skills during training sessions and maintenance of these skills between lessons. The *Functional Speech and Language Training for the Severely Handicapped* (Table 5-1, item 6) also employs an extensive record form to chart each session.

Naturally structured techniques are typically based on less rigid or structured training and data collecting procedures. The general setting for this type of approach is a group language session or in the natural environment, which would include classroom and home daily living situations (e.g., eating, toileting, and interacting with siblings and peers), rather than specific individual sessions. Group sessions allow the student to receive language models from peers as well as from the instructor. In addition, staff time may be more efficiently used. The instructor must be skilled in group techniques to encourage all group members to participate to the best of their ability.

The severity of the handicapping condition often seems to dictate the language training environment. Group lessons are typically not chosen for students with severe handicapping conditions. However, as discussed in Chapter 2, several studies (Flavell et al., 1978; Oliver & Scott, 1981; Storm & Willis, 1978) found group training to be an effective format for training some skills, even with people having severe to profound cognitive delays.

It is very important that people with severe handicaps be included in a "talking environment." Dolan and Burton (1976) have indicated that it is vital that parents and instructors continue to talk to nonspeakers even if progress in speech seems extremely limited and the individual appears not to be interested in speaking. Unfortunately, in classes for students with severe disabilities language is sometimes only programmed into specific language lessons. The instructors may receive so little communication feedback from the students that they may not attempt communication with some students unless it is included in the training schedule. Too often classroom language is limited to directives ("put in _____," "give me _____") and test questions ("Where is _____ ?" and "What's this?"). This lack of communication interaction may exist also with family members of nonspeaking children or adults. To avoid this type of situation, naturalistic language training techniques should be used, such as those described in Chapter 2 and summarized in Hart (1985). Hart and Rogers-Warren (1978) compared the individual training session approach with a naturalistic technique and concluded that the naturalistic approach has three positive features: (1) it is less expensive; (2) it is more conducive to generalizing behavior because the individual does not leave the normal flow of verbal social activities; and (3) it teaches the function of language, not just its form.

As discussed previously, Brown, Nietupski, and Hamre-Nietupski (1976) also presented a case for less individual training and more communication concentration in groups or in the natural environment. They indicated that individual training may be appropriate for some part of the day, but not as the only structured language training. Too often, while individual training is going on the other class members are left on their own, which may result in perpetuating self-stimulating behavior or continuing social isolation.

Direct instructor–student interaction time may be limited due to the logistics of feeding, positioning, and toileting demands; therefore, communication training must be inserted into these tasks (Musselwhite, 1986a), and the time without direct instructor–student interaction must be filled with constructive learning opportunities. Table 5-4 presents suggestions for inserting communication training during routine daily living activities.

Sample activities for filling periods without direct instruction are listed below.

1. Listening to taped stories while viewing slides made from matching story books; the student activates a switch to advance the slides (Goossens' and Crain, 1985a, pp. 145–147)
2. Working at a learning center with a language master
3. Practicing vocalizations with a talk-back animal
4. Positioning two physically disabled students with a shared activity, such as a play board (Carlson, 1982) or an activity frame (Musselwhite, 1986a).

It may be necessary to make an either/or choice between artificially and naturally structured approaches. The communication specialist and classroom staff can plan the day to allow time for both types of approaches. In addition, the naturally structured approach may also be

TABLE 5-4
Telescoping Communication Training During Daily Living Activities

Daily Living Activity	Instruction Opportunity to Be Inserted
Diapering	Commenting on actions (e.g., hiding behind a clean diaper and playing peek-a-boo) Vocal turn-taking Commenting on items/events (child's clothing, Mom's cold hands)
Positioning	Vocal imitation Labeling/commenting on prearranged pictures mounted within student's vision Labelling/commenting on objects suspended from an Activity Frame
Feeding	Choice making (selecting desired food items) Working on yes/no response patterns Group feeding, allowing opportunity for peer interaction and turntaking at meal time

carefully planned; the instructor can set up an activity in which goals are predetermined and data are collected on one student at a time within the group setting.

Comprehension and Production

The issue of whether to train comprehension before requiring production from people with severe handicaps was presented in Chapter 2. Careful scrutiny of the vocal language programs reviewed in this chapter revealed that during the assessment process some programs divide test items into receptive language tasks (comprehension) and expressive language tasks (production), which may lead to separate training of these skills. Until recently, there has been little disagreement among researchers that normally developing children and communication-disordered children appear to understand language before they can express themselves. However, there is now some evidence that the first words spoken are not necessarily the first words understood (Bloom & Lahey, 1978). Our view is that concurrent training of comprehension and production is more desirable than the separation of these skills.

Many language programs are likewise divided into sections in which receptive language training tasks are presented separately from expressive language tasks. This ordering appears to follow the premise that compre-

Vocal Communication Strategies

hension precedes production. Orelove and Sobsey (1987) reviewed data that basically support this premise. However, they suggested that it is important to avoid "the artificial isolation of reception and production in training" (p. 290). MacDonald (1985) stressed that the interactive process between communication partners helps to eliminate separating these two language functions.

Language programs that divide training objectives into receptive language training and expressive language training typically do not require that a student progress through the training sequence in all the receptive objectives before beginning expressive training. However, Siegel and Spradlin (1978) strongly supported a need for concurrent training of receptive and expressive language material. Cuvo and Riva (1980) have reported that severely handicapped children can be taught productive vocabulary before comprehension. They indicated that teaching "production first" was as effective as the traditional "comprehension first" sequence. In Kent's program (Table 5-1, item 11) the student moves back and forth between the verbal-receptive section and the verbal-expressive section as vocabulary expands, and as a review of material previously learned is undertaken.

Guess, Sailor, and Baer's program (Table 5-1, item 6) begins with the naming of objects in Step 1. Step 2 requires recognition of the objects learned in Step 1. Their premise is that verbal expression best allows an individual to manipulate and control the environment and, therefore, is in itself immediately reinforcing. Each new area of content is approached in this manner.

The current focus on interactive communication programming (Hanna, Lippert, & Harris, 1982; MacDonald, 1985; Warren & Rogers-Warren, 1985) has reduced the separation between comprehension and production training. We agree with Siegel and Spradlin (1978) and Reichle and Keogh (1985) that concurrent training will yield the most functional communication programming.

Content

Most of the programs reviewed in this chapter stress the need to select carefully the content or specific vocabulary in teaching communication skills. The actual responsibility for selecting the most functional language for an individual generally lies with the instructor, who must coordinate input from caregivers and consider all the settings in which the individual will communicate. When an augmentative system is selected, particularly a communication board, the number of words that can be utilized may be restricted significantly by the physical make-up of the system (see Chapter 8). This is not the case with a vocal language program where there is an almost infinite choice of words that could be taught.

Researchers in language acquisition of normal and disordered speakers have attempted to suggest rules for selecting an initial lexicon (vocabulary) for training functional language (Bloom & Lahey, 1978; Holland, 1975; Lahey & Bloom, 1977). Relevant findings in this area are presented in Chapter 2. The realization that knowledge about specific objects and actions is dependent on age, interest, and actual experiences of the individual makes the selection of words an ongoing process. As the person's experiences increase, so will the need for expansion of the vocabulary to allow for communication in new situations. The strategies presented in Chapter 2 for selecting initial content should be considered relative to choosing words as the entries (e.g., client preference, frequency of occurrence). In addition, strategies specific to vocal language programs will be discussed in this section.

Functional language, the language needed by the individual to meet his or her immediate needs, is the primary concern when planning a program. For example, Lahey and Bloom (1977) rejected the early use of color words in training children with language disorders, because such words have little communicative value. Special education classrooms have often over-emphasized color training because color words are easily illustrated. Similarly, body part labels, while relatively easy to teach, offer limited opportunity for communicative interaction. Thus, initial teaching of low-interest and nonfunctional words may stifle spontaneous interaction.

Another caution in vocal language programming, is the overuse of carrier phrases, such as "I want a _____, please," which may result in "robotic" sounding speech. If carrier phrases are used to increase the length of an utterance, a variety of phrases should be modeled to yield a more natural language pattern (e.g., I'd like a _____, Give me a _____, Can I have a _____ ?). Horstmeier and MacDonald (1978) suggested that insisting on social phrases like "please" or "thank you" too early with a child with a language disorder may limit his or her use of appropriate labels; it may be easier for the child to say "please" and point to what is wanted, rather than to use the correct word.

Input from communication partners is vital in selecting initial content for training. After words are selected, they must be used consistently when communicating with the individual in all settings. For example, toileting skills can become confusing if the label for the voiding receptacle is varied (e.g., toilet, potty, commode, water closet).

Several factors should be considered in determining the ease of production and discrimination of training words. Bloom and Lahey (1978) noted that there are no definitive guidelines on which word configurations are easiest to produce and discriminate. Nevertheless, they suggested the following:

1. Consider those sounds the child is already producing
2. Consider using short words because they are easier to produce than polysyllabic words (the first words of normally developing children tend to be of one syllable such as "no," or a repetition of one syllable: "dada")
3. Consider selecting words that are acoustically distinct from each other in order to reduce confusion (e.g., do not include "stop" and "shop" in the same training session).

Content selection involves many decisions based on input by care-givers, training staff, and the individual's particular needs and desires. Learning a limited number of words may be necessary for a person with a severe communication disorder, but it is vital that those words be functional and allow for combining the words for a variety of messages.

Context

The actual setting and circumstances that accompany a communication attempt represent the context of that language event. McLean and Snyder-McLean (1978) suggested that two bases of context must be considered when planning intervention strategies: (1) *physical context,* and (2) *communication context.*

The instructor must arrange a physical context, or setting, that provides increased opportunity for the child to manipulate materials in many ways, such as shaking, assembling and disassembling objects, and pouring. An effective communication context requires that there be someone with whom the child can communicate about situations that occur within that physical setting. This often involves careful arrangement of a classroom to present opportunities for optimal communication. McLean and Snyder-McLean suggested creating "natural-environment learning corners" (e.g., a toy kitchen or bedroom) and role-playing natural actions in these settings. Constable (1983) described numerous ways to manipulate the environment to provide support for communication attempts. Refer to Chapter 2 for more details.

Hart's (1985) naturalistic training techniques also take advantage of the natural environment for stimulating and modeling functional language. In her view, the generalization of new language content may be facilitated by demonstrating and emphasizing the immediate use of words and actions. Creating situations in which a person needs to use a variety of communication functions enhances spontaneous communication. Table 5-5 presents some examples of environmental manipulations designed to elicit a variety of communicative functions.

TABLE 5-5
Environmental Manipulations Designed to Elicit a Variety of Communication
Functions

Function	Manipulation	Reference
Requesting	Use a general statement ("I have cheese") without specifying what to request	Olswang, Kriegsmann, & Mastergearge, 1982
	Withhold turns or items "accidentally" ("forget" to push one child on a swing, neglect to give one student a dessert)	Constable, 1983
Commenting (on action)	Produce unexpected actions (allow a wind-up toy to walk off table)	Musselwhite (1986a)
Commenting (on object)	Produce an unexpected object (wave machine, harmonica) or place object in an unexpected location (plastic spider on face of a clock)	McLean, Snyder-McLean, Jacobs, & Rowland, 1981
Negating/protesting	Violate an object function (give a child an entire jug of milk instead of glass) or manipulation (comb hair with a spoon)	Constable, 1983 Musselwhite, 1986a

The instructor in a naturalistic setting should be available to respond by commenting, answering, and reinforcing the communication attempt. Rieke, Lynch, and Soltman (1977) cautioned that the instructor must resist talking too much. The role of the instructor is summed up in the "3Rs" of their strategy, whereby the instructor responds, reiterates, and reinforces the behavior the individual initiates. MacDonald and Gillette (1986) stressed the importance of establishing turn-taking with communication to encourage message exchanges. The communication partner is encouraged to speak just one step higher than the child's current functioning level to reduce the verbal overload the child hears. For example, if the child is not using words yet, the person interacting with the child should use one word utterances as much as possible. MacDonald and Gillette's conversation routines within the *Ecological Communication System* (Table 5, item 14) cautions against turns being dominated by the adult communication partner.

The role of a communication specialist in a class for students with severe disabilities may follow several models. The communication specialist may serve primarily as a consultant to the classroom staff in assisting in program planning and evaluation of progress. When a naturalistic approach is utilized, language training is integrated into all daily activities. Thus, it is the classroom staff that insures continual communication instruction. Individual therapy sessions may be conducted by the communication specialist on a regular basis, or as trial sessions to experiment with new techniques with a particular student, or to demonstrate various techniques to other staff so they may incorporate these techniques into their daily activities.

The team approach to training the individual with severe disabilities, as presented in Chapter 4, focuses on the people involved in program planning and implementation. The context of training involves a variety of settings in which the individual must function and the variety of people with whom the individual must interact. The staff should be open to flexible roles and flexible scheduling to allow for the blending of individualized training and stimulating communication growth in a more natural, interactive environment.

Generalization

As stated previously, creating as natural an environment as possible in which to nurture communication attempts most likely will enhance generalization of communication skills. Siegel and Spradlin (1978) stated that "training across settings involves teaching and reinforcing the child for emitting certain behaviors in situation after situation until the child can demonstrate the skill in a situation never previously encountered, without additional training" (p. 390). It is vital that the initial instructor not be involved in all new situations, as the individual must learn to perform independently of the instructor and the original training environment.

Stokes and Baer (1977) used the term "training loosely" to stress the features of planning generalization procedures that require the instructor to be flexible and creative in changing the stimuli from trial to trial, from session to session, and in different settings to determine if generalization has occurred. Stremel-Campbell and Campbell (1985) cautioned that this technique must be applied systematically. Careful planning and gradual introduction of varied stimulus conditions can encourage generalization without confusing the learner.

Most vocal language programs reviewed in this chapter provide suggestions for encouraging the use of new skills across settings and among people. Makohon and Fredricks (1985) presented standard generalization statements with slight variation for most expressive language objectives. These statements suggested that items taught during individual sessions be tracked in a variety of other settings with unstructured use of a time delay procedure. These brief directives may not be sufficient to offer the support needed to implement a successful generalization program.

MacDonald and Gillette (1986) in the *ECO System* presented more specific support for training in the natural environment by communication partners, such as parents. They used a calendar of conversation sounds to remind family members to practice and record interactions with their youngsters. Owens (1982) in the *PALS* program (Table 5, item 15) emphasized generalization of all program objectives by providing many ideas for incidental teaching of trained behaviors in everyday situations. For example, giving the student wrong items or not enough items to perform a task may provoke spontaneous requests that might not be generated otherwise. These suggestions appear before the formal training procedures are presented, which highlights the need for continual communication interactions under natural circumstances.

Within the classroom, group activities can be designed to reinforce concepts initially taught in individual sessions. The mechanics of recording data to chart generalization progress may pose some problems due to the unstructured and often spontaneous nature of reviewing skills in different settings. The use of a paraprofessional as group leader might allow the teacher to act periodically as an observer to record specific comments about each child's interaction in a particular activity. The mastery assessment form designed by Williams and Fox (1977) and reprinted in Chapter 2 of this book may help the instructor keep data on several aspects of generalization.

The ultimate goal of any training procedure is to teach a concept or a skill that the student will be able to use in a variety of situations with a variety of people. Evidence of this generalized use of new information is most positive when the student spontaneously uses the concept or skill without assistance, and completely on his or her own initiative. This is a difficult task for people with severe handicaps and requires careful planning and encouragement from everyone involved with the student.

Family Involvement

McCormack and Audette (1977) viewed training severely handicapped learners as a 24-hour job. They stressed that programming must involve "whole person planning" (p. 210), which considers the person's physical, emotional, social, and intellectual needs. Integrated and cooperative planning must be implemented by establishing a relationship between school and home environments (family or institutional). Striving for cooperative involvement of home caregivers is important, but the instructor must recognize that commitments (e.g., jobs, other children, illness) will play a part in the quality and quantity of time available for carrying out specific programs or charting specific behaviors at home.

During the 1970s, the focus of researchers and program planners appeared to be client-centered; how do we change the client's ability to communicate? During the 1980s, it may be said that the family of the person with a handicap has become the focus of much needed research and discussion. Not only have parental attitudes and needs received attention, but the special roles of siblings have been studied. The titles of four recent books demonstrate this new focus.

1. *Severely Handicapped Young Children and Their Families: Research Review* (Blacher, 1984)
2. *Families of Handicapped Persons: Research, Programs, and Policy Issues* (Gallagher & Vietze, 1986)
3. *Brothers & Sisters: A Special Part of Exceptional Families* (Powell & Ogle, 1985)
4. *Handicapped Infants and Children: A Handbook for Parents and Professionals* (Tingey–Michaelis, 1983).

Each of these books is annotated in Appendix B.

The demands placed on families who have a member with a handicap are ongoing; they do not end with the end of a work day, as they do for most professionals. The ultimate decision as to the appropriate care and planning for the handicapped individual lies with the family unit, with input from the professional community. Communication becomes vitally important in assisting families in meeting the needs of each family member.

Parents and other family members should be involved in communication programming from the beginning to help in selecting vocabulary and in describing family routines and family interests. This family-oriented information can be used by the instructor in selecting the content and contexts that will be meaningful to the individual when he or she is at home. The home environment is also full of powerful incidental learning opportunities as the child interacts with his or her immediate family and extended family members.

Schumaker and Sherman (1978) viewed parents as intervention agents who interact with their children naturally. They offered many suggestions to enrich interactions rather than to interrupt daily activities with specific, scheduled language-training sessions. They regard "incidental teaching episodes" as more effective in establishing spontaneous use of language than structured training sessions. The key to home teaching is making the activities enjoyable not only for the child but for the family member, also. Too much pressure on the child to talk *now* can have a negative effect; it is better to create a *desire* to speak, rather than to demand speech. For children, planning home communication activities around an appropriate toy(s) from a toy lending library (Musselwhite, 1986a, Chapter 13) can provide needed structure in a pleasant environment. This method may have the added advantage that the child may actually initiate play sessons by bringing the toy to the caregiver.

Family members, particularly fathers, may indicate that they do not know what to say to their handicapped child. Schumaker and Sherman (1978) suggested that family members describe what they are doing when they are bathing, dressing, changing, feeding, consoling, and playing with their child, to facilitate communication. Other situations, such as driving a car, shopping, or viewing television programs together, could be added to the list of times parents can encourage language-sharing. Since parents of children with limited speech are deprived of the natural reinforcement of vocal feedback from their children, talking "around" the child may become the pattern at home, rather than making an effort to include the child in ordinary conversations.

Several programs reviewed in this chapter offer clear and useful suggestions for targeting language intervention at home (Table 5-1, items 5, 8, 9, 13, and 14). *Ready, Set, Go: Talk to Me* and the *ECO System* are written for parents by professionals, including a parent of a handicapped child. Both programs assist parents in capitalizing on daily events to reinforce vocal communication. The *ECO System* introduces conversation routines that develop communication turn-taking from whatever the child is interested in at a particular time. Manolson's parent guide book *It Takes Two To Talk* used the following analogy to describe the game of learning to communicate.

> Learning to communicate is like learning to play ping-pong. When one player is better than the other, he must constantly adjust his way of playing to help his partner hit the ball and learn the game. Likewise, the parent or teacher must learn to adjust his way of communicating in accordance with the child's ability. (p. 3)

Her guide book offers many creative ways to keep conversations going, many prompts for better turn-taking, and means for initiating play to create opportunities for language learning.

In summary, the communication specialist may utilize many features of selected programs to help devise suggestions for family members to use at home. Basically, the family needs to know that they are already doing much to influence and encourage their child. Supporting their efforts in providing a variety of experiences and explanations about these experiences becomes an important supplemental role of the instructor. Leo Buscaglia (1975), in his book *The Disabled and Their Parents: A Counseling Challenge,* stated that parents are people first, with very special feelings regarding their children. Each family faces the limitations of each child in a unique way, and creates a unique response to each limitation. Each family usually has several people who interact with the handicapped person. Initially, the instructor may solicit the help of one family member to implement an activity or report about communication interactions at home; then, gradually, other family members should be instructed and encouraged to participate to assure generalization across settings and people. Professionals must deal with family members as patiently, empathetically, and realistically as possible. Just as planning language training for a client must be individualized, so should planning the involvement of family members. Each home represents a unique environment for language enrichment.

Part III: Augmentative Communication Systems

Chapter 6
Augmentative Communication: An Overview

If you want to know what it is like not being able to speak, there is a way. Go to a party and don't talk. Play mute. Use your hands if you wish but don't use paper and pencil. Paper and pencil are not always handy for a mute person. Here is what you will find: people talking; talking behind, beside, around, over, under, through, and even for you. But never with you. You are ignored until finally you feel like a piece of furniture. If you are working with nonspeech people I challenge you to experience this. Then you will have an idea of what it is like for nonspeech people.
— Rick Creech, paravocal communicator (augmented communicator)

The suggestion quoted above comes from a person who has been a paravocal communicator throughout his life. He feels strongly that those working with people who have severe communication handicaps should perform this experiment in order to develop a better understanding of the needs and feelings of nonspeaking people. Clearly, such a temporary simulation cannot provide a full picture of the needs and frustrations of nonspeaking people, but it may help to develop understanding and identify areas of concern. At the least, this experience should help the individual develop more appropriate ways of interacting with nonspeaking people.

The recent surge of interest in augmentative communication options is staggering. The last 10 years has seen a tremendous growth in the number of articles, pamphlets, newsletters, and textbooks relating to the use of augmentative communication approaches. The number and variety of communication devices has also increased dramatically, with formation of new companies and laboratories and expansion of already existing ones. Appendix C presents a list of major companies dealing with augmentative devices. A number of organizations also provide information and services concerning augmentative communication. These organizations, and the services provided by each, are presented in Appendix D. Chapters 6, 7, 8, and 9 will attempt to synthesize and explore existing information on augmentative systems and approaches.

Functions of Augmentative Systems

A variety of different functions have been suggested for augmentative communication systems, but the following have been found to be the most appropriate uses of these systems:

1. An *alternative communication system*, substituting to some extent for a vocal mode. This may be temporary use for a client who is learning to use vocal communication. The goal here is to transmit information through nonvocal means.

2. A *supplement* to vocal communication for the client who has difficulty with formulation or intelligibility, but who has some usable speech. The term *augmentative* is often used to describe this function.

3. A *facilitator* of communication, with emphasis on speech intelligibility, output and organization of language, and/or general communication skills.

The first function listed may indicate that the augmentative system is being used as a substitute for vocal language, a position which some researchers (Harris & Vanderheiden, 1980) find untenable. However, if we are truly concerned about being communication-oriented, as Silverman (1980) recommends, and if our primary concern is interaction, as some authors suggest (Harris & Vanderheiden, 1980; Kraat, 1985a), transmitting information through a nonvocal system is an acceptable function, at least initially. In addition, an augmentative system may serve a primary function as an interim communication system for a client who is receiving speech therapy, such as a laryngectomee.

The *supplemental function* is inherent to some communication systems, such as Cued Speech (Cornett, 1975) and initial letter cueing (Beukelman & Yorkston, 1977). These systems, by their very nature, are supplemental and must be combined with speech. Other systems, such as Blissymbolics or Signed English, can be made supplemental, either by using the system with vocal language simultaneously, as in signed speech (e.g., Schaeffer, 1980) or by employing the system to provide context or to clarify utterances (e.g., Abkarian, Dworkin, & Brown, 1978).

Use of augmentative systems as alternative communication systems, or as supplemental to vocal language, was represented visually on the non-vocal/vocal continuum presented in Chapter 2. As that continuum indicated, the difference between an alternative and a supplemental system may be to a great extent a matter of degree. The possible change in emphasis across time was also illustrated on that continuum.

There is, understandably, a great deal of interest in the use of augmentative systems *to facilitate a variety of behaviors.* Augmentative systems have been found to increase speech intelligibility (Beukelman & Yorkston, 1977), improve the ability to communicate, and increase attempts at speech (see Silverman, 1980, Tables 2-1 and 2-2, for reviews of a number of studies). In addition, Shane (1981) suggests that some augmentative systems, particularly aided systems, such as the Fitzgerald Key (Fitzgerald, 1949), may help the user to organize language output through their explicit visual content. Concerning all these studies, Silverman (1980) asserts that "intervention with nonspeech communication modes can be rationalized for the purpose of speech facilitation as well as improving message transmission" (p. 45).

In summary, augmentative communication systems may serve a variety of functions for the individual. The functions of these systems can apply singly or in combination at different points in time.

Implications of Using Augmentative Systems

We must be aware that electing to use an augmentative system will have definite implications for our clients. For example, people in the non-speaker's environment may interpret the use of the system to mean that we have "given up" on speech, and may do likewise by not encouraging the individual to vocalize. Ways to avoid or deal with this situation were suggested in Chapter 4. Persons in the environment are likely to interact with the nonspeaker differently, from the natural speaker, and will have to be taught appropriate means of interacting. These implications will be discussed briefly in the following two chapters.

Another major implication of using an augmentative system is that, as Harris and Vanderheiden (1980) pointed out, "nonvocal techniques are not a direct substitute for speech, and communication and interaction patterns as well as the overall communication development process may follow different courses for vocal and nonvocal children." They asserted also that "communication interaction patterns are very specific to the *speed* of communication, much more so in fact than they are to the *mode* of communication" (p. 245). The difference in speed, the time it takes to transmit a message, means that normal communication routines and strategies will not be directly transferred to augmentative systems. This is somewhat dependent on the augmentative system chosen. For example, some of the unaided communication systems can parallel spoken language, at least in total utterances produced if not in time taken to produce them. The parallels to spoken English in terms of propositions, sentence structure, and transmission time, will be discussed separately for each augmentative system presented in Chapters 7 and 8.

All of the implications mentioned relate to using an augmentative system instead of vocal language. Obviously, for the person who has no successful, conventional communication system, introduction of an augmentative system may have many highly desirable implications. The potential impact on intelligibility, speech attempts, and communication success were noted earlier and are considered in more detail in Silverman (1980). Silverman also reported a number of other positive effects of augmentative communication modes, such as increased attention span and reduced frustration.

Clearly, awareness and consideration of both positive and negative potential implications should help in implementing augmentative systems. At the very least, they should aid in avoiding or confronting resulting problems.

Communication Needs of Augmented Communicators

A number of authors have explored the range of communication needs that must be considered for individuals using augmentative communication systems (e.g., Beukelman, Yorkston, & Dowden, 1985; Vanderheiden, 1987; Vanderheiden & Lloyd, 1986; Yoder & Vanderheiden, (1986). Beukelman and colleagues developed a needs-assessment form (Figure 6-1) that includes five areas, as summarized below and illustrated in Figure 6-1.

1. *Positioning.* Examples are, in bed (supine, prone), related to mobility (in various wheelchairs, with a lapboard), and with other equipment (while intubated, with environmental control units)
2. *Communication Partners.* Sample partners may include those who cannot read or have poor vision or hearing.
3. *Locations.* Factors related to multiple locations, amount of light or noise, and movement may influence this feature
4. *Message Needs.* A wide range of communicative functions may be needed by a single user (e.g., call attention, give opinions, perform calculations, take notes)
5. *Mode of Communication.* This includes general communication needs such as conversation, writing, drawing, and computer access (Vanderheiden & Lloyd, 1986), plus specific needs such as talking on the phone.

Previously, intervention has focused primarily on conversation needs, with a rather hodge-podge approach to meeting other needs. For example,

Figure 6-1
Needs assessment form. From Beukelman, Yorkston, and Dowden (1985). *Communication augmentation: A casebook of clinical management.* San Diego: College-Hill Press. Reprinted with permission.

AUGMENTATIVE COMMUNICATION CENTER
DEPARTMENT OF REHABILITATION MEDICINE
UNIVERSITY OF WASHINGTON HOSPITAL

Name:

Date:

Interviewer:

Responders:

Please indicate whether the needs listed are:
M - Mandatory
D - Desirable
U - Unimportant
F - May be mandatory in the future

Positioning

In bed:
    While supine
    While lying prone
    While lying on side
    While in a Clinitron bed
    While in a Roto bed
    Wile sitting in bed
    While in arm restraints
    In a variety of positions
Related to mobility:
    Carry the system while walking
    Independently position the system
    In a manually controlled wheelchair
    In an electric wheelchair
    With a lapboard
    While the chair is reclined
    Arm troughs
Other equipment:
    With hand mitts
    With arterial lines
    Orally intubated
    While trached
    With oxygen mask
    With electric wheelchair controls
    Environmental control units
Other needs related to positioning:

Communication Partners

Someone who cannot read (e.g., child or nonreader)
Someone who has no familiarity with the system
Someone who has poor vision

Someone who has limited time or patience
Someone who is across the room or in another room
Someone who is not independently mobile
Several people at a time
Someone who is hearing impaired

Other needs related to partners:

Locations

Only in a single room
In multiple rooms with the same building
In dimly lit rooms
In bright rooms
In noisy rooms
Outdoors
While traveling in a car, van, and so forth
While moving from place to place within a building
At a desk or computer terminal
In more than two locations in a day

Other needs related to locations:

Message Needs

Call attention
Signal emergencies
Answer yes-no questions
Provide unique information
Make requests
Carry on a conversation
Express emotion
Give opinions
Convey basic medical needs
Greet people
Prepare messages in advance
Edit texts written by others
Edit texts prepared by the user
Make changes in diagrams
Compile lists (e.g., phone numbers)
Perform calculations
Take notes

Other needs related to messages:

Modality of Communication

Prepare printed messages
Prepare auditory messages
Talk on the phone
Communicate with other equipment (e.g., environmental control units)
Communicate privately with some partners
Switch from one modality to another during communication
Via several modalities at a time
    (e.g., taking notes while talking on the phone)
Communicate via an intercom
Via formal letters or reports
One pre-prepare worksheets

Other needs related to modality of communication:

Matt, a nine-year-old child with severe cerebral palsy, might be provided with an electronic communication device that meets some conversation needs but fails to take into account the variety of message needs required (e.g., quick responses necessary for fourth-grade humor), the locations at which he needs to communicate (adaptive swimming program, noisy lunchroom), and positions in which he needs to communicate (supine during physical therapy). Thus, Matt clearly will need a supplement to his electronic device in order to meet all of his needs (e.g., using a flotation ring marked with messages during swimming, eye gazing to words/phrases on a stimulation vest worn by the therapist during physial therapy).

Shane (1986) identified a number of intervention goals for augmentative communication that will be achieved if the previously listed communication needs are met to some degree. The goals are:

1. Equalize the gap between comprehension and production
2. Promote greater participation in the school setting
3. Enhance vocational opportunities
4. Promote interpersonal and social interaction
5. Reduce frustrations associated with communicative failure
6. Enhance language comprehension
7. Facilitate speech development
8. Serve as an organizer of language
9. Enhance speech intelligibility.

Consideration of both communication needs and potential intervention goals for an individual will help in developing a comprehensive augmentative communication system.

Unaided and Aided Modes

The next two chapters describe and discuss the use of unaided and aided communication modes respectively. Unaided communication includes systems which necessitate movement of the body, typically, the arms and hands, but do not require access to equipment or devices separate from the body. Since unaided gestures are not enduring and frequently involve movement or change, they may also be termed "dynamic" (Vanderheiden & Lloyd, 1986). Examples are sign languages, sign systems, and pantomine. Aided communication systems require some type of external assistance in the form of an aid or device. Access to graphic symbols, such as Blissymbols, rebuses, or words, is typically included under aided systems. These relatively permanent symbols may also be termed "static" (Vanderheiden & Lloyd, 1986).

Harris and Vanderheiden (1980) pointed out that the augmented speaker "does not usually have access to any one technique that can be as primary and powerful as speech is for the vocal child" (p. 246). Therefore, all augmented speakers should have access to a range of communication modes: vocal, paralinguistic, unaided, and aided. The following examples highlight how augmented speakers might use multiple modes in a variety of communication situations.

Vocal. Listener feedback in the form of the approximation of "uh-huh" to maintain a conversation. Attention-getting within a group situation through vocalization. Vocal indication of desired choice(s) from a set of items presented verbally by the partner (e.g., at meal time Mom asks: "What do you want on your hot dog? Slaw?... Chili?... Ketchup?").

Paralinguistic. A device user may indicate emphasis by pointing to an item repeatedly and/or firmly. A signer may demonstrate stress by repeatedly enlarging, or emphatically producing the sign(s). When physically possible, use of facial expression can help to emphasize a point or express intent (e.g., eyebrows raised to indicate question).

Unaided. A severely physically handicapped person may have a small core of gross gestures to share important information with primary caregivers (e.g., eyes up means "yes," arm raised means "Get my communication device").

Aided. In addition to a formal communication device, an augmented communicator might use items in the environment to provide cues and set topics for a conversation (e.g., point to clock to ask when an event will occur; eye-gaze to painting of a dog then to a TV to get the topic to Lassie). A usually unaided communicator may rely on writing to clarify misunderstood messages.

Each of these modes can be combined by an augmented speaker during one interaction. For example, in a conversation with her mother, Melinda may get her mother's attention by vocalizing and pointing emphatically to a topic setter, such as "camp," on her device.

Several factors need to be considered in matching communication modes, individuals, and situations, since these modes differ in their portability, adaptibility, message potential, social interaction, and flexibility. Table 6-1 illustrates these five factors as they relate to aided and unaided modes. Consideration of these factors in relation to client and situational variables can help a communication team determine the best modes for a given individual across various environments. For example, an augmented speaker might use a communication device with printed or vocal output in the classroom, but a combination of vocalizations, speech, natural gestures, and eye-pointing with close friends.

To summarize, although aided and unaided systems will be covered in separate chapters, it is our view that a multimodal approach will best meet the communication needs of most augmented communicators. While one mode may assume the primary role in a given situation, other modes will help to supplement communication interaction.

TABLE 6-1
Primary Considerations in Selecting an Unaided and Aided Communication System

Unaided Systems	Aided Systems
Portability Unaided systems are quite mobile; however, use of gestures may interfere with use of hands for other activities (e.g., eating, driving).	Communication displays may be less mobile due to factors such as weight, size, power source, and physical impairment (transporting while using crutches). Smaller, more portable displays may be used for various settings.
Adaptability Unaided systems may be adapted to physical impairment. Sample adaptations are: one-handed vs. two-handed signs; use of gross vs. fine motor signs. Adaptation may also be made in response to cognitive/experimental limitations. Examples of these adaptations are: restriction in sign content (e.g., fewer, more concrete signs) and use of gross vs. fine motor signs.	Numerous physical adaptations are available: indicating by eye gaze, switches; vocal, printed, or video output. Adaptations in device may suit needs in various settings, such as classroom or field trips. Cognitive/experiential adaptations include modification of symbol type (objects vs. symbols; embellished vs. unembellished symbols) or organization (e.g., single vs. multiple display; complex retrieval strategies).
Message The unaided system (e.g., Signed English) must be taught to all communication partners. This is especially difficult if the person lives in an "open environment" (e.g., lives at home, goes to school, has many speaking friends). No options are available within sign systems to allow delayed reception (e.g., for homework), or a permanent record. Thus, the individual must learn another system, such as traditional orthography, or a sign-linked graphic system.	Some symbol systems (e.g., Blissymbols) require printed words with symbols to help eliminate the need for special training of message receivers. Some confusion may persist if words or ideas are formed through combinations of symbols. Vocal or printed output is available to help clarify message reception. With some systems, a message can be read at leisure with a permanent record. Partners must learn to request and expect certain types of responses, depending on the type of communication device used.

Unaided Systems	Aided Systems

Social Interaction

Use of an unaided system requires total attention to the message sender in order to see the signs. This may enhance eye contact and general interaction.

The message receiver must concentrate on the display, unless spoken output or a permanent visual display is used. This reduces eye contact and makes it difficult to communicate in a group.

Flexibility

Vocabulary can be increased spontaneously for some users (i.e., the individual can make up new words as needed, or a partner can look them up). Grammatical structure may be taught, though exact parallel to a spoken language may not be realistic due to physical limitations, the pace of natural conversation, or cognitive limitation.

For many displays, vocabulary will be limited due to lack of space; supplementary notebooks may increase vocabulary, or words may be produced by letters or phonemes. Grammatical structure may be indicated to some degree (e.g., inflectional markers on display). Exact parallel to a spoken language may not be realistic, due to constraints of time, or physical impairment.

Chapter 7
Unaided Communication Systems and Strategies

Speech is a mirror of the soul. As a man speaks, so is he.
— Publius Syrus Maxim, 1073

An ever-growing list of publications documents the success of unaided communication systems for individuals with severe communication impairment. Some types of unaided systems have been used with nearly every population of severely communication-impaired individuals, including both children and adults. Considerable success has been reported with a wide variety of clients, ranging from preschool cognitively delayed children (Simpson & McDade, 1979) to adolescents with autism (Schaeffer, 1980) to adults with aphasia (Skelly, 1979). Within and across populations, different effects of introducing unaided communication can be seen, particularly in the area of communication and emotional adjustment.

In some cases individuals gain only a core vocabulary for expressing basic needs, while in other cases they achieve communication skills which parallel or facilitate spoken English. However, unaided communication training has been found to be only minimally useful for some individuals (e.g., Kimble, 1975); consequently, this mode, while not a panacea, appears to have considerable usefulness with many individuals having severe communication impairment.

Unaided communication systems have been used frequently with language-impaired children for speech and language facilitation. Romski and Ruder (1984) reviewed research showing that manual sign training can facilitate initiation of spoken words and word approximations. However, a careful review revealed that there are individual differences in performance, with manual signing having a beneficial influence on speech acquisition for some students and a detrimental influence for others. Thus, Romski and Ruder recommended that "speech–language clinicians should exercise caution in the automatic adoption or rejection of manual sign with speaking developmentally delayed children" (1984, p. 300).

This chapter covers several primary concerns in unaided communication: assessment issues; types of unaided systems; selection of initial content; methods of training; and support of unaided communication.

Assessment for Use of an Unaided System

Primary questons to consider when assessing an individual for possible use of an unaided system include:

- To what extent is the individual a candidate for an unaided system?
- Which unaided system best meets the needs and abilities of the individual?
- What are the initial training goals to be introduced or expanded (e.g., preliminary skills, lexical items, forms, and functions)?
- What methods of training are best suited to the individual?
- What are the capabilities and needs of the communication partners and facilitators?

Clearly, assessment issues as complex as these cannot be answered through a single evaluation, but will require an ongoing assessment process, including procedures such as interviews, observation, and formal assessment.

Use of Interview and Intake Forms

It is extremely important to document information such as current modes of communication, communication functions already established, and environmental success of those modes and functions. For example, Fran, a 41-year-old woman with severe physical impairment, had developed an extensive set of idiosyncratic gestures that she used quite successfully with her brother. However, until they were asked directly about this, neither had thought to inform the home health workers, who had been struggling to achieve successful communication for more than four months! Three versions of an intake form (preschool, school-age, adult) are presented in Goossens' and Crain (1985a). Light, McNaughton, and Parnes (1986) have prepared an extensive facilitator questionnaire to determine the needs and abilities of nonspeaking severely handicapped adults.

Use of Structured Observations

Structured observation can be used to gain information about each of the assessment questions listed previously. For example, observing that the individual typically points and gestures when her verbalizations are misunderstood would lend support to consideration of an unaided system as a back-up. Similarly, observation of a person's preferred items (book, food, etc.) could aid in choosing training goals, such as lexical items to be introduced. In terms of efficiency, it is important that this observation be structured to provide the maximum possible information as efficiently as possible. Dunn (1982) developed an informal pre-sign motor observation form to assess spontaneous behaviors (e.g., repetitive movements? patterned movements?), lead hand (preference shown?), repertoire behaviors (what movements, in relationship to the body and handshapes, are seen during object manipulation?), and imitative behaviors (which repertoire behaviors are imitated?). Thus, her assessment considers primarily the motor movements involved in sign production, and the individual's imitative ability, leading to decisions regarding system and sign selection.

Dennis, Reichle, Williams, and Vogelsberg (1982) observed that common prehension patterns, such as squeezing, and movement patterns, such as bringing one's arm across midline, are used in the production of ASL signs. Since many sign systems used with nonspeaking hearing people are based to some extent on ASL signs, they recommended observing specific activities of daily living, such as combing hair or dialing a phone, to assess these patterns. Assessment is structured by use of charts for common prehension and movement patterns, listing daily living activities that can be used for assessment of those motoric skills. This information can aid in determining the extent to which an individual is a candidate for an unaided system, the system(s) most appropriate, and the conventional signs that would be easiest to produce.

Light, McNaughton, and Parnes (1986) have developed a coding sheet for determining communicative functions and modes in naturally occurring contexts, including a social-interaction context (e.g., game play) and a needs-and-wants context (e.g., mealtime). Additional information could be coded indicating the mode of expression of each function observed. They also provided a coding sheet for assessing facilitator behaviors in naturally occurring contexts (e.g., structures the environment, paces the interaction).

Clearly, many additional areas will need to be observed in order to make decisions regarding assessment questions. For example, the behavioral assessment of cognitive skills developed by Goossens' and Crain (1985a) can be helpful if there are questions regarding cognitive readiness for signing (see Chapter 3 in this book).

Use of Elicitation-Based Assessment Tools

These assessment tools set up specific situations on which individuals are assessed. The tools may or may not be standardized, and can aid in answering many of the questions posed regarding unaided systems. Several traditional, standardized assessment tools may be helpful. For example, Hobson and Duncan (1979) observed that initial scores on the *Peabody Picture Vocabulary Test* (revised version, Dunn & Dunn, 1981) correlated significantly with vocabulary learned after six weeks, and retention after two months, for profoundly retarded, institutionalized persons. Topper-Zweiban (1977) reported that the *Manual Expression Subtest* of the *Illinois Test of Psycholinguistic Abilities* (Kirk, McCarthy, & Kirk, 1968) appeared to be the most reliable indicator of success for the nonspeaking profoundly retarded subjects in her study. However, she noted problems such as uncommon items (e.g., eggbeater) which were not familiar to persons in institutions.

Several elicitation-based assessment tools have been developed specifically to meet the needs of nonspeaking hearing people. For example, Goossens' and Crain (1985a) developed an elicitation procedure for determining the individual's preference and potential for using an aided versus an unaided communication mode.

Shane and Wilbur (1980) determined the motor requisites for signs by a task analysis of handshapes, locations, and movements. They then calculated the percent of occurrence of the various motor components from an analysis of a core vocabulary of 696 signs selected as being an appropriate initial vocabulary set for nonspeaking individuals with severe handicaps. Fifteen motor components were identified that are used in at least five percent of the analyzed core vocabulary. The ability of an individual to perform each of the motor acts can be determined through imitation, observation (by parent, teacher, clinician), physical shaping, or verbal analogy (e.g., "act like Tarzan," to elicit hand to chest action). Table 7-1 presents the 15 motor components, plus sample signs and play materials that can be used for assessment.

House and Rogerson (1984) included a manual skills battery in their screening assessment tool. In this tool, tasks are presented directly and scored on a five-point rating scale. Subtests include: I — Manual Training Prerequisites (Inhibition of Neurological Reflexes and Reflexive Behavior, Posturing); II — Movement Patterning (Passive Range of Movement, Active Range of Movement, and Purposeful Movement); III — Cognitive Correlates for Manual Communication (Presymbolic Skills, Symbolic Skills). The focus of this battery is to determine candidacy for use of an unaided system, in terms of both motor and cognitive skills.

TABLE 7-1
Motor Components of Signing Used for Assessment

Motor Component*	Sample Signs†		Play Materials/Activities‡
Locations			
Chest	ME	PLEASE	Hug doll or stuffed animal
Hand	MORE	ON	Two hand puppets play together
Face	EAT	MOMMY	Put on face makeup
Handshapes			
Flat Hand	ON	PLEASE	Play hand clapping games
Index Finger	GO	YOU	Activate finger puppet
Curved Hand	BALL	MIRROR	Hold a large ball
Fist	SHOE	PURSE	Beat a tom-tom
Thumb Touch	MOMMY	HIDE	Make "thumb-print" pictures
Movements			
Linear	WHERE	GO	Play a give-and-take game
Handshape			
Change	THROW	GIVE	Throw a small ball
Rotate or Twist	MIRROR	COOK	Put sticker in palm, have child look
Circular	WHO	THIS	Dial a toy telephone
Arc	POUR	SING	"Direct" a band with a wand
Hold	HELP	LOVE	Balance a toy on top of another
Repeat	MORE	SHOE	Hit a punch ball attached to wrist

* Motor components identified are from research by Shane and Wilbur (1980).
† Imitation of these signs can be elicited in a play setting, with a model demonstrating signs and receiving objects (e.g., sign SHOE, get dress up shoes) or events (sign SING, hear a silly song).
‡ Motor components can be observed through play activities listed.

Dunn (1982) has developed a formal presign motor assessment that considers five areas: (1) movement in relation to the body (e.g., toward midline); (2) hand usage patterns (e.g., dominant/assistor); (3) basic handshapes (e.g., "A" handshape); (4) intermediate handshapes (e.g., little-finger isolation); and (5) complex motor patterns (e.g., multiple movement). Motor patterns are assessed through observation and elicitation in an imitative format, yielding information for determining candidacy, selecting a system, and choosing signs.

Light, McNaughton, and Parnes (1986) included eliciting contexts for assessing expression of needs and wants and social interaction in severely handicapped adults, with space provided for indicating the mode used. This can provide information regarding existing, emerging, or needed communicative functions that can be expressed through the unaided mode.

Duffy and Duffy (1984) developed a set of pantomime tests intended to investigate the nonverbal communication abilities of communicatively disordered adults, such as aphasics. Recognition and expression of pantomimed abilities, as well as referential abilities, are assessed through pantomime. The authors suggest that these tests might be useful with other populations of individuals having severe communication impairment, including children.

This section has presented sample assessment procedures and tools for answering questions relative to using an unaided system. Clearly, this is not an exhaustive listing, as many other observational and elicitation-based tools can be applied.

Types of Unaided Systems

A number of unaided communication systems have evolved or have been designed to serve the needs of persons with severe communication impairment, especially deaf individuals. These systems may be divided into categories based on the origin, type, and intent of the systems:

• *Sign Languages,* such as American Sign language and Chinese Sign Language. These have been developed out of a contextual need to communicate and are not universal; that is, each has developed its own structure and rules.

• *Educational Sign Systems,* such as Signed English and Signing Exact English. These have been developed fairly recently to represent spoken English. Many of the educational systems used in the United States are based to some extent on American Sign Language and/or the American Manual Alphabet.

• *Gestural Language Codes,* such as Cued Speech and fingerspelling. These serve to represent the letters or sounds of a language such as English.

• *Other Unaided Communication Systems,* such as Amer-Ind or natural gestures. These consist of a wide range of formal and informal systems.

Matching these unaided symbol systems to the needs and capabilities of individuals is a difficult task requiring a thorough knowledge of available systems. The following discussion will focus on a number of unaided systems that have been or could be used with individuals having severe communication impairment. For each major system, the following information will be presented:

What — a description of the system, including features such as history, content, and structure

Why — a consideration of the functions of the system
Who — a consideration of potential candidates and appropriate audience, plus a brief review of the literature on applications to various populations
When — a suggestion of the time period for optimum introduction
How — a discussion of training methodology concerning learning by both instructors and users
Where — a brief list of sources of further information regarding the system and its implementation.

Recently, systems have been developed that combine sign and symbol representation of referents, or use sign-linked symbols. Examples are Worldsign and Sigsymbols. Each of those systems will be covered in Chapter 8, "Aided Communication Systems and Strategies," as the signs they use are primarily those used in other unaided systems, such as American or British Sign Language.

Sign Languages

A number of sign languages have developed in various countries to serve the conversational communication needs of deaf individuals. Woodward (1976) has identified several sign families. For example, the French sign language family includes sign languages currently used in three countries (France, Denmark, and the United States). However, sign languages from the same family are not mutually intelligible. Thus sign languages cannot be considered to be universal, but must be studied as distinct languages. This chapter will cover only one sign language, American Sign Language, since it is the principal system used in the United States and Canada. A brief section will introduce British Sign Language.

American Sign Language

WHAT. American Sign Language (ASL), or Ameslan, is the language used among most deaf adults in the United States and Canada. In fact, it is the fourth most common language in the U.S. (Mayberry, 1978). Traditionally, ASL is reported to have been brought to the United States by Thomas Gallaudet, an educator who went to Europe to learn about methods for educating the deaf, and Larent Clerc, a deaf French man. Gallaudet and Clerc established a school for the deaf in America, using a sign language based on Old French sign (Lane, 1977; Wilbur, 1976). However, Woodward (1976; 1978) presented sociological and linguistic evidence suggesting that many of the signs in ASL were derived from sign languages already used by American deaf people before Old French Sign was introduced. It is important to recognize that ASL is a language, not merely a code to represent English or any other language. Thus there is often not a one-to-one correspondence between ASL signs and words in English, French, German, or any other language. In addition, even if the best English gloss is assigned to each ASL word, word-by-word translations from one language to the other would not be equivalent, since the structure of the two languages differ as well. For example, the ASL signed sequences THEY FINISH EAT NIGHT or FINISH EAT NIGHT THEY could be translated in English as "They have already eaten their dinner" (Mayberry, 1976). Each of these is an acceptable utterance relative to its own language, but they are clearly not parallel in structure.

Signs in ASL have traditionally been described by three parameters (Siple, 1978; Stoke, 1980):

1. *Location:* where a sign begins and ends with relation to the signer's body, also termed the place of articulation (e.g., chest, face)
2. *Handshape:* the distinctive configuration(s) of the hand(s) used to make the sign (e.g., flat hand, index finger isolated)
3. *Movement:* the motion of the hand(s) forming the sign (e.g., circular, linear).

A fourth parameter, orientation of the palm of the hand, may be needed to distinguish between some sign pairs (e.g., THING/CHILDREN). Wilbur (1987) noted that several additional pieces of information may be needed to provide a full description of a sign, such as the contact of the hand with another body part, speed of signing, and facial expressions.

The Dictionary of American Sign Language (Stokoe, Casterline, & Croneberg, 1978) described 19 handshapes, 12 locations, and 24 types of movement (which can be combined in clusters). Markowicz (1977) noted that the exact number of each of these may vary, as do the number of vowels in English, depending on the dialect. As with other languages, ASL has formational rules that specify the possible combinations for signs.

Each of the four major parameters can illustrate minimal contrasts. For example, the signs CANDY, APPLE, and JEALOUS are all formed with the same location, movement, and orientation; only the hand configuration distinguishes them (Klima & Bellugi, 1979). Similar examples exist for other parameters of sign formation (see Bornstein & Jordan, 1984, for examples of possible confusions of more than 300 basic signs, based on differences in these parameters).

Wilbur (1987) presented a review of current approaches to describing ASL. The major difference is that the traditional approach treats sign structure as simultaneous (i.e., movement, location, and handshape all occur at once), while recent approaches consider sign structure to be sequential (i.e., there are syllables in ASL, with features such as handshape and movement occurring simultaneously within segments).

Several authors (Baker & Padden, 1978a; Frishberg, 1979; Wilbur, 1987) have reviewed a number of historical modifications in ASL signs that have increased ease of production or reception. Wilbur divided these modifications into five categories:

1. *Increase in symmetry.* For example, signs below the neck have tended to change from one-handed to two-handed (DEAD, HURRY)
2. *Fluidity.* The location, movement, and handshape of some signs has been modified to yield a sign that is more fluid than the compound from which it is formed (e.g., contact points and handshapes have been simplified to form HOSPITAL from SICK plus HOME)
3. *Centralization.* Older signs have moved in from the side, up from the waist, and down from the face
4. *Changing role of the head and face.* Frishberg (1979) reported that many signs once requiring body and head movement, facial gesture, or environmental contact in their citation forms, are currently limited to movements of the hands only (e.g., COMPARE)
5. *Borrowing from English through fingerspelling.* Initialization, the use of a handshape from the manual alphabet to make a sign correspond to an English word, can be used to extend possible meanings of an ASL sign (e.g., forming FAMILY, CLASS, from the ASL sign GROUP).

The primary reason for the evolution of these modifications was to enhance production and reception of ASL. As Baker and Padden (1978) asserted, "ASL signs are 'natural' — they are shaped to be seen and efficiently produced by the human body" (p. 11).

Just as shades of meaning can be provided to spoken language through voice-related qualities such as pitch, stress, and intonation, a variety of simultaneous behaviors can add nuances of meaning to sign language. Baker and Padden (1978b) reviewed a number of studies which, as they stated "have clearly revealed the fallacy of assuming the hands to be the only carriers of linguistic information in signed discourse" (pp. 27–28). For example, some lexical items are formed or supplemented by facial expressions such as SAD (with a sorrowful expression) and BITE (often accompanied by a biting motion of the mouth). Nonmanual signals can also code grammatical functions, as discussed later in this section.

Klima and Belllugi (1979) reported that "although signs are produced at half the rate of words, the rate of producing propositions does not differ in the two modes" (p. 194). While 50 percent more spoken words than signs were used in a comparison study by Bellugi and Fisher (1972), they were produced in the same amount of time, as spoken words take considerably less time to produce than signs. Wilbur (1987) asserted that this may suggest "that at some level of processing, there is an optimum time or rate for transmission of information regardless of modality" (p. 183). She also noted that the finding that signed English sentences for the same story increased story time — but not the number of propositions — by 50 percent may indicate a potential problem for use of signed English relative to perception, production, and memory processing. The reason that propositions can be transmitted in ASL in the same time frame, but using fewer entries, is that ASL economizes by coding information in many ways, such as omitting some English grammatical morphemes. However, the information coded in those morphemes is not lost in ASL, as can be demonstrated through translation from English to ASL, then from ASL back to English. A variety of methods are used for compacting linguistic information in ASL to make the language more efficient while still retaining its effectiveness in coding propositions. As Wilbur (1976) noted, "what needs to be indicated sequentially in auditory languages, by using markers and word order, often can be indicated simultaneously in ASL" (p. 194). Numerous examples of this efficiency can be provided.

Klima and Bellugi (1979) reported several general procedures for compacting linguistic information. One procedure is the *structured use of space*. For example, in a narrative, a sign central to the meaning may be made in the first sentence (e.g., DOG) and followed by a classifier (e.g., ANIMAL). Subsequently, that locus in space may be reserved, and later signs (e.g., FEED, PAT) may be directed toward the locus reserved for the dog. This saves time because the signer is not required to sign DOG each time the animal is referred to. A time line may also be used with the space directly in front of the body indicating the present, slightly more forward indicating the future, and greater distances forward indicating very distant future. Movement backward along the time line would indicate the past (Wilbur, 1987). ASL, like some spoken languages (e.g., Malay) uses the convention of marking the time of the conversation at the beginning of the conversation, after which no marking is necessary until the time reference is changed. The preceding examples are only two of the ways in which the structured use of space can increase efficiency in ASL.

Another procedure for increasing efficiency is the *superimposed modulations of the movement of signs* (Klima & Bellugi, 1979). For example, native signers observing various productions of the sign SCARED could determine, through qualitative changes in the movement, whether the signer intended translation of "was scared" or "became scared." Similarly, slight modulations of movement may be seen in noun–verb pairs, in which the manner of movement is restrained and movement is repeated for the noun (e.g., FLY/AIRPLANE, SWEEP/BROOM) (Suppalla & Newport, 1978).

A third procedure for simultaneous coding is the *simultaneous use of facial expression for grammatical purposes*. For example, use of a negating signal (side-to-side headshake, turned down corners of mouth) can negate an otherwise positive statement.

Several authors (Baker & Padden, 1978b; Liddell, 1978; Wilbur, 1987) have discussed the variety of nonmanual signals used in ASL. For example, Baker and Padden analyzed several nonmanual behavioral changes (face, brows, head, blink, gaze, hands, body). They noted that many synchronous behaviors occur during signing of conditional sentences. They concluded that the configurations of these nonmanual behaviors carry meaning, rather than any single behavior.

WHY. As with other unaided systems, ASL can serve as a successful facilitator of language (Simpson & Mcdade, 1979). Since it is a rich and complex language, ASL can also serve as a long-term communication system, and in fact does fill this role for the adult deaf community in the United States and Canada. Thus there is an already-existing audience of ASL users, and a large number of potential teachers. Its capabilities for simultaneous coding of several pieces of linguistic information makes ASL desirable from the aspect of efficiency. This is a positive feature since more time is required for forming a sign than for uttering a word.

WHO. As noted, American Sign Language developed as a communication system for the deaf and is widely used by the population in the United States and Canada. Success has been reported in the use of ASL with a variety of other populations, including persons with mild to profound cognitive delay (Hobson & Duncan, 1979; Simpson & McDade, 1979; Stremel-Campbell, Cantrell, & Halle, 1977); individuals with autism (Bonvillian & Nelson, 1978; Carr, Binkoff, Kologinsky, & Eddy, 1978; Fulwiler & Fouts, 1976; Konstantareas, Oxman, & Webster, 1978); and other nonspeaking individuals with multiple or undiagnosed disabilities (Konstantareas et al., 1978; Koselka, Hannah, Gardner, & Reagan, 1975). However, in many cases the clients in these studies have demonstrated success with lexical entries of ASL in isolation, or with two- and three-sign strings only, rather than with ASL as a total system. In addition, some authors (e.g., Stremel-Campbell et al., 1977) reported the use of ASL signs but in English word order, as in signed English. We are not suggesting that nondeaf individuals with severe disabilities cannot make full use of ASL as a language, but that to date it has typically been used in a limited manner.

Candidates for ASL should possess the following skills, or should be expected to acquire them:

1. *Good motor control of both hands,* in order to produce the variety of handshapes
2. *Good range of motion with both arms,* in order to produce signs at a variety of locations and with a number of movment patterns
3. *Good control over facial musculature,* in order to achieve nuances of meaning through facial expressions

4. *Good visual acuity and visual discrimination,* if the individual is to receive as well as produce sign
5. *Sensorimotor Stage 5* (Chapman & Miller, 1980) *or Stage 6 intelligence.*

The issue of nonmanual signs is important in selecting a sign system for use with an individual with severe communication impairment. If the individual is expected to use ASL as a communication system, it will be important to capitalize on using these nonmanual behaviors as well as the manual signs. Indeed, Baker and Padden (1978a) suggested that nonmanual behaviors be considered as basic building blocks of ASL, along with manual components such as handshapes.

The question of *who?* also relates to the potential audience if ASL is to be used as the primary means of communication. Baker and Padden reported that ASL is used by approximately 500,000 deaf Americans and Canadians of all ages, thus providing a large population of potential communication partners. However, the nonspeaking hearing individual is not likely to have access to the deaf community, making it necessary to train communication partners.

Signs have traditionally been described as having a degree of transparency, referring to the ease with which the meaning of a sign can be understood from its form alone. Klima and Bellugi (1979) studied the transparency of commonly used ASL signs (e.g., APPLE, BOY, EARTH, WEEK) presented to hearing subjects who knew no signs. They found that 81 of the 90 signs were not guessed by any of the 10 subjects. A second group of ten subjects scored no better than chance in selecting the signs on a multiple-choice test. Thus it is apparent that most of the ASL signs on this list were not readily transparent. However, the authors demonstrated that many of the signs could be considered translucent; "that is, nonsigners essentially agree on the basis for the relation between the sign and its meaning" (p. 10). Iconicity in signs can often be stressed or invented to serve as an aid in remembering signs. Thus, although it will be necessary for those in the environment to directly learn most signs, once meanings have been attached, they will, in most cases, be relatively easy to remember. However, native speakers of English will have to learn the syntax of ASL in addition to the vocabulary. This can be extremely difficult, especially if they do not have frequent access to persons fluent in ASL. Thus finding or training an audience for the individual who becomes fluent in ASL may be a significant problem.

HOW. As with most unaided systems used with nondeaf individuals with severe communication impairment, ASL is typically "taught," rather than learned as a natural language. Since it is a true language, it would seem more appropriate to introduce ASL as a natural language, through an environmental approach. Wilbur (1987) reviewed studies demonstrating that ASL is acquired spontaneously by hearing and deaf children who are exposed to it in the home. Unfortunately, most parents would have some difficulty in this respect because learning ASL as an adult constitutes learning a second language (Stokoe, 1980). It is unlikely that most families of hearing children with severe communication impairment would choose ASL as their primary communication system. In addition, the hearing, nonspeaking individual may not have any peers who use ASL.

If specific therapy sessions are to be used, training may be similar in many respects to training for other unaided systems (to be discussed in this chapter). However, the differences in structure of ASL suggest that instructors should employ specialized techniques for introducing ASL versus, for example, Signing Exact English. If ASL is intended to serve as a full communication system for the individual, the structure specific to ASL must be considered. In addition, nonmanual signals, such as facial expressions, body orientation, and eye gaze, which are related to lexical entries and structures of ASL, may require specific training. For example, it may be necessary to carefully model the combination of behaviors that signal production of a yes–no question (head and shoulders leaned forward, chin forward far enough to keep the face vertical, and eyebrows raised) (Liddell, 1978), in contrast to behaviors that signal a WH-question (brows raised and drawn together) (Baker & Padden, 1978a). Baker and Padden (1978b) have developed a list of some functions of eye movements and facial movements in ASL discourse which may help bring nonmanual behavior to a level of consciousness for both the instructor and the learner.

The preceding discussion on training nuances of ASL assumes that the instructor is a fluent user of ASL. This may be far from true for those of us who have learned sign from a book and/or a course, and have little or no opportunity to practice discourse with native ASL users. This may be especially problematic for communication specialists living in rural areas. A number of manuals available to help a potential instructor learn ASL are listed in the *Where* section. The communication specialist who is not bilingual in English and ASL may want to consider a number of alternatives:

1. Increase fluency in ASL through further course-work and preferably, practice with a native ASL signer prior to or concurrent with beginning training of clients
2. Locate a fluent ASL user to supplement instruction, at least temporarily[1]

---

[1] Contact the Registry of Interpreters for the Deaf, Inc., 814 Thayer Avenue, Silver Springs, MD 20910.

3. Limit ASL training to teaching of vocabulary and basic syntax, either as a facilitative or early communication system, or as a system for an individual whose language is not expected to reach a high level of complexity

4. Select a system whose structure more closely parallels English (e.g., Signing Exact English, Signed English), so that it is not necessary to learn a new structure as well as new vocabulary forms.

Several training programs have been designed or adapted for teaching ASL or ASL signs to various populations (e.g., persons with cognitive impairment, autism). These programs typically have a very limited scope. The communication specialist teaching ASL to individuals with higher-level language skills might find a second-language approach helpful. This would be especially true for some individuals who become nonspeaking after acquiring language.

WHERE. A great amount of information and research is available on American Sign Language (e.g., Klima & Bellugi, 1978; Stokoe et al., 1978; Wilbur, 1987). A sampling of the wide range of materials for teaching and learning ASL is:

- *Dictionaries* (see Appendix B): *American Sign Language: A comprehensive dictionary* (Sternberg, 1981); *Signs Across America* (Shroyer & Shroyer, 1984)
- *Training Materials: A basic course in American Sign Language* (Humphries, Padden, & O'Rourke, 1980); *American Sign Language: A beginning course* (Kettrick, 1984); *Intermediate conversational sign language* (Madsen, 1982); *Signing — How to speak with your hands* (Costello, 1983); *Teaching American Sign Language as a Second/Foreign Language* (1982)
- *Manufacturers/Distributors* (see Appendix C): A variety of materials such as games, signing trinkets, and songbooks, can be purchased from Joyce Media, Inc., and Sign UP
- *Organizations* (see Appendix D): Resources such as informational booklets, journals, games, flash cards, and translation exercises can be obtained from the following sources: Gallaudet University, The National Association of the Deaf, Regional Centers for Services to Deaf-Blind Children.

SUMMARY AND DISCUSSION. A number of myths and misconceptions persist concerning American Sign Language, such as it is ungrammatical (Markowicz, 1977). Many of the myths can be laid to rest simply by recognizing that ASL is a unique language, not just a coded representation of another language, such as English. Viewing it as a separate language, we can see that:

- *ASL is not a universal language,* it is merely the sign language used by most deaf persons of the United States and Canada. Deaf individuals of other countries (e.g., Japan, Denmark) use sign languages which differ from each other, just as spoken languages of those countries differ.
- *ASL is no more concept-based than other languages,* such as Norwegian. In fact, both words and signs are based on concepts.
- *ASL is not ungrammatical,* though utterances translated from ASL to English may appear ungrammatical, just as utterances translated from French or Italian frequently appear ungrammatical. ASL is based on a large number of grammatical rules which govern its use.

As a language of the deaf community, ASL has a rich history of use, dating back more than 160 years. Its use with hearing persons having severe communication impairment is of much more recent origin. In a limited fashion, success has been demonstrated in application of ASL to individuals having a wide range of communication disabilities. There is a future for extended use of ASL with hearing populations, due in great measure to its efficiency and the large audience of ASL users.

British Sign Language

The British Sign Language family comprises a number of widely used sign languages, including British Sign Language (BSL), Australasian Sign Language, Old Catholic Scottish Sign Language, and Modern Scottish Sign Language (Wilbur, 1987). Like ASL and other sign languages, it has evolved over a period of time, and has developed a structure and rules.

Recent research (reported in Kiernan, Jordan, & Saunders, 1978) suggested that about half of the signs in everyday use are performed with one hand, while over one-third involve two hands in symmetrical handshapes. As with ASL, many of the signs that originally had an iconic basis now appear arbitrary, as the meaningful link has been forgotten.

For further information on British Sign Language, see *Perspectives on British Sign Language and Deafness* (Woll, Kyle, & Deuchar, 1981) and *Language in Sign: An International Perspective on Sign Language* (Kyle & Woll, 1983). The latter publication also includes papers on other sign languages (e.g., Swedish Sign, Norwegian Sign).

Educational Sign Systems

Educationally based sign systems, often termed pedagogical systems, have been designed to meet certain educational needs. Regarding the developers of early educational sign systems, Gustason (1985) asserted that the main concern of the original group was the consistent, logical, rational, and practical development of signs to represent as specifically as possible the basic essentials of the English language. This concern sprang from the experience of all present with the poor English skills of many deaf students, and the desire for an easier, more successful way of developing mastery of English in a far greater number of such students. (p. 11)

The parallel to spoken and written English can be expected to benefit communication partners as well as potential users. Gustason, Pfetzing, & Zawolkow (1980) noted that roughly 90 percent of the parents of hearing-impaired children (in the United States) are hearing, with most of those parents having English as a native language. Thus, it would be helpful for those primary trainers to use a communication system that can be related to English, rather than requiring learning of a new set of grammatical rules in addition to new representations for lexical items.

Several educational sign systems (e.g., manual English, Seeing Essential English, Signing Exact English, Signed English) have some features in common as they are based to some extent on American Sign Language and the American Manual Alphabet. However, Wilbur (1987) noted that these systems do not simply take "the signs of ASL and put them in English word order," but also "drastically alter the morphological and phonological processes that users of ASL are accustomed to producing and perceiving" (e.g., reduplication, blending, assimilations) (p. 250).

Fristoe and Lloyd (1978), and Goodman, Wilson, and Bornstein (1978), sent questionnaires to special educators, the majority of whom worked in programs serving individuals with severe cognitive delay. These questionnaires dealt with the use of augmentative systems (primarily sign) in special education programs. One important finding was that many teachers reported using ASL while in fact they used only ASL signs in English word order, without the additional features of ASL. Fristoe and Lloyd (1978) suggested "either that they do not recognize that there are differences in sign systems or else that they are not aware of the importance of the differences" (p. 101). They also noted that respondents often gave misinformed reasons for choosing one system over another, such as stating that Signing Exact English is simpler than other systems (in fact, signed English is less complex). Therefore, the communication specialist must be aware of the distinctions among systems when matching a sign system to an individual user. Three systems that are widely used and/or can meet the needs of hearing individuals with severe communication impairment are covered in depth in this chapter (Signing Exact English, Signed English, Duffysigns). Several systems used less widely in North America, or less appropriate to the needs of severely speech-impaired persons, are covered briefly.

Paget-Gorman Systematic Sign

This system was the first English-based educational sign system. It was developed by Sir Richard Paget (1951), and was initially named "A New Sign Language." Because it developed in England, this system does not use ASL signs. Paget-Gorman Systematic Sign (PGSS) includes over 3,000 primarily pantomimic signs which include combinations of 21 standard hand positions and 37 basic signs representing general concepts (e.g., ANIMAL, PERSON, COLOR, BUILDING). The basic signs serve to group signs with a common concept, such as FOOD and ANIMAL, while the hand configurations indicate specific entries within each group. For example, *Dentist* is formed by PERSON and TOOTH, and *red* consists of COLOR and BLOOD. For each of these signs, the first hand would form the basic sign, while the second sign would indicate the signifier. The combination of basic signs and signifiers to form single signs yields a high percentage of two-handed constructions, with each hand forming a different handshape. This increases the complexity of sign formation, and increases the difficulty of production for individuals with physical impairment.

The PGSS system includes various grammatical features such as inclusion of common affixes (e.g., plural, possessive, past tense, adverb), pronominalization (e.g., signs for I, YOU, and IT, plus variations) and formation of compound and complex words.

Although PGSS was developed with the intention that it should be highly pantomimic, Jones and Cregan (1986) noted that a high level of world knowledge would be required to decode the representational nature of many of the signs. Thus, hearing adults might be able to use the pantomimic connections to learn and retain signs in a way unavailable to persons who are young or cognitively delayed. In a similar vein, Craig (1976) observed that, while the internal structure (basic sign plus signifier) appears to be opaque to children learning the system, it can have considerable value to hearing adults, as an aid to memory in learning the system.

Several resources are available for further information on the system: *American Sign Language* (Wilbur, 1987, Chapter 10); *The Paget-Gorman Sign System* (Paget, Gorman, & Paget, 1976); and *Sign and Symbol Communication for Mentally Handicapped People* (Jones & Cregan, 1986).

Seeing Essential English

Seeing Essential English (SEE 1) was the first educational sign system developed in the United States. It was developed by David Anthony (1966, 1971) as a simplified system for use with deaf, cognitively delayed individuals. Two sign systems, Linguistics of Visual English and Signing Exact English, have been derived from Seeing Essential English. This book will not cover Seeing Essential English, as it is not widely available and does not seem to have gained widespread use with persons having severe communication impairment. See Anthony (1971) or Bornstein (1973) for further information on this system.

Linguistics of Visual English

This sign system was intended for use with preschool and kindergarten children. It is a morpheme-based system; signs are intended to represent morphemes rather than word roots, prefixes, and suffixes. Morphemes are distinguished on the basis of similarity of two of three characteristics: sound, spelling, and meaning. The signs of ASL are paired with English bound and unbound morphemes. For example, Mayberry (1976) noted that the word *carpet* would be made through the ASL signs CAR plus PET (translated "auto" plus "physically stroke"). Linguistics of Visual English follows English word order and uses English function words and inflections, such as pronouns, articles, tense markers, and auxiliaries. Further information on this system may be found in Mayberry (1976).

Signed English

WHAT. Signed English, as conceived by Bornstein and his colleagues (1973; 1983) is a "language-like tool" consisting of two types of signs: more than 3,100 sign words (e.g., DISNEY, LAUGH, and REPTILE), and 14 sign markers (e.g., past tense, -ed, and adjective; -y). This formal, contrived system is intended to parallel spoken English more closely than ASL. The signs do not represent sounds, syllables, or phonemes, nor do they represent English spelling. Rather, Signed English signs represent only the specific English word with all its various meanings. The basic vocabulary list was assembled from published lists of the spoken language of children and from "language logs" provided by parents and teachers, listing vocabulary used in the homes and classrooms of deaf children. Several additional rules were used in sign selection (Bornstein, Saulnier, & Hamilton, 1983):

- One sign (gesture) is designed to represent one English word (e.g., different ASL signs are used for GLAD and HAPPY)
- Where possible, a sign from American Sign Language is used (to encourage signing with pidgin ASL users)
- Signs represent meaning, rather than sound or spelling of a word (e.g., the noun LAND and the verb LAND have different sign representations).

The 14 sign markers included in Signed English are illustrated in Figure 7-1. They are used to represent very basic and common English word form changes, usually inflections and endings. All but one of these markers is used after the sign. The frequently used markers are formed by the right hand only, in the "resting" position (the position assumed during pauses), to minimize effort and time expended to produce markers. In general only one sign marker is added to each sign word, to maintain the simple structure considered necessary for consistent use. It is recommended that fingerspelling be used for words and word forms not covered by the vocabulary and sign markers.

WHY. Signed English has been successfully used as a communication system, as well as for speech and language facilitation, with people having severe handicaps (e.g., Kimble, 1975; Kopchick & Lloyd, 1976; Schaeffer, 1980). Factors that may make this system especially desirable for some nonspeakers are its focus on a vocabulary appropriate to young children, paralleling of English word order, use of a limited set of sign markers, and availability of a wide range of support materials.

WHO. Signed English candidates should meet the same requirements as candidates for ASL, with the exception that good control of facial musculature is less crucial. The reason for this distinction is that nonmanual behavior is not used to code as much linguistic information in Signed English, since it uses English structure. Although designed for use with deaf children, Signed English has been used or advocated for use with a variety of populations, including people who are severely cognitively delayed (Kimble, 1975; Kopchick & Lloyd, 1976); autistic (Schaeffer, 1980); and adventitiously nonverbal (Abkarian, Dworkin, & Brown, 1978).

With regard to communication partners, signs in this system would likely not be highly transparent, as many are based on ASL signs. Thus, it would be necessary for parents, teachers, and others to directly learn the system. However, several factors should theoretically make it easier to learn than ASL or the SEE systems for competent speakers of English. First, since it is designed to parallel English, it will basically be necessary to learn only a vocabulary of signs based on English words, rather than a new set of grammatical rules, as is necessary for ASL users. Second, the vocabulary is restricted to 3,100 signs, while ASL and Signing Exact English have more than 5,000 signs each. Signed English has also been restricted to 14 sign markers, compared to more than 50 markers for Signing Exact English. These features would, of course, also make Signed English relatively easy to learn for clients having competency in English, such as persons with severe spastic dysphonia. It is feasible to consider learning Signed English from one of the many available books.

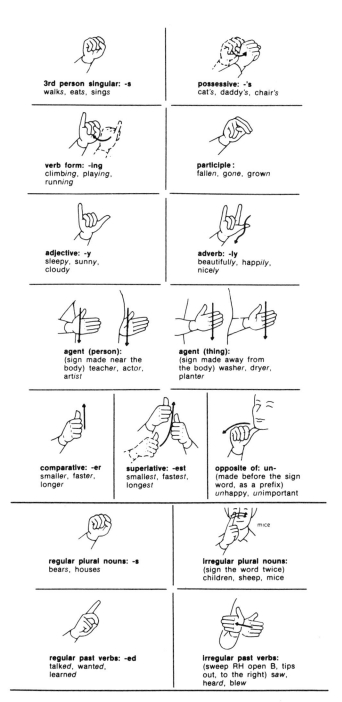

3rd person singular: -s
walks, eats, sings

possessive: -'s
cat's, daddy's, chair's

verb form: -ing
climbing, playing,
running

participle :
fallen, gone, grown

adjective: -y
sleepy, sunny,
cloudy

adverb: -ly
beautifully, happily,
nicely

agent (person):
(sign made near the
body) teacher, actor,
artist

agent (thing):
(sign made away from
the body) washer, dryer,
planter

comparative: -er
smaller, faster,
longer

superlative: -est
smallest, fastest,
longest

opposite of: un-
(made before the sign
word, as a prefix)
unhappy, unimportant

regular plural nouns: -s
bears, houses

irregular plural nouns:
(sign the word twice)
children, sheep, mice

mice

regular past verbs: -ed
talked, wanted,
learned

irregular past verbs:
(sweep RH open B, tips
out, to the right) saw,
heard, blew

Figure 7-1
Sign markers in Signed English. From Bornstein and Saulnier (1985), *The Signed English Starter*. Washington, DC: Gallaudet University Press. Reprinted with permission.

WHEN. It is generally suggested that exposure begin as early as possible; for example as soon as a child is diagnosed as deaf. Signed English could be used as input to clients with cognitive skills below Stage 5 sensorimotor development.

HOW. As always, training procedures will depend primarily on the needs of the client and the realities of the environment. Training procedures specific to use of Signed English, especially for chronologically or developmentally young children, involve use of the many training aids available. Varied formats are provided, such as posters, storybooks, nursery rhymes, and songbooks. According to Bornstein (1974), each teaching aid uses pictures to present the child with "a consistent and accurate relationship between the printed word, signed word, and appearance of the lips" (p. 340). Each teaching aid is self-contained so that it may be used without the need of other materials. Thus parents can learn Signed English and become primary teachers of the system for their children. A songbook (Musselwhite, 1985) presents more than 100 basic Signed English signs, plus goals and teaching ideas in the areas of cognition, communication, and motor skills.

WHERE. Information about Signed English may be obtained by requesting a guide to the system from Gallaudet University Press (see Appendix C). Teaching aids such as storybooks, sign/word flashcards, and posters may also be purchased from that organization.

• Books (see Appendix B): Functional Signs: A New Approach from Simple to Complex (Bornstein & Jordan, 1984); The Signed English Starter (Bornstein & Saulnier, 1984); The Comprehensive Signed English Dictionary (Bornstein, Saulnier, & Hamilton, 1983); Songbook: Signs and Symbols (Musselwhite, 1985); The Signed English Schoolbook (Bornstein & Saulnier, 1987); Signed English Storybooks; Signed English for the Classroom (Bornstein, Saulnier, & Hamilton, 1979a); and Signed English for the Residence Hall (Bornstein, Saulnier, & Hamilton, 1979b).

DISCUSSION AND SUMMARY. The Signed English system is an attempt to represent English manually. However, it is more limited (in terms of vocabulary represented by signs) and less complex (in terms of sign markers) than other educational systems reviewed in this chapter, such as Signing Exact English. The potential of Signed English for use by people having severe communication handicaps appears quite broad, due in great measure to its simplicity and available support materials.

Signing Exact English

WHAT. Signing Exact English, often referred to as SEE 2, developed from a January, 1969 meeting in southern California, in which concerned parents, educators, and deaf adults met to discuss appropriate, effective ways to represent English in the gestural mode. Signing Exact English was initially quite similar to Seeing Essential English (SEE 1) (Anthony, 1966), but has evolved separately from that system.

A brief history of the development of SEE 2 is quite interesting. Bornstein (1973) reported that the developers were former members of the Seeing Essential English group who felt that that system needed improvement. The three women primarily responsible for developing materials for SEE 2 (Gustason, Pfetzing, & Zawolkow, 1980) have had considerable experience with deaf individuals. The first author, who was deafened at age six, has earned several advanced degrees, and has taught extensively in various programs for the deaf, including Gallaudet College. The second author was the mother of a deaf child, served as Head Interpreter in a public school, and taught adult education courses to parents and teachers working with young deaf children. The third author, the daughter of deaf parents, grew up using American Sign language and now serves as an interpreter and a consultant to many programs using sign language.

Signing Exact English currently consists of nearly 4,000 signs, including more than 70 commonly used English affixes. The system has undergone considerable modification during the first decade of its use. Following are the basic principles around which the system was developed, plus examples of rule application.

1. *English should be signed in a manner that is as consistent as possible with how it is spoken or written.* For example, idioms such as "hanging around" or "cool it" should be signed exactly and inflections such as kiss-*ing* should be indicated.

2. *A sign should be translatable to only one English equivalent.* However, additional principles regarding basic, compound, and complex signs have been developed to clarify this rule.

3. *"Basic words" are words that can have no more taken away and still form a complete word.* Examples are *boy, drink, an,* and *more.* A three-point criteria of sound, spelling, and meaning is used. If any two of these three factors are the same, the same sign is used. Thus, one sign would be used for various forms of *drop* (DROP the plate, a DROP of water), while different signs would be used for *to, two,* and *too.*

4. *"Complex words" are defined as basic words with the addition of an affix or inflection.* Examples are *boys, drinking, drank.*

5. *"Compound words" are two or more basic words put together, only if the meaning for the words separately is consistent with the meaning of the*

words together. For example, *doorknob* = DOOR + KNOB. However, UNDER-STAND has its own represenation, rather than being formed from *under* + *stand,* as its meaning is not derived from those two base words.

6. *When a sign already exists in ASL that is clear, unambiguous, and commonly translates to only one English word, this sign is retained.* This provides for maximum possible overlap with ASL, while still retaining the principles of Signing Exact English.

7. *When the first letter is added to a basic sign to create synonyms, the basic sign is retained wherever possible as the most commonly used word.* For example, the common verb MAKE is not initialized, while C-hands (using the C handshape) are used for CREATE, and P-hands (using the P handshape) for PRODUCE.

8. *When more than one marker is added to a word, middle markers may be dropped if there is no sacrifice of clarity.* For instance, *examination* can be signed EXAM + TION (with omission of the medial INE).

9. *While following the above principles, respect needs to be shown for characteristics of visual-gestural communication.* This principle refers to avoidance of awkward or difficult movements, whenever possible.

Wilbur (1979, 1987) has pointed out inconsistent applications of these basic rules. For example, rather than following the two-out-of-three principle, some words are broken down into morpheme divisions ("Scotch" = SCOT + H) or syllable divisions ("nursery" = NURSE + ER + Y). It is difficult to see how these purely arbitrary deviations were determined, since SEE 2 is a contrived sign system, rather than a naturally evolving language such as ASL. However, comparison of the manual (Gustason, Pfetzing, & Zawolkow, 1980) with an earlier version (no longer in print) suggests that inconsistencies are gradually being reduced.

Guidelines are also presented for developing additional signs. Gustason and colleagues (1980) first advise seeking or modifying an existing sign, or considering fingerspelling. If a new sign must be invented, they offer specific guidelines for sign formation, considering principles such as the signing space and the number of handshapes per sign. Fourteen guidelines are also presented for developing clear, expressive signing. Several of these guidelines relate to ASL techniques, such as indicating a *wh*-question by a slight frown or indicating the direction of the action of a verb. The overall purpose is to provide supplemental meaning not present in the citation forms of the signs.

WHY. The SEE 2 system was developed as a manual communication system to represent English for educational purposes. The use of a large number of affixes and a large vocabulary of English words is intended to help the user develop a good base for understanding and producing idiomatic standard English, whether signed, spoken, or written. Jordan, Gustason, and Rosen (1976, 1979) noted that there has been a great increase of Total Communication in schools in the United State States, with a predominance of texts of sign systems designed to represent English, such as Signing Exact English. Gustason, Pfetzing and Zowolkow (1980) stressed that SEE 2 is not a replacement for ASL.

WHO. SEE 2 was designed for use by hearing-impaired or deaf children, and by their parents, families, friends, and teachers. Gustason and colleagues (1980) observed that SEE 2 is not widely used by adults, although some of its signs are being incorporated into common ASL usage. Also, students are now graduating from high schools who have grown up with SEE 2. Candidates for this system should meet the same basic requirements as for Signed English, with one exception. The relatively greater emphasis on use of pronouns and affixes will require that the individual be expected to develop a fairly high level of English competence. Thus, its use would seem to be less appropriate for individuals with severe cognitive delay. The addition of affixes may also increase the difficulty of motor planning and execution, which may make this system too difficult for many physically disabled individuals.

Since it closely parallels spoken English, Signing Exact English might be appropriate for some individuals who have acquired competence in English but cannot produce it for some reason (e.g., vocal fold paralysis). The close approximation with English should also make SEE 2 simpler for hearing adults (e.g., English-speaking parents of nonspeaking children) to learn than ASL, assuming that full use of the structure is desired. Due again to its close relationship to English, this system should be appropriate for individuals who are expected to develop reading skills, although this premise has not yet been proven.

WHEN. As with the other sign systems presented in this chapter, Signing Exact English is intended for use, at least as an input system, as soon as feasible, as early as Stage 2. Production of signs should be expected to begin at a similar developmental level to other signs, at approximately Stage 4.

HOW. As with other systems, teaching methods will depend to a great extent on features related to the learner, such as current level of linguistic competence and the intended function of the system (e.g., as a second language system for a person with an acquired disorder). A wide variety of materials has been developed specifically to support Signing Exact English. Selected materials, such as videotapes and student workbooks, are intended for use with individuals learning the system to serve as teachers or communication partners (e.g., college students, parents, family members), while other materials, such as the storybook collection, are designed for use directly with hearing-impaired and/or nonspeaking individuals. Since word order and sentence structure parallel English to a great extent, it should be possible for English-speaking adults to learn SEE 2 through introductory sign courses and/or printed or videotaped materials, followed by extensive practice.

WHERE. Materials and training suggestions for this system are available through Modern Signs Press, Inc. (see Appendix C). Sample materials are:

- *Books: Teaching and Learning Signing Exact English* (Gustason, 1983a); *Signing Exact English* (Gustaston, Pfetzing, & Zawolkow, 1980); *Student Workbook* (Gustason, 1983b)
- *Materials: Signing Exact English Vocabulary Development Kits* (Cenoplano, Gustason, & Zawolkow, 1981); *The Talking Fingers Storybook Series*
- *Videotapes: Beginning Curriculum A* (7 hours); *Sign What You Say* (30 minutes); *Mothers Look at Total Communication* (45 minutes). A quarterly newsletter (*See What's Happening*) is also available.

SUMMARY AND DISCUSSION. This is a well-developed sign system designed to represent spoken English for educational purposes. The system has grown in a number of ways over the past 15 years, including the number of signs represented, the number and variety of users, and the quantity of support materials available. The motoric and linguistic complexity of the system will limit its expressive use with many persons having severe communication impairment.

Duffysigns

WHAT. This sign system is the result of a master's thesis by a special education teacher in a class for students with moderate mental retardation and physical handicaps (Duffy, 1977). The system was developed following observation and trial therapy with students having severe handicaps. Each sign was then tested with four students, ages 7 to 15, who were medically diagnosed as having quadriplegic athetoid cerebral palsy. The speech of these students was limited to vowel sounds and a few consonants (/b/, /p/, /m/, /n/).

The sign system comprises 471 signs that are formed by gross gestures such as raising one hand or placing one hand on the knee or the wheelchair armrest. Some signs are accompanied by vocalizations. For example ONE = "un" + raise one hand, while TWO = "ooo" + raise two hands. A few of the entries consist of vocalizations only. An example is the letter

U, which is indicated by the sound /u/. For some signs alternate methods of production are suggested. For example, *K* can be indicated either by touching the chin with the hand or touching the chin on the wheelchair armrest. Wherever possible signs are iconic, such as crossing the legs for *X,* or pantomiming pulling up pants for PANTS.

The system is logically organized. Many of the categories are preceded by a general sign. For example, the general sign for time precedes most time-category signs (e.g., 1:00 = TIME + ONE). A general sign can also be used to indicate "I am spelling," or "numbers will follow." Within lexical groupings a logical base can also be seen. Days of the week are formed by the sign for DAY plus the number of the day (*Sunday* = DAY + ONE; *Monday* = DAY + TWO). Similarly, months are indicated by the sign for time plus the first letter of the month and a vocal sound (*May* = TIME + M + "aaah"; *December* = TIME + D + "eee"). Questions are indicated by making the sign QUESTION followed by the appropriate sign (WHO, WHAT, WHERE). Facial movements and whole body movements are often used in expressing feelings. For example, one set of feelings requires the user to bounce up and down in the chair while executing arm movements and/or signs for facial expressions (EXCITED, UPSET, SURPRISE, LUCKY). In addition to the categories of letters, numbers, time, and emotions, a wide variety of other categories are covered. Examples are persons, places, adjectives, prepositions, verbs, and pronouns. With the exception of producing questions by using QUESTION + question word, no specific structural rules are presented for this system.

WHY. Of all the sign systems presented in this chapter, Duffysigns requires the least motor control. It would be likely to be used only as an output system, since users who could decode this system, with its emphasis on numbers and letters, could likely decode speech or an augmentative system presented at a faster rate (e.g., fingerspelling or Signed English). Duffy (personal communication) suggested that this system might be used as an interim system while vocal communication skills are being developed. It may prove to facilitate speech because many of the signs require vocalization. Duffysigns could also be used as a supplement to another communication system (e.g., a symbolic communication board using Blissymbols) since it is portable and requires learning a relatively small number of signs.

WHO. This system was designed for people with severe physical handicaps, particularly cerebral palsy. Execution of signs requires the following:

1. *Volitional control over gross motor movements of all limbs,* since some signs are two-handed (TIME) and some involve active use of the legs (X)

2. *High level of cognitive-academic development,* if the spelling aspect is to be used. However, many signs based on numbers or letters could be memorized without regard to their component parts
3. *Moderate control over facial musculature,* since some signs involve the use of the lips (F) or facial expression (ANGRY)
4. *Volitional control over some vocalizations,* primarily vowels, since some signs require supplemental use of vocalizations (CUP, MAY).

This system may also be of some use to persons with hemiplegia and symbolic deficiencies (e.g., aphasics) since many signs are iconic and all require only gross motor movement.

Duffysigns would not be a difficult system for those in the user's environment to learn. The small number of signs, the iconicity of many signs, and the logical basis of the system should aid in rapid acquisition by non-impaired adults.

WHEN. A number of the simple iconic signs (PANTS, CUP) could be taught to a person with cognitive development at about the sensorimotor Stage 5 or 6. Some of the more academic signs (e.g., letters, numbers, time) could be taught if and when the person demonstrated readiness.

HOW. Duffy (1977) recommended that the trainer initially teach from a wheelchair because several of the signs involve touching a part of the wheelchair. In addition, for clients who are in wheelchairs, this will provide an appropriate model of positioning. Other teaching procedures follow general sign training methods, with adaptations made according to the person's physical limitations.

WHERE. Duffy has prepared the following materials relating to Duffy-signs: a text describing the need and the project and presenting all 471 signs, with illustrations where necessary; a 10-minute slide presentation including 72 slides, an 18-page script, and a cassette tape; and a short videotape demonstrating the use of the system with three students having severe cerebral palsy. The text and slide set may be borrowed from the Univeristy of Nevada, Las Vegas, library.[2] Other materials may be rented and/or purchased from The Info Bank.[3]

SUMMARY AND DISCUSSION. Duffysigns consists of 471 gross motor signs, with some signs supplemented by vocalizations. Although this system has not yet achieved widespread use, it does appear to be a viable

---

[2] Request the following call numbers: LC/4580/D8 (text); LC/4850/D81 (script and slide set).
[3] Box 852, Layton, UT 84041.

choice for some people with physical disabilities. Rate of output would likely be slow due to the necessity, in many cases, of producing several gestures to encode one concept. However, this feature also makes the system more applicable to persons with physical disabilities, since a relatively small number of gross motor movements can be combined to yield 471 signs. Thus, for nonspeakers who are motorically unable to use a more extensive unaided system such as Signed English, Duffysigns could prove very useful. A major use might be for communicating with a small audience who had learned the signs, such as family members, when an aided system was not available or not desired (e.g., the user wishes to communicate directly with the body, rather than through a display). For persons without a vocal output communication aid, Duffysigns can also serve the need for communicating from a distance. For example, Scott, a six-year-old child with cerebral palsy, could use Duffysigns to communicate with his father while his father is cooking dinner and is unable to look closely at a communication display.

Gestural Language Codes

Gestural language codes are systems which allow the user to code a specific language, such as English or Finnish. Amer-Ind, to be described later in this chapter, would not fit into this category since it does not code a language. In the systems included here gestures represent segments of a spoken language (phonemes, syllables) or a written language (letters of the alphabet). For each of these gestural language codes the structure is that of the language it represents. The codes presented in this section are intended to represent English or other languages based on the Roman alphabet, although modifications can be made for applying the codes to other languages, such as Russian.

Fingerspelling

WHAT. Fingerspelling is a code that uses handshapes to represent letters of the alphabet. The fingerspelling system used with languages based on the Roman alphabet includes 26 distinct handshapes to represent the 26 letters of that alphabet, as illustrated in Figure 7-2. The system used in the United States is often termed the American Manual Alphabet. The fingerspelling system used to represent the English language in England is two-handed, compared to the one-handed system of the United States. Manual alphabets are used to represent many languages. For example, the Russian Manual Alphabet has 32 symbols that stand for the 32 symbols of that alphabet. In 1963 the Fourth Congress of the World Federation of the Deaf adopted an International Fingerspelling Alphabet. Wilbur (1987)

Figure 7-2
The American Manual Alphabet. From Bornstein and Saulnier (1984). *The Signed English Starter.* Washington, DC: Gallaudet University Press. Reprinted with permission.

reported that this alphabet, while not universal, has gained some acceptance in Europe. Illustrations of the International Fingerspelling Alphabet, plus manual alphabets from 45 countries, are presented in Carmel (1982). The major parameter to be considered in any manual alphabet is configuration, although motion may also be important (e.g., for the letters J and Z in the American Manual Alphabet). A left-handed manual alphabet has been developed (Chen, 1968; 1971), in which the gestures depict alphabet letters as closely as possible. Wilbur (1979) noted that fingerspelling is slow in comparison to signing or speech.

Moores (1980) reported that the use of fingerspelling as a tool in deaf education has been documented as far back as 1620. Simultaneous use of speech and fingerspelling is referred to as the *Rochester Method* in the United States, and *neo-oralism* in the Soviet Union.

Regarding the execution of fingerspelling, Wilber (1987) observed that skilled fingerspellers form words as units rather than as simple sequences of letters. Akamatsu (1982; 1985) referred to this as the "movement envelope" containing handshape changes rather than a sequence of handshapes with transitions between them. This may create a perceptual problem for the message receiver because the center letters of a word may be assimilated to the surrounding letters and the formation of the letters may be blurred. Thus, the receiver must make successive guesses regarding what is being perceived, much as one does in speechreading. A thorough knowledge of the grammar of the language is required in order to narrow the possible choices of the words being presented. Wilbur (1987) supported Akamatsu's (1982) argument that "early acquisition of fingerspelling is heavily movement-shape dependent, rather than handshape-sequence dependent" (p. 223).

WHY. Moores (1980) reported that "investigators comparing fingerspelling with oral-only programs and with oral-manual programs consistently favor the use of fingerspelling with speech but without signs" (p. 42). He reviewed several studies concerning this issue, all conducted with deaf or hearing-impaired subjects. The findings support the use of fingerspelling to improve skills such as written language, reading, and speechreading.

Fingerspelling is also used widely by deaf persons as a link between sign language or sign systems and the spoken language. For example, proper nouns and words not represented in the sign language may be fingerspelled.

Fingerspelling is quite easy to learn by those who already know how to spell; in fact, it is a code learned by many adolescents to serve as a secret communication system after they outgrow "Pig Latin." Thus many adults working with people having severe communication handicaps will already have learned the basic handshapes representing their language. Considerable practice is needed, however, in order to develop fluency in the system.

Since it can be readily learned by persons with good motoric and spelling capabilities (e.g., laryngectomees), fingerspelling could be an excellent choice for an interim system (e.g., while learning esophageal speech) or as a back-up system (e.g., on days when the client has a cold). Although not documented in the literature, it is feasible to use fingerspelling as a supplemental system. Beukelman and Yorkston (1977) used an alphabet–number board for initial letter cueing with clients having dysarthric speech. A similar procedure could be used with fingerspelling. That is, a person with intelligibility problems could fingerspell the first letter of every word spoken, or just those words that are unclear to the listener. This typically results in a slightly reduced speech rate, which might further facilitate intelligibility (see Chapter 8, initial letter cueing, for further information).

WHO: Fingerspelling has several basic requirements for input and/or output:

1. *Good motoric control of one hand.* Fingerspelling requires small, rapid movements with a considerably greater degree of motoric coordination than signing (Wilbur, 1987). Note that some manual alphabets (e.g., the one used in England) may require two-handed productions.
2. *Ability to spell.* The user must encode and decode words that have not been memorized. However, it is possible to memorize the movement envelopes of a small core of fingerspelled words, without learning the actual spelling of the word (Akamatsu, 1982; 1985).
3. *Good visual discrimination skills* (for input): Letters are often blurred together during production.
4. *High level of cognitive development.* Cognitive stages range from late preoperations to early concrete operations (Chapman & Miller, 1980).

Moores (1980) reported that fingerspelling is widely used with deaf children in the Soviet Union, but employed in only a handful of programs in the United States. Reports of successful use of fingerspelling with other populations of nonspeaking people are rare, although Chen (1971) did use a manual alphabet combined with manual sign gestures for several clients, including persons with aphasia, dysarthria, and laryngectomy. Potential candidates, in addition to deaf people, would be persons who had developed good language and spelling skills and have good motor control of at least one hand. Potential audiences can learn the basic code quickly; however, as Wilbur (1987) pointed out, it is difficult to perceive and read fingerspelling produced at a fast rate. It may be necessary for the user to fingerspell very slowly, which could interfere with features such as intonation patterns and communication interaction.

WHEN. Wilbur (1987) suggested that "although a child may combine two or three signs into an utterance at about 1 year 6 months, fingerspelling does not emerge until much later" (p. 271). This is not surprising since the ability to spell is important to productive use of fingerspelling. Thus fingerspelling would generally not be introduced, at least as a primary output system, until the potential user has developed or demonstrated a readiness to learn spelling skills.

HOW. Since fingerspelling is typically introduced at a higher cognitive stage than signing, it may be possible to use a second-language approach to training, utilizing formal training with emphasis on drill and practice. Materials and guidelines for teaching in this manner are presented in Babbini (1974a; 1974b). Numerous books and games are also available for teaching fingerspelling to children or adults. As an input mode, fingerspelling may be introduced in a more natural manner, paired with speech.

WHERE. A variety of resource materials are available to aid in teaching or learning fingerspelling.

- *Books* (see Appendix B): *A Look at Fingerspelling* (Gallaudet College Bookstore); *Expressive and Receptive Fingerspelling for Hearing Adults* (Guillory, 1966); *Fingerspelling Fun* (Adler, 1980); *Manual Communication — A course for instructors* (Babbini, 1974a); *Manual Communication — A course for students* (Babbini, 1974b); *Signs for All Seasons: More Sign Language Games* (Kirchner, 1977)
- *Distributors* (see Appendix' C): Gallaudet College Bookstore, Joyce Media, Sign UP
- *Organizations* (see Appendix D): National Association for the Deaf.

SUMMARY AND DISCUSSION. Fingerspelling is a deceptively simple system. While it is easy for an unimpaired person to learn the core of handshapes, those handshapes may be quite difficult for persons with poor motoric control. The difficulty receiving messages transmitted at high rates of speed may also be a problem, as the normal flow of speech and intonation are interrupted. However, for a person who does not attempt to speak and fingerspell simultaneously, this may be less of a barrier. If a major goal is communication of basic wants and needs, a fairly slow rate may be acceptable.

Fingerspelling may have a limited population of potential users due to the motoric and spelling capabilities required. However, for persons who can learn it, fingerspelling may be extremely helpful. It can serve as a primary communication system, or, more likely, as a supplemental system to be used with a specific audience or under certain conditions, such as a noisy environment.

Gestural Morse Code

Silverman (1980) suggested that the dots and dashes of the Morse Code, which represent letters and numbers, can be signalled gesturally. The code can be signalled by producing a single gesture (an eye blink) of two durations, or by producing entirely different gestures (look to right or left) to represent the dot and the dash (Vanderheiden & Grilley, 1976). This system could be adapted to meet the needs of individuals with severe physical impairment but intact cognitive abilities. Silverman noted that this system would be especially appropriate for persons who had learned Morse Code prior to the onset of the impairment (e.g., an individual with myasthenia gravis who was an amateur radio operator).

Cued Speech

WHAT Cued Speech was developed for use with and among individuals with hearing impairment. In this system one hand is used to supplement the information visible on the lips to make a spoken message clearly understood by the speechreader. Eight handshapes (for consonants) and four hand positions (for vowels) are used in synchronization with natural speech as illustrated in Figure 7-3. The result is a visually different pattern for each syllable of the spoken language. Thus, "syllables which look alike on the lips look different on the hand. Syllables which look alike on the hand look different on the lips" (Henegar & Cornett, 1971, p. 14). It is the combination of cues and mouth patterns that allows the partner to gain meaning, as the hand serves only to identify a group of three or four sounds that differ visually on the lips. For example, one handshape allows the partner to narrow the choice of consonants to /h/, /s/, and /r/. Observing the speaker's oral patterns will enable the partner to determine which of those three consonants is actually being produced. Vowels are cued by hand positions plus information at the lips. Thus consonant–vowel pairs (e.g., "ma") may be represented by superimposing the consonant handshape on the vowel hand position, resulting in increased efficiency of movement. Intonation can be indicated to some extent by altering the inclination or orientation of the hand forming the cue. Similarly, increased stress can be indicated by increased emphasis of the hand movement while cuing the stressed syllable. Silent letters are not cued, and digraphs such as "ch" (chair), "sh" (share), and "ph" (phone), which must be spelled out in fingerspelling, are represented by a single cue in Cued Speech. For example, production of the word "telephone" requires nine configurations in fingerspelling (*T-E-L-E-P-H-O-N-E*), but only four (*te-lu-foe-n*) in Cued Speech.

It should be noted that cues are not the equivalent of signs, as cues do not have meaning in isolation. Cued Speech is a method of making a spoken language (English, French, Thai) visible. It has been adapted to more than 40 languages, including Hindi and Marathi, and to dialects such as British and American English. Thus it is a tool for representing a language, not a language or a sign system.

WHY. The primary purpose of Cued Speech is to aid in verbal language development for hearing-impaired individuals through providing a method of clear communication (Cornett, 1975). Cued Speech may also be helpful in speech production training, because the learner may be instructed, through Cued Speech, where to place sounds that have been learned in articulation training. Thus, errors would be those of execution, not of intention (Cornett, personal communication, as quoted from Alexander Graham Bell). That is, the individual would know where sounds should be placed in a word, even if he or she were unable to produce those sounds correctly.

Cornett (in Beaupre, 1984) noted that he developed Cued Speech from a systems approach (listing what the system needed to accomplish, what conditions of use it must satisfy, what means it could employ, and so forth). For this reason it is a highly logical system, adding to ease of learning and retention for proficient speakers.

WHO. As noted, Cued Speech was designed for use with hearing-impaired persons, and has been used primarily with this population. Requirements for application of Cued Speech as an input or output system include:

- *Moderate motoric control of at least one hand,* sufficient to produce basic handshapes in four different positions near the face
- *Good visual acuity and discrimination,* for decoding the cues and lip information, if it is to be used as an input system
- *Good oral-motor control,* as production requires cues plus information at the lips
- *Cognitive development of at least Sensorimotor Stage 5 or 6.*

While it is not clear yet what cognitive level is required, a higher cognitive level would likely be required than for most sign systems. In sign systems the gesture (sign) can be related directly to the referent, while in Cued Speech a single gesture (cue) may be used for several different referents (e.g., *ham, roof,* and *sit* have the same cues), and the partner must pair the cue with the oral pattern to decode the word. Thus Cued Speech may initially be more difficult than a sign system, which may be introduced via a small number of highly iconic signs.

Based on the requirements listed above, several populations would appear to be potential users of Cued Speech. Individuals with hearing impairment would be the most likely candidates, with research studies

VOWEL CODE & CUESCRIPT CHART

(note: vowels alone are cued with *OPEN* handshape)

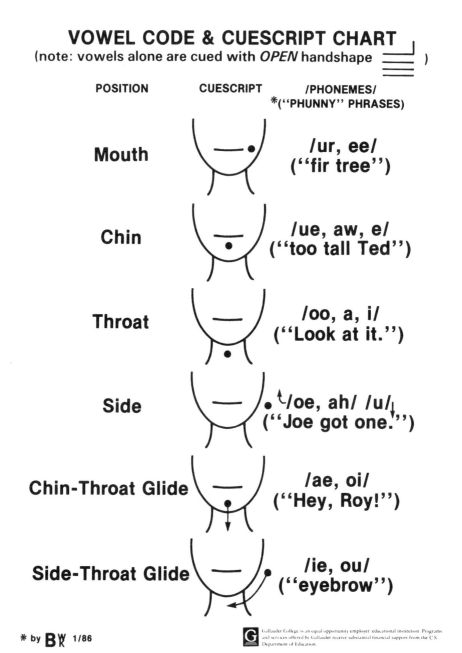

POSITION	CUESCRIPT	/PHONEMES/ *("PHUNNY" PHRASES)
Mouth		/ur, ee/ ("fir tree")
Chin		/ue, aw, e/ ("too tall Ted")
Throat		/oo, a, i/ ("Look at it.")
Side		/oe, ah/ /u/ ("Joe got one.")
Chin-Throat Glide		/ae, oi/ ("Hey, Roy!")
Side-Throat Glide		/ie, ou/ ("eyebrow")

* by **BW** 1/86

Gallaudet College is an equal opportunity employer educational institution. Programs and services offered by Gallaudet receive substantial financial support from the U.S. Department of Education.

CONSONANT CODE & CUESCRIPT CHART

HANDSHAPE	CUESCRIPT	HANDSHAPE CODE NUMBER	/PHONEMES/ *("PHUNNY" PHRASES)
	 ——	1	/d, zh, p/ ("déjà pu")
	——	2	/ᵗH, k, v,z/ ("the caves")
	≡	3	/h, r, s/ ("horse")
	 ≣	4	/b, hw, n/ ("By when?")
	 ⌐	5	/m, f, t/ ("miffed")
	⌐	6	/w, l, sh/ ("Welsh")
	⌐	7	/j, g, th/ ("joggeth")
	 ＞	8	/ch, y, ng/ ("Chai Yung")

*by Karen Koehler 1/86

Figure 7-3
Cued speech handshapes and hand positions. Reprinted with permission from
Gallaudet University Press.

documenting success on skills such as increased comprehension of sentences and key words within sentences (Clarke & Ling, 1976; Nicholls, 1979). Other populations that could theoretically benefit from use of Cued Speech for output include those in which individuals have the requirements listed but lack normal voicing. This would include individuals with laryngectomy, aphonia, spastic dysphonia, as well as persons having progressive disorders, such as myasthenia gravis, yielding a very weak voice.

WHEN. Ideally, Cued Speech should be initiated as soon as the impairment is diagnosed. Thus parents and teachers may begin cuing to young infants. However, infants or preschoolers should not initially be expected or required to begin cuing. Hengar and Cornett (1971) noted that "usually, a child spends several months in the initial receptive stage before he reacts expressively, even after he demonstrates a great deal of receptive understanding" (p. 75).

HOW. While Cued Speech can be used for both input and output, for the young child developing language the initial focus will be on input. Henegar and Cornett stressed that Cued Speech should not be taught to prelinguistic deaf children; rather, they should be exposed to it naturally, much as young hearing children are exposed to spoken language in conjunction with meaningful events and actions. Cornett (1985) stressed the importance of a high quality and quantity of language exposure through Cued Speech. It is recommended that brief work sessions be carried out in addition to a variety of activities such as puppetry and games.

For older deaf individuals, a two-way approach can be used, with Cued Speech used for communication and taught as a system. Henegar and Cornett suggested that Cued Speech be taught as much as possible through the communication system the person is already using, whether that is signed, written, pictured, or spoken.

Hearing parents, teachers, and hearing users with an intact language system (e.g., persons with laryngectomy) could also use a systematic training approach composed of drills and exercises. A wide variety of materials is available to aid in this learning. The eight handshapes and four positions can be learned in a matter of hours, but learning to use and comprehend them takes considerably longer.

WHERE. Information is available on Cued Speech through the Cued Speech Team, Department of Audiology, Gallaudet University, which also distributes a newsletter, *Cued Speech News* (see Appendix D). The National Cued Speech Association (see Appendix D) distributes a journal, *Cued Speech Annual.* Additional materials are available from the Cued Speech Center, Inc. (P.O. Box 31345, Raleigh, NC 27622).

- *Books* (see Appendix B): *Cued Speech Instructional Manual* (Sbaiti, 1983); *Gaining Cued Speech Proficiency: A Manual for Parents, Teachers, and Clinicians* (Beaupre, 1984)
- *Videotapes:* Intro to Cued Speech, C.S. Lessons for Hearing Persons (available through Cued Speech Team)

SUMMARY AND DISCUSSION. Cued Speech is a phonemically based tool for representing a spoken language. As with other systems that represent letters or sounds (such as fingerspelling or Morse Code), Cued Speech has limited usefulness until the entire system is learned. However, once it is learned, virtually anything that can be said can be cued understandably, including nonsense sounds and songs. Although the system appears to have potential for hearing but nonspeaking persons, its primary applications to date have been with hearing-impaired individuals.

Other Unaided Communication Systems

A number of unaided systems do not fit into any of the categories described earlier. That is, they are not sign languages or sign systems, nor do they gesturally code a language. These systems range from the informal use of pantomime or natural gestures to the more formal use of a codified system such as Amer-Ind. Only one of these systems, Amer-Ind, will be described in detail. The remaining systems will be covered briefly, along with suggestions for sources of further information.

Several communication systems, such as the Tadoma method and the Glove method, have been developed primarily for use with deaf-blind individuals. These are not unaided systems in the sense that they have been described in this book. For example, the Tadoma method involves having the deaf-blind person decode speech by placing one or both hands on the face of the speaker in a prescribed manner (Norton, Schultz, Reed, Braida, Durlach, Rabinowitz, & Chomsky, 1977). Coverage of these systems is beyond the scope of this book. For those interested in further information, Jensema (1979) described a number of communication systems for individuals who are deaf-blind.

Natural Gestures

Hamre-Nietupski and colleagues (1977) observed that nondisabled persons use body movements in communication, including many generally understood gestures such as shaking the head from side to side to indicate *no*. These are referred to in this section as natural gestures. One major advantage for using natural gestures with adults having acquired communication impairment is the normative nature of these gestures. Since they are used by nondisabled individuals, natural gestures may have a high rate of acceptance among persons who might reject other forms of communication augmentation. This may also be true for families of nonspeaking children. Hamre-Nietupski and colleagues noted two additional advantages of using natural gestures:

> Natural gestures are usually understood by teachers, parents, or other students without any specialized training;
>
> Natural gestures often involve gross motor movements, which can be an important factor when selecting a system for use with individuals having severe motoric and/or visual impairments. (p. 100)

A system of natural gestures is limited in terms of its usefulness in comparison to sign languages or systems, but it may be useful as an interim system, or as a supplement to another communication system. For example, a child with severe dysarthria might use natural gestures to establish context when a communication breakdown occurs by motioning for a person to come and remove an obstacle in front of the wheelchair. Natural gestures could also serve as an introduction to sign training, or a facilitator of other modes of communication. For example, persons with acquired symbolic deficits (e.g., aphasia) often retain or readily relearn these natural gestures, which can serve as an immediate communication mode, and a possible bridge to other systems.

As Vanderheiden and Lloyd (1986) observed, "when used by severely impaired individuals, these gestures may have only a partial chance of being identified by strangers and some may be totally unrecognizable" (p. 76). Research has indicated a fairly high recognition rate (77 percent) by individuals working with severely handicapped persons (Fiocca, 1981), with a much lower recognition rate (44 percent) for 24 retarded adults in sheltered workshop settings (Doherty, Karlan, & Lloyd, 1982).

Hamre-Nietupski and associates (1977) provided a list of more than 160 generally understood gestures. Curricular strategies for teaching production and comprehension of those gestures are also included.

Pantomime (Mime)

Mime is an art form based on the technique of conveying information or ideas through pantomime, or simulation of an activity. Silverman (1980) noted several differences between pantomime and other unaided systems, such as sign languages or Amer-Ind.

- Pantomime uses the musculature of the entire body, not only that (or primarily that) of the upper extremities
- The gestures tend to be more dynamic
- More gestures usually are needed to convey a message than with manual systems

- The gestures are an analogue of the message — that is, they are a dramatization of the message. (p. 72)

Pantomime is a very basic form of communication that may be used to reach individuals who are not able to communicate through the auditory–vocal channel. It may have potential, therefore, as an input system for some individuals. It may also be used as a supplemental output system. Many individuals who become nonspeaking attempt to communicate through pantomime, though perhaps not very effectively.

Several anecdotal reports have indicated use of pantomime with individuals having a variety of disabilities. However, use of pantomime as a primary communication system has not been documented, and would not be expected, due to its relative inefficiency and limited scope. Pantomime may serve as a back-up system for some persons or situations. For example, Janette, a four-year-old with a limited repertoire of signs, used pantomime to add to her signed message (e.g., showing a baby crawling) or to convey information to individuals who did not understand her signs.

One requirement that differs from most unaided systems is the need for a rich experiential background, in order to have experiences to draw from. This is important if an individual is to initiate topics for which pantomimic routines have not been taught.

Since pantomime is not a widely used augmentative system, training materials and strategies are limited. Often, a communication specialist will assist an individual in improving existing mimetic routines as a means of temporary or supplemental communication, while introducing more flexible long-term modes of communication.

Limited Systems of Idiosyncractic Gestures

Several limited gestural systems have been developed at various hospitals, nursing homes, or residential centers. These provide users with a small number of gestures for basic needs such as COME HERE, I'M HOT, or I HAVE PAIN. Silverman (1980) described several of these unaided systems. Typically, they require only moderate control of one hand. Since the number of gestures is limited (often fewer than 20) persons in the environment can learn them quickly. These limited systems may be very useful as interim systems; for example, for an individual who is too ill to learn or use a full communication system. They may also be useful as supplements to other systems, such as aided symbol systems.

Supplemental gestures should be considered for all nonspeakers using an aided system since, by definition, aided systems require access to symbols extraneous to the body (Musselwhite, 1984). Thus there will be times, such as bathing, toileting, or during physical therapy, when aided systems will be unavailable or difficult to access. At a minimum, individuals should be able to directly signal messages such as GET MY BOARD. Many individuals will develop their own set of idiosyncratic gestures, which should be clarified if necessary and catalogued for sharing with all communication partners. Most nonspeakers can build a repertoire of usable signals from gross movements similar to those used in Duffysigns (Duffy, 1977). Bottorf and DePape (1982) suggested several criteria for selecting communication signals that can be applied to selection of idiosyncratic gestures:

1. Ease and speed of production
2. Minimal fatigue
3. Ease of recognition by partners
4. Low frequency of involuntary movements that could be confused with the signals.

These criteria can be used systematically to assess controlled movements used by an individual, to develop a core of signals that can be used to provide unaided communication.

Creativity and flexibility may be necessary in developing a set of idiosyncratic gestures. For example, Cathy White and her mother Harriet White developed a gestural system for Cathy based on leg movements, because Cathy has a severe hearing loss combined with athetoid spastic cerebral palsy including severe upper extremity involvement. This system, "White's Gestural Systems for Lower Extremities," consists of approximately 125 "leg signs" (Huer, 1987). Signs require from one to five body movements/positions per sign. The system uses approximately 34 leg, 20 foot, 33 toe, 26 heel, 16 knee, 19 ankle, 8 calf, and 7 thigh touch points of movements or positions. A variety of linguistic categories are included (people, actions, objects, questions, attributes, yes/no, places, comments, animals). Huer reported reliability ratings greater than 95 percent for a set of 100 signs across three different listeners, with the signer in two positions.[3]

Thus, idiosyncratic signals may be developed for several individuals within a single setting, or for one individual in one or more settings. In either case these gestures, as well as conventional signs, should be described on a Communication Report Form (see Kollinzas, 1983) which is posted near the user or in a book that accompanies him or her.

Amer-Ind Gestural Code

WHAT. Amer-Ind is neither a language nor a sign system. It does not have a linguistic base but is, rather, a code or signal system. It is based

---

[3] For further information, please contact Mary Blake Huer, 164 North Franklin Street, Whitewater, WI 53190.

on universal American Indian Hand Talk, which was used by a variety of Indian tribes to accommodate their large number of spoken languages (more than 550 distinct languages, according to Farb, 1968). Recently, Hand Talk has been adapted to serve the needs of persons who are non-speaking, resulting in the development of Amer-Ind. American Indian Hand Talk has been authenticated, to the extent that this is possible, through records written by non-Indians in limited contact with American Indian cultures (Clark, 1885; Mallery, 1881; Tomkins, 1931, 1969), and through the memories of Hand Talk users still living throughout the United States. Skelly and associates have also modernized the code, eliminating signals that are no longer applicable and adding signals needed as a result of the changes of 20th-century life. The new signals have been developed on the same principles as the ancient signals, such as concrete reference and ease of interpretation. Each new signal was submitted to one or more tribal elders for approval. Skelly, the primary developer of Amer-Ind, is part American Indian, and was taught Hand Talk as a child by her Iroquois relatives.

Skelly (1979) described several primary characteristics of Amer-Ind:

- It is *nonlinguistic;* therefore, it should not be interpreted by exact translation
- It is *concept-oriented,* yielding what is described as "kinetic photographs of ideas" (p. 110)
- It is *action-oriented* rather than nominally organized, although clarifying signals can be used if necessary to indicate an object or person
- It is *reality-oriented* and conveys messages through a string of related signaled concepts
- It is *telegraphic,* using the fewest possible signals for encoding.

Since signals represent concepts rather than words, Amer-Ind signals are discussed in terms of a repertoire instead of a vocabulary. The current clinically tested signal repertoire includes 250 concept labels.[4] Each concept can stand for several English words since Amer-Ind does not follow a signal-for-word translation. For example, the concept label QUIET, made by holding the index finger of the hand to the lips, has the following synonyms: calm, dormant, hush, low (noise), mute, noiseless, serene, silence, silent, still, and tranquil. The intended meaning is determined through context. As a result, the repertoire of 250 labels has an English vocabulary equivalent to approximately 2,500 words. In addition, this vocabulary equivalent may be extended through the process of agglutination, to be described later. It should be noted that, just as there is no one correct word

---

[4] This text follows the convention of printing Amer-Ind concept labels in capital letters, with the series of synonyms for each label printed in lowercase letters.

which translates a signal, a specific concept can often be indicated through use of one of several signals. For example, while NO can be interpreted as denial, disagreement, negation, or refusal, the basic concept of negation can be coded by signals with the following concept labels: NO, REJECT, STOP, DEFY.

Eighty percent of the clinical repertoire can be executed using only one hand. Most of the remaining signals can be adapted for one-handed execution, using suggestions provided by Skelly (1979). For the 11 signals that cannot be readily adapted, Skelly suggested alternative signals for substitution. Skelly described several features related to the transmission of Amer-Ind:

• *Transposition,* the process of encoding in signals.

• *Clarification,* the methods designed to assist signalers having difficulty in transmitting messages. For example, a flat hand thrust can distinguish object from action, and the user may add the signal for PAST or FUTURE as needed. Several other methods are suggested, including slowing the rate, adding information, and trying an alternative signal.

• *Agglutination,* the principle allowing invention of new ways to express a concept for which a specific signal does not exist; typically, a string of signals is used, beginning with the most general and adding further information. Examples are:

teacher   = PERSON + GIVES + KNOWLEDGE (know)
ambulance = DRIVE + PAIN + SHELTER + FAST
insane   = BRAIN + REJECT, or BRAIN + FLY + DISTANT

• *Execution,* the way in which signals are produced. Signals may be static (the hand position is held, such as HEAR), kinetic (a specific movement is required, such as LITTLE), or repetitive (a specified movement is repeated three times, such as MONEY). In addition, there are three criteria for effective signaling — precision, consistency, and completion.

WHY. Amer-Ind appears appropriate for a variety of purposes relative to people with severe communication handicaps. Skelly asserted that

the American Indian Code's low symbolic level, ease of acquisition, flexibility, speed, lack of grammatical structure and rules, and use of concrete, demonstrable referents, which enable the viewer to interpret without formal instruction, make it acceptable to the use of many patients who are unable to speak. (p. 7)

It would appear to be an especially appropriate system for persons who are unable to learn other unaided systems or are uninterested in other systems due to the limited audiences they provide. Amer-Ind seems especially useful as an interim communication system due to the relative transparency of signals, which should increase ease of acquisition, at least for cognitively unimpaired learners. These aspects, plus its action-oriented base, also make Amer-Ind useful as an input system. Preliminary evidence (Skelly, 1979, pp. 30–37) suggested that Amer-Ind may serve to facilitate both language and speech. Thus, Amer-Ind has the potential of serving a variety of functions for persons with severe communication handicaps. Some of the potential limitations of the system are considered in the summary and discussion section.

WHO. Skelly (1979) listed several prerequisite skills for introduction of Amer-Ind: eye contact, attending, physical imitation, pointing, and shaping skills. Other requirements for use of Amer-Ind include

- *Moderate degree of motor control of one hand,* to allow execution of a limited number of hand configurations
- *Good range of motion in one arm,* for executing signals at various locations and with various movements.

Amer-Ind has been used with varying degrees of success by persons having a wide range of disorders, including severe dysphonia, severe dysarthria, oral–verbal apraxia, severe and profound mental retardation, surgical deficits such as total glossectomy, total laryngectomy, laryngectomized total glossectomy, and aphasia. (See Skelly [1979] for reviews of 10 projects by a number of researchers dealing with acquisition of Amer-Ind across a wide range of populations.) Skelly suggested that, while Amer-Ind may be used appropriately with clients from any of these populations treatment approaches would differ. She identified three main client groupings:

1. *Intact auditory comprehension of language,* in which the user retains skills such as normal symbolism. Examples of client populations are persons having severe dysphonia, severe dysarthria, oral–verbal apraxia, surgical deficits such as glossectomy or laryngectomy, and aphasia with adequate auditory reception of language.

2. *Impaired auditory reception of language,* in which the person has problems of symbolization and/or conceptualization. Examples of clients in this group are persons with moderate to severe adult aphasia, and mild to moderate cognitive delay.

3. *Developmental impairment,* particularly characterized by concept deficits. Examples of clients include persons with severe to profound cognitive delay.

For many individuals, the use of Amer-Ind will be temporary. For example, Skelly reported use of Amer-Ind as an interim system for persons with dysphonia during voice rest, and for others (e.g., persons with glossectomy or oral–verbal apraxia) while speech and/or language skills are being improved. In addition, it may serve as a supplemental system for many persons, either following communication breakdown or when speech is temporarily unusable due to physical problems (e.g., at the end of the day, for a person with myasthenia gravis).

It is also important to determine who can interpret Amer-Ind. Skelly reported results from a number of research projects involving signal transmission, indicating transparency rates of 80 to 90 percent. However, recent research indicates that Amer-Ind is approximately 50 percent transparent for nonretarded young adults, such as college students, with lower ratings for cognitively delayed individuals (Daniloff, Lloyd, & Fristoe, 1983; Doherty, Daniloff, & Lloyd, 1985).

HOW. A natural language approach, as used for example with American Sign Language, is not recommended for Amer-Ind. Skelly (1979) presented three treatment programs designed for the three client groupings listed earlier.

Treatment Program A is intended for persons with intact auditory comprehension of language. The overall goal of this program is "use of signals at a level equivalent to propositional speech" (p. 138). The user's knowledge and understanding of English (or any spoken language) is employed in training sessions, with explanations of aspects such as the rationale behind signal meaning. Modifications are provided for use with persons having oral–verbal apraxia, as those clients are often hemiplegic and may require a slower treatment pace. Oral facilitation procedures are also suggested.

Treatment Program B is a nonverbal, nonlinguistic approach designed for clients having impaired auditory reception of language. Amer-Ind may be used as an input mode as well as an output mode for persons in this category. For this approach, sessions are more structured and content is more repetitive. Repeated demonstrations using real-life objects in naturally structured situations are used in place of artificially structured drills. The primary goal for Program B is to establish the use of 50 signals for basic social and need situations, plus 10 habituated signals (HELLO, PLEASE, COME), in 12 to 24 weeks.

Treatment Program C is intended for use with persons who are developmentally impaired. The goal of this program is "communication of basic needs in Amer-Ind with approximately fifty signals acquired over a period of one year" (p. 175). As in Program B, the instructor communicates with the potential user only in signals. Programmed segments of five weeks each are used for training groups of five signals. However, the objective is different for each week of a segment. The progression of objectives is: first week — imitation with necessary assistance; second week — unassisted imitation; third week — replication of the signal after the model is removed; fourth week, retrieval from memory; fifth week — initiation of signals.

Skelly (1979) also presented an Amer-Ind Scale of Progress, designed "to record as briefly and meaningfully as possible the results of treatments by certain methods at certain levels of acquisition, execution, and transmission by the patient" (p. 97). Daniloff and Schafer (1981) later modified this scale to meet the needs of users with severe to profound cognitive delay. For example, they did not require participants to maintain eye contact as a prerequisite to training, and they deferred signal recognition until students could retrieve signals for several stimuli.

Skelly noted that "because Amer-Ind has been easily interpreted by untrained viewers, many persons have concluded that it may be just as easily acquired and executed by the uninstructed signaler" (p. 114). She stressed that this assumption is false, and that communication specialists planning to teach or do research projects on Amer-Ind must learn the system fully. She recommends that Amer-Ind be learned from an experienced, knowledgeable signaler.

WHEN. This system has been used with people who have lost the ability to speak, due to conditions such as aphasia, apraxia, or laryngectomy. For these persons, training in Amer-Ind would likely be initiated as soon as the need becomes evident (e.g., poor prognosis for rapid relearning of functional speech) and a physician's approval is obtained. Skelly recommended delaying direct training until prerequisite skills such as eye contact, attending, and physical imitation have been learned. However, other researchers (e.g., Daniloff & Shafer, 1981) demonstrated success in Amer-Ind training with severely cognitively delayed students who did not demonstrate those skills prior to training.

WHERE. Information on Amer-Ind is available in both print and video format.

- *Books/Articles* (see Appendix B): "A gestural communication program for severely and profoundly handicapped children" (Daniloff & Shafer, 1981); *Amer-Ind Gestural Code Based on Universal American Indian Hand Talk* (Skelly, 1979)
- *Videotape: Amer-Ind Code Repertoire* (Auditec of St. Louis, 330 Selma Avenue, St. Louis, MO 63119).

SUMMARY AND DISCUSSION. Amer-Ind is a gestural code based on American Indian Hand Talk, and is intended for use with persons who are nonspeaking due to a variety of etiologies. Amer-Ind differs from other unaided systems presented in this chapter because it is not linguistically based. However, its signals are also different from natural gestures because it is codified and allows extension of the repertoire through agglutination. The basic features of Amer-Ind, such as its low symbolic level, flexibility, and lack of grammatical structure, make it especially suitable for some users, but restricts its application with others. As Skelly (1979) pointed out,

Amer-Ind is especially useful for clients with symbol deficits. On the other hand, persons with a high level of linguistic competence who have lost (or never had) the physical capability for vocal production may choose not to use Amer-Ind because it does not parallel the spoken language. Thus, many individuals who are physically capable of using Amer-Ind (e.g., persons having a glossectomy/laryngectomy) will find that it is not powerful enough to meet all communication needs.

Selecting an Unaided Communication System

Many factors must be considered in matching an unaided symbol system to an individual with a severe communication impairment. The primary consideration should relate to the needs and abilities of the potential user. When a profile of user needs and abilities is developed, several systems can often be eliminated from consideration. The decision-making team should recognize, however, that an unaided symbol system will typically be only one component of a multi-component communication system. Therefore, a system may not need to be eliminated if it fails to fulfill only one need. Clearly, this matching process requires a good working knowledge of a variety of unaided symbol systems.

In addition to the needs listed in the checklist reprinted in Table 1-1, several client abilities and needs should be considered specific to selection of an unaided symbol system. Several factors are presented below, with brief discussion of each factor, as it relates to the unaided systems described in this chapter.

Motoric Capabilities

Motoric capabilities differ for individuals, and motoric requirements differ for various unaided systems. Some basic differences can be seen in the various systems; systems based on American Sign Language require approximately 20 different handshapes, while Duffysigns uses only gross limb movements. Several systems (e.g., Amer-Ind, Cued Speech, finger-spelling) are essentially one-handed, while others (e.g., Paget-Gorman Systematic Sign) make extensive use of two-handed nonsymmetrical signs. The team should consider the motoric requirements of the system (e.g., number and complexity of handshapes, movements, locations, number of hands required, percent of symmetrical signs) in relation to the abilities of the potential user. The assessment section presented numerous tools for determining user abilities, and each *Who* subsection listed the general motoric requirements for the systems.

Cognitive Abilities

The cognitive requirements vary to some extent for various systems, ranging from entry level at the Sensorimotor Level 4–6 (natural gestures, ASL-based systems, Duffysigns) to the Preoperational Level (fingerspelling, Cued Speech). This factor is listed for each system in the *Who* section.

Size of Vocabulary

The available vocabulary size varies from system to system. While most systems permit some form of spelling, nonspellers will be limited to the signs included in the system. This ranges from a basic vocabulary of fewer than 500 signs or signals (Amer-Ind, Duffysigns) to systems having more than 3,000 signs (Signed English, Signing Exact English, Paget-Gorman Systematic Sign), to sign languages, which may have more than 5,000 entries (ASL). In some cases (e.g., Amer-Ind), gestures may be combined to form additional entries. The decision-making team must determine if the vocabulary size of a system under consideration will limit a potential user.

Grammatical Structure of System

This may range from no structure (Amer-Ind) to the structure of the language represented (fingerspelling, Cued Speech, Signed English, Signing Exact English), to its own structure (sign languages such as ASL). Individual needs will determine the appropriate structure. For example, if the user is expected to verbalize with the signs, either immediately or in the future, a system that parallels the structure of the spoken language, such as Signing Exact English or Signed English, will be needed. A parallel structure system may also be desirable to enhance academic skills.

Ease of Learning

While existing research studies (e.g., Doherty, 1985; Luftig, 1984) have considered learning a single system, rather than providing comparisons of several systems, several conclusions may be drawn from the research, and from clinical observation. Motoric factors that affect learning, such as number of handshapes, were discussed previously. Other factors are:

• *Transparency and translucency.* These factors have been found to influence sign learning, both for the user and for communication partners. Unaided systems differ in their transparency and translucency rates. Systems range from highly transparent (e.g., natural gestures) to moderately

161

transparent (e.g., Amer-Ind) to minimally transparent (e.g., ASL-based systems) to opaque (e.g., Cued Speech). However, some of the minimally transparent systems have a high degree of translucency, meaning that learners may be able to retain the signs once the meaning connection between the sign and the referent are known. This situation would apply for sign languages, ASL-based systems, and Paget-Gorman Systematic Sign.

• *Availability of Communication Partners and Teachers.* This factor can greatly influence learning. For example, if only one individual serves as the primary teacher, or if no one is fluent in a system selected, the rate and extent of acquisition may be slowed. Thus, the existence of potential teachers and communication partners already fluent in a system may be one factor in a selection protocol. This may vary in different regions or settings. If an individual has close contact with many ASL users, or lives in an institution where many residents used Signed English, this factor should be one, though not the only, consideration.

• *Availability of Support Materials and Training.* This factor may influence the availability of communication partners and/or teachers. For example, one community might offer coursework in Signing Exact English, while in another ASL might be taught. Unaided systems have varying degrees of support materials. For example, Signed English has an extensive set of storybooks that can be used to aid sign learning for a child as well as for parents, teachers, and other partners. The *Where* sections above provide a summary of available support materials for each system covered in depth.

To summarize, a profile of needs and abilities of the individual user must be matched with the capabilities of each system in order to choose the optimal system. This decision must be made on an individual basis, although considerations of the individual social environment will also influence the selection.

Selecting Content

A number of strategies may be helpful in choosing the initial content for unaided communication programs. In some cases, selection may be determined by the unaided system or program to be used. For example, Skelly (1979) suggested initial Amer-Ind concepts for training, and the *Revised Makaton Vocabulary* (Walker, 1976) includes approximately 350 British Sign Language signs arranged into eight stages for training purposes. However, vocabulary selection decisions will typically be made by persons familiar with the individual. Potential selection strategies are divided into two categories for ease of consideration.

Functionality of Signs: The Need Variable

Luftig (1984) noted that concept functionality has been the overriding basis for inclusion of sign or concepts in initial sign lexicons. Functionality can be considered from several perspectives. Fristoe and Lloyd (1979) compiled a list of 850 words appearing in two or more sign manuals from various systems. They noted that those signs with the highest frequency of occurrence (CHAIR/SIT, BED/SLEEP, GOOD, STOP, and TOILET/BATHROOM/POTTY) "would seem to be taught more for the convenience of the trainers in controlling the client than for their interest value for the client" (p. 366). Thus, one aspect of functionality may be the usefulness from the point of view of trainers.

A second aspect of concept functionality involves the ability to communicate about events, materials, or ideas of high interest to the user. Individual preference should be carefully considered in any sign selection protocol. Preference can be determined through careful observation and interview of significant others. A closely related factor is the reinforcement value of signs. This is especially important in the selection of early signs, and is typically highly individualized. For example, an aide might report that Katie is especially fond of taped music, and whimpers and taps the tape recorder when the music ends. Given this observation, a music-related sign (ON/MUSIC) would rate high in preference and reinforcement potential.

A third consideration regarding concept functionality is the social validation of lexical items. Karlan and Lloyd (1983) investigated initial lexicons to determine whether items were functional and therapeutically or socially significant for severely mentally retarded individuals in their natural environment. Lexical items were drawn from a 1980 study by Fristoe and Lloyd of vocabularies in sign manuals for mentally retarded persons. The lexicon was evaluated by people who dealt with language-impaired mentally retarded individuals on a daily basis (e.g., parents, teachers, institutional direct-care staff). Two lexicons were developed (elementary and adolescent/adult), with concepts categorized (essential, useful, could be useful, no value) and rank in each lexicon. Other vocabulary lists felt to be functional for persons with severe handicaps are available, though they have typically not been exposed to extensive social validation procedures. For example, Schwartz and McKinley (1984) prepared lists of survival language for a variety of settings (food preparation, grocery shopping, restaurant, clothing care, pharmacy, car, mass transit, money/banking). Also see the word lists referenced in Chapter 8 of this book.

Learnability Variables

Following an extensive literature review, Luftig (1984) identified eight learnability variables to be considered in initial sign lexicons. Doherty (1985) identified many of these same variables. These eight variables can be divided into three subcategories: (1) physical production; (2) referents which the signs represent; and (3) perceived relationship between sign and gloss.

Physical Production

Research data have indicated that the following physical aspects influence sign learning: (1) number of hands required (two-handed signs are learned faster than signs made with one hand); (2) physical contact of hands on the body (contact signs are learned more efficiently than noncontact signs); 3) symmetry of hands (symmetrical signs are learned more easily than asymmetrical signs); (4) visibility of sign (signs highly visible to the learner are easier to learn); and (5) repetitiveness (repetition is facilitative to sign learning). Four assessment tools suggested previously (Dennis et al., 1982; Dunn, 1982; House & Rogerson, 1984; Shane and Wilbur, 1980) are useful in assessing the motor patterns of the individual. Dunn (1982) has provided description of each of these factors, plus strategies for analyzing signs.

Bornstein and Jordan (1984) analyzed the 330 most frequently appearing words from the Fristoe and Lloyd (1979) examination of 20 sign manuals for handicapped children in the United States. They identified sign characteristics (movement, handshape, and location) that were not necessary for a sign to be understood by most persons familiar with the sign. A simpler sign form that is still highly understandable they termed *robust*, while a sign that requires a cluster of information in order to be understood they termed *fragile*. Of the 330 signs, 21 were judged to be robust on all characteristics. For example, the signs BABY and DRINK were understandable even if any of the three features were missing, making those signs excellent choices for early instruction, all other variables being equal. An additional 54 sign words were robust on two characteristics and fragile on none (e.g., CLIMB, PLEASE). This information, which is presented in very simple fashion, can be combined with assessment of the sign characteristics and used to aid in sign selection. A case example will help to illustrate.

Stacy, a three-year-old child with Down syndrome, was assessed using Dunn's *Formal Pre-Sign Motor Assessment* (1982) and Shane and Wilbur's assessment protocol (1980). Stacy produced most of the movement patterns, and all of the sign locations, but only three of the handshapes attempted. Therefore, one variable may be selection of signs that are robust when handshapes have been simplified, using the Bornstein and Jordan (1984) information.

Referents Which the Signs Represent

Two variables referring to the referents (glosses) have been found to influence sign learning: (1) concreteness/abstractness (more concrete referents are more easily learned); and (2) concept frequency (high frequency facilitates learning in both children and adults). Concreteness/abstractness ratings can be obtained from studies by Paivio, Yuille, and Madigan's (1968) ratings for nouns, and Lippman's (1974) ratings for verbs. Word frequency ratings can be found in the frequency tables developed by Thorndike and Lorge (1944). Reichle, Williams, and Ryan (1981) observed that emphasis has frequently been placed on frequency of vocabulary used by normal populations, which may not be appropriate for all learners. They recommended that parents and educators keep a diary of the learner's activities to determine objects, actions, and events most frequently encountered by the learner.

Perceived Relationship Between Sign and Gloss

Among naive signers (those who are learning signs), signs judged to be relatively high in translucency (the degree of perceived relationship between a sign and its meaning, when both are given) are learned more easily. Translucency ratings are available for ASL signs (Luftig, Page, & Lloyd, 1983) and Amer-Ind signals (Daniloff, Lloyd, & Fristoe, 1983).

Making Decisions in Selecting Initial Lexicons

Luftig (1984) noted that, for the adolescent/adult lexicon evaluated, the only variables used were concreteness/abstractness and word frequency, plus, to a lesser extent, translucency. None of the eight learnability variables described by Luftig were used in the elementary lexicon. Thus, it would appear that those lexicons, especially the elementary one, were based primarily on the variable of functionality. Luftig asserted that, while functionality is critical in an early lexicon, learnability variables should be considered as well. Table 7-2 presents a sample sign selection checklist that can be used to choose an initial core of signs with a high probability of success for the learner. Doherty (1985) reviewed the literature on sign acquisition and suggested that highly translucent, one-handed contact signs be included in the first five signs taught, and symmetric two-handed contact signs be included in a later lexicon. However, consideration of the learnability variables should not mean that an individual will be denied training on needed lexical items simply because the sign is initially too complex motorically; if a specific lexical item is needed, it should be made available. If the sign is too difficult, the instructor could first consult Bornstein and Jordan (1984) to see if the conventional sign is likely to be understood if it is simplified. If the sign will be too unclear with characteristics simplified, it may be necessary to develop an idiosyncratic gesture, using the physical production information cited previously, plus the sug-

TABLE 7-2
Selection Features for Choosing Initial Sign Content

Sign	Functional			Motoric Factors					Learnability		Score
	User Preference	Two-Handed	Physical Contact	Symmetrical	Within Vision	Repetitive	Simple Handshape	Simple Movement	Concrete	Frequently Useable	
MORE	+	+	+	+	+	+	/	+	/	+	9
TOILET	−	−	−	NA	+	+	−	−	/	/	3
EAT	+	−	+	NA	/	+	/	+	+	+	7
MUSIC	+	−	−	NA	+	+	+	/	+	+	6.5

Instructions: Using input from family and other team members plus sign pools, select a vocabulary pool of at least 15 items. Rate each sign relative to each feature, using the following code:

+ = sign meets this feature (1 point)
/ = sign partially meets this feature (1/2 point)
− = sign does not meet this feature (0 points)

Example: Four signs were rated for Sandy, a four year old in a developmental preschool. Sandy is cognitively delayed and demonstrates low muscle tone and emerging motor imitation skills. Note that some factors (e.g., within vision) are standard across signers, while others (e.g., preference, frequency of occurrence in environment) are highly user-specific.

gestions in this chapter for developing idiosyncratic gestures. Another mode (e.g., a graphic symbol) may also be appropriate for representing items that are motorically complex.

Methods of Teaching Unaided Communication

Intervention methods selected will be determined by several factors, such as the communication system chosen, the capabilities and background of the learner, and the intended function(s) of the system. Individual variability in rate of acquisition (Skelly, 1979; Snyder-McLean, 1978) suggests that training programs must be individualized.

Several unaided symbol systems are accompanied by training materials and/or programs (e.g., Amer-Ind, Signing Exact English). In each case, however, flexibility is suggested. With the growing use of systems designed for one population applied to other populations, flexibility must be stressed. For example, use of Signed English with adults, and with individuals who are cognitively delayed or autistic, requires somewhat different strategies than those employed for using it with preschool deaf children, for whom it was originally intended. Further, some systems (e.g., ASL, Cued Speech, Signed English) were not intended to be directly taught to their target population, deaf individuals; that is, environmental learning, rather than classroom or therapy instruction, was intended. However, with application to a wider range of populations, this concept may have to be changed.

The capabilities and background of the learner enter into the decision regarding the type of training approach. For example, for the individual who has already developed motor imitation skills, training strategies will likely capitalize on this skill. Similarly, individuals who have acquired language competency will probably be taught through a modification of a second language approach rather than a natural language approach.

The intended function(s) of the unaided system will also affect the training strategies. For example, if the intent is to have a language facilitation system, the focus may be on factors such as language concepts. If the intent is for a primary communication system, the proper execution of signs will likely be emphasized at some point in the intervention process, as well as the individual's success in transmitting messages. If the system is to serve primarily as an input mode (e.g., Cued Speech for a deaf child), the emphasis will be on the learner's reception of the message.

These major factors should be considered in designing or selecting a program for training the use of gestures or signs. Programs and strategies specific to individual systems have been suggested throughout this chapter. The present discussion will center on general training strategies for use with unaided communication systems.

Teaching Unaided Communication

This section will cover various options in developing intervention programs for unaided communication. Options presented include selection of methodology, logistical considerations, methods of teaching sign production, and methods of teaching and extending sign use.

Selection of Methodology

Several authors have opted to use a naturally structured format of less intrusive strategies for training in unaided communication (Culatta & Blackstone, 1980; Hamre-Nietupski et al., 1977; Skelly, 1979). Thus, while specific targets may be focused on in a session, interactive, conversational techniques should be used, as opposed to rote learning and drills. This is especially true for an individual learning an unaided system as a first language. However, Skelly (1979) also applied a naturally structured approach, with emphasis on objects and activities of daily living, for persons having normal language competence (e.g., a laryngectomee).

Other programs (e.g., Carr, 1981; Potoki, Miller, & Canosa, 1980) use more intrusive intervention, with artificially structured activities such as drills. This approach, which typically follows a preplanned antecedent-behavior-consequnence pattern differs from the less intrusive approach in the assumed communicative intent. Researchers in the field of communication and communication disorders have stressed the importance of factors such as contextual support and communicative intent (Bates, 1976; Bloom & Lahey, 1978). These factors may be especially applicable to training persons not having functional communication systems.

It may be possible to combine the two approaches. For example, the treatment programs outlined by Skelly (1979) specify antecedent events, learner responses, and potential consequences. However, antecedent events are typically based on real situations (e.g., presentation of a bar of soap to elicit WASH). Learner behavior may be equally tied to reality, such as signalling WASH and washing hands. Whenever possible, consequences should also be natural, such as fulfilling a request. If drills are deemed necessary, procedures can be designed to increase the interactional nature by contriving context or communicative intent. For example, the question "What is that?" can be meaningful, rather than merely a request for display of knowledge, if the learner can see the referent (e.g., a doll hiding behind a box) which is out of the instructor's vision. Culatta and Blackstone (1980) offered numerous creative suggestions for developing clinician-evoked and situation-evoked sign production.

Logistical Considerations

While there are many potential logistical considerations in developing a sign training program, this section will cover only three examples. One very simple but often ignored factor is the position of the learner and the instructor. Dunn (1982) recommended that the instructor sit next to and at the same level as the learner. If the learner is seated on a chair, factors such as trunk stability and support of the feet should be observed and modified as needed, in order to optimize use of the upper extremities.

The instructor's presentation of gestures or signs can also influence success. For example, Dunn provided several suggestions for improving presentation: (1) present the sign slowly, exactly, and clearly; (2) if necessary, break the sign into its component parts (e.g., demonstrate handshape, then add movement to the location, with exaggeration as needed); (3) consider the learner's needs or limitations (e.g., if signs produced within the learner's vision are easier, help the learner to make the sign within vision, then move it to the appropriate location).

A third logistical consideration is the grouping of signs for initial training. Several authors (Goossens' & Crain, 1985a; Griffith & Robinson, 1980; Mills & Weldon, 1983) have suggested that including formationally similar signs (e.g., those that are similar in two of the three characteristics) in a learning set interferes with learning.

Methods of Teaching Sign Production

Mayberry (1976) reported the use of three major methods of teaching gesture/sign production; molding, handshaping, and imitation. Each of these general methods will be presented, with brief discussion relative to sample research and applications.

MOLDING. This refers to placing the learner's hand(s) around an object, and may be used for teaching gestures that take the shape of the object they represent (BABY, BALL, CUP). Kriegsmann, Gallaher, and Meyers (1982) suggested that this is an especially appropriate procedure for individuals functioning below Stage 4 level, as the association between the referent and the sign may be clearly shown. Goossens' and Crain (1985b) have identified Signed English signs and Amer-Ind signals with potential for molding the handshape on the referent.

HANDSHAPING. This refers to the instructor initially shaping the learner's hand(s) into the desired position(s), followed by fading of physical assistance. Bornstein and Jordan (1984) suggested that the instructor emphasize fragile characteristics in training (for example, a handshape that could cause confusion of the sign for another). They observed that the analysis of the specific sign might suggest the best way to emphasize the fragile characteristic. Sample techniques for emphasizing a fragile characteristic are (1) *pointing* (e.g., pointing to the place of articulation for the sign FATHER, so it is not confused with the sign MOTHER); (2) *touching* (e.g., touching the index finger to indicate the need for index finger isolation in the sign CANDY, to avoid confusion with APPLE); (3) *tracing-in-air* (e.g., tracing the motion for OPEN in the air, to avoid its confusion with BOOK); and (4) *emphatic physical action* (e.g., emphatically forming the up/down movement for *yes*, so it is not confused with the letter *S*. Dunn (1982) also suggested prompting techniques to facilitate sign production. She recommended that movement be prompted first, with as little physical assistance as possible, then prompting correct production of the handshape. Dunn observed that beginning instructors typically touch the fingers that should not be isolated (e.g., holding down other fingers when working on index finger isolation), rather than touching only those fingers that should be isolated. The result can be a drawing away of attention from the targets (e.g., index finger or thumb isolation), which can add confusion for individuals who already have difficulty with proprioceptive muscle feedback for imitation. Thus, she recommended touching target fingers to enhance proprioception. Dunn has also suggested numerous adaptive techniques to facilitate sign production. These are listed as techniques to try if students have difficulty performing specific movements (e.g., problems imitating gross arm movements, supinating forearms, performing handshapes out of vision, performing dominant/assistor patterns).

IMITATION. This refers to having the instructor or another model produce the sign, with the learner reproducing it. Intention can be provided to imitative activities. For example, signs can be selected, and then taught, through songs that include them or have been written around the target sign words (Musselwhite, 1985; 1986a). Musselwhite suggested that early signed songs should meet several criteria: (1) ease of acquisition (simple, short songs); (2) acceptability to children and staff; (3) provide teaching opportunities (e.g., communicative goals for content, form, and use); and (4) provide opportunities for generalization (interactive component within song, opportunities for later practice). Since movement imitation is typical in songs for young children, intentionality can be provided for sign imitation. The key motor components of sign production, as identified by Shane and Wilbur (1980), can also be practiced through imitation in play activities (see Table 7-1) and through art activities (see Musselwhite, 1986a, Table 16-3).

Teaching and Extending Sign Use

Four sample intervention strategies will be described for teaching and extending sign use. These strategies focus on a less intrusive training methodology.

PROVIDE A COMMUNICATIVE ENVIRONMENT. Many of the strategies reviewed in Chapter 3 of this volume will aid in encouraging sign use.

Culatta and Blackstone (1980) provided particularly creative suggestions for developing clinician-evoked sign production. For example:

> to encourage use of the sign OPEN to a child who enjoyed water-play, the clinician offered a few granules of detergent in many separate cans, small amounts of water in many separate jars, and single paper towels in many paper bags. Incentive to communicate was built into the presentation as the clinician either withheld the containers until the child produced the sign or arranged for the containers to be impossible for the child to open without assistance. (p. 39)

Gradually, these clinician-evoked sign productions should be faded to situation-evoked productions (e.g., the clinician arranges for the child to discover in the environment enticing containers that she cannot open alone). Various forms of environmental manipulation and "creative stupidity" can yield situations that require use of previously learned signs, with the learner unaware that the situation is being manipulated.

A variety of communication functions should be modeled and evoked. Many structured communication programs overemphasize labeling and requesting (Carr, 1981; Potoki et al., 1980), at the expense of other important functions (e.g., attention-getting, protest, comment on referent). A related idea is to avoid predetermination of which signs the individual should learn (Kriegsmann et al., 1982). Thus, instead of repeatedly "teaching" the signs for CRACKER, POUR, and JUICE, the instructor might offer naturalized input ("These CRACKERS are GOOD. I'm HUNGRY. WANT MORE JUICE?") and allow the learner to attach meaning and to use the vocabulary and functions he or she selects.

EXPECTANT TIME DELAY. Several authors (e.g., Goossens' & Crain, 1985b; Halle, Alpert, & Anderson, 1984; Snell & Gast, 1981) have observed that expectant time delay (described in Chapter 2 of this volume) is an especially effective and efficient procedure for sign training. Goossens' and Crain (1985b) described an errorless learning time delay procedure in which hand-over-hand physical assistance (in which the instructor puts the child through sign formation) is initially given for all sign components (configuration, location, movement), after which a delay is introduced between the cue and the assistance. In this way, assistance is faded so that the learner gradually assumes control over the movement, then the location, and finally the configuration of the sign. Individual variation may require that the delay time or the sign components to be physically guided be modified to meet the needs and abilities of the learner. Time delay procedures are especially useful when combined with clinician- and situation-evoked procedures, as described in the previous section.

EXPANDING SIGN USE THROUGH BARRIER COMMUNICATION GAMES. Barrier communication games can be modified to be used by signers, in order to require greater specificity of reference. In the basic task, the speaker must code a message about a set of materials (e.g., a puzzle), which the listener must decode in order to manipulate a duplicate set of materials. A barrier is placed between the sets of materials, requiring the sender to be very specific in his or her information. For adaptation to signers, the barrier must be set up so that each partner can see the signs but not the materials of the other partner. For example, adult cognitively delayed partners might sit on low stools on either side of a counter, with food items placed on snack tables below the level of the counter top. One partner could instruct the other in the completion of a task (making the perfect hot dog, assembling a flashlight, washing dishes) that he or she has learned through a vocational training program. Specific rules and additional examples of barrier communication tasks for expanding communication use are presented in Musselwhite (1986a, pp. 130–132; 139).

ENHANCING NONVERBAL COMMUNICATION. For some unaided communicators, training of nonmanual aspects of communication may be desirable. A number of texts cover this information. For example, Schwartz and McKinley (1984) included activities for expressing meaning by facial expression. Leathers (1986) covered aspects such as kinesic communication systems (e.g., facial communication, including a facial meaning sensitivity test), and suggested methods for observing, classifying, and measuring the quality of nonverbal communication.

Evaluating Progress in Unaided Communication

It is necessary to provide ongoing evaluation of individual progress to determine the appropriateness of the unaided system, its content, the intervention procedures, and to identify goals for further intervention. Montgomery (1980a) suggested six points to consider in evaluating the effectiveness of communication aid use (see Chapter 8 in this book). Adapting those points to unaided systems, the instructor would

- Establish meaningful exit criteria
- Determine how frequently conversation is initiated
- Count the number of peer interactions
- Assess the degree to which the system serves as a learning tool
- Decide whether there is a need for a more complex system
- Note how the individual uses the system for various communication functions.

These general areas should be considered in evaluating the success of an unaided system. For example, exit criteria for an adult laryngectomee using Amer-Ind might be the equivalence of propositional use of English.

Unaided systems are often more open than aided systems; that is, the individual may draw from a potentially large vocabulary, as compared to the limited content available to many communication aid users. In addition, gestures or signs may be more open to interpretation than graphic symbols on a communication display, as they are more dependent on factors of client execution, such as precision, consistency, and completeness (Skelly, 1979). Therefore, a criterion regarding execution of gestures and successful message transmission should be added. Execution of gestures should be evaluated in context rather than in citation form. For example, partners with whom the individual regularly communicates could engage in conversation, judging each gesture or gestural string as successful (e.g., correctly interpreted on first trial) or unsuccessful. If an experienced signer also judges these gestures, information can be gained by the instructor regarding whether the breakdown is on the part of the nonspeaker or the partner. Response of both the nonspeaker and the partners to communication breakdowns would also be important to observe.

Involvement of Staff and Family in Unaided Communication Training

It is essential to involve parents, spouses, and other family members and communication partners in developing any communication system. This family involvement may be even more difficult when introducing an unaided system. Training must also take place throughout the day, not just during designated "therapy" sessions. Bonvillian and Nelson (1978) noted that most studies they reviewed indicate a relatively low exposure to fluent sign communication. This lack of frequent exposure, combined with lack of exposure to fluent users of the system, could severely limit the rate of acquisition and the level of competence obtained. Clearly, the more partners who know the system, and the more fluent they are, the better the prognosis for the learner. Kriegsmann and colleagues (1982) noted that some staff members may have more opportunities to communicate with an individual than do some family members. Thus, they observed that it may be more crucial for the lunch aide and the bus driver to learn the child's sign system than for the grandmother, who may not understand why signs will help her grandchild. The set of communication partners will vary for each individual, and must be identified and reached if communication training is to be maximally successful. Kriegsmann and colleagues suggested three major areas of staff and family training that should be considered.

Affective Concerns

Kriegsmann and colleagues identified three areas of concern that should be discussed regarding family affect: (1) feeling awkward and self-conscious, especially with regard to signing in public; (2) family reaction, including feelings of siblings and grandparents; and (3) anxiety about the child's response (e.g., Will this keep her from learning speech? What if the rate of acquisition is very slow?). For some family members, merely verbalizing these concerns may provide needed reassurance. In some cases, group sharing sessions with other parents, spouses, or siblings may offer support and encourage family members to voice their concerns.

Support in Sign Acquisition

There are a variety of methods for teaching a core of functional signs to communication teachers and partners. Sample strategies are described in the following section.

Group Training Sessions

This method has the advantage of offering group support to deal with concerns such as those listed in the Affective Concerns section above. Skelly (1979) suggested scheduling these training sessions for relatives during therapy time of clients seen on an outpatient basis. She also recommended having family members and friends share in the transportation of a client so that a large number of persons may participate in training. Skelly also observed that production of gestures seems to facilitate learning, even if the primary goal is for the relatives to learn to receive the gestures, indicating that training of relatives should involve gesture production as well as gesture reception. If differing schedules make planning group sessions difficult, family members and staff can be provided with information on sign classes available at local community colleges or churches. One caution with this approach is that the sign system taught in a community course might differ from that chosen for a nonspeaking individual.

Self-Learning of Sign Systems Through Various Media

A variety of materials can be purchased or borrowed to aid in sign acquisition. Samples of various media are:

• *Videotapes.* Professionally produced videotapes are available for learning most of the sign systems or languages described in this chapter. These can be used at a central location or in an individual's home.

• *Sign Dictionaries.* Many of the sign systems have sign dictionaries that offer sufficient illustrations and descriptions for acquiring signs. However, this is most effective if the person has initial direct training (e.g., to learn basic handshapes and movement patterns). Some dictionaries (e.g., Bornstein & Saulnier, 1984; Christopher, 1976) include sentences for practicing sign reception and/or production.

• *Storybooks.* Several systems (e.g., Signed English, Signing Exact English) offer storybook sets that are self-contained; this provides smaller sign acquisition goals, and may be less overwhelming for many new signers than a large sign dictionary.

• *Music.* Learning signs through music can be a very nonthreatening approach. Several signed songbooks are available (*Songs in Signed English* [Saulnier, 1974]; *Music in Motion* [Wojcio, Gustason, & Zawolko, 1983]; *Songbook: Signs and Symbols for Children* [Musselwhite, 1985]).

Each of these sign acquisition strategies will require considerable effort on the part of the family or staff member. Some of the parent involvement strategies suggested in Chapter 4, such as having parents write contracts, could help to establish family support. For example, parents could make a commitment to learn 10 new signs per week, or to present each new sign at least one time each day at home. Sobsey and Bieniek (1983) noted that there are alternatives to the traditional model of training parents as "mediators" between the instructor and the learner. They conducted a research study in which three language-delayed brothers and their mother were taught signs for words selected as potentially functional in the home and concluded that family training (training of and by the entire family, including siblings) could be used as an adjunct to parent training. In their study, the children filled both the roles of student (learning signs from the instructor) and mediator (teaching signs to the parent and other siblings), to enhance family interaction.

Special Strategies for Siblings and Peers

Sign training can be accomplished through training sessions for older children and game-type formats for younger children. Setting specific targets, such as the "sign-for-the-day," can encourage use of the gestures introduced. All of the formats listed for self-learning with adults can be applied with nondisabled children, with some modifications. For example, an appropriate sign language dictionary for children is *Sesame Street Sign Language Fun* (Bove, 1985), in which Sesame Street characters are illustrated engaging in activities and Linda Bove, the deaf actress who often appears on the Sesame Street television program, is pictured demonstrating signs.

Training Techniques and Interactions

It is very important that all communication partners of a severely communication-impaired individual use the same teaching strategies and share the same expectations. If a time delay procedure is being used by the professionals involved, family members should be taught to apply it at home as well. Untrained staff or family members will frequently have inappropriate expectations; for example, requesting only imitative signing, or expecting verbalizations accompanying every sign. Strategies that may increase consistency among communication partners are providing opportunities for sharing expectations; use of printed materials describing training techniques, such as expectant time delay; and providing the opportunity to observe clinician–client interactions and to practice facilitative interaction techniques while being observed by the clinician.

Summary

This chapter has presented many issues relative to unaided communication, including assessment, types of unaided systems, selection of content, methods of training, and involvement of others in implementation. Throughout the entire decision-making process, the overriding issue of the interrelatedness of all these issues must be considered. For example, the choice of an unaided system is highly related to decisions regarding content, training, and involvement of partners. Further, the interrelatedness between unaided communication and other modes of communication, such as vocal and aided, must always be considered. Only by maintaining a focus on how combined modes will work for an individual user can an effective multi-component system be developed.

Chapter 8

Aided Communication Systems and Strategies

The limits of my language mean the limits of my world.
— Ludwig Wittgenstein

Aided communication systems have become both more widely used and more sophisticated over the last two decades. In fact, new graphic symbol systems are still under development to meet identified needs of augmented communicators. Numerous organizations and newsletters have been developed to provide information to professionals, families, and aided communicators. One reason for the wide application of aided systems is that they may be used with individuals who have very severe physical impairments.

There is great diversity in the types of aided communication systems, and in the method of accessing, displaying, and teaching the use of those systems. This chapter focuses on a number of aided symbol systems, and issues involved in the use of those systems, such as assessment, intervention, and involving communication partners. The focus in this chapter is on nonelectronic communication systems and displays. Chapter 9 covers electronic devices and other technology issues.

Assessment for Use of an Aided System

Since individuals being assessed for possible use of aided systems often have severe motoric disabilities, assessment can be quite overwhelming. Several factors should be considered as "givens" when undertaking such an assessment. First, as stressed in Chapter 4, the team approach is essential. It is crucial to have input from appropriate professionals in determining optimal components such as positioning, a means of accessing an aided system, and the ideal size, boldness, and spacing of symbols. Second, initiating assessment from a needs framework (as discussed in Chapters 1 and 6) will ensure that issues important to the user, family, and other communication partners will be considered. This also helps to avoid a shotgun approach to assessment, with all possible components assessed through trial and error. Within a needs framework, assessment can be more carefully directed, yielding an assessment that is both more accurate and more effective. A third "given" is the ongoing nature of assessment for a multi-component augmentative system. Components should be evaluated frequently through performance trials, with more in-depth assessment occurring at critical decision-making points, such as transition from preschool to elementary school, or home to group home setting.

Yorkston and Karlan (1986) have described three basic purposes of assessment tools for determining capabilities and making system recommendations:

• *Comprehensive Capability Profiling.* This approach requires determination of maximum level of performance in target areas of interest (e.g., language, spelling, fine motor skills). While this may be a very thorough approach, it requires a massive commitment in terms of time and expense. The tools used may be standard assessment tools (e.g., assessment of receptive language through the *Test for Auditory Comprehension of Language* [Carrow, 1973], assessment of spelling through the *Wide Range Achievement Test* [Jastak, Bijou, & Jastak, 1978]). General purpose assessment tools have also been developed specifically for augmentative communication, as described in the following sections.

• *Criteria-Based Profiling.* Beukelman, Yorkston, and Dowden (1985) described this approach, which asks the question "is the level of performance on a series of cognitive, language, motor, or visual tasks sufficient to allow the individual to use a given approach?" (p. 10). Thus, the evaluator would assess minimal levels of performance on a particular skill. As Yorkston and Karlan (1986) noted, this approach can expedite assessment, as a series of branching decisions can allow the team to omit a number of possible questions and proceed to critical decisions. For example, a standardized spelling test might be started; if the individual passes items at the third or fourth grade level, the evaluator may decide not to complete the entire test, if that level is judged sufficient for the environment.

• *Predictive Profiling.* Yorkston and Karlan (1986) described this approach as administration of carefully constructed tasks, with performance then used to predict the efficiency with which an individual could use a given aid or technique. For example, Goossens' and Crain (1985a) provided specific assessment tasks for diverse goals such as determining optimal response mode or ability to use an initial letter/sound cueing approach.

Specific areas that must be evaluated are related to the assessment questions to be answered. For example, the team must answer the following questions:

1. To what extent is the individual a candidate for an aided system?
2. How will the individual access the aided symbols?
3. Which aided symbol system(s) will best meet the needs and abilities of the individual?
4. What lexical items should be placed on initial displays, and how should the displays be organized?
5. What are the initial training goals to be introduced or expanded (e.g., preliminary skills, lexical items, forms, and functions)?
6. What methods of training best suit the individual?
7. What are the capabilities and needs of the communication partners?

A variety of types of tools can be used in an ongoing assessment, including procedures such as interview, observation, and formal assessment.

Use of Interview and Intake Forms

Bottorf and DePape (1982) asserted that "ignoring previously effective modes of expression may have a negative effect on both the nonspeaking person's and others' acceptance of the new system" (p. 58). For this reason, the assessment must include information on current communication strategies, as well as other pertinent information (e.g., preferences, typical environments and partners). An interview and/or intake form can provide this type of information. Numerous forms are available, serving various purposes. For example, Goosens' and Crain (1985a) have developed three versions of an intake form (preschool, school-age, adult) for general purposes. Light, McNaughton, and Parnes (1986) included in their protocol a facilitator questionnaire to determine background information on the facilitator and client, general impressions, current communication status, and potential assessment contexts. A Communication Profile for Severe Expressive Impairment (Grabowski & Shane, 1986) can be used to document both standard and nonstandard communicative behavior for individuals with severe expressive impairment. Intake and interview forms are also available in a computerized format. For example, the Augmentative Communication Evaluation System[w] is an integrated software/hardware program for IBM computers. It includes an extensive "Client Information

---

The superscript letters following some products refer to their manufacturers and distributors. See Appendix C for names and addresses.

System," covering areas such as personal information, current communication ability, and motor skills. The information entered is then available for rapid summary, comparison, and updating. Interview and intake forms can provide support for the assessment purposes suggested by Yorkston and Karlan (1986). For example, an extensive questionnaire can help to determine comprehensive capability profiling. In-depth interview in more specific areas may provide support for threshhold functioning levels used in criteria-based profiling (e.g., knowledge that the individual with ALS has a college degree may negate the need for extensive testing of spelling skills).

Use of Structured Observations

Structured observations can be useful for gaining information such as the number and frequency of communicative functions used by an augmented communicator and/or partner in specific contexts. However, Kraat (1986) cautioned that "protocols based on normal spoken language models and discourse rules judge these individuals against a standard that may not be effective, functional, or possible" (p. 226). This could in turn lead to inappropriate intervention decisions. Kraat suggested several questions to be considered when collecting a communication sample through observation: (1) what is the main purpose of the observation (overall impression? in-depth information about interaction with unfamiliar partners?), with the answers helping to determine the focus of the observation; (2) what communication and language behaviors should be observed (if the target behavior is initiating requests, a more contrived, elicited context may be needed); (3) what level of client performance is of interest (typical performance? best performance? both?); (4) what context (partners, environments, activities), sampling techniques, and sample lengths best provide the desired information? (pp. 227–229). Thus, observation should be carefully structured, with goals determined in advance. For naturally occurring situations, several observation protocols are available. For example, the *INteraction CHecklist for Augmentative Communication* (Bolton & Dashiell, 1984) provides a systematic observation of three separate initial and follow-up recordings of interactions between augmented communicators and partners. The protocol by Light, McNaughton, and Parnes (1986) includes coding of two naturally occurring contexts (social, and needs and wants). Kraat (1985a, Appendix E) has provided reprints of a variety of additional structured observation forms (e.g., a conversation intent inventory). A general overview of human variables (e.g., readiness, signal, expressive communication) is provided in "The Assessment for Non-Oral Communication" (Mills & Higgins, 1983), with the evaluation based primarily on observation of natural activities, and supplemented by elicited activities. Again, information gained in structured observations can be used for several purposes. For example, taken as a whole, the observations from the Mills and Higgins assessment can support comprehensive capability profiling. In contrast, a specific level on an observation subtest (e.g., Mills & Higgins, 1983) may be predetermined as the entry level for criteria-based profiling (e.g., if the individual can use direct selection at a predetermined level, in-depth assessment of switch use may not be undertaken at that time).

Use of Elicitation-Based Assessment Tools

Elicitation-based tools set up specific situations on which individuals are assessed. These may or may not be standardized. Elicitation-based tools may be borrowed from other disciplines or developed specifically to assess augmented communicators.

Tools Developed for General Populations

A wide range of standardized elicitation-based tools can be used to gain information for various purposes. Several strategies can be used to modify standardized tests, as described in Table 8-1. For more in-depth suggestions for test modifications, see Dawson (1982); Goossens' and Crain (1985a, pp. 54-57); Wasson, Tynan, & Gardiner (1982). Lists of standardized tests that are appropriate for use in modified form with persons with physical impairment are available in Fairweather, Haun, and Finkle (1983, pp. 9-13); and McDonald (1987, Appendix).

Tools Developed for Aided Communicators

A number of formal and informal elicitation-based tools have been developed to assess various components of aided communication, such as those presented in the assessment book by Goossens' and Crain (1985a). Samples of broad-based tools appropriate for use in comprehensive capability profiling are "Assessment Procedures for Nonspeaking Persons" (Lipschultz & Shane, 1980), *Comprehensive Screening Tool for Determining Optimal Communication Mode* (House & Rogerson, 1984), *The Non Speech Test* (Huer, 1983), and "Systematic Evaluation of the Nonspeaking Child" (Bristow & Fristoe, 1984). The Augmentative Communication Evaluation System[w] described previously includes an extensive battery of evaluation tests administered through use of an IBM computer with specialized hardware and software. For example, computer-generated tasks are provided for assessment of visual skills (e.g., auditory acuity, and visual perception), auditory skills (e.g., auditory memory), and motor skills (e.g., activation of a range of switches with various body sites).

A number of specifically oriented assessment tools are also available, such as *The Non-Oral Communication Assessment* (Fell, Lynn, & Morrison,

TABLE 8-1
Sample Strategies for Modifying Tests for Augmentative Communication

Strategy	Example
Use existing stimuli with slight modifications	Enlarge stimulus plates to allow hand pointing or eye gaze Separate stimulus items (e.g., on Etran frame, on choice board) Place items on a scanning display (e.g., rotary scanner) for switch selection Place a number, shape, color code below, next to, or above each choice Frame picture stimuli with darkened lines, to provide more contrast
Vary the response method	Allow person to use eye gaze, a headstick, a light beam, or an electronic device Use an encoding system, with each choice coded; user indicates number/color/shape Use partner assisted scanning with yes/no response (partner points to choices)

Adapted from Dawson (1982); Goossens' and Crain (1985a); Wasson et al. (1982).

1984) designed to assess motoric functioning for switching and for pointing, and communication capacity. These tools can assist in criteria-based profiling and predictive profiling, as can clinician-developed tools to examine specific abilities.

Several elicitation-based communication sampling procedures have been developed for use with augmented communicators and their partners. In their assessment tool for adults, Light and colleagues (1986) included a protocol for assessment of eliciting contexts. Kraat (1985a, Appendix C) provided three sample structured contexts for children (snack routine, picnic routine, attention-getting script). She also presented transcription and coding systems used in the study of communication interaction between aid users and others (1985a, Appendix D).

This section has provided an overview of sample assessment tools used for a variety of purposes with aided communicators. Each of the tools described in this section is annotated in Appendix B. Specific subsections within this and other chapters suggest assessment tools for decision-making with regard to specific questions.

Indicating Messages Elements

The development of a clear, reliable means of indicating message items is essential to successful communication. This may also be referred to as the "transmission technique." If message indication is not clear to the communication partner, communication breakdowns are inevitable, resulting in a reduction in rate and an increase in frustration for both partners. An accurate means of indicating message elements is important in assessing cognitive and linguistic skills, and allows an individual to be a more active partner in the decision-making process, such as helping to select vocabulary. Several general methods of indicating desired messages can be used with nonelectronic displays. In determining the most appropriate means of indicating for an individual, several factors should be considered (Musselwhite, 1987):

- *Accuracy.* While pointing directly with a hand is conventional, pointing with a mouthstick or using encoding might allow smaller symbols to be indicated, with fewer errors
- *Speed.* Speed in indicating contributes to output rate and must be optimized to increase the potential for successful interactions
- *Effort.* A high degree of effort will slow the rate and contribute to fatigue
- *Cognitive Demands.* Scanning and encoding require greater cognitive demands from the user than direct selection
- *Listener Demands.* The effort required of the communication partner (e.g., learning the coding system, verifying responses) may determine whether the user is free to communicate with a large number of partners, or is limited to those willing or able to interpret the message.

Direct Selection

With direct selection, the individual directly indicates the desired message element from the selection set through pointing. The body part (finger, thumb, fist, eyes, elbow, or any other part) may be used alone or with an accessing aid, such as a handpointer, headpointer, or optical light pointer.

Assessment of direct selection skills involves determining the individual's targeting skills with regard to features such as accuracy, range of motion, speed, effort, and reliability of response. Goossens' and Crain (1985a) discussed both commerically available and homemade equipment for determining optimal targeting skills.

As with many other areas, determination of potential should often follow a period of diagnostic therapy, with the instructor introducing adaptations as needed. These may include (1) altering positioning (e.g., adding a stabilizing bar for the nonpointing hand to increase trunk stability; modifying the wheelchair to enhance trunk stability), (2) adjusting the height, angle, or stability of the display to facilitate ease of pointing (e.g., using an adjustable easel), (3) experimenting with use of accessing tools such as mouthsticks, light beam indicators, head or chin pointers, or handsticks (see Goossens' and Crain, 1985a, pp. 99–101; 1985b, pp. 28–29). Fishman (1987) summarized functional differences between headsticks and light pointers. For example, a light pointer requires less range of motion than a headstick, and is cosmetically less interfering, which enables the user to select items within a large area. A headstick, unlike a light pointer, can also be used to manipulate or activate objects or devices (e.g., to turn pages).

Table 8–2 illustrates application of sample adaptations in assessing and optimizing a hand pointing response. Input from an occupational therapist is essential for both selection and training of adaptations.

Numerous suggestions for adaptations to enhance direct selection are presented in Charlebois–Marois (1985). Specific activities for facilitating use of headsticks and optical pointers are provided in a publication by the Swedish Institute for the Handicapped (Eriksson, 1985).

TABLE 8-2
Sample Adaptations in Assessing and Optimizing a Hand Pointing Response

Factors	Sample Considerations	Sample Adaptations
Range	Size of effective area Movement patterns Effect on opposite extremity	Alter height and angle of display Place entries in optimal positions Alter size of display
Accuracy	Ability to isolate thumb/fingers Potential item spacing Visual monitoring of hand	Use weight cuff Use appliance (e.g., T-stick) Place guard on display Alter size/spacing of entries Encourage middle finger pointing
Speed	Length of response time Area for quickest response	Use sliding pointer, to maintain hand on board Alter organization of entries Place frequent entries in quickly reached positions
Effort	Reasonableness of effort Motivation of user Overflow movements	Use stability bar for nonpointing hand Use sliding pointer, to keep hand in pointing position Reassess positioning (e.g., use of strap for head control)

Adapted from Musselwhite (1987).

Scanning

With scanning, message elements are presented one at a time with the user indicating the desired element. A wide range of nonelectronic scanning techniques can be used, all of which are partner-assisted. For example, in auditory scanning, the partner calls out message elements, with the user indicating the desired message in some way (e.g., vocalizing, producing a prearranged signal such as closing the eyes or nodding the head). The simplest example of visual scanning would be for the partner to indicate message elements on a display one at a time until the user signals a choice. Clearly, this type of nonelectronic, partner-assisted scanning can be extremely slow. Some users may be able to indicate groupings on a display (e.g., through a fist point or eye gaze), with the partner scanning through individual items within the indicated area. Thus, an individual who has only gross targeting skills can access a display with far smaller message elements.

Assessment considerations for auditory partner-assisted scanning would involve determination of memory skills (i.e., can the individual retain the possible choices in his or her memory). For both auditory and visual scanning, the user must have one reliable, consistent, voluntary movement (e.g., blink, brow lift) to indicate an affirmative response (Rothschild, 1986).

The technique of auditory scanning is most efficient if elements are ignored until the desired element is reached; that is, the user should not indicate "no" responses, but should wait to indicate only the "yes" response. A vocal response can enhance the flexibility of the technique, because the partner does not need to closely watch the user, and can even communicate from another room. The partner may want to present the "menu" of possible choices first, as illustrated in the following example. Sharon is in the den and her spouse is in the kitchen fixing a snack. He first lets her know what is available, then scans through the choices to allow her to make a choice. "We have butter pecan, rocky road, and vanilla. What'll you have? Butter pecan ... rocky road ..." (Sharon vocalizes to indicate her choice). Auditory scanning can also include groupings to increase speed. For example, for auditory scanning through the alphabet, the partner can present groupings of letters first, ("A to G ... H to M ... N to T ... U to Z"), followed with letter by letter presentation for the grouping indicated (H ... I ... J ... K ...").

Rothschild (1986) has presented numerous samples and guidelines for developing visual partner-assisted scanning techniques. For example, display features should be carefully determined, including the size, and number of items in each grouping, and the arrangement of the groupings. Other important factors are the positioning of partners and the use of confirmation to minimize communication breakdown. A sample display for use with partner-assisted scanning is presented in Figure 8–1A.

Encoding

With encoding, a pattern or code of signals are used to indicate message elements. As Vanderheiden and Lloyd (1986) observed, encoding techniques can increase the number of items that can be selected, or decrease the amount of time required to select a target item. The code is typically indicated by direct selection, either manually (e.g., user points to large numbers to enter a number code for items on a display) or visually (e.g., user eye-gazes to colors on a plexiglass interface frame to indicate desired message elements within a grouping).

In assessing potential use of encoding techniques, cognitive factors are important. For example, the user must be able to understand that one item indicated (e.g., a color square) represents a message element (e.g., the symbol bordered by that color within a grouping). Skills such as color matching and number matching will also be necessary for some encoding techniques. Sequencing skills should also be assessed, if a two-movement encoding technique is to be used; the user may need to indicate two numbers or two colors in sequence to indicate a specific entry on a separate display (e.g., 2, 4 indicates the entry in column 2, row 4, or 24 indicates entry number 24 on the communication display).

Manual encoding can be used with an individual who has only gross targeting skills, but needs a large number of message elements. For example, in the display pictured in Figure 8–1B, items within groupings are color-coded to allow the user to point to the grouping, then point to the color block whose position and color correspond to the target item.

For visual encoding, users often use a plexiglass or lexan interface frame (often referred to as an "etran display") to eye-gaze to the code elements. Message entries can be displayed directly on the chart, as illustrated in Figure 8–1C, requiring the user to first indicate the location of the grouping, then indicate the position of the target entry within that grouping. An example of an early visual encoding technique using this strategy is the location, color-coded entran system illustrated in Figure 8–1D. Van Tatenhove (1986c) has developed specific steps for constructing and introducing a location, color-coded entran. Goossens' and Crain (1985b) presented numerous examples of encoding displays using eye gaze. They also provided addresses for commercially available displays, as well as directions for constructing both an adjustable eye-gaze frame and eye-gaze communication vests, in which the partner wears a vest with objects or symbols affixed for the partner and user to indicate. Seery (1985) has developed a set of eye-gaze communication games, activities, and interactions for use in a classroom setting.

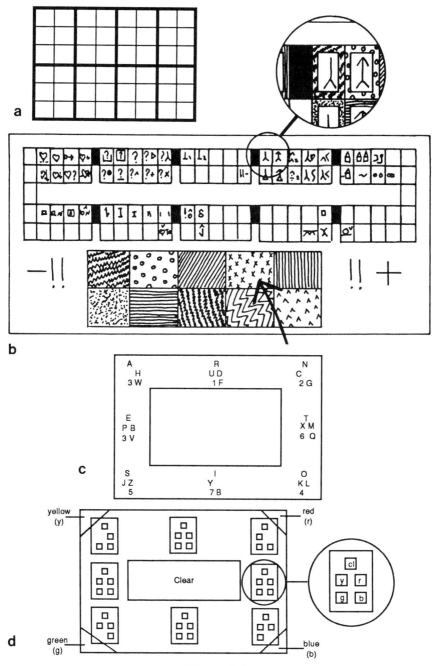

Figure 8-1

Means of indicating with nonelectronic displays. A. Partner assisted scanning, display with items separated with colored tape as marking boundaries (Roths-child, 1986, p. 22). B. Manual color-position display (Charlebois–Marois, 1985, p. 92). C. Two-movement encoding using Etran (Vanderheiden & Lloyd, 1986, p. 117). D. Area-color encoded format (Goossens' & Crain, 1985, p. 156).

Summary

The importance of developing a clear, reliable, nonfatiguing means of emphasizing message elements cannot be overstressed. Often, combinations of the basic techniques will be used, with desirable features of each combined; an example would be pointing to large numbers that are used for encoding. Many users employ a variety of means of indicating, to effectively and efficiently communicate across a range of situations and communication partners, as illustrated in the following case study.

When seated in her adaptive chair, with her communication display affixed to an angled easel on her laptray, Marie–Pierre is able to use her left index finger for pointing. In the bathtub, she relies on eye gaze to point out objects, and to a small laminated display. When she is on the floor and communicating with familiar partners, she points to a grouping, with her partner assisting in scanning for the target item. She often uses partner-assisted auditory scanning to indicate messages that are not on her display, and when her display is not available.

RESOURCE. The primary resources for assessing and developing a means of indication for nonelectronic displays are: *Augmentative Communication: Assessment Resource* (Goossens' & Crain, 1985a); *Augmentative Communication: Intervention Resource* (Goossens' & Crain, 1985b); and *Everybody's Technology* (Charlebois–Marois, 1985).

Aided Symbol Systems

The aided symbol system covered in this section can be divided into four major categories:

1. *Object Communication Systems.* These represent life-sized or miniature objects used as communication symbols.

2. *Representational Symbol Systems.* These systems primarily include symbols that suggest their meanings, such as pictures, photographs, and line drawings. Symbol systems include primarily pictographs and ideographs (e.g., Blissymbolics, PICSYMS).

3. *Abstract Symbol Systems.* For these systems, the meaning is not suggested by the symbol's appearance. Examples are Yerkish lexigrams and Premack-type shapes.

4. *Symbolic Language Codes.* These consist of codes representing the letters or sounds of a language such as English or Italian. Examples are alphabets, phonemes, words, alphabetic clusters, Braille, and Morse Code.

Each of these aided symbol systems will be reviewed in this chapter. Several systems will be covered in some details, using the what, why, who format introduced in Chapter 7.

Object Communication Displays

WHAT. Object displays can use either real objects or objects that represent other objects or events. For example, the student can select an actual bottle of bubbles, or a duplicate bottle of bubbles can be selected to represent the bottle that will be used. Miniature objects can also be used. Sources of miniatures are objects from dollhouse sets, objects found in novelty stores (e.g., miniature electronic keyboards), erasers, and magnets. Caution should be used in introducing miniatures, as some individuals may find them as abstract as photographic or pictographic representations. Figures 8–2 and 8–3 illustrate sample commerical and constructed object communication displays, with regard to the types of objects used and the ways they are organzied and presented to the user.

Several potential problem areas should be considered in designing object communication displays:

• *Safety.* Miniaturized objects may produce risks to some students, particularly with regard to choking. For those students, items should be carefully selected for size, small removable parts, and sharp edges. It may be necessary to affix objects to a board or to insert them into a protective covering (e.g., sealed bags, plastic sealant, plastic box).

• *Durability.* The display must be designed to minimize damage to objects, and to reduce loss of objects. Covering the display and/or the objects are examples of strategies for enhancing durability. For example, miniature objects can be placed on a backing (e.g., a masonite sample clip)

a **b**

Figure 8–2
Commercially available object communication displays. A. Choice Board. B. Symbol Training Display. (Photos by Don Johnston Development Equipment, Inc.).

A. Eye gaze communication vest
(Goossens' and Crain, 1985b, directions
pp. 205–208)

B. Object box (Porter et al., 1985)

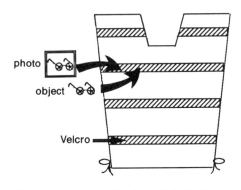

photo

object

Velcro

Note: Objects are affixed by stickyback
hook Velcro

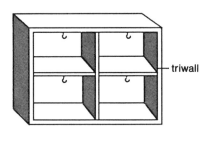

triwall

Note: Objects can be placed on shelves
or suspended by hooks.

C. Keep Box (available at variety and hardware stores)

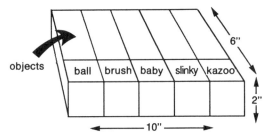

objects

ball | brush | baby | slinky | kazoo

6"

2"

10"

Note: Letters represent symbols that are
placed in slide protector squares

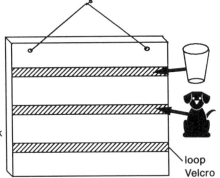

D. Object communication display
(Triwall covered in contact paper)

Note: Objects are affixed with stickyback
hook Velcro.

loop
Velcro

Figure 8-3

Constructed object communication displays. A. Eye gaze communication vest
(Goossens' & Crain, 1985b, directions pp. 205–208). B. Object box (Porter et al.,
1985). C. Keep box (available at variety stores). D. Object communication display
(Triwall, i.e., three-layer cardboard, covered in contact paper).

and covered with clear non-glare plastic (e.g., Envirotech or Ultro-Glo), available at craft supply stores.

• *Flexibility*. Permanently affixed object displays have extremely limited use, except perhaps for assessment purposes. Ideally, objects should be added or replaced quickly, using no tools, or tools that are easily obtainable.

WHY. To ensure future conversational control and prevent learned helplessness, it is important to provide some type of communication display as soon as the child is cognitively ready. Also, for the older individual with severe cognitive delay, waiting until he or she reaches the representational level of recognizing photographs may be extremely limiting. Thus, object displays may serve a useful introduction to augmentative communication. They may also aid in the transition to pictographic displays.

WHO. Object displays are most appropriate for young children or cognitively delayed individuals. Requirements for using objects would be less demanding in terms of cognitive level and visual discrimination skills.

WHEN. Object displays using realistic, full-sized objects can be introduced at the Stage 3 level of sensorimotor development. Thus, an individual who repeats chance actions to reproduce an interesting change or effect may be ready for introduction of an object display.

HOW. Musselwhite (1986a, Chapter 7) and Porter and associates (1985) have suggested numerous strategies for introducing objects for use in decision-making, and developing object displays for communication purposes. This decision-making using objects should be incorporated into all daily living activities, such as dressing, feeding, playing independently, and outdoor play.

Goossens' and Crain (1985b, pp. 57–62) offered a variety of strategies for generalizing from objects to pictures. First, a pairing process (Van Tatenhove, 1978) should be used, with a previously learned representational level (e.g., miniature object) paired with a higher representational level (line drawing). For example, adhesive Velcro can be used to affix both a miniature pair of funny glasses and a drawing of the glasses onto a stimulation vest, as illustrated in Figure 8–3A. The lower level representation should be gradually faded (e.g., distancing the miniature from the drawing). Goossens' and Crain (1985b) also recommended using "object pictures" to promote a smooth transition from objects to pictures. In this process, a cross-section of the real object is mounted on a surface to yield a three-dimensional picture. Raised pictures are next introduced, with the height of the raised picture decreased, until a flat surface is achieved. Samples of objects that can be used for this procedure are small cereal box, yogurt container, small cardboard book, plastic car. Other strategies helpful in moving from objects to pictures are taking an instant photo of an object and allowing the person to watch it develop, pointing back and forth from the object to the photo or placing the object (e.g., spoon, bottle) on a piece of sturdy paper; tracing around the object, then adding details to yield a symbol representing the target object. Again, point back and forth from object to symbol, and pair the two for training.

WHERE. Resources for developing object communication displays are *Adaptive Play for Special Needs Children* (Musselwhite, 1986a, Chapter 7) and *Augmentative Communication: Intervention Resource* (Goossens' and Crain, 1985b).

Representational Symbol Systems

The majority of aided symbol systems used by nonspellers falls in the category of representational systems, meaning that most symbols used in the system suggest their referents. This connection may be directly suggested, as in the case of a pictograph (e.g., a drawing of a tree that clearly depicts the trunk, limbs, and leaves) or an ideograph (e.g., a symbol that evokes an idea of the referent, such as a happy face or a heart plus an arrow pointing up to denote the concept *happy*). Over one dozen representational symbol systems are currently in use. Several of those systems are described in some detail in the following section.

Pictures, Photographs, and Line Drawings

WHAT. A great variety of materials may fall under the category of pictures, photographs, and line drawings. Mirenda (1985) suggested that these sets can be divided into two general categories: (1) those that are commercially available, and (2) those that are constructed from commonly available materials. Sample symbol picture sets from the first category are presented in Figure 8–4. One symbol set, Picture Communication Symbols, is presented in more depth as it is extensive, widely available, and frequently used for both clinical and research applications. Constructed picture sets can include black or white and color photographs, cutouts from magazines, catalogs, coupons, or packaging materials, and hand prepared line drawings, either black and white or colored. Table 8–3 presents a comparison of advantages and disadvantages of commerically prepared versus constructed picture sets.

Several authors (e.g., Lapidus, Adler, & Modugno, 1984; Silverman, 1980; Williams & Fox, 1977) refer to a hypothetical "abstraction continu-

SYMBOL SET/ DISTRIBUTOR	EXAMPLES	QUANTITY/ SIZE	COMMENTS
PICTOGRAM IDEOGRAM COMMUNICATION (PIC) Developmental Equipment P.O. Box 639 Wauconda, IL 60084		400 2 × 2 5/8 × 5/8	White foreground pictures on black background intended to minimize figure-ground discrimination for persons with visual impairment; includes cards and stickers.
PICTURE COMMUNICATION SYMBOLS Mayer-Johnson Company P.O. Box AD Solana Beach, CA 92075	dog sad look, see under	1800 1 × 1 2 × 2	Simple line drawings organized by categories in binders (See description in this chapter).
TOUCH 'N TALK Imaginart Communications Products P.O. Box 1868 Idyllwild, CA 92349		420 1 1/2 × 1 1/2 5/8 × 5/8	Simple black-and-white line drawings representing a variety of language concepts; pressure-sensitive stickers, with doubles presented of most commonly used pictures.

Figure 8-4
Samples of commercially available picture sets.

SYMBOL SET/ DISTRIBUTOR	EXAMPLES	QUANTITY/ SIZE	COMMENTS
COMMUNIMAGE Asso. de Paralysie Cerebral du Quebec 525 Boul. Hamel Est Quebec, QC G1M 2S8		600 3/4 × 3/4 1 1/4 × 1 1/4 2 × 2	Black-and-white line drawings are presented with French labels; target audience is children age 3–10 years; 26 categories are included.
OAKLAND PICTURE DICTIONARY P.O. Box 639 Wauconda, IL 60084		500+ 1/2 × 1/2 1 × 1 2 × 2	Simple black-and-white line drawings divided into 20 categories; includes alphabetical and categorical indexes.
PEEL AND PUT Communication Skill Builders 3830 East Bellevue Tucson, AZ 85733		880 2 × 2	Color illustrations on pressure-sensitive stickers; categories represented include nouns, verbs, prepositions; indices list by sound, language concept, category.

Figure 8–4 *(continued)*
Samples of commercially available picture sets.

TABLE 8-3
Advantages and Disadvantages of Commercially Prepared Versus Constructed Picture Sets

Advantages	Disadvantages
Commercially Prepared Picture Sets	
Ready availability	Lack of color cues
Relatively low cost	Typically small in size
Excellent picture quality	Predetermined pictures may discourage selection of appropriate lexicon or personalization of pictures
Constructed Picture Sets	
Can be totally individualized regarding type and size of picture	Typically time-consuming to develop
Typically very low cost	Staff may not have necessary skills for total system design
Families/caregivers can be involved	May be difficult to reproduce
May be easily expanded	

Adapted from Mirenda (1985).

um," in which photographs are assumed to have a relatively low level of abstraction, while line drawings demonstrate a relatively high level of abstraction. The amounts of detail and the extent to which the foreground stands out from the background are assumed to influence the complexity of a pictured item. Mirenda (1985), takes exception to the idea of a fixed order of complexity, and the resulting assumption that if a student is not successful learning to use the least complex of the pictorial systems in the hierarchy (i.e., photographs with simple backgrounds), then attempts at more "advanced" types of pictures (i.e., line drawings) would be futile. Mirenda pointed out that learners who seem to process information in idiosyncratic, perhaps unpredictable ways (e.g., persons with autism) may not follow this assumption.

WHY. Pictures, especially those that are highly representative of the referent (e.g., a label from a toy carton), may provide an intermediate step between real objects, events, and people, and more abstract aided symbols such as PICSYMS, rebuses, or Blissymbols. They may be adapted to the needs of the individual by using photographs or drawings of people, objects, and events familiar to the user. However, note that some symbol systems, such as PICSYMS and Picture Your Blissymbols, allow modification of symbols in order to represent life experiences of symbol users (e.g., draw-

195

ing in glasses to clarify the symbol of an individual). Thus, the need for a picture set, as opposed to a symbol system, is a highly individual decision.

WHO. Picture sets may be helpful for learners with severe handicapping conditions, such as mental retardation or autism. Picture sets can be located or developed to meet specific needs of individual learners, such as size (many commerical sets are limited in size), exact-match requirement (using labels from food containers or toy boxes), and inclusion of background details (color photographs, showing setting of objects).

The potential audience for comprehending picture systems would vary, depending on the complexity of the pictures or of their use. For example, pictures of specific objects will typically be highly transparent, while use of a magazine photograph of bologna to indicate "you're full of bologna" would be more open to misinterpretation. Some pictures might be difficult to guess, due to possible background/foreground confusion. In that case, alternate pictures should be chosen or pictures should be labeled with words.

HOW. Several authors suggest procedures for teaching clients that pictures represent specified referents. A basic procedure followed in many training programs is a match-to-sample task, with the user matching the picture to an object, event, or person (Keogh & Reichle, 1985). This may be preceded by match-to-sample tasks involving matching objects to objects. Clearly, these procedures may be used with a variety of symbol sets or systems. Several authors have suggested specific techniques for demonstrating that pictures represent three-dimensional objects. For example, McDonald (1980) suggested that the trainer take an instant photograph of the referent (e.g., the toilet) and allow the client to watch it develop. To enhance the transition to line drawings, Libergott (1980) recommended pointing to the referent, such as a baby bottle, then placing it on a sheet of paper and tracing around it. In both of these examples, the picture is produced while the client watches, with the trainer indicating back and forth between the picture and the referent.

WHERE. See Goossens' and Crain (1985b, pp. 123–128) for a listing of a variety of graphic communication sets that are commercially available. See also figure 8–4 in this chapter.

SUMMARY AND DISCUSSION. The category of pictures, photographs, and line drawings includes a wide range of commercially purchased and clinician-prepared materials. One concern with picture sets is that most are limited in terms of ideas that can be expressed, with a focus on noun and verb entries. Since these compilations do not form true communication systems, often rules for preparing items are lacking or unclear. For that reason, it may be difficult to expand a picture set as new communication needs arise. This does not rule out the potential for use as an introductory system, particularly for persons who are chronologically young or developmentally delayed.

Picture Communication Symbols

WHAT. Picture Communication Symbols (PCS) is a set of line drawings specifically designed for use by augmented communicators. Symbols are drawn with bold strokes, and comprise primarily simple, clear drawings, as illustrated in Figure 8-4. They are intended to be photocopied rather than hand-drawn. The set is basically nongenerative (Whitley, 1985), as no rules exist for developing new symbols.

The symbols are presented in one-inch and two-inch sizes in two sturdy three-ring binders, or in stamp form (one-inch size only). Book I includes 700 introductory vocabulary items divided into six categories: people, verbs, nouns, descriptive, social, and miscellaneous. A brief PCS guide is included with sample ideas for use of the symbols. Book II presents an additional 1,100 symbols, providing expansion of the categories in Book I. New topic areas are also presented, including religion, sexuality, computers, and leisure. Basic faces and heads are provided to allow customized symbolization of a particular individual. Conversational discourse phrases such as "please repeat," "my turn," and "not on this board" are also represented pictorially. An index includes vocabulary from both books, for ease of reference.

WHY. This set was designed while the author was working with trainable mentally retarded teenagers, some of whom needed an augmentative communication system (Johnson, 1985). Johnson felt the need for a system that could be easily learned, either because of limited cognitive abilities in her students, or because the symbols would be needed for only a short period of time. Thus, PCS was developed as a versatile, relatively inexpensive picture set offering a large vocabulary of clearly presented drawings. The primary goals for the set are that it

- Be easily learned
- Be appropriate for all age levels
- Have simple, clear drawings for visual clarity
- Be easily reproduced on copying machines, making it inexpensive to use
- Have easily separated categories of symbols, so that the users need only use the symbols appropriate

- Have standardized sizes so the symbols could be neatly and easily put on standardized grids.

WHO. These symbols are suggested for use with a variety of disabilities, including aphasia, apraxia, autism, retardation, cerebral palsy, and postoperative conditions. As indicated previously, an attempt has been made to design symbols that are appropriate across all age levels.

WHEN. Research with normally developing two-year-olds indicated that they were able to identify 65 percent of a subset of Picture Communication Symbols (Small–Morris, 1986). The task required pointing to the target symbol, presented in a field of four items arranged in a two-by-two matrix. The set of symbols consisted of 29 nouns and verbs, judged by the parents and teachers of the subjects to be within the receptive vocabulary of all subjects. Nouns and verbs would appear to be the most easily recognized categories in the set; therefore, the entire set may be less guessable for young children. Also, it is not known how these findings relate to nonspeaking children.

HOW. There is not a structured training program for PCS. However, a variety of teaching materials are available to assist in teaching use of the symbols. Samples are:

- *Practice Communication Cards:* cards to teach 42 target words, with a guide suggesting various training activities and gems, scoring systems, and so forth
- *Life Experiences Communication Kit:* provides 11 "lesson plans" for activities, including Mini Communication Boards for activities such as making juice, washing hands, and working a computer. Training suggestions are provided
- *Read-A-Bol Books:* symbol books presented in three levels, with increasing numbers of symbols, plus ideas for training (note that these books include some symbols not in the PCS set).

WHERE. Most PCS materials can be ordered through Mayer–Johnson Company (see Appendix C). The *Read-A-Bol Books* are available through the Read-A-Bol Group (see Appendix C).

SUMMARY AND DISCUSSION. Picture Communication Symbols form an extensive set of symbols that are applicable to both children and adults. The symbols can be readily photocopied, and most can be hand-drawn with some practice. The large vocabulary of entries designed specifically for augmented communicators, and the available support materials, combine to make this a widely-used system.

Rebus

WHAT. The term *rebus* comes from a Latin word meaning "thing" (Woodcock, 1968). The meaning of the word can be indicated by a thing such as a geometric form or a picture, rather than by the orthographic form of the word (Clark, Davies, & Woodcock, 1974). Rebus symbols represent entire words or parts of words. It is not a closed symbolic system, since anyone can design rebus symbols. The rebuses described here as a system are those included in the *Standard Rebus Glossary* (Clark et al., 1974), and used in programs such as the *Peabody Rebus Reading Program* (Woodcock, Clark & Davies, 1969).

Rebus symbols may be classified into three basic categories, with combinations of the symbols yielding a fourth category (Figure 8–5).

The combination of symbols and letters is described as the "semiphonic" potential (Woodcock, 1968). With this tactic, a rebus such as *in* forms the main portion of the word, and an initial consonant, consonant blend, or digraph is used with the rebus. Letters may be added either before or after the rebus. It should be noted that this semi-phonic approach typically yields words in which the rebus is not related to the meaning. A related tactic is use of a rebus that pictures a homonym of the intended word; again, the pictorial representation will not match the meaning of the word. This practice can yield a single rebus for two or more words with different meanings, such as *be/bee, wood/would,* and *two/to/too.* With regard to this semi-phonic approach, Clark and Woodcock (1976) explain that "the reader decoding words represented by the rebus principle is required to transfer the meaning of the pictographic symbols into sound chunks, then process the sound chunks into new or second-order meaning" (p. 554).

Since this system allows the addition of letters to rebuses, any morphological inflections may be produced. Therefore, it is possible for the syntax of Rebus to parallel English or another language.

WHY. Rebus symbols were developed as an aid to learning reading, particularly for culturally disadvantanged children. They were later adapted to the communication needs of nonspeakers. Rebuses have been standardized to some extent, and are available commercially in rub-on form, thus increasing the ease with which they may be used on communication displays.

WHO. Rebuses have been used for different purposes, with a variety of populations, including people who are culturally disadvantaged (Woodcock, 1968), hearing impaired (Clark, Moores, & Woodcock, 1975), and mentally retarded (Apffel, Kelleher, Lilly, & Richardson, 1975). It is likely that rebuses would not be accepted well by nonspeaking adults, due to the childish nature of many of the rebuses.

1. *Concrete symbols* — these primarily depict objects or actions:

| see | she | be | wood |

2. *Relational symbols* — these primarily depict locations or directions:

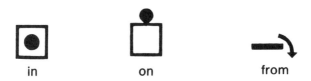

| in | on | from |

3. *Abstract symbols* — these are primarily arbitrary symbols, although some are ideographic:

| the | if | could |

4. Combinations —
   a. *compound symbols* in which two or more rebuses are joined:

| into | somewhat |

   b. *combined symbol using affixes* in which a root word is joined to an affix such as present progressive "-ing", past tense "-ed", or plural "s":

| doing | theirs |

   c. *combined symbols using letters* in which rebuses are joined with letters of the alphabet:

| son | sat | sand |

Figure 8–5
Symbolic communication strategies using rebuses.

Persons using rebuses as symbols for an aided communication system would need the following skills:

• Good visual discrimination skills, in order to distinguish among the rebuses, many of which have minimal differences
• Sensorimotor Stage 4 cognitive development, for decoding the pictographic symbols. For symbols using letters, higher cognitive skills would be required
• Skills in sound blending, in order to decode combined symbols (unless they are learned in a rote manner).

The audience for rebuses would be broad, as many symbols are iconic. Musselwhite and Ruscello (1984) found rebus symbols in their study to be highly guessable for the older subject groups (ages 9 and up), and significantly above chance levels for the younger groups (ages 3 and 6). In addition, rebuses are typically displayed with the English word printed below each symbol, making them easily decoded by the English-reading community.

WHEN. As noted previously, deciding pictographic symbols should be possible at the Stage 4 or 5 level of sensorimotor development. Symbols requiring use of traditional orthography may need to be delayed until the child is at the preoperational stage of development.

HOW. A variety of materials and several programs are available for teaching the use of rebuses. It should be noted, however, that many of these programs were designed to teach reading, rather than as symbols for communication use. Recent approaches have focused on teaching rebuses as an aid to functional communication. For example, the *Clark Early Language Program* (Clark & Moores, 1984) provides grammatical instruction as well as practice in using several parts of speech and simple sentence constructions. A series of 55 developmental lessons are included for teaching functional language through a total communication approach, using approximately 150 rebus symbols, spoken language, and (optionally) Signed English. In the United Kingdom, modifications have been made to use rebuses in conjunction with British Sign Language (van Oosterom & Devereaux, 1984).

WHERE. Materials related to the rebus system are available from the American Guidance Service (see Appendix C).

• *Books* (see Appendix B): *Clark Early Language Program* (Clark & Moores, 1984); *Learning with Rebuses* (Devereaux & van Oosterom, 1984); *Rebus Glossary* (van Oosterom & Devereaux, 1984); *Standard Rebus Glossary* (Clark, Davies, & Woodcock, 1974).

SUMMARY AND DISCUSSION. Rebuses may be used as entries on communication displays, especially for children. The liberal use of traditional orthography in combined rebuses, and the lack of semantic basis for many symbols, may make it difficult to learn the entire system. As Jones and Cregan (1986) noted, combined rebuses that use a letter of the alphabet plus an iconic symbol may be conceptually confusing, because the iconic part will have a greater impact than the symbol as a whole.

PICSYMS

WHAT. PICSYMS is an open-ended visual graphic symbol system based on the language of young children (Carlson, 1985). It is highly structured, comprising a system rather than a mere set of picture symbols. The name PICSYMS is derived from the words PICture SYMbolS.

The *Categorical Dictionary* (Carlson, 1985) presents more than 800 symbols in one-, two-, and three-inch sizes.

PICSYMS were developed according to several logical principles to enhance meaning (see Figure 8–6):

• *Semantic Groupings.* A shape or manner of representation can key the user into a semantic category. For example, characters and occupations are shown with solid rather than stick figures, to accommodate uniforms. Buildings without distinct shapes take the basic building shape, with the front used as a billboard, on which is displayed a PICSYM of the function or feature of the building (Figure 8–6A).

• *Relative Abstraction.* Concrete concepts such as objects are represented in a more realistic manner, while more abstract concepts are depicted with less realism. To illustrate, feelings are shown by the circular happy face, plus use of the forehead as a billboard for symbolizing ideas, plus addition of related symbols (Figure 8–6B).

• *Developmental Progression.* Both immature and mature forms are presented for many PICSYMS, to allow for variations in developmental level. Language concept maturity was also considered. For example, target elements are often depicted by bold lines and with background visual information shown in light or broken lines, to avoid confusion when parts of pictures, such as a nose, are presented in isolation (Figure 8–6C).

• *Customizing Symbols.* Symbols for both objects and people can be customized to match items and people within a user's experience (Figure 8–6D).

• *Creation of New Symbols.* New PICSYMS can be created by following the principles and rules outlined in the *Categorical Dictionary* (Carlson, 1985).

• *Aesthetic Appeal.* Carlson (1985) asserted the need to create symbols that are attractive and appealing to the general public, to encourage greater symbol use.

A. SEMANTIC GROUPINGS

1. Characters/Occupations

2. Buildings

Butcher	Santa Claus

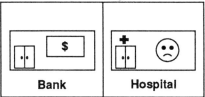

Bank	Hospital

B. RELATIVE ABSTRACTION

1. Concrete Concepts

2. More Abstract Concepts

Jack-in-Box	Ice Cream Cone

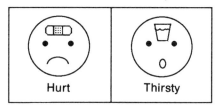

Hurt	Thirsty

C. DEVELOPMENTAL PROGRESSION

1. Immature/Mature Forms

2. Background visual information

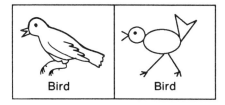

Bird	Bird

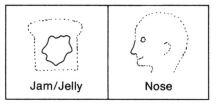

Jam/Jelly	Nose

D. CUSTOMIZING SYMBOLS

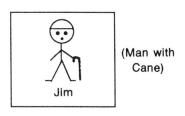

(Man with Cane)

Jim

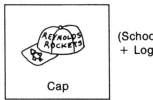

(School Colors + Logo)

Cap

Figure 8-6
PICSYMS: Logical principles. A. Semantic groupings. B. Relative abstraction. C. Developmental progression. D. Customizing symbols.

PICSYMS is a highly logical system based on 28 rules of composition. The depiction of pronouns illustrates several rules such as: #2, *Line Contrasts* (solid line for target elements, broken line for defining elements); #6, *Generic People* (sex designated by hairline, no sex differentiation unless necessary); #8, *Relationships* (figures within relationships hold hands; figure in between used for more distant relationships); #11, *Things or Undifferentiated Objects* (possession denoted by figure holding object). The pronouns presented in Figure 8-7 illustrate these rules of composition.

Since they are based on a grid (8 squares by 6 squares), PICSYMS can be easily drawn by hand, either through use of a grid, tracing, or a template. Carlson presented numerous suggestions for accurately reproducing the symbols. She also provided specific ideas for creating new PICSYMS, in addition to the 28 rules for composition previously described. PICSYMS are also available on a computer software program entitled *Magic Cymbals* (Schneier Communication Unit, Appendix C).

WHY. This system evolved through Carlson's work with young nonspeaking children. She felt that many available systems were too abstract or did not provide needed symbols. Drawing pictures to meet the needs of individual children was successful but too time-consuming. In addition, not all communication partners were found to be equally successful in their artistic attempts. Carlson saw the need to develop a system of symbols that would be easily recognizable, flexible, and open-ended. Several children's dictionaries were consulted to determine needed vocabulary, supplemented by direct experience with young nonspeaking children and their siblings and friends, as well as continuing parental requests. Ease of symbol reproduction and symbol creation were also important criteria in system development.

WHO. Although PICSYMS were intended for young nonspeaking children, Carlson reports that they have been helpful with other populations as well. Potential users include children with language or learning disabil-

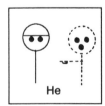   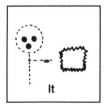

Figure 8-7
PICSYMS: Pronouns as illustration of rules of composition.

ities (to aid in concept learning and reading) and people with dysarthria, apraxia, aphasia, and mental retardation. Carlson observed that current applications with some of these populations are limited; more research and study is needed before the range of usefulness is known.

WHEN. Anecdotal reports indicate that PICSYMS have been useful with children as young as 18 months of age. A study by Small–Morris (1986) found that two-year-old children identified 67 percent of a subset of PICSYMS. A total of 29 nouns and verbs comprised the task. All referents included were judged by parents and teachers of the subjects as being within the receptive vocabulary of all subjects. Since nouns and verbs are likely the most easily recognized categories of PICSYMS, the entire set may be less guessable for young children.

HOW. Numerous teaching strategies are presented for teaching specific rules for PICSYMS (Carlson, 1985). A songbook also presents over 100 PIC-SYMS, with suggestions for introducing the symbols through signed music (Musselwhite, 1985). No formal teaching methods are presented for the system.

WHERE. Supportive materials are available through several sources:

- *Books* (see Appendix B): *PICSYMS Categorical Dictionary* (Carlson, 1985); *SONGBOOK: Signs and Symbols for Children* (Musselwhite, 1985).
- *Materials*: PICSYMS on cardstock (Baggeboda Press); *Magic Cymbals* software program (Schneier Communication Unit).

SUMMARY AND DISCUSSION. PICSYMS is a logically based set of graphic communication symbols designed for communication with children who are nonspeaking. The logical basis of the system may make it easier for cognitively able persons to learn and/or retain symbols, once the rules are learned. Logical rules clearly help in creation of new symbols. For individuals who have difficulty creating new symbols, even with the extensive support provided, the 800 PICSYMS currently available may be too limited a system. The style of symbol formation has been noted by nondisabled children and adults as being "friendly" (Musselwhite, 1982). However, some adults may feel that the symbols are somewhat childish. PIC-SYMS are quite easy to reproduce by hand, but are less clear when photocopied. The ability to draw symbols quickly and easily can have great advantages, as discussed in the section, *Selecting Symbol Systems* (p. 233).

Blissymbolics

WHAT. Blissymbolics is described by McNaughton and Kates (1980) as "a graphic nonalphabet communication system" (p. 305). It was created by

Charles K. Bliss over a period of more than 20 years, and was intended to serve as an international communication system. A number of factors led to his development of the system. First, because his birthplace was near the Russian border of Austria, Bliss was exposed to the misunderstandings created by different languages (Bliss & McNaughton, 1975). His father was a combination of optician and electrician who introduced his son at an early age to the logic of blueprints and the symbols they contain. As a young man, Bliss was also introduced to the logical languages expressed in chemical and mathematical symbols, through his training as a chemical engineer. The idea for the Blissymbolics system was finally conceived while Bliss was in China, where he learned to read Chinese ideographic writing. The system Bliss developed was termed "Semantography" (from Greek, "a meaningful writing"), and is extensively described in the book, *Semantography* (Bliss, 1965). The first application of Blissymbolics as an augmentative communication system was in 1971 at the Ontario Crippled Children's Centre (Kates & McNaughton, 1975).

Blissymbolics is primarily a semantically based system formed from a small number of basic shapes, some of which are geometric. Blissymbols can be divided into four classes (McNaughton, 1985). The four basic classes of Blissymbols, and the organization of Blissymbols into categories of simple and compound symbols is illustrated in Figure 8-8.

Several factors determine symbol meaning. The most important of these are:

- *Configuration* (slight shape change may alter meaning):

tree	umbrella	number	cloth

- *Size* (different sizes of the same basic shape have different meanings):

enclosure	thing	thing indicator
		▫

- *Location* (relative to an imaginary skyline and earthline which serve to guide the drawing of symbols):

earth	subtraction	sky

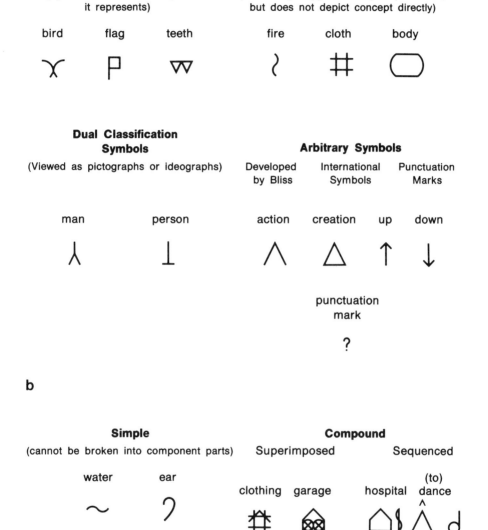

a

Pictographs
(Symbol look like the object it represents)

bird   flag   teeth

Ideographs
(Form may suggest concept represented, but does not depict concept directly)

fire   cloth   body

Dual Classification Symbols
(Viewed as pictographs or ideographs)

man   person

Arbitrary Symbols

Developed by Bliss	International Symbols	Punctuation Marks

action   creation   up   down

punctuation mark

?

b

Simple
(cannot be broken into component parts)

water   ear

Compound

Superimposed   Sequenced

clothing   garage   (to)
hospital   dance

Figure 8–8
Blissymbols. A. Basic classes of Blissymbols. B. Simple and compound Blissymbols.

207

- *Distance* (between parts of a symbol):

- *Size of angle* (right angle or acute angles can signify different meanings):

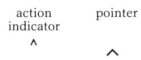

- *Orientation/Direction* (orientation of symbol element can modify meaning):

- *Pointer* (may identify particular part or significant area of a symbol):

- *Numbers* (can be used with other symbols to create new meanings, such as personal pronouns or symbols relating to time):

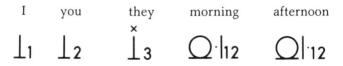

- *Positional Reference* (e.g., direction of arrow, location of dot):

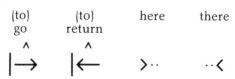

Several system features allow considerable expansion of the Blissymbol vocabulary, including the use of the negative symbol, indicators, strategy symbols, and combined symbols. The negative symbol can change the meaning of a symbol from positive to negative. Indicators serve to identify grammatical categories within the Blissymbolics system. For example the action indicator consists of a small version of the full size symbol denoting "the action." This indicator, like all others, is placed one-fourth of a space above the skyline. Examples of use of several indicators are:

drink	(to) drink	drinks	drank	will drink
	∧	×	)	(

Strategy symbols may be used to change or create new symbol meanings. These include symbols such as opposite meaning, part of, and intensity, which change the meaning of a symbol in a specific way. Figure 8–9 presents a variety of strategies used in Blissymbolics.

Should a symbol be inappropriate or too difficult, or should space be limited, new meanings can also be derived by sequencing symbols and enclosing them within combination indicators. A sample combined symbol is:

community
center

A recent addition to Blissymbolics is *Picture Your Blissymbols* (McNaughton & Warrick, 1984), offering pictographic enhancements of Blissymbols. A functional vocabulary comprising of 312 Blissymbols was designed "to promote cognitive, linguistic, psychosocial and interactive development." Strategies are suggested for using the approach to modify symbols from the full Blissymbol vocabulary to "personalized" symbols, to meet the needs of individual users. Sample embellished Blissymbols are depicted in Figure 8–10. Enhancements are typically presented in light pink, contrasting with the black of the standard symbol.

Four theoretical syntax models have been identified for Blissymbol communication by English-language persons who lack functional speech (McNaughton, 1985, pp. 85–87): (1) The Bliss model, formulated from *Semantography* (Bliss, 1965), includes features such as simple tense indicators, questions and commands signalled at the beginning of an utterance, negatives appearing prior to verbs, and the absence of verb auxiliaries; (2) The developmental model, applies stages of language development to Blissymbolics; (3) The English model, formulated using articles, auxiliary verbs, and function words, allows production of messages that resemble an English utterance; and (4) The telegraphic model, in which the only symbols used are those needed for transmission of essential meanings.

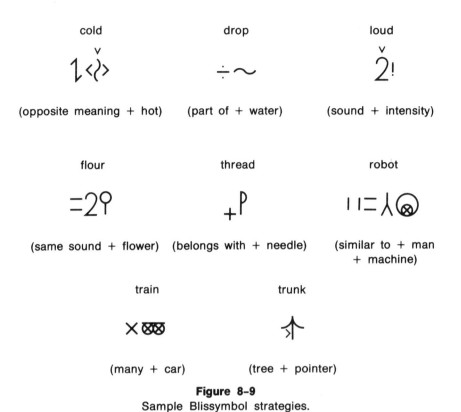

Figure 8-9
Sample Blissymbol strategies.

Currently, several output options are available with Blissymbolics. Symbols can be viewed directly, such as on a communication display, on a monitor for an Apple microcomputer (using software such as the *Talking Blissapple*), and printed on paper (hardcopy of the symbols from the Apple monitor). Vocal output is also possible, through dedicated electronic devices such as the VOIS 136 or microcomputer applications.

In summary, Blissymbolics, originally designed for the purpose of international communication, is currently used with a wide range of augmented communicators. It is a logical, visual–graphic system using symbols formed from a small number of basic components.

WHY. The semantic base of Blissymbolics allows a small number of symbol elements to be combined into a large number of entries. The pictographic and ideographic nature of many of the symbols allows them to be

Figure 8-10
Sample standard and embellished Blissymbols.

easily learned and retained. This makes the system ideal for individuals who are not ready for traditional orthography alone, but who have the potential to learn large vocabularies. Thus, Blissymbolics may be appropriate as a primary communication system for many people who are nonspeaking. Since traditional orthography is paired with symbols, extended use may enhance reading skills, as suggested by case reports (Silverman, McNaughton, & Kates, 1978). However, controlled research on the influence of Blissymbolics on reading acquisition is needed.

McNaughton and Kates (1980) noted that applications of Blissymbolics have greatly expanded, from its initial use as an augmentative communication system primarily for people with severe physical disabilities, to include a broad range of experimental uses. They report that:

> Blissymbolics is being explored as an educational tool for blind, deaf, and autistic students; for pre-reading activities; for remedial reading programs; for

visual-perception remediation; for second language teaching; for concept and language development; as an enrichment activity; and for communicating with students with severe behavioral and emotional problems. (p. 313)

Despite this range of applications, Blissymbolics is not intended as a panacea for all nonspeaking persons and all problems. McNaughton and Kates list both advantages and disadvantages of the system, as well as positive and negative effects on symbol users.

WHO. Blissymbolics have reportedly been used with success by symbol users having a wide range of disabilities, including physical disabilities (Kates & McNaughton, 1975), mild to severe developmental delay (Harris–Vanderheiden, 1976; Song, 1979), multiple handicaps (Elder & Bergman, 1978); deafness (Goddard, 1977), and adult aphasia (Saya, 1979). The following skills are typically necessary for successful acquisition of Blissymbolics:

- Good visual discrimination skills, in order to distinguish small differences in features such as size, configuration, and orientation of symbols
- Cognitive skills at the late preoperations or early concrete operations stage (Chapman & Miller, 1980)
- Moderate to good auditory comprehension and visual matching skills appear to be necessary for use with people having aphasia (Saya, 1979); these criteria may also apply to other populations

For sophisticated use of Blissymbolics, involving aspects such as creation of needed vocabulary items by combining symbols, the user should have a higher cognitive level (at least concrete operations) and a rich experiential background. This will enable the user to understand the logic of the system and its meaning-based symbols, rather than assigning meaning in rote manner to visual configurations.

Thus, while Blissymbolics is "particularly valuable to physically handicapped persons whose physical limitations restrict them to a specific number of symbols" (McNaughton & Kates, 1980, p. 311), the system also has great potential for a variety of applications to a wide range of symbol users.

The audience of Blissymbol users includes, theoretically, persons who can read English. However, English meaning cannot always be determined by reading the words above the symbols. In order to decode messages from sophisticated users, partners must have some understanding of the basic logic of Blissymbolics. For example, understanding use of the metaphor strategy should help the partner understand that the symbol sequence GET OFF MY BOX, preceded by the metaphor symbol, could be translated as "get off my case." The logical base of the system and the small number of basic components (e.g., cross hatches representing woven threads) used in numerous symbols (e.g., TABLECLOTH, KNIT, DRESS, SNOWSUIT) should make this a relatively easy system for a nonimpaired adult to learn.

WHEN. McNaughton and Kates noted that studies are needed to determine the earliest cognitive level at which Blissymbols can be used functionally. Blissymbols have been used successfully with preschool children as young as two years of age (Silverman et al., 1978; Waugh & Gibson, 1979). *Picture Your Blissymbols* (McNaughton & Warrick, 1984) may allow earlier introduction of Blissymbols. Warrick (1985) suggested that this symbol enhancement approach can be useful for students who have the potential to use the full capabilities of the system of Blissymbolics.

HOW. Although a vast array of instructional materials is now available, no rigid teaching methodology is suggested. The application of Blissymbolics depends on the goals for an individual, determined through thorough assessment and consideration of current and future needs. Thus, a very slow learner who requires continuous drill and shows no interest in creating new symbols would require a different training approach from one who learns symbols quickly and readily attempts to create new symbols. Three instructional models for Blissymbol learning have been identified, relating to the language abilities and needs of the symbol user (McNaughton, 1985; Silverman et al., 1978). These models should not be considered to be rigid or mutually exclusive.

• *Model One* — using Blissymbolics as an expressive language to augment a developed, receptive native language. This model assumes that the symbol user has reduced language experience rather than impaired language capability. Blissymbolics is therefore introduced as a functional expressive mode, with use of numerous symbols, a vast number of sentences, and varied sentence patterns. This model would be appropriate for interim use (e.g., a temporarily aphonic person) or long-term use (e.g., a person with severe cerebral palsy).

• *Model Two* — using Blissymbolics as an expressive language paralleling and contributing to the development of native language. This approach assumes the importance of normal language learning, and offers Blissymbolics as a medium for allowing the young child to interact with the environment while learning language. It can be applied to developmentally based language teaching programs for people with moderate developmental delay. Thus, this model could be applied to existing vocal language programs (e.g., MacDonald & Gillette, 1986).

• *Model Three* — using Blissymbolics as a surface communication system. This model offers use of Blissymbolics as a communication medium at the surface level. A small number of symbols would be presented for rote learning through highly structured programming. Primary candidates are individuals with severe developmental delay, for whom limited learning potential is predicted.

Sample introductory programs are offered (McNaughton, 1985, pp. 156–160) for using each of the three models. This type of programming can provide the support needed for a beginning symbol instructor, while allowing flexibility and room for creativity. Several monographs from the Blissymbolics Communication International (BCI) offer additional teaching strategies, as do articles in the magazine, *Communicating Together.*

WHERE. Blissymbolics are now in use by nonspeaking people throughout the world, with support services available in the form of resource centers, seminars, printed materials, videotapes and other media. The primary source of information is The Blissymbolics Communication International (BCI) a program of the Easter Seal Communication Institute, Toronto, Canada (see Appendix D). Specific resources are highlighted below:

• *Books* (see Appendix B): *Blissymbolics: Independent Study Guide* (Blissymbolics Communication International, 1985); *Blissymbols for Use* (Hehner, 1979); *Communicating with Blissymbolics* (McNaughton, 1985); *Teaching and Using Blissymbolics* (McDonald, 1980b); *Picture Your Blissymbols* (McNaughton & Warrick, 1984)
• *Magazines* (see Appendix B): *Communicating Together*
• *Monographs: Blissymbol Application Readings* (Monograph #2, Blissymbolics Communication International, 1985); *Teaching Aids and Ideas — From Handbook of Blissymbolics 1978* (Monograph #9, Blissymbolics Communication International, 1985).

Sigsymbols

WHAT. The Sigsymbol system was developed to serve as an alternate to primarily pictographic systems (e.g., PCS, simple rebus), in which it is difficult to depict abstract referents, and more complex systems such as Blissymbolics and traditional orthography (TO) (Cregan & Lloyd, 1988). The term *Sigsymbol* is a contraction of "sig," from manual signs, and "symbol," from graphic symbol. Individual symbols called Sigs. As illustrated in Figure 8–11, the three types of Sigsymbols are:

• *Simple Pictographs,* used where a referent can appropriately be pictured (e.g., CAT, RUN).
• *Simple Ideographs,* used for pronouns, possessives, and directional or relational terms, following rules such as using blobs to represent unspecified things, and using red (or bold) lines for specific purposes (e.g., for the significant apsect in adjectives).

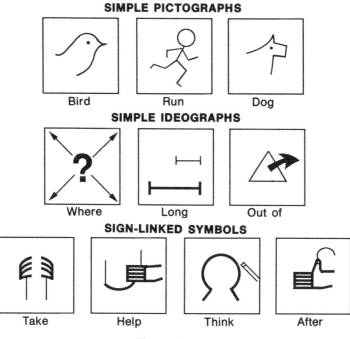

Figure 8-11
Sigsymbols.

- *Sign-Linked Symbols,* used for more complex or arbitrary referents, but drawn with a minimum of detail. Sign-linked Sigs are simple drawings of manual signs. They are intended only "to act as a kind of shorthand to jog the memory rather than as a complete sign representation" (Jones & Cregan, 1986). Sign-linked Sigs in the initial set (Cregan, 1982) represent British Sign Language. An American edition bases Sigs on ASL and Signed English signs (Cregan & Lloyd, 1988).

Sigsymbols, like PICSYMS, are enclosed in a box for several reasons: (1) the box is felt to aid perception, as it is isolated and stands out against the background; (2) opposites are more easily shown in relative scale; and (3) joining of boxes reinforces visually the conceptual unity of a phase or sentence (Jones & Cregan, 1986). The Sigsymbol vocabulary was developed to meet the needs of early communication and language development in a school environment. The original *Sigsymbol Dictionary* (Cregan, 1982) includes more than 350 referents, with the American edition (Cregan & Lloyd, 1988) presenting 352 referents. With regard to the design of Sigsymbols, Cregan (1982), and Cregan and Lloyd (1988), have described and illustrated both general criteria (e.g., decodability, clarity, reproducibility) and specific rules (e.g., a triangle is used as the point of reference in positional prepositions and certain adverbs of place, with red blobs or arrows to specify the meaning). Sigsymbols are designed to avoid minimal pairs, or two symbols that differ on only one feature, such as bold and fine lines. The guidelines and rules can be applied to expand the vocabulary set yielding Sigsymbols that meet the needs of individual users.

WHO. These symbols were developed for a group of institutionalized young teenagers, all of whom had severe mental handicaps. Cregan and Lloyd suggested that Sigsymbols are primarily intended for use with individuals who are learning or have learned manual signs. They cautioned that the decision team must decide whether to use sign-linked symbols or other graphic representations for individuals not learning sign. Other persons for whom Sigsymbols may be appropriate include those with early or basic expressive language impairment (e.g., persons with hearing impairment, autism, or aphasia).

WHY. Sigsymbols were developed to reinforce or elicit signed or spoken language. They can serve as a stable visual cue to support language learning and expression in nonreaders (Vanderheiden & Lloyd, 1986). Cregan and Lloyd (1988) identified two bridging functions for Sigsymbols: (1) from concrete pictographs and ideographs to abstract TO; (2) between aided and unaided communication. Full use of the system would require:

- Cognitive level of at least Stage 4. This is the stage at which individuals have been noted to begin to use aided and unaided symbol systems
- Minimal visual discrimination skills. Symbols are not visually complex, and are designed to avoid distinctions based on a single feature
- Moderate motoric control of both hands. This would be necessary if the signing component of the system is to be used
- Receptive and/or expressive use of a core of signs. This would allow the sign-linked symbols to be meaningful

WHEN. As reported by Cregan and Lloyd (1988), the original population of Sigsymbol users had an average expressive language age of just under two years. They suggested that it might be applied to a lower functional level if initial concentration were on the pictographs.

HOW. Cregan and Lloyd have offered numerous general training suggestions, such as strategies for introducing Sigsymbols, transferring to TO, and adapting for various populations (e.g., for potential signers, replace pictographs and ideographs with sign-linked symbols). Cregan (1982) presented numerous activity cards for training specific entries (TOILET, PLEASE, THANK YOU, FLOAT/SINK), and specific skills (e.g., matching objects and Sigsymbols, answering questions). A revised set of teaching activities is also included in Cregan and Lloyd (1988).

WHERE. Two primary sources of information on Sigsymbols are available. In Britian, the source is the *Sigsymbol Dictionary/Teaching Pack* (Cregan, 1982), while the primary reference in the United States is the *Sigsymbol Dictionary: American Edition* (Cregan & Lloyd, 1988).

SUMMARY AND DISCUSSION. Sigsymbols represent a simple bridge between pictographic systems and TO, and between manual signs and graphic representations. They were developed by a teacher in an applied setting. The symbols are easily drawn, with the potential for quickly adding new symbols as needed. As this is a recently developed system, little research is currently available regarding its use.

Worldsign

WHAT. Worldsign can be described as "a multi-sensory system of communication which takes three forms: a signed form, a written form and a form of symbol animation" (Orcutt, 1985, p. 24). The symbols in Worldsign are evocative. Each symbol is part of a whole concept, and is intended to evoke that concept (Warrick, 1984). The developer of Worldsign, David Orcutt, is an artist, puppeteer, and film animator who used the concepts of multimedia communication in the creation of this new system. Worldsign was intended to serve as a language link for people of different countries and linguistic communities (e.g., the French- and English-speaking people of Canada).

The three forms of Worldsign were designed to be interconnected and interactive. Following is a brief description of each form:

• *Worldsign Signing.* This form includes approximately 700 basic manual signs, which can be used to yield thousands of possible compounds. Orcutt suggested that the special needs of signing for hearing people must be considered, such as a less developed visual sense, in comparison with deaf people. Thus, signs selected are easy to make and to interpret, with iconic signs given priority in selection. Signs chosen also must lend themselves to good graphic realization and effective, distinctive animation. The "kinesthetic satisfaction" in making a sign was another important consideration in sign selection. Signs were drawn from several sources. The largest number came from American Sign Langauge, followed by "Gestuno" and North American Indian Sign. Various other sources yielded a few signs, such as sign languages of other countries (e.g., Japan), and Southern Indian dance mudras.

• *Worldsign Writing.* This form includes graphic symbols corresponding to the manual signs (see Figure 8–12). Two primary types of symbols are (1) pictographic symbols, which directly represent the referent, and (2) kinegraphic symbols, representing some aspect of the way the symbol is

PICTOGRAPHIC SYMBOLS

tree   world   house   flower   forest

KINEGRAPHIC SYMBOLS

some   think   big   to   get/take

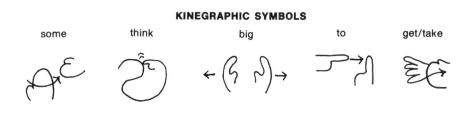

ALTERING DEGREE OF ABSTRACTION

me   me   me   crazy   crazy

COMPOUNDS: SEQUENTIAL AND "WHOLE-WRITES"

same   think   agree   learn   space   school

GRAMMATICAL FEATURES

going   to see   teach + person teacher   houses   our book

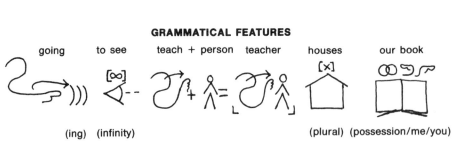

(ing) (infinity)   (plural) (possession/me/you)

Figure 8-12

Worldsign. A. Pictographic symbols. B. Kinegraphic symbols. C. Altering degree of abstraction. D. Compounds: Sequential and "whole-writes." E. Grammatical features.

signed. The degree of abstraction can be altered by adding or removing details. Compounds, or "gestalts," are an important component of World-sign, with compounds presented sequentially or as "whole-writes," in which symbols are enclosed, touch, overlap, or are initimately associated with another symbol. A variety of grammatical features are possible with-in Worldsign.

• *Worldsign Symbol Animation.* This third form uses symbols that are basically the same as in the written form. The primary difference is that each symbol has its own distinctive animation, which Orcutt terms its "ki-netic signature." A different set of rules determines how animated symbols can be related. Orcutt has noted that, in the animated form, symbols can have a time-, space-, and intensity-varying capacity, such as suddenly ap-pearing or disappearing, changing size, moving in any direction, being su-perimposed on each other or the background, fading or dissolving. In addition to animation through film, video, and microcomputers, Worldsign symbols can be animated in live stage performances in a variety of low-budget ways: (1) Symbols can be animated in a curtain of light by manipu-lators covered in black cloth; (2) Fluorescent symbols can be attached to black-clothed manipulators, or are free-standing and are manipulated as they move about in ultraviolet light; (3) Two dimensional "puppet-sym-bols" can be animated by an instructor-manipulator — the puppet-sym-bols would be on individual stands on a table in front of a blackboard, while different hand positions can be formed using Velcro attachments, and symbols such as CLOUDS can be drawn on the blackboard.

Orcutt has identified numerous options for combining Worldsign with other systems, such as using nonspoken symbolic sounds (e.g., a baby cry-ing) with a Worldsign symbol, and using spoken or written words with Worldsigns. Also, Worldsign symbols in either the written or animated form can be combined with any visual image that is recognizable. This allows Worldsign to incorporate pictures from any of the picture systems (e.g., PICSYMS, Core Picture Vocabulary, Oakland Picture Dictionary).

WHY. As indicated previously, Worldsign was developed to serve as a wholistic communication system between people who do not speak the same language. It was designed to have the characteristics of both picture-based and kinesthetic-based languages. Relative to individuals needing augmentative communication, Orcutt (1985) noted a growing acceptance of a multiple-system approach. However, he also observed that the workload required to learn more than one system may be excessive if the systems used are very different (e.g., Blissymbols and Signed English) and not mu-tually supportive. Anecdotal evidence suggests that it may be easier to teach the signed and written forms (of Worldsign) together than to teach either one separately. Orcutt has hypothesized that when the form of symbol animation is added, combined with sound and imagery, the learnability of the signed and written forms will be greatly enhanced. This hypothesis is based on the observation that knowing the signed form enables the learner to have a kinesthetic experience when reading the written form, and being familiar with symbol animation allows the Worldsign reader to imagine the symbols being animated. Each of these interconnections could have the effect of increasing the salience of the graphic symbols. While these suggestions have not yet been proven, they are reasonable assumptions and would be interesting research topics. Orcutt (personal communication) has also suggested the possibility that Worldsign might be used as a bridge into conventional reading and writing for some individuals.

WHO. To date, there is little information on application of Worldsign with persons having severe communication impairment. This system is one that should be considered for persons with strong needs in both the unaided and aided modes. Orcutt (1985) suggested that "because of its multi-sensory capacity and because the symbols used are concept-based, rather than being syllabic or alphabetic, wide areas of the brain are involved in this communication process" (p. 24). This may have implications for persons with left-hemisphere damage, a theory as yet undocumented.

WHEN. The lack of widespread use of the Worldsign system means that an optimal time for introduction cannot be identified. However, the evocative, ideographic nature of many of the symbols would suggest that the written form should not be introduced as an early communication system. Orcutt (personal communication) suggested that a style of the written form that contains solid areas (enclosed spaces) may be more recognizable than the written line style, and should be introduced first. He noted that this enclosed solid area style (e.g., symbols such as HOUSE, FOREST) have advantages for use on flannel boards, two-dimensional puppets, and with microcomputer graphics, further supporting their early introduction.

HOW. The symbol animation form would appear to be an excellent medium for training use of the written symbols. This could be accomplished in several ways. For example, an instructor could use a "live" symbol animation technique, as described previously. Computer programs could also promote independent, interactive learning of the static and animated graphic symbols of Worldsign. Orcutt (1985) has suggested that animated symbols could be stored in the form of floppy discs, hard discs, or simultaneously recorded videotape, to enable each facility to develop learning materials suited to the needs of the learners.

WHERE. A limited set of materials is available to support Worldsign at the present time. For more information, please contact the Worldsign Communication Society (Perry Siding, Winlaw, BC, Canada, V0G 2J0).

- *Books: The Worldsign Symbolbook* (Orcutt, 1984); *Worldsign Exposition* (Orcutt, 1987)
- *Video: Communication With Symbol Animation* (Worldsign Communication Society, 1986).

Abstract Symbol Systems

Abstract shapes and abstract logographs have been developed in recent years. While each of the abstract shapes or symbols represents a word, they are considered abstract because the form does not suggest any meaning. One abstract logograph system (lexigrams) and one abstract shape system (Premack-type symbols) are briefly described. Each of these systems stemmed from research originally conducted with nonhuman primates to study their ability to acquire and use abstract language (Vanderheiden & Lloyd, 1986). For this reason, the logographs/shapes were deliberately designed to allow no relationship between form and referent.

Yerkish Lexigrams

Yerkish is a synthetic language designed for use in Project Lana, a nonhuman primate language research project. A correlational grammar was written for Yerkish, with lexigrams (distinctive geometric figures that function as words) used as Yerkish symbols. Lexigrams are composed of nine geometric design elements (e.g., a dot, a line, a diamond, and a circle) used singly or in combination of two, three, or four to form symbols (Romski, White, Millen, & Rumbaugh, 1984). Word classes are potentially differentiated by the background color. For Project Lana, and for communication training with severely retarded persons, lexigrams have been used as keys on a computer keyboard developed to highlight the symbols (Romski, et al., 1984). Selecting and depressing those keys yields visual facsimilies, so the user and communicating partner can see which symbols have been produced. A computer monitors all linguistic events, evaluates them grammatically, and records them. The computer used in Project Lana can honor correctly formed requests such as "Please machine give piece of apple." The training project involving nine severely language-impaired mentally retarded persons included training within a communicative context (Romski et al., 1984). Subjects demonstrated linguistic achievement ranging from a small symbol vocabulary to generalized conversational skills, with high rates of retention over an 18-month period. With regard to a comparison to traditional orthography, Romski, Sevcik, Pate, and Rumbaugh (1985) observed that while letters are sequenced to form words, lexigrams are superimposed to form symbols. A research study with nine institutionalized severely retarded individuals indicated that both symbol-naive and symbol-experienced groups responded more accurately and more quickly to lexigram elements than to traditional orthographic letters. For more information on lexigrams, consult the following sources: Romski and colleagues (1984; 1985); Savage–Rumbaugh (1986); and the Yerkes Primate Research Center, Emory University, Atlanta, Georgia.

Premack-Type Shapes

The symbols used in this system are different plastic or masonite shapes, each of which represents a word. They are based on Premack's work with chimpanzees (Premack, 1970). An example of the use of these shapes is the Non-SLIP symbols, developed for the Non-Speech Language Initiation Program (Carrier, 1976; Carrier & Peak, 1975). Each symbol has a unique shape, is color-coded, and is keyed to indicate the sequence of the program in which it is to be used. The English word is printed on each symbol. The symbols are manipulated by placing them in the appropriate sequence on the form board. Deich and Hodges (1978) suggested modifications in the use of Premack-type symbols to make them more usable as a functional communication system.

Symbolic Language Codes

This category includes systems that represent a spoken or written language. The most common of these systems is the alphabet. Under this classification, traditional orthography is used to represent a written language such as English, while phonemic alphabets may be used to represent spoken languages. Numerous variations exist for both traditional orthography and phonemic alphabets, some of which may be useful as aided systems for augmented communicators. Finally, symbol systems have been designed to represent either traditional orthography or phonemic alphabets, similar to the unaided systems of fingerspelling, gestural Morse Code, and Cued Speech. The aided symbol systems of Morse Code and Braille are examples of systems that represent traditional orthography, while NUE-VUE-CUE represents a phonemic alphabet. Each of these major subcategories of symbolic language codes will be discussed separately.

Traditional Orthography and Variations

WHAT. Traditional orthography refers to the written alphabet, such as the Roman alphabet used to represent English. In English, there is often no one-to-one correspondence between sounds and letters, due to the frequency of silent letters, and letters that make different sounds in different words. A number of approaches have been devised to provide added cues to traditional orthography as an aid to the process of learning to read. Clark and Woodcock (1976) divided these into *controlled traditional orthography* and *elaborated traditional orthography*. The controlled approaches emphasize what is termed the linguistic aspect. The spelling patterns of traditional orthography are controlled, yielding sentences such as "A man ran a tan van" (p. 560). Several reading programs developed according to this approach are described by Clark and Woodcock. They noted that findings on the success of these programs are equivocal and that "the value of learning to read words in isolation with a de-emphasis on reading for meaning has been questioned" (p. 562).

The elaborated approaches involve alteration of the shape and size of letters, or embellishment of letters, without modifying the spelling. Programs based on this approach use strategies such as color coding of vowel phonemes (Bannatyne, 1968), a *Diacritical Marking System* (Fry, 1964), and *Symbol Accentuation* (Miller, 1968), in which words are embellished to represent meaning, such as adding stripes to the word "candy" (Miller, 1968). Clark and Woodcock (1976) reported that results of research on these systems are inclusive, but that reading ability seems to be enhanced while the system is being learned, with enhancement diminishing as the system is faded.

Even if traditional orthography is not altered, it may be presented differently on communication displays. For example, many displays include the 26 letters of the alphabet, although another aided symbol system, such as Blissymbols, is used. Traditional orthography may also be combined with other symbols to add meaning. For example, words may be printed on abstract symbols such as Premack-type shapes or printed above or below graphic symbols such as PICSYMS. Letter or letter combinations (prefixes, grammatical markers) may also be added to symbols such as rebuses to change their meaning. Beukelman and Yorkston (1977) suggested use of an alphabet-number cueing board, with the user pointing to the initial letter of each word spoken, as illustrated in Figure 8–13. Letters can also be chunked, or combined in ways based on frequency of occurrence in the language of interest, as in the WRITE[t] approach (Goodenough–Trepagnier, Tarry, & Prather, 1982). Chunking refers to combining frequently occurring letter sequences in order to reduce the number of selections needed to communicate a word. Traditional orthography can also be used in larger groupings, such as words, phrases, or sentences. A sample layout for WRITE 200 is presented in Figure 8–14. It includes the 200 most frequent WRITE units in alphabetic order.

Orthographic symbols could be used on communication displays in the following ways: traditional orthography (alone or in conjunction with other symbols); in the form of letters, syllables, or words; elaborated orthography, provided to help the user or partners decode the entries. Controlled traditional orthography would not be useful as an aided symbol system, but might be considered in training.

A B C D E

REPEAT WHAT YOU HEARD

START AGAIN

F G H I J K

WAIT

I HAVE SOMETHING TO SAY

L M N O P

YOU MISUNDERSTOOD

Q R S T U

THIS IS IMPORTANT!

ASK ME AGAIN LATER

V W X Y Z

1 2 3 4 5 6 7 8 9 0

Figure 8-13
Alphabet-number cueing chart.

WHY. Traditional orthography has the advantage of being a normative system and having a large audience of potential users and partners. If the alphabet is used by an individual with good spelling skills, the available vocabulary is unlimited. Traditional orthography also has many applications in combination with other aided symbol systems, and there is some evidence that written words may be learned without direct teaching by pairing them with symbols such as Blissymbols (Silverman, McNaughton, & Kates, 1978).

WHO. Traditional orthography and variations have been used with a variety of disability groups such as persons with cerebral palsy and those with acquired disorders such as amyotrophic lateral sclerosis (ALS). Entry level requirements for use of traditional orthography and its variations would include:

a	about	ac	ad	h	ha	had	n	n't	nd	t	ta	te	ter		
al	all	an	and	have	he	her	ne	ng	ni	th	that	that's	the		
any	ar	are	as	here	hi	ho	no	not	nt	them	then	there	they	I	z
at	b	ba	be	i	i'm	if	o	of	oh	on	they're	thing	think	3	4
because	bo	but	c	il	in	ing	one	or	other	out	this	ti	time	5	6
ca	can	ce	ch	ion	ir	is	p	pa	pe	to	too	ty	u	7	8
ci	ck	co	could	it	it's	j	just	people	pl	ugh	un	up	ur	9	10
course	ct	d	day	k	ke	ki	know	qu	r	us	ut	v	ve	o	SPACE
de	di	do	don't	l	la	le	ra	re	really	w	wa	ver	vi	.	,
down	e	ed	el	li	like	little	ri	ro	rt	was	way	we	well	?	...
en	er	es	f	ll	lo	ly	ry	s	sa	says	were	what	when	!	
fa	fe	fl	for	m	ma	me	school	se	see	sh	wi	with	work	'	's
from	g	ge	get	mean	mi	mo	she	si	so	some	would	x	y		
ght	go	going	good	got	much	my	ss	st	sta	su	yeah	year	you	z	

Figure 8-14

Sample WRITE 200. From Goodenough-Trepagnier, C., Tarry, E., & Prather, P. (1982). Derivation of an efficient nonvocal communication system. *Human Factors, 24,* 163–172. Reprinted with permission.

- Good visual discrimination skills, in order to recognize small differences between characters
- High level of cognitive development, especially if the individual is expected to encode as well as decode words (Chapman & Miller, 1980, suggested late preoperations to concrete operations stages of cognitive development)
- Good spelling skills, if the person is expected to use letters to encode words, with level dependent on the needs (e.g., fourth-grade equivalency may be sufficient for some environments, while higher-level skills will be needed for environments such as college or competitive work in business)
- Knowledge of the structure of language, in order to pair written words with spoken words.

These requirements may be reduced somewhat if the person is expected only to decode a limited number of words (sightread), and not to encode words (spell) as well. The use of elaborated traditional orthography, especially with accentuation of symbols, may further reduce the cognitive and linguistic requirements. For example, Clark and Woodcock (1976) reported that the Symbol Accentuation system was originally designed for use with persons having severe cognitive delay, but has also been used with adults having aphasia and children with severe hearing impairment.

A number of spelling tests can be used to determine spelling level and error patterns. Sample tests are: *Test of Written Spelling* (Larsen & Hammill, 1976) or the spelling subtests of the *Wide Range Achievement Test* (Jastak, Bijou, & Jastak, 1978).

Use of initial letter cueing, as suggested by Beukelman and Yorkston (1977) would be especially useful as a supplemental system for persons with intelligibility problems (e.g., dysarthria, apraxia). This approach has the advantages of (1) decreasing the rate of speech output, possibly further adding to intelligibility, and (2) placing minimal demands on spelling skills. Candidates for initial letter cueing are persons who typically omit initial letters, can indicate the first letter of words that they speak, and retain syllabic integrity (i.e., produce all four syllables in a four-syllable word). Goossens' and Crain (1985a) have developed an initial letter/sound cueing test to aid in determining candidacy for an initial letter cueing system.

Thus traditional orthography and its variations may be useful for persons with a wide range of etiologies. The target audience would be all persons who read the language.

WHEN. As noted in the entry requirements, a relatively high level of cognitive development is required, at least for spelling. Even with elaborated systems it is unlikely that this would be an initial system for augmentation with individuals having congenital disabilities. However, it is often combined with a primary system (e.g., symbols) with the intent of fading out the symbols as reading skills develop. For individuals with adventitious communication disorders such as laryngectomy or ALS, traditional orthography may serve as an interim system (e.g., until esophageal speech is mastered) or as a primary system. The requirements would be that the individual was a reader/speller before onset of the disability and retained those abilities.

HOW. The procedures for teaching these systems would be those used for teaching reading and spelling. The approach chosen depends on the system selected (e.g., training procedures may accompany various elaborated systems), and user characteristics, such as cognitive level. General training procedures have been designed for teaching selected reading and spelling skills to persons with moderate to severe cognitive delay (Snell, 1983; Wulz & Hollis, 1980). The area of teaching reading is primarily the realm of the special educator and reading specialist. The communication specialist can play a role in providing input regarding content, with the intent of transferring reading skills learned to use of a communication display.

In summary, the question of how to teach may be answered in part by considering the type of symbols and the user's abilities. It is recommended that a reading specialist with experience in training persons with severe disabilities be consulted if possible.

WHERE. Primary resources for teaching reading and/or spelling skills to persons with severe disabilities are: "Graphic systems of communication" (Clark & Woodcock, 1976); "Functional reading" (Snell, 1983); and "Word identification and comprehension training for exceptional children" (Wulz & Hollis, 1980).

SUMMARY AND DISCUSSION. It must be stressed that use of traditional orthography for encoding (spelling) and for decoding a small set (e.g., sight words, phrases, sentences) involves very different levels of processing, and yields quite different potential. Use of words and larger groupings can increase the speed of transmission since the user need only point to one entry, rather than a series, to produce a word or sentence. However, this apparent increase in efficiency is true only for words or sentences included on the display; when a needed entry is not available, other strategies (spelling, indicating clues, engaging in "20 Questions") must be used. In addition, the time saved in indicating a whole word or sentence may be offset by the time needed to locate or retrieve it (e.g., visually scanning a display to locate a desired entry, turning to the page of a supplemental notebook containing the entry). When possible, many individuals choose to combine all formats (alphabet, words, phrases, sentences) in order to increase efficiency (the ability to indicate a long entry with a single point), while retaining openness of vocabulary (the ability to spell any word desired). For prespellers, if a word or sentence approach is used, the selection of entries to be displayed is particularly crucial, as described in the section on selecting the content.

Symbol Systems That Represent Traditional Orthography

WHAT. This section will describe two widely used systems that represent traditional orthography. These systems require a higher cognitive level than the language codes previously described because the user must understand that the codes represent traditional orthography, while traditional orthography represents the intended referent. Thus, these systems are two steps removed from the referent. The two codes to be described are Braille and Morse Code.

The *Braille symbol system* is a tactile system invented for use with individuals who are blind. Characters in Braille are formed by raised dot patterns based on a six-location cell. Grade 1 Braille consists of Braille cell configurations for each letter of the alphabet, while Grade 2 and Grade 3 use additional contractions and codes to reduce the number of cells necessary to spell out a word or sentence (Vanderheiden & Lloyd, 1986). Samples of additions are frequently used words such as *for* and letter combinations such as *please*.

The *International Morse Code* is a system that encodes letters and digits, plus a few additional elements (e.g., punctuation, error signal) through a series of dots and dashes. It is basically a technique for transmitting messages based on traditional orthography.

Both of these systems may be encoded by an individual using adaptive devices. For example, interface switches can be used to transmit Morse Code. The individual can use two switches, one transmitting a dot and one a dash. Alternatively, one switch can be used with a short duration indicating a dot and a long duration indicating a dash.

To locate devices or software using these systems as input or output, the ResourceBooks (Brandenburg & Vanderheiden, 1987a; 1987b; 1987c) should be consulted; examine Index 2, which lists products by input and output features. For example, the Adaptive Firmware Card[ap] allows access to standard microcomputer software through a number of input methods, including Morse Code. A number of portable communication devices also accept Morse Code input, such as the Light Talker,[pr] Portable Voice II,[w] or ScanPAC/Epson.[a]

WHY. Braille may be selected because of user impairment (blindness). Morse Code may be chosen as an efficient input system for switch users. For example, an individual who is visually impaired and uses two switches could access a device using Morse Code at a relatively efficient rate, as compared to scanning. With regard to Morse code, Newell (1974) reported that on the average fewer than three operations are required per letter entered. Since both of these systems represent traditional orthography, they would be especially useful to clients who learned how to read and spell before onset of their condition.

WHO. Braille is designed for individuals who are blind, while Morse code has been adapted primarily for use with individuals having severe physical impairment. Some of the entry requirements would be the same for the two systems:

- High level of cognitive development, since the user must be able to understand and use the codes (Chapman & Miller [1980] recommended stages of cognitive ability from late preoperations to concrete operations)
- Good spelling skills would be helpful since these codes are based primarily on traditional orthography

In addition, reading Braille requires good tactile perceptual skills, since the individual must be able to recognize and interpret the patterns of

---

The superscript letters refer to manufacturers. See Appendix C.

raised dots of the system. Use of Morse Code requires the ability to produce two distinct signals, for example by activating two switches or by activating one switch with two durations (e.g., sip or suck on an air tube). If the output of the aid is the code, the audience must also learn the code. In most cases, the device will yield output in the form of traditional orthography or synthetic speech, so that the potential target audience is wide.

WHEN. Since these codes are based on traditional orthography, they may be introduced readily to persons with spelling abilities (e.g., persons who become nonspeaking adventitiously). However, for persons with developmental delay, the systems may replace traditional orthography, and may be introduced when spelling skills would normally be introduced.

HOW. Teaching Braille is primarily the responsibility of a teacher of the visually impaired. Communication specialists may wish to learn to encode or decode Braille to aid in their work with visually impaired persons. The best choice is to take a course in Braille from a college or university. If that is not possible, correspondence courses are available through organizations such as the Hadley School for the Blind, which offers several levels of instruction in Braille. Manuals are also available for teaching sighted persons; an example is the one by Ashcroft & Henderson (1963; see Appendix B). A number of software programs are available for teaching Braille, as located in Brandenburg and Vanderheiden (1987c). Samples are Audio Braille Game Tutorial[s] and Braille Trainer.[r]

A number of resources are available to help interested persons learn Morse Code. The best alternative is to take a course from a licensed instructor. For the name of the nearest instructor, contact the American Radio Relay League (see Appendix D). There are also a number of resources that can aid in learning Morse code. *Tune in the World with Ham Radio* is a self-teaching package that trains for successfully passing the requirements for the Federal Communications Commission Novice license. One area covered is Morse Code, which is taught by use of a cassette tape, with the goal of training use of the code at five words per minute. The entire package can be obtained on tape from the Courage Center. The American Radio Relay League also offers a book, *ARRL Program for the Disabled* (American Radio Relay League, 1985). This book describes numerous equipment modifications for users with a variety of impairments. Plans are included for projects such as an audio transducer for persons with severe hearing impairment, a spectacule-mounted code blinker for individuals with severe physical impairment, and a Braille tactile transducer for persons who are blind. Software for training Morse Code is also available, and can be located by consulting Brandenburg and Vanderheiden (1987c). Samples are Morse Code and Scanning Practice[wr] and Morse Code Drills.[p]

WHERE. Further information about teaching and learning Braille may be obtained from the following sources: American Foundation for the Blind, America Printing House for the Blind, and National Library Service for the Blind and Physically Handicapped (see Appendix D). The National Library Service offers a free reference circular, *Braille Instruction and Writing Equipment,* which lists manuals for teaching Braille, Braille correspondence courses, Braille writing equipment, and a selected bibliography.

Information regarding Morse Code may be obtained from the American Radio Relay League (see Appendix D).

SUMMARY AND DISCUSSION. Both Braille and Morse Code offer input and output potential for persons with severe impairments. Since they represent traditional orthography, they are ideally suited for individuals who can already read and spell.

Phonemic Alphabet Systems

WHAT. A number of phonemic alphabets have been devised to represent spoken languages. This discussion will focus on phonemic alphabets that represent English, since the sound–letter correspondence between spoken and written English is poor. Phonemic alphabets can also be used on some voice output electronic devices, such as the VOIS.[pe] For example, a modified version of the standard International Phonetic Alphabet (IPA) is used with the VOIS 136. The phonemes available for that device include IPA symbols, and variations of IPA designed for use in diphthong combinations or to indicate stress or durational differences. These entries are used in generating synthetic speech. The Wolf[ad] is another example of a device using a phonemic alphabet to generate synthetic speech.

Either IPA or the Initial Teaching Alphabet (i.t.a.) symbols may also be useful in phoneme cueing systems, similar to the alphabet cueing system suggested by Beukelman and Yorkston (1977) and described in the previous section. Instead of indicating the initial letter of a word, the individual can indicate the symbol for the initial phoneme. For young children, sound–meaning correspondence graphics can be added to aid learning (e.g., snake is used for /s/ sound; motorboat for /p/ sound).

Another adaptation of the phonemic alphabet is SPEEC[t] (Goodenough–Trepagnier & Prather, 1981), with a French version entitled Par lē si la b. These systems were developed to increase speed of expression by chunking sounds, as the WRITE system chunks letters. The entries for SPEEC and Par lē si la b are phoneme sequences that have a high frequency of occurrence in spoken English or French respectively, plus a set of single phonemes. These are represented in a consistent, simplified orthography. This syllabary, as it is termed, is intended "to provide an optimal middle ground between the alphabet and word lexicon" (Goodenough–Trepagnier, 1978, p. 422). Two versions of SPEEC are available, one of 256 and the other of 400 units. Each presents the units in one of two arrangements — a traditional alphabetic arrangement and a frequency-of-occurrence arrangement. To illustrate the system, the chunk of sounds SUHN is included in the system as it occurs frequently in words (*son, sun*) and as part of words (*Sunday, person, messenger*).

NU-VUE-CUE provides a multi-lingual approach to representing spoken language. Clark (1980; 1984) has adapted the sound based Cued Speech system (described in Chapter 7) for use as an aided system, typically accessed through eye gaze. The system, termed NU-VUE-CUE, uses a Plexiglas interface frame for display. Consonant sounds (indicated by graphic hand cues and letters) are located at the eight points of a Tic-Tac-Toe arrangement, while vowels and diphthongs are located at the outer corners, as illustrated in Figure 8–15. Mouth configurations (such as tip-alveolar or bilabial) can be represented by color codes on the inside edges of the rectangle. As the system includes only eight hand configurations, five vowel/diphthong sets, and four colors, many motorically involved individuals will be able to use eye gaze or direct selection to indicate an unlimited set of messages. Sound chunks are combined to form words. For example, T + E + CH + UR + Z = *teachers*. From those chunks, a variety of words can be formed including *easy, cheese, church, eat,* and *tea.* A wide range of materials is available to support the NUE-VUE-CUE system, including guidelines manual, charts, a plexiglass viewing chart with a stand, a sticker book for young children, videotapes, and computer programs (for the Apple IIe and the Texas Instruments 99/4A).

WHY. Goodenough–Trepagnier and Prather (1981) observed that sound-based systems are more economical than spelling-based systems for several reasons. First, English sounds may be represented in varied ways through traditional orthography, but are generally represented through only one symbol in a phonemic alphabet systems. For example, Shane and Melrose (1975) noted the efficiency of the International Teaching Alphabet relative to traditional orthography by pointing out that eight different Roman alphabet letters are needed to represent the phoneme /u/, while only one i.t.a. symbol is needed. In addition, a sound-based system can ignore silent letters and can use one symbol rather than two to indicate a digraph such as "sh."

Studies have documented the efficiency of phonemic alphabets. Goodenough–Trepagnier and Prather, developers of the SPEEC system, reported that letter-by-letter spelling requires 2.44 times as many selection gestures as SPEEC-400. Goodenough–Trepagnier and Deser (1980) compared the rate of output in structured speech with a SPEEC board and a Canon Communicator,[c] which uses an alphabetic symbol system. They found that while the user produced more entries per minute on the Canon (27.2) than the SPEEC

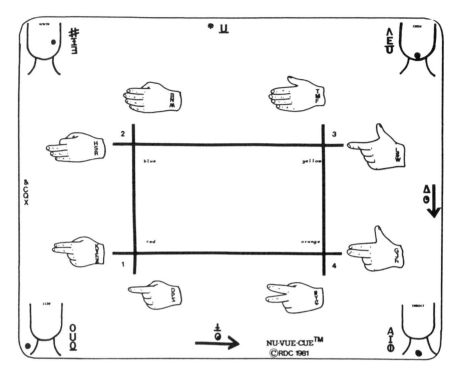

Figure 8-15
NU-VUE-CUE chart. Drawing by R. D. Clark, Inc.

(11.3), the resultant output in words per minute was lower for the Canon (4.8) than for the SPEEC (7.2). Thus, while the smaller entry field of 26 letters yielded more rapid selections, the larger entry field using phoneme chunks ultimately resulted in more efficient communication for the user. The effect of fatigue could also be less for more efficient systems, because fewer gestures would be required. The final determination of relative efficiency will need to be made on an individual user basis.

WHO. Use of the phonemic alphabet systems described here has been reported primarily with persons having severe physical impairment, such as individuals with cerebral palsy. Entry level requirements would be:

• Good visual discrimination skills, in order to recognize differences between phonemes and phoneme sequences
• High level of cognitive development to comprehend the relationship between abstract symbols and sounds (likely late preoperations to early concrete operations stages)

• Good sound-blending skills, or capability of developing them in the future.

Goodenough–Trepagnier and Prather (1980) suggested that clients who have not yet acquired English orthography may be able to master SPEEC since it does not involve the extremely complex set of rules and exceptions found in traditional orthography. However, there is currently not enough data to support this assertion.

The audience for these systems would depend on the type of output. If the system is used on a vocal output communication aid, the audience is virtually unlimited. Goodenough–Trepagnier and Prather demonstrated that visual output from the SPEEC system may be comprehended by reading adults with a low error rate after minimal training sessions (30 to 45 minutes).

WHEN. As noted previously, it is not clear when phonemic alphabet systems can be introduced, though it appears that this may be earlier than for traditional orthography, if use in encoding messages is compared.

HOW. If the phonemic alphabet system is used to generate speech for an electronic device, training procedures may focus on using the system through use of the aid. Training may also relate to aspects of phonemic alphabet training, such as sound blending. A manual for teachers of SPEEC is available (Goodenough–Trepagnier & Prather, 1982).

WHERE. Information on use of phonemic alphabets with vocal output devices can be obtained from the appropriate vendors. Information regarding SPEEC and Par lē si la b is available from: Biomedical Engineering Center of Tufts-New England Medical Center (Appendix C). Information about NU-VUE-CUE can be obtained from R. D. Clark, Inc.

SUMMARY AND DISCUSSION. Phonemic alphabets can be used on both electronic devices and nonelectronic displays. They may provide a clear match between the spoken language and symbols used to represent that language, and can provide a more efficient system than traditional orthography.

Selecting Symbol Systems

The choice of aided symbol system(s) for an individual can have long-range implications. For example, a system that is cognitively difficult may require directing a disproportionate amount of time and effort on symbol acquisition, rather than on learning strategies for communicating effectively. A system that is too limited for an individual's communication development may need to be replaced within a short period of time, causing problems such as modification of displays and teaching of new symbols to represent old vocabulary items. Clinicians are increasingly choosing to use an eclectic approach. Thus, a primary system (e.g., Blissymbolics) may be selected for an individual, but symbols may also be taken from other systems to represent selected entries (e.g., animals from the PICSYMS system). These decisions should be based on individual needs, with symbols selected to reflect the person's life experiences and to facilitate future communication development.

In making decisions of system selection, a variety of factors should be considered. Both Lloyd (1982) and Musselwhite (1987) have described criteria that relate to symbol system selection. The importance of each factor will vary with individuals using communication augmentation. Sample factors of importance are:

• *Acceptability.* This factor is of major importance to both user motivation and partner interaction. For example, traditional orthography is a highly normative system, and would be expected to have high acceptance for cognitively able users. Beukelman and Yorkston (1982) suggested that age and life experiences may also influence the perceived acceptability of a system. For example, many adults will not tolerate restricted vocabulary sets that are readily accepted by children. Exposure to a system may also influence acceptability. For example, a system that initially appears difficult to understand may be accepted once the potential user or partner understands the underlying logic of the system.

• *Ease of Acquisition.* In general, research has suggested that representational symbol systems (e.g., Blissymbolics, PICSYMS, rebuses) are more readily learned than abstract systems (e.g., Premack-type shapes), which in turn are more easily acquired than symbolic language codes such as traditional orthography. Musselwhite (1982) provided a review of that literature.

• *Efficiency.* This factor reflects the number of entries required to yield a sufficient vocabulary, and the number of movements necessary to indicate a word. A trade-off may be necessary. For example, systems that allow agglutination, or combination of entries to form new entries (e.g., traditional orthography and variations, Blissymbolics) typically require fewer entries, but more movements to produce a message (note that Blissymbols may either be agglutinated, such as PERSON + GIVE + KNOWLEDGE = TEACHER, or used as whole-word entries, such as the compound symbol for TEACHER). Several symbolic language codes (NU-VUE-CUE, SPEEC, WRITE) demonstrate attempts to compromise between the number of entries and the number of movements required to produce the maximum possible vocabulary with the minimum possible effort.

• *Flexibility.* Several subfactors determine the flexibility of an aided symbol system. The *adaptability* of a system may be of great importance to some users. For example, both Blissymbolics and PICSYMS are adaptable; embellishments can be added to produce symbols that reflect life experiences of an individual user. The available *vocabulary size,* and the *utility of the vocabulary,* relate to the specificity of message production for a nonspelling symbol user. To illustrate, the *Standard Rebus Glossary* (Clark et al., 1974) includes more than 2,000 words. However, a review of the entries suggests that many of them were chosen primarily for their ease of being pictured, rather than for their potential usefulness. For example, 53 compound symbols are formed with "over." However, many of these (e.g., *overbook, oversell, overwinter*) would be minimally functional for most augmented communicators.

A related subfactor is the *expansion capability* of a system. This is unlimited for systems based on traditional orthography or phonemic systems. It is extensive for Blissymbolics (through use of strategies and combining) and for Sigsymbols and PICSYMS (through guidelines for creating new symbols and use of tactics). The expansion capability of some systems (e.g., PIC) is extremely limited, as symbols are difficult to draw, and guidelines for designing symbols are not included.

The *ease of symbol reproduction* is another subfactor of flexibility. This is reflected by the ease of reproducing symbols with regard to accuracy, cost, time, spontaneity, and output type. Blissymbolics, PICSYMS, Sigsymbols, Worldsign, and symbolic language codes such as the alphabet all rate high on this feature. Symbols from each of these systems can be readily and inexpensively prepared by hand, with or without use of a template. This can add to spontaneity. For example, a partner can quickly draw a string of Blissymbols, to reflect the sequence of symbols indicated by the user, for purposes of clarification, feedback, and sentence structure learning. In addition, symbols that can be hand-drawn can be added to a display while the user watches, greatly enhancing acquisition of the symbol.

• *Intelligibility.* This refers to the ease with which symbols can be identified without use of added cues such as printed words or verbal prompts, and is also termed "symbol transparency" or guessability. Symbol intelligibility may be important to both the aided communicator and the communication partners. For example, Musselwhite and Ruscello (1984) found that a set of 30 PICSYMS and rebus symbols were significantly easier to guess than was the set of Blissymbols for four age groups (ranging from 3 years to 21 years). This was especially notable for subjects under 6 years, 11 months, as those subject groups achieved only random scores for Blissymbolics on a closed-choice format symbol test. The needs assessment will determine whether this factor is important for a given individual. For example, a user who has one significant partner who is nonreading (e.g., a sibling), or several frequent partners who are nonreading (e.g., Cub Scouts), may need access to a symbol system with high intelligibility, at least for use with those partners.

One approach to symbol system selection is to rule out inappropriate systems based on factors such as cognitive level and communicative environment. Then the needs and preferences of the user and the communication partners should be considered to select a system that will provide the greatest possible support. The primary system should be supplemented as necessary for specific entries.

Selecting the Content

Vocabulary selection decisions can be crucial to the success of an aided system. Too often, the vocabulary selected is so precise, boring, or infrequently needed that the display is used only when all other attempts have failed. Kraat (1985b) recommended an "interactional approach" to vocabulary selection, with vocabulary or sentences selected according to the social impact and interaction that can occur. She also observed that "vocabulary selection should follow the development and selection of client goals which, in turn, influence the language units that are chosen" (Kraat, 1986, p. 246). Thus, if one goal is interaction with speaking peers in a Brownie meeting, language units should reflect that goal. Sample entries could be: *"Will you be my 'buddy'?"; "Look at mine";* and *"Can you help me?"* A college student using communication augmentation might have as one communication goal ease of contributing to small-group discussions. Potential entries would be: *"I have an idea about that . . . I'll get back to you"; "I don't really agree because . . .";* and *"That's a good point. I agree."* This section presents approaches for selecting and adding to early vocabulary, with an emphasis on capitalizing on communicative interaction. The goals for the user and communication partners must always be clearly identified and considered while selecting content.

Selecting an Initial Core Vocabulary

The initial core vocabulary chosen for a nonelectronic display can have a great impact on the individual's motivation, and on ultimate success or failure of the system. This becomes a more important issue when the person, due to physical and/or cognitive limitations, can initially indicate only a small number of items. If choices are restricted to "The Big Three," *eat/drink/toilet,* desire to communicate may be extremely minimal. Thus, early selections should be especially powerful for the individual. Ideally, these early choices should represent items or events that meet the criteria listed in Table 2–1.

Choosing and Using Topic Setters

Some individuals will initially have extremely restricted vocabulary, due to physical limitations (e.g., Taylor is learning to successfully control a light pointer; Becky is learning an eye-gaze encoding system that will expand her access; Maggie is gaining control on switch activation). General topic setters can yield interactions that are user initiated, more than one turn in length, and vehicles of partner training. Examples include:

• *Instruction Block:* "Hi! I'm Katie. When I look at a picture, it means I want to talk with you. Please read the topic, then ask me questions that I can answer by looking at something or answering *yes* (by blinking my eyes) or *no* (by looking away). Remember — let me have a turn every time you have a turn!"

• *Topic Setters:* Messages should be of interest to the individual, but generic enough to apply to anyone. Ideal topics are those people have in common (families, homes, pets, interest in TV, books, music). Examples: *Tickle* = I'd like a tickle, but you have to guess where. *Family* = I have a mom, a dad, three sisters, and a baby brother (whew!). How about you?. *Collection* [pictures: necklace, sticker, wind-up toy] = I have 3 collections. Bet you can't guess what they are. Do you have a collection? The user indicates the topic and the partner reads and responds to the message.

• *Organization:* Topic-setter cards can be inserted into plastic recipe protectors and affixed to the laptray, with the symbol facing the user, and the message facing the partner. An alternative is to cut out and laminate symbols on circles with Velcro backing, which can be affixed to a colorful Velcro bracelet. "Spare" topic setters can be affixed to a board with strips of Velcro and hung on the wall. This provides quick access and allows the user to request a topic setter (e.g., by eye-pointing and vocalizing to the topic display), then to select the specific topic setter desired (e.g., collections, music).

Extending Vocabulary Selection

Mirenda (1985) has applied the Ecological Inventory Approach (Brown et al., 1980) to vocabulary selection in aided communication. This approach will be used as a framework, with suggestions from other authors added where appropriate.

1. DETERMINE THE CURRENT AND SUBSEQUENT SCHOOL AND COMMUNITY ENVIRONMENTS IN WHICH THE INDIVIDUAL FUNCTIONS. Carlson (1981) suggested that the clinician, in conjunction with the parent/caregiver (and hopefully, the user), systematically list settings where the individual spends time, such as school, home, Grandma's house, rehabilitation hospital. The frequency or amount of time spent in each setting should be determined, then one or two major settings (e.g., school) should be chosen for further description. Within that setting, areas where the individual spends time should be identified (e.g., classroom, computer lab, physical therapy room,

gym), with one subarea selected for initial vocabulary selection (e.g., computer lab). To encourage thinking about environment, a checklist of sample environments and activities can be provided to communication partners.

2. CONDUCT DETAILED ON-SITE ANALYSES OF THE COMMUNICATION REQUIREMENTS (NEEDS) OF NONDISABLED PERSONS DURING ACTUAL ACTIVITIES IN THOSE ENVIRONMENTS. For example, observe nondisabled students using several programs in the computer lab. Carlson suggested developing a vocabulary pool, considering activities that are participatory (e.g., making a card using the Print Shop software program) or observatory (e.g., watching peers play "Where In The World Is Carmen Sandiego?"). Organize the list into categories (people, actions, places, feelings, silly words) to facilitate selection or words for syntactic structures. Enlist the help of peers, siblings, spouses, and so forth to ensure that items selected are meaningful and appropriate. (See van Tatenhove [1987] for strategies for training caregivers and facilitators to select vocabulary.)

3. CONDUCT ON-SITE INVENTORIES OF THE NONSPEAKING INDIVIDUAL RELATED TO THE SAME ACTIVITIES AND ENVIRONMENTS. For example, observe students with disabilities activating several computer programs. The same forms may be used, adding information, and coding it to represent additional vocabulary needed (e.g., *Move my switch*).

4. CONDUCT DISCREPANCY ANALYSES TO DETERMINE THE COMMUNICATION DEFECITS AND NEEDS OF INDIVIDUALS WITH DISABILITIES. Typical limitations will be in the areas of restricted vocabulary sets and extremely reduced speed. Therefore, some stock phrases and sentences may be added to the list. Rothschild (1985, pp. 17–18) presented an extensive list of phrases and sentences that can be used as samples to indicate the diversity possible for different individuals. She used alternate styles (formal, polite, tactful, direct, jargon), and organized the information into useful categories. Samples are:

- *Needs and Wants:* Discomfort (*My strap hurts*); Problem (*I can't reach my switch*); Activities (*Let's play a computer game*); Outings (*Let's go to the computer lab*); Specific Situations (*Ha Ha! I gotcha!*); Help (*Please turn up the monitor*); General Requests (*Something is not working*)
- *Social Comments:* Greetings/Closings (*What's up, Doc?*); Negative Comments (*Hey, You cheated!*); Positive Comments (*Nice move!; This is really fun!*); General Comments/Questions (*I don't know*)
- *Interaction Strategies:* Initiation (*Would you like to play with me?*); Repairs (*No symbol; you'll have to guess*); Feedback to Speaker (*Tell me more*); Termination (*I'm ready to quit*).

As Rothschild noted, these sentences should not be used as an entire communication display, but only as an adjunct to novel messages produced through spelling or combining words.

Baker (1986) has suggested the Dialogue Method for developing a core vocabulary of truly useful messages for use with the MINSPEAK system. He provided five rules for developing dialogues, that can be used after topic subareas have been developed using Rothschild's categories. Four of these rules are appropriate to nonelectronic displays:

1. *Assure that the Language is Colloquial.* This will reduce the robotic effect of many aided messages. Thus, "I would like to play a computer game with you," could be changed to "Let's play a computer game."

2. *Consider Age or Cognitive Appropriateness.* This goal reflects Strategy 2, considering appropriate vocabulary for a nondisabled person in the same situation. Clearly, an individual with severe cognitive delay will need language more in tune with receptive abilities.

3. *Develop Vocabulary Richness.* A wide variety of words should be used, "salting" the dialogue with useful words obtained from composite vocabulary lists such as the Non-speaker Composite Vocabulary List, NSC-2/9 (Yorkston, Marriner, Smith, Dowden, & Honsinger, 1987). That list represents 744 words that appear in two or more of nine user vocabulary lists. For a nonspelling individual, vocabulary richness should also include descriptive words and topic setters. For example, a child might refer to *spaghetti* as "long red food," or *bubbles* as "round, wet, for playing."

4. *Ensure Reusability.* Entries should be multipurpose, or useable in a variety of contexts. For example, *Want to play?* would be easier to reuse than *Want to play a computer game?*, and *Fix it* would be more generic than *Fix my light.* It may be necessary to use several short, reusable utterances to equal one long novel utterance. Tennell (1986) suggested that reusability can be increased by use of "half-sentences" composed of introductory phrases (*do you, I want to go with, I talked to, what are we*) and carrier phrases (*at school today, call my friend, play a game*). The issue of reusability is important for words as well as longer utterances. For example, van Tatenhove (1986b) noted the need for considering vocabulary versatility when selecting and organizing vocabulary sets, with single words (e.g., run) used for multiple purposes. Blau (1983) also noted that single words can serve multiple functions when combined with residual oral and paralinguistic skills and nonverbal expressions. Thus, the entry *understand* may be used as a question when accompanied by facial expression, and as a backchannel response (similar to "Oh, I see") when accompanied by a head nod. Baker (1985) observed that a set of about 700 collocations (words that often occur together) make up about 20 percent of spoken speech. A large percentage of these collocations are formed by a small subset of function

words, illustrated in Table 8–4. These words can be combined in a variety of ways to facilitate grammatically appropriate, normalized communication.

Using these guidelines, imaginary dialogues can be written and practiced, developing a core of highly functional, multipurpose utterances. An example of core messages, with application to dialogues in various settings, is presented in Table 8–5.

TABLE 8-4
Sample Frequency Occurring Collocations in English

Personal Pronouns	Modals	Auxiliaries	Semi-modal Phrases
I	shall	am/are/is	have to
you	will	was/were	used to
he	may	be/been	to be + going to
she	might	have/had	would like to
it	can	do/does/did	to be + able to
we	must		ought to
they	would		
	should		
	could		

TABLE 8-5
Sample Core Messages Useable in Various Dialogues

Core Message	Dialogue	Potential Intent/Event
I'm not sure	Math Class	"Maybe I can stall until the answer comes to me."
	Eating Out	"Give me a minute while I make up my mind."
	Work	Answer to "Did you get the latest budget report?"
What do you think?	Dressing	"How does this outfit look?"
	Shopping	"Does this fit me well?"
	Politics	Follow up to "I'm against nuclear power."
Can you fix this?	Computer	Switch is malfunctioning . . . again.
	Leisure	Tape is stuck in recorder.
	Art Class	Paintbrush has come loose from holder.
It's too big.	Shopping	Shirt is a size too large.
	Art Class	The nose Jean drew is too big for the face.
	Mealtime	The bite is too big to chew safely.
I don't like it.	Mealtime	"Real kids don't eat spinach quiche."
	Dressing	"That sweater looks terrible with this skirt."
	Music Class	"That's not the best choice for the recital."

5. INTERVIEW SIGNIFICANT OTHERS REGARDING COMMUNICATION NEEDS. Clearly, this strategy should be used throughout the vocabulary selection process. However, it can be especially useful in choosing specific utterances, as that can be quite a time-consuming production for nonspellers. One time-efficient and highly effective way to select phrases and sentences is as follows: (1) Use Rothschild's (1986) category list to select ideas that should be conveyed within a given environment; (2) Based on your knowledge of the individual, plus input from others (peers, parents, siblings), plus use of Baker's (1986) guidelines, develop a multiple-choice listing of possible ways to represent an idea; (3) Present the list to the individual for selection. The option "None of the above" should also be available, in which case the user can select another choice, or reject the concept entirely.

6. CREATE INSTRUCTIONAL ADAPTATIONS. This step involves the actual preparation of overlays or booklets, entering vocabulary into a device, and so forth. The section on organization presents numerous ideas for developing displays.

RESOURCES. Primary references for selecting content include: *Augmentative Communication: Intervention Resource* (Goossens' & Crain, 1985b); "How to Establish a Core Vocabulary through the Dialogue Method" (Baker, 1986); "Training caregivers and facilitators to select vocabulary" (van Tatenhove, 1987); and "Vocabulary selection in augmentative communication" (Blau, 1983).

Organizing Nonelectronic Displays

Anderson (1980) asserted that "communication aids sometimes seem to be built to conform more to the wheelchair tray or needs of observers than to the specific needs and abilities of their non-speaking users" (p. 41). It is clear in observing the variety of displays in a single classroom of successful aided communicators that the "one-size-fits-all" assumption has given way to careful display customization to meet user needs and abilities.
The organization of a display refers to features such as the design of a display, the way in which entries are arranged, and logistical factors concerning entries. The overall organization will be determined by abilities of the users (e.g., using a headstick) and needs (e.g., portable displays for various situations).

Design of a Nonelectronic Display

The design of a nonelectronic display can have a negative or positive impact on features such as the rate of communication, the accuracy of indication, and interaction potential within specific situations. Design features that must be considered include portability, ease of access, and design type. Portability, while of greatest concern to ambulatory individuals, should be considered for all aided communicators. For example, a bulky display is unlikely to be dragged to outings such as picnics. In addition, a display affixed to a child's laptray will have little utility when that child is on the floor watching TV. Portability can be particularly troublesome for persons using eye pointing, requiring creative problem-solving. Examples of portable eye-gaze displays are a floor mount for an interface frame, so the frame can be used while the child is lying on the prone positioner, and use of plastic slide protector pages, with the page divided into four sections using PVC tape — the center column is left clear to facilitate reading the user's eye gaze (see Figure 8-16). Charlebois–Marois (1985) described a number of portable displays that can be used or adapted. Portability needs will often require that an individual have access to multiple communication displays, because needs in different settings can rarely be met by a single display.

Ease of access is closely related to portability. It involves features such as mounting of a display, if necessary. This may be as simple as placing Velcro on the back of the child's display and on the laptray surface. In some cases, it may be helpful to use a mounting system (e.g., the Prentke-Romich wheelchair mounting kit), with the display placed on the back of a clipboard which is secured with its clip to the mounting kit (Rothschild, 1984). A variety of special laptrays or mounting surfaces are described in Charlebois–Marois (1985) and Goossens' and Crain (1985b).

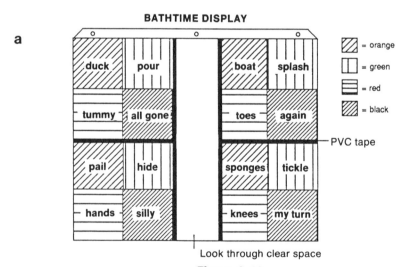

Figure 8-16

Situation specific displays. A. Eye gaze portable display using slide protector sheets. B. Grandma's "Surprise Box" display.

(Surprise symbol covered by Post It Note)

Note: A person with intact reading skills would need to tell the children less obvious messages (ex: "You fooled me!") until the children learn them.

Figure 8-16 *(continued)*

Several basic design types can be identified, each of which may fit the needs of various users, or which may be used by a single user in various situations.

SINGLE SHEET DISPLAY. This approach presents all vocabulary entries for all situations on a single nonelectronic display. While this was the standard design for early displays, current applications typically offer a broader selection to an aided communicator. It is inefficient and unreasonable to place vocabulary needed for all situations on a single sheet. In current practice, several single sheet displays are typically used as miniboards for specific purposes, thus minimizing time needed for locating entries. Detailed instructions for constructing and training in the use of miniboards is presented by Cook (1987) and Goossens' and Crain (1985b;

243

1986). Semi-permanent displays can be placed throughout the user's environment, as illustrated in the following example (see Figure 8–16):

• *Topic-Specific Miniboard.* Carlos, an adolescent with mild cognitive delay and cerebral palsy, used a topical miniboard affixed to his laptray to tell others about his experiences at the Very Special Arts Festival. Items included line drawings and instant photos with captions.

• *Situation-Specific Miniboard.* An early miniboard used by Barry, age 4, included bathtime vocabulary (*duck, pour, more, my turn*), with square laminated symbols placed in a slide album page. The middle column was left empty to allow eye-pointing, and the display was hung from a hook in the bathtub.

• *Function-Specific Miniboard.* Stuart, age 8, used eye gaze to use a joke board, in which joke-telling entries (*Want to hear a good joke; Bet you can't guess; Turn it over; Ha-ha, fooled you again*) were color coded and jokes were written on Post-It notes.

• *Partner-Specific Miniboard.* Julia, a woman who was aphasic following a stroke, used a play board to promote interactions with her prereading grandchildren, ages two and four. This display was affixed to the lid of "Grandma's Surprise Box," with at least one entry added before each visit from Julia's grandchildren.

MULTIPLE DISPLAYS. Vicker (1974) suggested use of multiple displays, which can take several forms. A Multiple Sequential Display consists of a combination of horizontal and vertical display areas. Either the user or the partner can flip to pages with additional entries. Since only one page is visible at a time, each page functions as a single supplemental display. This might be accomplished in a notebook format, with pages pulled from a laptray compartment, or from a flip chart, as illustrated in Figure 8–17. As Vicker noted, if pages are set up in linguistic categories (e.g., pronouns and prepositions on one page, verbs on another), all linguistic categories would not be available on a single page, making it difficult to form syntactically complete sentences without changing pages, which would be laborious and time-consuming. A Multiple Simultaneous Display would allow nearly all linguistic categories to be exposed at the same time, though not all entries within a category (e.g., nouns) would be visible simultaneously. Vicker suggested that this type of display might remind a user to include relational words (auxiliaries, prepositions) which are frequently omitted.

SUPPLEMENTAL NOTEBOOKS. These may be similar to notebook-organized Multiple Sequential Displays, except that they are used only when requested by the user. For example, while a broad range of proper names or photos is often included on a display, observation indicates that most are used infrequently. Thus, proper names, along with other highly specific

a

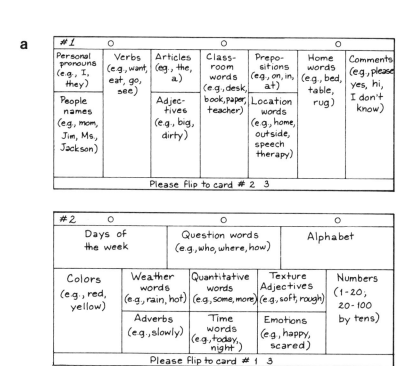

b

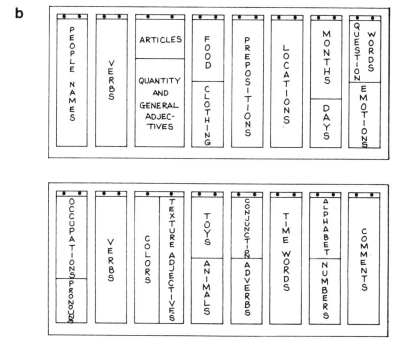

Figure 8-17

Multiple displays. A. Multiple sequential display. B. Multiple simultaneous display.

245

categories (e.g., many noun subcategories, seldom-used adjectives) can be included in a supplemental notebook, with the user requesting the partner to get the notebook, turn it to a menu page, then turn to the page requested.

COMBINATION OF DISPLAY TYPES. Just as the supplemental notebook, by its nature, must be combined with one or more displays, the other basic display types can be combined to meet user needs. Two examples of combination displays will be used to give an idea of the possibilities. Figure 8–18 illustrates a combination of thematic displays, plus a core vocabulary. The thematic displays are mounted on a vinyl backing and rolled into position when requested (e.g., by pointing to a color which frames the thematic display). A Plexiglas grid overlay serves the dual purpose of facilitating pointing and acting as a holder for core entries (e.g., *WH*-questions, conversational control sentences). Goossens' and Crain (1985b; 1986) have described several additional designs for combination displays. The multiframe core plus supplemental display illustrated in Figure 8–18B uses a central core of frequently used entries. Frames reflect supplemental vocabulary needed in specific environments or activities (e.g., church, ballpark, cooking class). The frames can be permanently affixed with rings, or

a

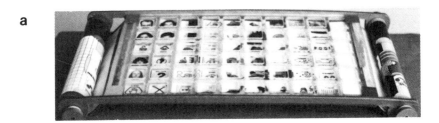

b

Figure 8–18

Combination displays. A. Thematic displays plus core vocabulary (Charlebois-Marois, 1985, p. 57). (Photo by Charlecoms.) B. Multiframe core plus supplemental display (Goossens' and Crain, 1985b, p. 168). (Illustration by Carol Goossens'.)

stored in appropriate locations (e.g., church frame stored in trunk of car), to reduce the everyday weight and bulk of the display.

Arranging Entries on a Nonelectronic Display

As with the design, the arrangement of entries may impede or enhance factors such as communication rate and interaction potential. Several features should be considered in arranging entries.

SPATIAL ARRANGEMENT OF ENTRIES. The traditional arrangement has incorporated a modified "Fitzgerald Key" (McDonald, 1980). This key, developed for use with hearing-impaired children, uses columns with an appropriate heading at the top of each to indicate the most common word in English. Categories in an adapted version might include who, what, where, verbs, modifiers, when, and so forth. An alternate approach would be to organize by frequency of use, with more frequent items placed where they can be quickly and easily accessed. As Mirenda (1985) observed, for individuals with severe cognitive handicaps, features related to visual scanning, visual attending, and motor planning skills should be considered. For example, some individuals may have better success in scanning top to bottom rather than left to right, or may be able to attend to only one picture per page. An individual who has difficulty crossing the midline might require pictures arranged on the dominant side (e.g., pictures arranged in top-to-bottom arrays on the fronts only, with pages turned in the opposite direction of the dominant hand).

Persons using eye-pointing will need entries arranged to promote speed and accuracy of indicating. For example, an early display for use with a play farmhouse might include four groups of four items each, with four subthemes chosen, such as: agents (*dog/pig*); actions (*eat/jump*); prepositions (*in/over*); and objects used as locations (*barn/wagon*). Coding subthemes by location and color (e.g., agents are in upper left-hand corner of each quadrant, bordered by yellow) would allow use of a single eye point in some elicited contexts (e.g., "Who wants to come out now?" could elicit the response of an agent). Other possible arrangements of entries for eye-pointing are described in the section Indicating Message Elements.

SIZE AND SHAPE OF DISPLAY. The optimum size and shape of a display will depend on the individual's effective range of motion. This can be determined by developing laminated pointing grids of varying cell size and recording the size individuals can accurately point to. Goossens' and Crain (1985a, pp. 91–93) suggested placing adhering stick-ons (e.g., Colorforms, Uniset picture clings) on strategic cells to provide a motivating task for assessment. Beginning with small, square grids and moving to larger grids as necessary, the evaluator can determine the optimal size of the display and those locations where no entries should be placed, thus outlining the optimal display shape.

SIZE AND SPACING OF ENTRIES. Goossens' and Crain (1985a) noted that communication displays have traditionally been designed with uniform cell size across the entire display. However, for some motorically involved individuals, targeting accuracy may vary greatly across the display area, meaning that cell size should vary as well. They presented an assessment procedure for customizing displays of variable cell size (Goossens' & Crain, 1985a, pp. 103–106). Another procedure involves placing entries in a checkerboard format, with alternating spaces and entries, to facilitate transitioning from a larger cell size to a cell size half as large.

COLOR CODING. As described in the section "Accessing Aided Displays," color coding can be used in an encoding system, for example with persons using eye pointing. Vocabulary sets can also be color coded to enhance classification and location of items, with standard colors suggested for some aided systems. For example, the scheme recommended for use with Blissymbolics is: (1) white = time and function (colors, alphabet, seasons, etc.); (2) yellow = people and pronouns; (3) blue = description; (4) orange = nouns; (5) green = verbs; (6) rose = special functions. McNaughton (1985) noted that some users may choose not to use color coding, feeling that it is visually confusing or childish. Van Tatenhove (1986b) further observed that color coding the vocabulary set may reduce vocabulary versatility. Thus, the person who is visually reminded that *fly* is a verb (since it is green and is located in the verb group), may be less likely to use it as a noun (that buzzing *fly,* zip up your *fly*), a modifier (another *fly* ball), or in its idiomatic usage (getting late — I've got to *fly*). When color coding is determined desirable, it can be accomplished by using fixed coloring materials (e.g., bordering symbols with colored pens, copying symbols unto colored paper) or removable coloring materials (e.g., acetate report folders), as described by Goossens' and Crain (1985b, pp. 144–145).

RESOURCES FOR DISPLAY ORGANIZATION. Several resources present illustrations, photos, verbal descriptions, and/or instructions for organizing nonelectronic displays. Primary resources are: *Augmentative Communication: Intervention Resources* (Goossens' & Crain, 1985b); Communication Systems for Persons with Severe Neuromotor Impairment (Munson, Nordquist, & Thuma–Rew, 1987); *Everybody's Technology,* (Charlebois–Marois, 1985); *Language Board Instruction Kit* (Oakander, 1980); "Designing pictorial communication systems for physically able-bodied students with severe handicaps" (Mirenda, 1985).

Issues in Intervention with Aided Communication Systems

In her book *Communication Interaction Between Aided and Natural Speakers,* Kraat (1985a) observed that, while there was a continuum of abilities for aided speakers using communication devices,

> there appears to be a large percentage of augmented speakers, both children and adults, who are under-utilizing these devices. They are primarily using modes of communication that were available prior to the introduction of a device, and/or interacting minimally in everyday social and communication environments. (p. 130)

This observation, based on an extensive literature review, suggests the need for training in a variety of areas for both the augmented speaker and the communication partners. Table 8-6 suggests areas to consider in planning intervention for the person using augmentative communication. This

---

TABLE 8-6
Intervention Planning for the Person Using Augmentative Communication

---

Individualizing the communication system
- Modes to be used
- Language content
- Construction/acquisition of aided boards and devices

Acquisition of nonspeech forms and techniques

Development of vocal/speech abilities

Development of language knowledge/reacquisition
- Language comprehension
- Language expression (content, form, use)
- Cognitive development
- General world experiences

Development of communicative interaction/use
- Development of general interaction/skills
- Social development/experiences
- Acquisition of adaptive strategies to accomplish various language and pragmatic tasks across partners and contexts
- Strategies to optimize speed and efficiency
- Attention to interfering nonverbal behaviors

Training abilities and skills for future augmentative systems (e.g., modes, techniques, language representation)

From A. Kraat (1986). Developing intervention goals. In S. Blackstone (Ed.), *Augmentative communication: An introduction.* Rockville, MD: American Speech-Language-Hearing Association. Reprinted with permission.

section will present sample strategies for selected areas of intervention with nonelectronic displays.

The intervention strategies selected will depend on a variety of factors related to the needs, interests, and abilities of the augmented communicator. For example, if the individual is using an aided system to facilitate oral language, the focus of intervention will be different than for an individual using an aided system as a primary communication mode. The age, cognitive level, language abilities, and interests of the user will also influence intervention decisions. For example, an individual with intact language skills (e.g., someone with a degenerative condition) may benefit from a second-language learning approach from the beginning, while an individual learning language for the first time will need to be taught through more naturally structured approaches, at least initially. Clinical observation suggests that intervention with aided communication often degrades to "show speech," with the user asked to answer rhetorical questions ("What are you wearing?"), label objects unnecessarily ("What's this?"), and respond using inefficient modes ("Say it with your board," although the child provided a clear request by pointing to the object). These noninteractive strategies may discourage an individual from communicating often and successfully. The section in this chapter on "Involving Communication Partners" presents ideas for facilitating the interactive skills of partners.

Kraat (1986) noted several *erroneous assumptions* that may be made regarding intervention, with the potential results of each assumption:

1. "The individual will receive sufficient communication experiences, reaction, interaction, and modeling from the environment to acquire communicative competence." This is not true; in fact, recent research has shown that the amount, frequency, and variety of communication experiences and overall interactions are often severely restricted in individuals needing communication augmentation.

2. "The language forms, content, and uses that surround the child or adult and that they are familiar with can easily be produced using augmentative components." This assumption is false, due to restrictions in size of available vocabulary (e.g., a 400 word display) and/or rate of output (e.g., 5 words per minute). Most augmented speakers will not be able to use a range of polite forms ("If you're not in too much of a hurry..."), sophisticated content ("ubiquitous," "phenomenal"), and varied functions (indicating sarcasm through vocal inflection) that are modeled for them. Thus, they may need to use altered content, forms, and functions, reducing the possibility for incidental learning in natural environments.

3. "The productive use of these aids and techniques is the same as the productive use of speech." This assumption is also false. Differences such as rate, vocabulary size, accessing technique, and partner understanding of

symbols all contribute to making augmented communication clearly at variance from spoken communication.

4. "The person using augmentative communication techniques does not have a language disorder or delay requiring special intervention." In reality, many persons using communication augmentation have communication impairments such as aphasia, cognitive delay, or other language disorders or delays, which must be addressed in intervention.

To summarize, teaching from a spoken output model, or focusing only on the technical aspects of augmentative communication (e.g., symbols, transmission techniques, device operations) will not meet all needs of augmented communicators. To develop truly interactive communication, considerations must also be given to modifications in life experiences, the content, form and use of language, the use of augmented techniques, and the specific language impairments of the individual.

Introducing Aided Communication

Introduction of aided communication may involve diverse skills such as (1) how to indicate (training transmission techniques such as direct selection using a chinstick), (2) how to communicate (helping the individual learn various communication modes, forms, and outputs, and when each is appropriate), (3) what to communicate (teaching content, including nonspeech symbols), (4) when to communicate (demonstrating timing, such as attention-getting, initiation, and responding), and (5) why to communicate (teaching the use of a variety of communication functions). Materials are now available for intervention in each of those areas, though they are fragmented and incomplete. For example, strategies for developing a means to indicate through adaptive play have been suggested by Goossens' and Crain (1985a) and Musselwhite (1986a, 1986b). This section will suggest sample strategies for introducing the content, form, and use of aided communication.

Provide Opportunities for Modeling Content, Form, Use

Bottorf and DePape (1982) emphasized the need to develop an "augmentative atmosphere," in which the environment can be designed and manipulated to incorporate components of the augmentative system into ongoing interaction. Several strategies can facilitate this.

OFFER TOTAL IMMERSION WITH THE SYMBOLS SELECTED. For most symbol learners, the opportunities for observing others using symbols for communication are so restricted that incidental learning opportunities are rare. Specific suggestions for providing immersion in symbols are provided by Bottorf and DePape (1982), Goossens' and Crain (1985b); McNaughton (1985), and Musselwhite (1986b). A summary of those strategies is (1) label the environment, (2) provide direct training on vocabulary learning within an interactive format or adapted games, (3) introduce vocabulary through augmentative music (Musselwhite, 1985), (4) provide language stimulation through the symbol system used by the individual. Each of those strategies can be facilitated by use of a stimulation vest (Goossens' & Crain, 1985b, illustrated previously in Figure 8-3). A stimulation vest is worn by the communication facilitator (teacher, therapist, parent), with the facilitator modeling aided symbols as they are spoken. One idea is to present new symbols in this way, making them available for modeling and eye gaze before they are added to an individual's display. In that way, the individual can learn the content (what "stop" means), the form (the graphic representation of *stop*), and the use (commanding the dog to *stop*) of the symbols without resorting to didactic teaching. For example, Norman is a four-year-old child activating a switch to send a battery-operated pick-up truck to the "store" to get some toys to bring home. The therapist wears a stimulation vest with symbols for *go* and *stop* on the shoulders, where Norman can easily eye gaze to them. Other symbols for introduction may include object labels (new symbols representing the toys for selection), "starters" (*I want, Get me*), and descriptors (*big, fast*). The therapist models appropriate language, pointing to key symbols on the vest and offering opportunities for Norman to eye gaze to GO or STOP at appropriate times.

Bruno (1986) presented a modeling procedure for increasing the use of communicative functions in communication aid users. This consists of training facilitators to model use of content, forms, and functions on the individual's device or display.

USE EXPECTANT TIME DELAY. The generalized strategy of expectant time delay (Halle, Baer, & Spradlin, 1981) has recently been applied to aided communication. Expectant time delay, as described in Chapter 2, can be especially powerful when combined with the use of interactive prompts (Olswang, Kriegsmann, & Mastergeorge, 1982). General statements can be presented to give an idea of what to request, without providing a direct model. This can be done nonverbally (pat pocket, point, and smile; hold up purse, shake it, demonstrating that something is inside) or verbally ("I have a crazy new toy...": "Erin has some grapes..."). In indirect model can also be used to specify what to request ("Let me know if you want a turn"; "If you need a paintbrush, tell Karen"). Offering a choice is a variation of the indirect model, ("Would you like a milkshake or a comb?"), with options presented, but not in the form of a direct model. Obstacle presentation, also known as "creative stupidity" or "sabotage," can be used to set the stage for expectant time dealy. For example, the facilitator can make a request ("Eat your dessert, Liz") for which the materials are not available (missing spoon or no dessert). If a direct model must be used, involvement of a third person ("Ask Grace . . .") can allow the request to have communicative intent. Glennen and Calculator (1985) paired expectant time delay with a "structured communicative event," in which the target item or event was shown to be both desirable and available for request ("Slinkys are really fun to stretch!").

USE COMMUNICATION SCRIPTS BASED ON SOCIAL ROUTINES. Social routines are a major part of communicative interaction, and can be used in both assessment (e.g., Cassatt–James, 1986) and intervention. Routines refer to interactions in which children participate in a sequence of events in which the accompanying verbal exchanges are similar each time the routine occurs. Gunter and Van Kleek (1984) identified four primary interaction formats: (1) nonverbal games (pat-a-cake) and verbal games (riddles, rhymes, fantasy); (2) social amenities and courtesies (please/thank you routine, greetings and closings, pardon me routine); (3) description of everyday activities (verbal accompaniments to caregiving routines, such as dressing and feeding and later routines for storytelling and narration); (4) formats and scripts (routines for situations such as mealtime, reading circles, and community events).

MacDonald, Gillette, Bickley, and Rodriguez (1984) presented a sample conversation routine designed to put language on display and offer "slots" for interaction in everyday routines for object play (e.g., water play), people play (e.g., waking up), teaching (e.g., colors), and spontaneous routines (e.g., in the car). These sample scripts demonstrate useful strategies (e.g., imitation and expansion of child utterances) and common problems (e.g., turn dominance by the partner). A variety of content, form and use goals can be modeled within a single communication script, with the child gradually taking responsibility for performing the routine. For example, Mary is a four-year-old girl who eye-gazes to one- and two-symbol utterances to communicate. During a water play activitiy, the script includes the following goals: (1) Content — introduction of symbols for *pour* and *splash*; (2) Form — modeling of "action + object" form (*splash baby; splash duck*); (3) Use — modeling protest (*"Baby says NO SPLASH!"*).

Frumkin (1986) suggested introducing communication scripts within role playing activities. Using this strategy, the clinician would prepare a script for an activity, present it to the client for approval, and develop the vocabulary display. The role-playing activity is then presented as a "Let's pretend" event, offering an opportunity to practice scripted dialogues for specific activities (e.g., playtime with necklace making; mealtime with friends).

These general strategies (modeling, expectant time delay, and scripting) can be modified and combined as needed for individual learners. In that way, acquisition and practice of content, form, and use can take place within meaningful contexts.

Extending Use of Aided Communication Systems

As Kraat (1985a) observed, it will often be necessary to train adaptive strategies to accomplish various language and pragmatic tasks across a range of contexts and partners. The following section presents sample tasks and adaptive strategies for aided communicators.

Establishing the Topic

Topic setting can be especially problematic to aided communicators who have a limited vocabulary set and are prespelling. As might be expected, the majority of topics are introduced by the natural speaker. Sample strategies that can be used for establishing a topic are (1) eye-gazing or gesturing toward a person, place, or object associated with the topic (e.g., looking at a wall calendar to establish the topic of dates and, ultimately, the topic of holidays), (2) indicating symbols on a communication display (e.g., pointing to *boy/little/home* to establish the topic of a new baby brother); (3) using a topic-setter notebook (see Figure 8–19) for predetermined topics of special interest. Often, the needed linguistic or environmental support will not be available to the aided partner. Kraat (1985a) suggested that success may relate to several factors: (1) the mode used; (2) the amount of shared information between participants; (3) the partner's skill in asking information-producing questions; (4) the relationship of the topic to available linguistic and environmental cues; and (5) the partner's willingness to pursue topic identification. This listing clearly indicates the interrelatedness between training the user and his or her communication partners. While intervention may increase the user's ability to set topics, that may be insufficient if partners do not also use appropriate topic setting strategies. Sample strategies for intervention that can affect both the aided and the natural speaker are:

• *Ensure that negotiation vocabulary is available, if appropriate.* Topic shifts may be negotiated more easily if the user has available symbols such as "Can I change the subject?" or "new topic/idea" (Kraat, 1985a). In addition, using dialoging (Baker, 1986) may help to determine needed vocabulary for establishing topics, such as a variety of descriptive words.
• *Provide direct training in topic establishment.* Aided communicators can be taught to set the topic through strategies suggested previously. Partners should model indication to objects, symbols, and topic setters to establish or shift the topic. Barrier communication tasks can also be used. For example, Chuck, an aided communicator, points to indicate symbols on a display with 50 entries. A facilitator selects the topic of movies and shares it with Chuck. Together, they brainstorm about ways to indicate that topic using his existing modes (e.g., eye gaze to TV, point to symbols for

---

Description. Topic setters can be inserted in the pages of mini photo albums, with additional information included on Post-It notes in the form of yes/no or auditory scanning questions. Open-ended questions should be used for persons with access to extensive communication displays.

Instruction block. To allow this system to be self-contained, specific instructions should be affixed to the inside cover of the book:

> Hi, my name is Sheela. Let's talk awhile. We can start by talking about a story in my book. If you turn the pages, I'll tell you which one I want. REMEMBER . . . please ask me questions I can answer by yes, no, or looking at an object. I say *yes* by smiling & saying "ahhh." I say *no* by closing my eyes. Let's go!

Use. Momentos from outings (napkins from Wendy's, church bulletin, "dead" balloon from circus) or tidbits that suggest events (swatch of hair from haircut, tag from new shoes) can be put into the book to tell about special activities. Simple pictures may also be drawn, or symbols can be used. Instant photographs can also represent special events (e.g., child wearing Special Olympics medal; child with pet during Pets Are Wonderful visit). Questions should be written on Post-Its, with answers on back.

Examples. Topic Setter 1: Straw from Western Steer restaurant. Question: (1) Who took Sandy out to dinner? (Nana & Boppy, grandparents); (2) Guess who spilled water (Boppy!); (3) What did Sandy have for dessert — jello, pie, or ice cream? (jello).

Topic Setter 2: Picture of computer screen with hand touching it, labeled Magic Switch. Question: (1) How did Kara make the computer work (put her hand on the screen); (2) What did Stickybear do (climb up, jump on box, go to sleep); (3) Who made Stickybear work (Kara).

Topic Setter 3: Instant photo of Sam making Monster Toast. Question: (1) Guess what we did in class today! (child points to *cook* on communication display); (2) Can you tell what this is? (Banana pudding, Monster Toast, applesauce); (3) Guess what we did with it at the end? (Sam indicates *eat . . . good!* on display).

Figure 8–19
Developing a topic-setter notebook. Adapted from a lecture by Beukelman to the North Carolina Augmented Communication Association, 1985.

long, and *go*). After developing a plan for topic setting, a third person is brought in and Chuck attempts to transmit the topic to that person.

• *Introduce a topic-setter notebook.* While this strategy will not provide a panacea for topic setting, it can help individuals establish predetermined topics. Figure 8–19 describes development and use of a topic setter notebook for sharing unique topics across barriers (Beukelman, 1985).

Preventing and Repairing Communication Breakdowns

Both the aided communicator and the partner have a role in preventing and repairing communication breakdowns. This section will review the role of the aided communicator. McBride and Blau (1985) offered general suggestions for preventing breakdowns, such as (1) using more complete forms with unfamiliar listeners, at least initially, (2) ensuring that partners understand the communication techniques used (e.g., through use of a message block and/or stock sentences such as *Please repeat words as I point*), (3) establishing eye contact to monitor partner's comprehension as the message is formulated.

If communication breakdowns do occur, a variety of strategies can aid in repair: (1) Indication that a breakdown exists (e.g., eye-gazing a symbol representing *Did you understand?*); (2) Repeating (indicating the misunderstood message again); (3) Use of another mode (e.g., moving from gesture to symbol use, or vice versa); (4) Clarifying the topic (e.g., using strategies suggested in the previous section); (5) Providing additional information; (6) Modifying the form used (e.g., *Wait a minute — I'll spell it*). Several of these strategies require that appropriate vocabulary is included on the display(s) available to the aided communicator, such as vocabulary for indicating a breakdown and descriptive words for providing additional information. Users must also be trained in the use of these strategies, through activities such as role playing (see Frumkin, 1986) and barrier communication tasks (see Buzolich, 1987c and Musselwhite, 1986a, pp. 130–132, 144–145).

Facilitating Peer Interaction

An important goal of augmentative communication is communicating with both speaking and nonspeaking peers. The subgoals and procedures for accomplishing this will vary according to the communication skills of all partners. Several general strategies should be considered. First, positioning of partners can influence success (Lytton, Carlson, DeSilva, Glass, Lake, & Pensa, 1987). For example, if symbol selection is made by means of pointing, students must be seated next to each other, while a partner should face an individual using eye gaze. Use of facilitators can greatly enhance successful peer interaction (Jolie, 1985; Lytton et al., 1987). Jolie stressed that "The overall goal of the facilitator is to set up a situation that allows the two peers to communicate independently without a mediator/interpreter" (1985, p. 19). She provided specific suggestions for facilitators, such as encouraging the participants to accept mutual responsibility for the balance of the interaction. She also stressed that each partner must assume responsibility for communicative competence, taking charge of factors such as determining when a partner does not understand, and negotiating the rules of conversation. Adaptations may be needed for facilitating communication between two or more users with aided displays. Examples are (1) using one user's system as a "common" system (e.g., Karoly accesses his display through encoding while Britt uses direct selection. Both individuals could be trained to use Britt's display for certain interactive purposes; see Jolie, 1985), (2) fabricating a common communication system for specific needs (e.g., placing vocabulary for a board game on a clear plastic rotary scanning device which John accesses with a switch, while Melinda eye-gazes to target entries), (3) using a "discussion group display" (topical displays of generic vocabulary on transparencies easily viewed by all participants via an overhead projection; as each student communicates on his or her own display, the facilitator repeats the message using the discussion group display; see Lytton et al., 1987).

Specific situations can be developed for modeling or teaching appropriate peer interaction skills. Each of these situations involves structuring "joint action routines" (Snyder–McLean, Solomonson, McLean, & Sack, 1984) with students working cooperatively on a joint effort, allowing for numerous interaction opportunities. Lytton et al., (1987) suggested that this approach can be applied to teaching peer interaction skills for augmented communicators and their partners. Sample situations and activities are:

• *Adaptive Games.* A variety of action games can be adapted to serve as a framework for peer interaction. As Robison (1986) noted, turn-taking can be very natural in game play. Sample games include (1) action games (e.g., Red Rover, adaptive switch games, ball play), (2) computer games, and (3) board games (e.g., variations on Concentration, Bingo; see Munson, Nordquist, & Thuma–Rew, 1987, and Warrick, 1987 for suggested games and adaptations).

• *Partner-Dependent Activities.* Joint action routines can be arranged with each student having part of the information for a specific project (e.g., finding a treasure; building a block castle with help of nondisabled peers; completing a scavenger hunt). Thus, cooperation and interaction are vital to the success of the activity.

• *Mealtime.* Carlson, Hough, Lippert, & Young (1987) suggested strategies for fostering interaction between augmented communicators and their partners during mealtime. Both group and individual objectives can be set, with a Mealtime Inventory Profile and Sample Daily Lesson Plans included.

• *Conversation Group.* Conversation groups can be developed including augmented communicators plus an adult facilitator (Ahlers, Bortnem, Bradley, & Leite, 1987). A similar group may be set up including speaking peers (Buzolich, 1987b). These conversation groups can offer very specific goals for both individuals and for the group. Buzolich developed a Pragmatic Protocol for assessing both verbal aspects (e.g., variety of speech acts, topic introduction) and nonverbal aspects (e.g., body posture, facial expression). Ahlers et al. (1987) presented sample group agendas for the activities of "shopping" (via role playing) and Wheel of Fortune.

• *Special Events/Activities.* Special activities such as the arts can also be used to facilitate peer interaction. For example, Stuart (1986) presented a strategy for using play acting to develop a variety of skills such as producing genuine didactic exchanges with peers and enhancing spontaneous problem-solving and repair of communication breakdowns.

RESOURCES. Primary resources for intervention in aided communication are:

• *Books* (see Appendix B): *Augmentative Communication: Implementation Strategies* (in progress; contact the American Speech-Language-Hearing Association); *Augmentative Communication: Intervention Resources* (Goossens' & Crain, 1985b); "Developing intervention goals" (Kraat, 1986)
• *Magazine: Communicating Together.*

Evaluating the Effectiveness of Aided Communication

Beukelman (1986) suggested that evaluation of effectiveness be based on all three levels of communication disorder as described in the model of disorder adopted by the World Health Organization: (1) *Impairment* (capability assessment, such as testing to determine changes in visual acuity); (2) *Disability* (assessment of functional communication, such as interaction patterns); and (3) *Handicap* (assessment of societal disadvantage, such as interview of attitudes of partners). Beukelman also observed that evaluating the effectiveness of augmentative communication intervention programs can assist in purposes such as assessing progress and introducing needed program modifications, supporting clinical research in identifying and refining effective strategies, and providing for accountability on an individual or a systems basis. Of key interest will be the measurement of functional communication. Many of the same procedures suggested in the assessment section of this chapter can be used in evaluating effectiveness. The staff at the Non-Oral Communication Center, Fountain Valley, California developed a list of points to consider in evaluating effectiveness (Montgomery, 1980a). This list will be used to demonstrate tools that can be used for evaluating effectiveness:

• *Establish meaningful exit criteria.* How far do you expect an individual to progress in what length of time? With what degree of speed or accuracy will the person communicate? In what way or ways will the person use the system? Checklists (e.g., Mills & Higgins, 1983) may be useful in determining appropriate exit criteria, based on pretesting information.

• *Initiation of conversation.* One of the highest levels of communication use is to generate or initiate discourse and not merely respond. Evaluation of this ability can involve direct observation in natural or contrived situations, using observation tools suggested previously.

• *Number of peer interactions.* The greatest amount of conversation or interaction time for all of us is that spent with peers. Using frequency counts or similar data, the number of approaches or incidents of peer interaction can be recorded. Pre-and post-system results, as used in the study by Calculator and Luchko (1983) may be determined. Performance evaluation measures used by Beukelman and Yorkston (1980) may also be helpful.

• *Serves as a learning tool.* We use language to solve problems, and to gain information and exchange it with others. Direct observation or use of questionnaires or checklists by partners such as teachers can be used to determine the level of this function.

• *Need for a more complex system.* The need for a more sophisticated approach (e.g., extensive message retrieval) or greatly expanded vocabulary is a sign that the system has been successfully implemented. Logs showing expansion of vocabulary or questionnaire responses by users and partners can aid in determining this information. A review and updating of the initial needs assessment can also indicate which needs are being met, and can suggest the need for a more complex system.

• *Expansion of purposeful use.* The use of an aided system for a variety of communicative purposes, rather than a restricted range of responding/ requesting can demonstrate effectiveness of use. A number of checklists or observation forms can be selected for this purpose, matching the tools to the needs and abilities of the user (e.g., Bolton & Dashiell, 1984; Buzolich, 1987b; Light, McNaughton, & Parnes, 1986).

Four questions can be used to provide a framework for the entire process of evaluating effectiveness (Beukelman, 1986). They are: (1) Is change occurring? (This assumes that baseline data has been taken which can be used for comparison.); (2) Is the expected change occurring? (The hypothesis about expected change will guide, and may restrict the scope of the effectiveness evaluation.); (3) Is change occurring at a different disorder level than anticipated? (For example, partners may improve their abilities to interact, so that the handicap is reduced, even though the impairment and disability are relatively static.); (4) Is change occurring that will support future improvment in other levels of performance? (For example, improvement in visual, motor, cognitive, or linguistic skills could allow the individual to move to an electronic communication device, which had previously not been feasible).

Involving Communication Partners in
Aided Communication Intervention

Involving others in the intervention process is crucial to the success of an aided communication system. An effective system will require some level of committment from all communication partners, including training staff (teachers, aides, therapists), family (parents, siblings, spouses, grandparents), and others (including peers, other school personnel, and community members). Kraat (1986) outlined general areas to consider in planning intervention programs with persons in the environment (see Table 8-7). The following discussion will review those and other areas of concern.

TABLE 8-7
Intervention Planning for Persons in the Environment

Understanding of the physical operation, maintenance, and set-up of aided system components

Acquisition of the meaning of signs and symbols; nonverbal behaviors, vocalization/speech; how to participate in aided techniques; how to receive communication through these system components

Development of language and communication skills in persons using augmentation

- Providing social, cognitive, and language experiences
- Facilitating language and speech acquisition
- Providing models and experiences in use of augmentative components

Development of communicative interaction skills in communicating with persons using augmentation

- How to talk to persons using augmentation
- Strategies for expanding and elaborating incomplete utterances of nonspellers
- Awareness of conversational patterns that either facilitate or inhibit interaction
- Adaptive strategies to increase speed (prediction and verification)
- Strategies for handling and repairing communication breakdowns
- Development of general adaptive strategies for interacting with persons using augmentation

From A. Kraat (1986). Developing intervention goals. In S. Blackstone (Ed.), *Augmentative communication: An introduction*. Rockville, MD: American Speech-Language-Hearing Association. Reprinted with permission.

Affective Concerns

Many of the affective concerns described in Chapter 7 are pertinent for aided communication as well. For example, it may be necessary to address concerns such as self-consciousness or the fear that the individual will not learn speech if an aided system is introduced. Norris (1985) discussed the issue of parents who reject organized communication systems for their child, due to a feeling that they can anticipate and interpret their child's needs through "private" systems of communication (e.g., vocalizations or idiosyncratic gestures). Strategies that may be used to demonstrate increased potential with use of a more formalized system are (1) discussion (e.g., pointing out that the parents will not always be available as interpreters), (2) education (e.g., demonstration of equipment, provision of reading materials), (3) simulations (e.g., trying to convey a new topic using only private systems), and (4) observation of a successful aided communicator (face-to-face or on videotape). Support groups can be especially helpful to parents of aided communicators. Norris noted that holding meetings of "neutral ground" might be helpful in building confidence. A group focus, such as learning a skill (switch-making, developing symbol overlays for toys in the toy-lending library) can also provide a common goal that can aid in developing a cohesive group.

Support in Technical Learning

This component involves assisting parents in learning the "how-to" of the communication system. In addition to obvious factors such as learning the meaning of signs and symbols, partners of nonelectronic display users must learn how to receive communication through the system components. For example, a partner of an ETRAN user must learn how to decode the entries and remember each entry to form a message. Individual users may employ specific strategies to increase efficiency, such as point-and-scan techniques, or pointing to category words and expecting partners to guess. Often, "co-construction techniques," or techniques for taking an active role in helping the nonspeaking conversational partner produce a message (Blau, 1983), will be needed. It is crucial that these strategies are clearly shared with partners. For example, an "instruction block" can present instructions for receiving the message, and for assisting in message production. Frequent partners such as parents and siblings should also receive direct training through strategies such as demonstration and role playing, to ensure they they are able to receive and participate in communication interchange.

Support in Direct Intervention

Parents and other family members can greatly enhance the success of an aided program through direct intervention. Their intervention can take on many forms:

• *Facilitating use of a transmission technique.* Practice in the motor skill of indicating an entry can be carried out in play activities at home. For example, a sibling could play a variety of games to help the user practice headstick use, eye gaze, or finger pointing. Numerous activities for using headstick or optical pointers are given in Eriksson (1985), and eye gaze activities are provided in Seery (1985). Many of these games, plus more traditional games, could be adapted for practice in skills such as finger pointing.

• *Facilitating symbol acquisition.* Parents and siblings can enhance the acquisition and generalization of symbols through a variety of strategies, such as labeling the environment, wearing a stimulation vest to model symbols during activities such as cooking, and introducing symbols on song strips during repetitive children's songs.

• *Developing materials.* The sheer logistics of developing materials for an individual with a growing communication needs requires that more than one individual be involved in the process. While all persons will not feel comfortable in symbol preparation, most families will have one member who can develop materials, such as symbols for use in labeling the environment, adding to children's books, and displaying on stimulation vests or song strips, topic-setter notebooks (see Figure 8–19), and vocabulary lists for addition to displays at home or school.

This is just a sampling of the way in which family members can provide intervention support. Additional areas of concern involve the development of language and communication skills in persons using augmentation, as listed in Table 8–7.

Training Partner Interaction Techniques

Aided communication using nonelectronic displays results in numerous barriers to interaction, such as (1) unfamiliar transmission techniques and symbols used (e.g., eye gazing to Blissymbols), (2) reduced speed (e.g., 2–10 words per minute), (3) altered content, form and use of language (e.g., more telegraphic messages with restrictions in specific vocabulary, polite forms, and variety of functions), and (4) altered conversational patterns (e.g., partner-dominated conversation). Partners can aid in minimizing these potential barriers to interaction. For example, a partner who clearly understands the encoding technique and symbol strategies used by the aided communicator will be a more successful partner. Several general areas of intervention for partners will be outlined, with resources suggested for each area.

Providing Appropriate Language Input

The context and content of modeling are very important to the development of interaction skills. A communicative context is essential, with opportunities to communicate about motivating topics and materials. Suggestions presented in Chapter 2 should assist in developing a communicative environment. Goossens' and Crain (1985b, pp. 34–42) have developed a strategy for establishing interactive symbolic communication. A major portion of this strategy involves providing appropriate language input. The illustrated examples they provide are appropriate for sharing with communication partners in printed form or, preferably, in combination with demonstration sessions.

Conversational Patterns that Inhibit or Facilitate Interaction

Conversational partners can have a positive or a negative influence on an interaction with an aided communicator. Research (e.g., Calculator & Luschko, 1983) has demonstrated that even relatively short training sessions can improve partner interaction patterns. Training can be accomplished through a variety of formats, including lecture and discussion, observation of demonstrations or videotapes, and role playing. Table 8–8 presents sample conversational patterns that can inhibit interaction, and patterns that can facilitate interaction. These patterns can serve as the core for inservice training. Goossens' and Crain (1985b, pp. 174–179) have provided an extensive listing for interactional problems introduced by the speaking partner (e.g., a tendency to talk more frequently or to use many questions), with therapeutic implications suggested for each problem. Appropriate facilitator strategies, with numerous examples of each strategy, are suggested by Light, McNaughton, and Parnes (1986) and McNaughton and Light (1986).

Repairing Communication Breakdowns

Some communication breakdowns can be prevented by intervention as suggested in the preceding sections (learning transmission and co-construction techniques, using patterns that facilitate interaction). Partners can also receive specific training in strategies for repairing breakdowns, depending on the needs of the augmented speaker. Sample strategies that may be used are: (1) Indication that a breakdown in communication exists ("Sorry — I didn't get that"), followed by a pause to allow the augmented communicator to make the first attempt to repair; (2) Repetition ("I missed that. Show me again"); (3) Clarification via another mode ("Could you show me on your board"); (4) Topic setting ("I'm confused. Are you talking about . . .?" or "What are you telling me about? Give me a clue"); (5) Alternative form ("Maybe you could spell the first word"). Kraat (1985a) has summarized existing research relative to the prevention and repair of communication breakdown. The strategy suggested by Higgins and Mills (1986) for communication training in real environments is especially helpful in

TABLE 8-8
Sample Conversational Patterns That Can Inhibit or Facilitate Interaction

Pattern	Example
Patterns that Inhibit Interaction	
Talking more frequently, monopolizing the conversation	Talking while the user prepares message Filling in gaps with extraneous talk Unnecessarily repeating questions
Using an excessive amount of questions ("show speech," yes/no, and closed-ended)	"What color is your blouse?" "Do you like TV?" "Where are you going this weekend?"
Talking "down" to the partner	Using "baby talk" or very simple language
Communicating from a distance	Call across room, meaning that partner with nonelectronic display can't respond
Patterns that Facilitate Interaction	
Structuring environment to promote communicative interaction	Position for optimal communication (e.g., move user side-by-side with peer) Ensure that activities are meaningful
Following the client's lead	Individual shows interest in cooking, so interactive cooking activities are used
Providing opportunities for communicative interaction	Take advantage of greeting opportunities Offer choices throughout all activities
Expecting communication/ interaction that is appropriate for the person	Consider physical status, cognitive abilities, and communication skills Allow chances to use new skills, but don't expect use of skills above current levels
Attending to the individual until the interaction is completed	Make user the focus of attention, ignore distractions, appropriately end interaction
Pacing interaction	Allow sufficient pause time/look expectant
Prompting	Signal for turntaking using minimally intrusive prompts (gestural: questioning facial expression; verbal: "what next?")
Providing appropriate language input	Use language that is appropriate to user's receptive skills; provide support through facial expression, body language, gesture
Providing models for user's expressive communication mode	Point to symbols on user's display Pointing to objects in environment

Adapted from Goossens' and Crain (1985b), McNaughton and Light (1986), and Light, McNaughton, and Parnes (1986).

teaching augmented communicators and their partners how to deal with communication breakdowns. That strategy incorporates a "buddy," or a facilitator who can intervene when communication breakdowns occur to ensure message completion. This can provide direct benefit in increasing successful completion of interactions, thus enhancing motivation for both the aided communicator and the partners. In addition, partners will observe appropriate strategies for repairing breakdowns, which can be used in future interactions. Major interaction problems (e.g., insufficient vocabulary to repair breakdowns) can also be identified by the buddy and modified as appropriate.

Facilitating Communication in Mainstream Settings

When an individual using communication augmentation is in a mainstream setting, appropriate partner training can be logistically difficult, however, such training is closely related to communicative success. This is especially true in settings where partners do not know the individual, and are not familiar with his or her communication system. Hill, Bennett, and Pistell (1985) have prepared an article that can be shared with communication partners. They suggest interaction strategies for several areas: (1) One-to-one communication (e.g., speak normally, let the speaking-disabled person know when you do not understand); (2) Group communication in academic settings (e.g., group members who are experienced listeners can interpret, or a member can read a prepared message aloud); (3) Group communication in social settings (e.g., avoid talking "in front of" or "for" the individual); (4) Course work (e.g., assist the speaking-disabled person with reading or note-taking).

Chapter 9
Technology for Aided Communication

If you can't explain it simply, you don't understand it well enough.
— Albert Einstein

Technology, although it is exciting and may expand horizons for many aided communicators, must be viewed in perspective. The interrelatedness of technology and issues such as nonelectronic displays, vocabulary selection, and interaction training should always be considered. Thus, most of the issues discussed in previous chapters will apply to the selection and application of appropriate technology.

It must be stressed that modifications in devices occur frequently, and that the array of devices on the market varies from year to year as well as from country to country. The devices illustrated in this chapter are included to provide samples of important features. While the devices will be upgraded or discontinued, the features for consideration will continue to be important.

Another issue that should be addressed at this point is that of computer use in augmentative communication. As Fishman (1987) observed, the distinction between "computers" and "dedicated speech devices" is being minimized as many augmentative devices are based on microcomputers (e.g., Words + Equalizer in Datavue computer)[w].

Superscript letters refer to manufactuers and distributors. See Appendix C for names and addresses.

Microcomputers can also be used for simulation of augmentative devices and training of augmentative device use. A wide range of materials is available in microcomputer use relative to augmentative communication. For more information, refer to the following books annotated in Appendix B (Behrmann, 1984; Burkhart, 1987; Brandenburg & Vanderheiden, 1987c; Hutinger, 1986; Wright & Nomura, 1985) and organizations: Activating Children Through Technology (ACTT); Closing the Gap; LINC Resources (see Appendix D for addresses).

There has been a recent shift of focus toward choosing a multi-component system based on a determination of individual needs, rather than on an examination of the features inherent in various devices (Beukelman, Yorkston, & Dowden, 1985; Vanderheiden, 1987). This chapter will approach exploration of technology for augmentative and alternative communication from a needs orientation.

Assessment for Aided Technology

Consistent with a needs orientation is development of a needs profile, such as the one provided by Beukelman, Yorkston, and Dowden (1985; see Chapter 7 in this book for a summary), Vagnini (1984), or the Multi-Component Communication Checklist reprinted in Table 1-1 of this book (from Vanderheiden & Lloyd, 1986). Beukelman and associates (1985, p. 8) suggested an interview approach, asking a series of questions relative to the needs statements:

1. Is the need currently being met satisfactorily by another approach? For example, the need to signal answers to yes-or-no questions is often met by head nods rather than by an augmentative device.
2. Is the need a mandatory one? If the answer is "yes," priority is given to finding a device that meets that need.
3. Is the need desirable but not mandatory? If the answer is "yes," a lower priority is given to meeting that need.
4. Is the need unimportant? If the answer is "yes," the need is no longer considered in system selection.
5. In the forseeable future might this need become mandatory?

Matching of the user and device is a formidable task that must be carried out using a team approach. A one-shot evaluation will have limited success for most individuals, due to variation caused by factors such as fatigue, novelty of the device, unfamiliar partners, and unfamiliar environment. Both current and future needs must be considered in the matching process. Kraat (1985b) outlined a three-phase process that can provide structure to a potentially overwhelming task. The three phases are:

• *Phase I — Augmentative Communication Evaluation.* This phase must determine the abilities and needs of both the individual and the environment. For example, user abilities to be considered are current modes used, controlled movement in various physical positions, and functional vision and hearing. Sample abilities of importance for primary and secondary partners include reading and spelling skills, vision and hearing, and attitudes regarding augmentative communication. Assessment tools for determining abilities are described in appropriate sections of Chapter 8 and this chapter. Sample user needs to be determined are those covered in the Beukelman and associates (1985) needs list. Needs for the partners include the type of communication they would like with the individual, and time or availability limitations.

• *Phase II — Selecting Electronic Aids for Trial Evaluation.* For persons found appropriate for electronic aid use, desired features should be compared to features available on various aids. The team will begin by considering all available aids, and will develop a list of potentially useful aids for the individual. Five major categories of features should be compared: (1) *Technique* (e.g., direct selection); (2) *Non-speech form* (e.g., symbols, sight words, spelling, access to prepared sentences); (3) *Outputs* (e.g., speech, printed); (4) *Portability* (e.g., battery-operated); and (5) *Special features* (e.g., training required and its availability). Each of these areas will be discussed later in this chapter.

• *Phase III — Assessment/Selection Process.* This phase involves assessment of the abilities of the user and the environment with regard to the specific techniques and devices under consideration. Can the user use and understand specific aid features such as codes and operation of levels? Are support services available for training and maintenance? Devices that are of greatest potential should be given trial use by the individual, with the "goodness of fit" determined, and the best match selected.

This condensed framework can be used in conjunction with information listing the features of communication devices under consideration. The chart "Features of commercially available communication devices" in Kraat and Sitver-Kogut (1985) is especially useful for that purpose. That chart lists devices according to all of the primary features. Other resources that can aid in determining features are *Communication, control, and computer access for disabled and elderly individuals* (Brandenburg & Vanderheiden, 1987a; 1987b; 1987c); and *Express yourself: Communication disabilities need not be handicaps* (Johnson, 1987). Computer simulation may also assist in device selection. For example, the Augmentative Communication Evaluation System^w program includes microcomputer hardware and software designed to simulate a range of electronic communication devices. In-depth information regarding specific devices can be obtained from vendors (see Appendix C).

Components of Communication Devices
Matched to User Needs

As described previously, Kraat (1985b) has identified five categories of features needed by an individual that can be matched to features of available aids. For ease of consideration, each of those feature categories will be discussed separately, although the potential for interrelatedness between and among categories should be remembered.

Transmission Techniques for Indicating Message Elements

This area involves the means of indicating, accessing the system, system control, or transmission techniques. Many factors must be considered when choosing the most appropriate transmission technique for an individual, after which a device with input capability can be selected.

Positioning

The positioning of an individual can have a major impact on the ease, consistency, and accuracy with which a transmission technique can be used. Thus, positioning is an important part of the needs assessment. If the transmission technique chosen (e.g., direct selection) can only be used when the person is in an adaptive chair, a secondary technique (e.g., encoding through eye gaze) will often need to be developed to meet communication needs in positions such as in bed or lying on the floor. Resources for assessing and intervening with positioning were presented in Chapter 4 of this book.

Overview of Transmission Techniques

With regard to input techniques for electronic devices, two basic types of input are used, direct selection and scanning. Encoding will be considered as part of the system process, to be discussed in another section.

DIRECT SELECTION. Many of the aspects of direct selection covered in Chapter 8, such as body parts used and potential accessing tools, apply to electronic as well as nonelectronic devices. However, some aspects differentiate the two. For example, not all techniques used in nonelectronic boards (e.g., encoding by eye-gazing to an etran display) can be transferred to electronic devices. Electronic devices also require either some degree of pressure (as with a key or membrane square) or use of an external indicator or activator (such as a magnet or LED sensor). Examples of widely used devices with various direct selection features are: Alltalk,[a] Special Friend,[sp] Touch Talker,[pr] VOIS 136[pe] (various size membrane squares); Cannon Communicator M[c] (medium size keys); Light Talker[pr] and lightpointer version of ACS SpeechPAC/Epson[a] (optical headpointer). Expanded direct selection displays are also available with computers (e.g., Unicorn Keyboard) and with portable communication devices (e.g., Words + Portable Voice II.[w]). Direct eye gaze is also possible, with the user gazing at entries, and with eye position "read" by the device (Eye Typer Model 300[ss]). See Figure 9-1.

A less obvious difference between electronic and nonelectronic devices is that an electronic device does not make allowances for "almost" activating the appropriate target. For example, assume that Pierre uses gross pointing skills, with the partner determining the desired item by context and experience cues. With an electronic device, this gross approximation could cause him to make frequent inappropriate activations, with resulting breakdowns in communication. Thus, in addition to range of motion and targeting skills, assessment for direct selection of electronic devices must consider factors such as ability to produce and maintain pressure for an appropriate time (but, in some cases, not long enough to reactivate the key), need for accessing tools, and need for grids to improve accuracy.

RESOURCES. In addition to the general information on direct selection reviewed in Chapter 8, information on electronic use of direct selection with electronic devices can be found in *Electronic communication aids* (Fishman, 1987), and "Communication systems and their components" (Vanderheiden & Lloyd, 1986).

SCANNING. While scanning with nonelectronic displays is partner-assisted, scanning with electronic displays is typically independent, with the user activating an interface switch to signal a choice. Scanning can be divided into several categories:

• *Linear Scanning.* With this pattern, items are scanned one at a time until the user indicates the desired item. Rotating pointers, such as the Dial Scan[d] or Communiclock[k] use linear scanning, with the pointer advancing item by item. As Vanderheiden and Lloyd (1986) observed, once the number of choices is greater than 16, this approach is too time-consuming, as the user spends excessive time waiting while the device indicates the wrong choices, before the target is reached.

• *Group Item Scanning.* The most widely used group-item pattern is row–column scanning. For this technique, the user first indicates the desired row (the one including the target item). Items in that row are then

a

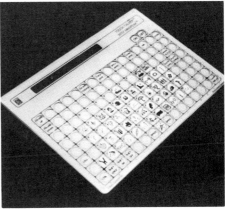

b

c

d

Figure 9-1

Samples of direct selection devices. A. Alltalk (Photo by Adaptive Communication Systems, Inc.). B. Touch Talker. C. Light Talker (Photos by Prentke Romich Company). D. ACS Speech PAC/Epson with optical head pointer (Photo by Adaptive Communication Systems, Inc).

e

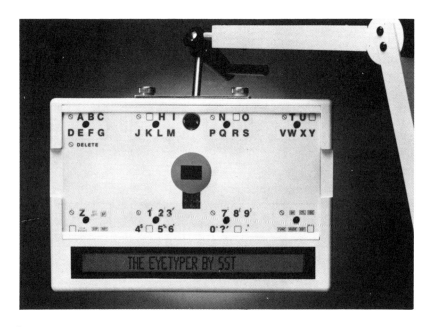

f

Figure 9-1 *(continued)*
E. Words+ Portable Voice II (Photo by Adaptive Communication Systems, Inc.).
F. Eye Typer 300 (Photo by Sentient Systems Technology, Inc.).

presented in sequence until the user selects the target item. Samples of devices that can use this technique are the Light Talker,[pr] Special Friend[sp] (Scanning version), ACS SpeechPAC[a] (Scan version), and Scan Writer.[z] Branching type matrices also use the group-item pattern. For example, the *Audio Scan* software program[d] groups items according to vocabularies (e.g., conversation, spelling), with categories listed under each vocabulary (e.g., under conversation, the categories might be greetings, follow-up, repairs, and so forth), while the *Message Maker* software program[b] groups words and phrases under corresponding letters of the alphabet.

• *Directed Scanning.* For this pattern of scanning, both the type or direction of movement and the timing of the movement influence item selection. For example, a joystick or an armslot control might be used to move the indicator up, down, left, right, or diagonally, with the user activating a switch to make the selection when the indicator is over the target item. Samples of devices that use this pattern are Light Talker,[pr] Scan Writer,[z] and Special Friend (scanning version).[sp] Variations can be made in switching functions or arrangement of items to make scanning more efficient. For example, with a step scanning pattern, a switch activation is required to move the indicator from each item to the next. With a latched scanning motion, the indicator will begin automatic scanning when the switch is activated, and will terminate scanning with the switch is released. Frequency of occurrence information can also improve efficiency of scanning. For example, the scanning version of the ACS SpeechPAC[a] uses a rearranged alphabet. See Figure 9-2.

Overview of Interface Switches

A switch can act as an interface between a user and a device. Switches used with communication devices are typically operated through momentary contact (Fishman, 1987). The switch is normally open, with switch closure following some type of activation from the user. When the activating force is removed, the switch returns to the open condition.

Switches can be differentiated according to the means of input (the type of activation). Table 9-1 lists the eight input types identified by Brandenburg and Vanderheiden (1987b), with a brief description and example of each input feature. Switches can also be differentiated according to output features (i.e., single switch, dual switch, joystick, or multiple switches). The Brandenburg and Vanderheiden resource book lists switches by both input and output features.

A number of other features should be considered with regard to interface switch selection. Kraat (1985) and Williams, Csongradi, and LeBlanc (1982) have identified additional features of potential importance: (1) Type and size of activating surface (push button, lever, touch plate); (2) Resis-

a

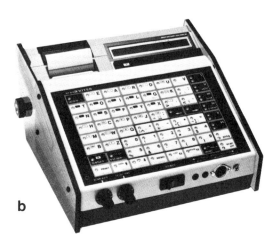

b

c

d

Figure 9-2

Samples of scanning devices. A. Dial Scan (Photo by Don Johnston Developmental Equipment, Inc.). B. Scanwriter (Photo courtesy of ZYGO Industries, Inc.). C. Special Friend, scanning version (Photo by Shea Products, Inc.). D. ACS SpeechPAC, rearranged keyboard (Photo by Adaptive Communication Systems, Inc.).

TABLE 9-1
Types of Input Switches

Input Type	Description	Examples
Air (Sip Puff)	Activation by intake/outflow of air; some versions allow dual activation	Pneumatic Switch[pr,t,z] Sip & Puff[k]
Contact (Zero Pressure)	Activation by skin contact or slight muscle movement	Cylindrical Touch[t] P-Switch[pr]
Eye Movement/ Eye Gaze	Reflection of an infrared beam closes switch; mounted on eyeglass frame	Infrared Switch[w]
Joystick/ Wobblestick	Movement in various directions causes activation of multiple switches	4-switch Joystick[z] PRC Joystick[pr]
Light Sensitive	Activation by light beam interruption	Photo Cell Switch[k]
Movement Activated	Movement of body part out of resting position causes switch activation	Eyebrow Switch[w] Tilt Switch[k]
Noise (Sound or Vocalization)	Detection of noise by a microphone causes switch activation	Voice Activated[k]
Pressure Sensitive	Varying degrees of pressure (less than 30 grams to more than 6 ounces) yields switch activation	Button Switch[k,t] Leaf Switch[k,t,z] Mounting Switch[d] Plate Switch[d,k,t,z]

List of switch input types from Brandenburg and Vanderheiden (1987b).
Superscript letter codes refer to vendors listed in Appendix C.

tance and pressure required; (3) Degree of movement required (the travel necessary for activation); (4) Type of movement required (e.g., pressure push versus turn/tilt of wrist or head); (5) Ease of placement (relative to body part and movement); (6) Feedback, including auditory (e.g., click), visual (e.g., degree of travel), or somatosensory (e.g., feel of surface or movement).

Mounting of Devices and Interface Switches

Mounting refers to positioning of a communication device or interface switch and attaching it to a foundation (laptray, desk, wheelchair frame) in some manner (Fishman, 1987). Appropriate mounting is crucial if a switch and/or device is to be accessed efficiently, effectively, and independently. As Fishman noted, even a device that is intended to be portable may be used as a desk-top stationary aid, because most caregivers will be unable to carry the device everywhere the user goes.

Mounting systems may be either commercial or customized (Fishman, 1987). For example, commercial mounting kits, including components such as wheelchair clamps, couplings, rods, and goosenecks. Goossens' and Crain (1985a, pp. 127–131) have provided a listing of commercially available mounting hardware. Custom-made equipment can include components from medical supply catalogues, as well as camera, music, and hardware stores (see Goossens' & Crain, in press).

Assessment and Selection of Interface Switches for a Scanning Technique

The user needs and abilities will determine the optimal choice of interface switch, control site, scanning pattern, and mounting. Goossens' and Crain (1985a, pp. 107–112) described a systematic single-input control assessment developed at the Hugh McMillan Medical Center in Toronto, Ontario. This includes two components: a clinical component designed to delineate three options, and a computer-assisted component designed to systematically and objectively evaluate the user's performance. Four key factors (abbreviated MSIP) are evaluated in the clinical component.

1. *M = Movement* (e.g., head movement such as lateral, tilt, flexion, extension, eyebrow raise)
2. *S = Control Site* (e.g., relative to head, could be top, eyebrow, chin, cheek, temple, back of head)
3. *I = Switch Interface* (varying on the input type and features listed previously, such as size and feedback)
4. *P = Positioning of Switch Interface* (e.g., chin mount attached to chest or affixed to wheelchair frame)

From this, three selected MSIPs are selected, then evaluated according to three different functional computer tasks, with a single-input control selected on the basis of performance data. The software program used is Single-Input Control Assessment.[d] This program is merely an example of available materials to support switch selection. Additional hardware (e.g., Ability Switch Tester[t]), software (e.g., Single Switch Assessment Program) and hardware/software combinations (e.g., Augmentative Communication Evaluation System[w]) are available for assessing switch use. These materials can be located by referring to cross-listings (e.g., assessment software) in Brandenburg and Vanderheiden (1987a, 1987b, 1987c).

Once the appropriate movement, site, interface, and position have been determined, the switch must be mounted. Williams and associates

(1982) developed guidelines for designing and assessing a mounting system for an interface switch, and Fishman (1987) summarized those guidelines. They are presented in Table 9-2. Goossens' and Crain (1985a, pp. 113–126) provided assessment and construction strategies for determining the optimal format for a laptray-mounted switches, including recessed switch mounts.

The most appropriate scanning pattern for an individual must also be determined, based on individual abilities and needs. For example, the user with only one controlled movement will be restricted to a linear or row-column scanning (though single switch Morse Code can be used if duration can be controlled). With two controlled movements, two way directed scan or two-switch Morse Code are also options, while ability to use multiple movements allows use of directed scan or multiple switches. Software

---

TABLE 9-2
Guidelines for Designing and Assessing a Mounting System

---

1. Identify What the Adaptive Fixture Needs to Do Based on an Evaluation for Identifying an Appropriate Control (e.g., activate a dedicated communication device, interface with a microcomputer, provide environmental control).

2. Identify Physical and Environmental Constraints.
   a. Does the user's range of movement limit potential placement?
   b. Does fixture need to be removable?
   c. Does fixture need to be adjustable?
   d. What characteristics such as aesthetics, are important to the user?
   e. How strong does the fixture need to be?
   f. How must the adaptive fixture fit into the user's existing scheme of assistive devices and environment (must not interfere).

3. Identify Possible Foundation for Attachment of the Fixture (e.g., table top, wheelchair frame, bed post).

4. Identify Possible Fixtures (components to create connector between foundation and switch).

5. Identify Method of Attachment of Fixture to Switch.

6. Evaluate Identified System. Take into Account the Considerations Listed Above, and the Following:
   a. Does the adaptive switch obscure transfers?
   b. Does it increase the overall width of the wheelchair and perhaps interfere with ability to manipulate chair in restricted areas?
   c. Does it create an appendage that can interfere with mobility?
   d. Is the fixture strong enough?
   e. Does it need to be easily moved or swung away?

Adapted from Williams, Csongradi, and LeBlanc (1982).

and hardware may be useful for assessing and training various scanning patterns (e.g., Catch the Cow;[j] and Target[b] software programs).

RESOURCES. The primary resources for selecting the appropriate transmission technique, interface switch, mounting system, and scanning pattern are *Augmentative communication: Assessment resource* (Goossens' & Crain, 1985a); *Communication, control, and computer access for disabled and elderly individuals* (Brandenburg & Vanderheiden, 1987a; 1987b; 1987c); *Electronic communication aids* (Fishman, 1987); and *A guide to controls* (Williams, Csongradi, & LeBlanc, 1982). All of those resources are listed in Appendix B.

System Process

As described by Beukelman and colleagues (1985), system process refers to the communication function performed by the system. Discussion here will also include the type of language content and nonspeech forms that can be included on a specific device (e.g., letters, sight words, symbols). Several general features of the system process will be considered.

Open/Fixed Content

For some devices, the content is fixed. For example, the Vocaid[ti] includes four preprogrammed levels, while the Say-It-All[i] presents content that is alphanumeric (alphabet plus numbers). Other devices offer totally open content. For example, the Alltalk[a] has no preprogrammed content. More typically, devices combine fixed and open content, including preprogrammed content such as alphanumeric entries, words and sentences plus user programmable memory of varying extent.

Flexibility of Nonspeech Form

This feature refers to the capability of using various nonspeech forms (pictures, symbols, sight words), in addition to alphanumeric entries. The representational level(s) required by the user will determine the importance of this feature. Many devices intended for use with reading, spelling users (e.g., Canon Communicator M;[c] personal computers; Special Friend[sp]) include alphanumeric entries, plus added functions such as a "speak" key. Other devices offer the possibility of using sight words chosen by the user (e.g., VOIS 136[pe]) or symbol overlays (e.g., ACS SpeechPAC/scan version;[a] Alltalk;[a] Light Talker;[pr] Touch Talker;[pr] VOIS 136;[pe] Wolf.[ad]

The size of square that can be easily programmed also varies according to the device. This can be important both relative to input (for direct selectors) and to the amount of information that can be visible at any one time. Devices that are based on alphaneumeric entries typically have fixed square size. For other devices, the square size can often be modified to some extent. For example, an 8-location and a 32-location operating kit are available to enhance programming of the Touch Talker[pr] or Light Talker[pr] for use of 8- or 32-location overlays respectively. Many other devices (e.g, Alltalk;[a] ACS SpeechPAC, Scan version[a]) can use squares of varying sizes, depending on the needs of the user.

Amount of Content Available

This feature refers to the capability of a device in terms of the number of "spaces" that are available at any one time, and the amount of information that can be stored in each space. Devices may range from a small number of keys (e.g., 16 keys for the VOIS 140[pr]) to a moderate number (up to 36 for the Wolf[ad]) to a large keyboard (e.g., 128 squares for devices such as Alltalk[pa] and Touch Talker[pr]). There is also a wide range of programming capacity, from a small memory capapcity (19 characters each for 5 keys on the Cannon Communicator M[c]) to a moderate memory capacity (600 words for the standard Alltalk[pa]) to a large memory (more than 45,000 characters for the Touch Talker with Minspeak software[pr]). For devices that offer text to speech capability, the potential content is unlimited (although it may be slow or difficult to access).

Vocabulary Expansion and Acceleration

As Baker (1984) wrote in *Conversations with Non-Speaking People,* "Life is conducted at a 'talker's pace' " (p. 42). With an average spoken communication rate at 175–200 words per minute, written communication rate at 35–46 words per minute, and aided communication at 2–30 words per minute (Goossens' & Crain, 1985a), it is clear that letter-by-letter spelling will not meet all needs, especially conversational needs, for aided communicators. Several approaches may be used to provide quick access to a large vocabulary of prestored words, phrases, and sentences.

USE OF LEVELS. As the individual's vocabulary needs grow, it is impossible to place all needed entries on squares of a single overlay. For this reason, levels are commonly used on communication devices. These have been described as "variable depth encoding systems" by Vanderheiden and Lloyd (1986). Use of levels can be compared to use of the shift key on a typewriter, to access upper or lower case letters. The level approach may be quite simple, such as the use of multiple overlays for various environments (e.g., VOIS 136;[pe] Wolf[ad]). This has the advantage of obviousness, but requires an "overlay shuffle," with the likelihood that needed messages are not available unless the overlay is changed. Since persons with physical impairment often cannot change overlays, independence may be restricted. Alternatively, a single overlay can indicate entries for two or more levels, with entries at various levels encoded by location or color (e.g., VOIS 136,[pe] as illustrated in Figure 9–3). While this is a straightforward approach, it has limitations for an individual with visual impairment and will not allow inclusion of numerous long entries on the overlay. Another option is use of a code to indicate the level, with the code listed separately. For example, the individual may choose the W page of the Special Friend[sp] device to store personal wants, with letters used to indicate specific wants (e.g., A = *Can I have my stuffed animal now?* B = *I need my backpack*). The codes for messages stored under each level may be posted in a notebook, laptray chart, or a wall poster, as an aid to memory. While this is not as obvious as including the message directly on the display, it allows for visual representation of longer entries. A disadvantage is the logistical difficulty of accessing the letter or number code, and having it available at all times.

USING ABBREVIATION EXPANSION. This approach, which can be used with all techniques including an alphabet in the selection vocabulary, allows the user to code and recall words, phrases, or sentences through a short abbreviation. Thus, just as acronyms such as ISAAC reflect the words they abbreviate, an abbreviation can be used to retrieve a prestored entry. A generic abbreviation expansion technique called QuicKey (Vanderheiden, 1984) allows generation of any other abbreviation expansion technique as a subset. The increase in spelling rate for normal conversation and logical abbreviations is up to 200 percent, with 300 percent or more efficiency for text on a familiar topic.

Logical Letter Coding (LOLEC) is an abbreviation/expansion technique used in the ACS SpeechPAC.[a] This technique allows assignment of two or three letter or number codes to messages. For example, a variety of messages related to homework might be stored using the "H" key as the first entry. Entry of the code is then used to retrieve the message. Initially, at least, it will be necessary to provide access to the code. The logical relationship between the code and the message should help aid memory for retrieval, at least for sentences. However, as the number of prestored entries increases, it may be difficult to select two or three entry codes that logically reflect each entry and promote recall. For example, both "I want a drink of water" and "I wish I had a new dress, hint, hint" might logically be encoded under "I-W-D." For words, a two-entry code would be highly desirable (because it is 50 percent more efficient than a three-entry code, and words are relatively short). Selecting two-entry logical letter codes for words may not be feasible, as so many words would be reduced to the

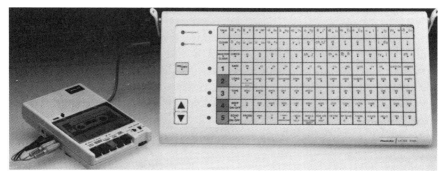

a

b

c

Figure 9-3
Samples of vocabulary expansion techniques used with electronic devices. A. Use of levels: VOIS 136 (Photo by Phonic Ear, Inc.). B. Coded levels: Special Friend (Photo by Shea Products, Inc.). C. Logical letter coding: ACS SpeechPAC (Photo by Adaptive Communication Systems, Inc.).

same two letter codes (e.g., work/walk, want/went, talk/take). Since the electronic device "remembers" the code, it is not necessary for the user to choose an obvious code. It would be possible to assign either the code "I-L-D" or "L-1" to the message "I'd really like a cold drink if you have one." However, for purposes of memory, cryptic codes should only be used for frequently used entries, where the time spent learning the code would be balanced by the frequency of use (Vanderheiden & Lloyd, 1986).

PREDICTIVE TECHNIQUES. Both letter prediction and word prediction techniques have been explored. In word prediction, the microprocessor offers the most likely word completions as the user begins to type a word, with the computer's guess revised each time an additional letter is entered; if the word completion is correct, the user enters a space or punctuation, or merely continues spelling following an incorrect guess. Another prediction technique is the word window approach, in which 10 numerically coded (0–9) probable completions of a word appear in the lower portion of the monitor. For example, the user enters the message "I'm feeling discouraged t-," then the computer offers 10 word choices (10 likely words to complete that word, all beginning with "t"). If the choice, "today," is coded #4, the user would enter "4," and the word would be completed. If the choice is not in the word window listing, the user would continue to type, and would see a revised list of 10 probable words. Vanderheiden and Lloyd (1986) observed that prediction techniques appear to be of greatest use to slow users accessing the device through slow techniques such as step scanning. In this case, the user has time to observe the display, and can achieve an increase in efficiency.

SEMANTIC ENCODING. As noted previously, memory-based encoding techniques become cumbersome as more messages are included for recall. The semantic compaction approach termed *Minspeak* is a mnemonic software system in which strings of polysemous (multiple meaning) icons (symbols) are used to recall strings of letters or sounds. *Minspeak* is used as software for the Touch Talker[pr] and Light Talker.[pr] The technique makes use of recognition memory rather than recall memory in aiding retrieval of words, phrases, or sentences (Baker, 1985). Individuals assign meaning to icons according to a variety of principles. Examples of potential meanings are: (1) *Primary meanings* (*apple* means apple; *sun* means sun); (2) *Category membership* (*apple* is a food; *eye* is a body part); (3) *Associated activities* (*apple* is to eat; *sun* is to shine); (4) *Salient characteristics* (*apple* is red; *sun* is hot); (5) *Conventionalisms* (*frog* is lucky; *elephants* never forget); (6) *Rebus, homophones, and puns* (*eye* may be "I"; *cactus* may be "wood or "would") (Stump, Weinberg, & Baker, 1987). Thus, icons selected for Minspeak must be rich in meaning, to allow multiple opportunities for developing recognition memory. Sample Minispeak icons are illustrated in Figure 9–4.

Icons can be used to recall words, although some degree of grammatical knowledge is necessary. Vanderheiden and Lloyd (1986) have suggested that storage of a small core of words would be more complex than use of levels or abbreviations; however, as the vocabulary size increases (over 800 words), semantic compaction would become less complex or cognitively taxing than the other retrieval techniques. The Words Strategy focuses on developing rationales for icon sequences (e.g., "walk" = SHOE VERB, because shoes are used for walking) and using logical storage/retrieval strategies (e.g., for verbs, the icon VERB always follows the meaning of related icons; the icon VERB + S is used as the final icon for third person singular verb forms). For recall of phrases or sentences, the Sentence Strategy is used, in which a sequence of icons recalls key semantic concepts underlying the message. Thus, the exact form of an utterance does not influence memory, as it would with abbreviation expansion techniques. For example, the forms "I would like a drink of water" and "A cold glass of water would sure hit the spot" could be encoded using the icons WANT (to signify a request) and OVER (showing the cup of drink overflowing). Alternatively, the polite form could be preceded by the icon GIRL (since polite girls get what they ask for). Samples of Minspeak icon sequences for words and sentences are illustrated in Figure 9-4. However, it must be stressed that, especially for the Sentence Strategy, icon sequences selected will be highly user-related.

A different use of levels is the "symbol theme" concept used with *Minspeak* software in the Touch Talker[pr] and Light Talker.[pr] For this approach, the user codes messages for a particular environment or situation using the same starting icon. For example, all messages concerning homework might be coded using the BOOK icon first. When retrieving these messages, a one symbol theme of BOOK can be entered, so that the icon BOOK is assumed before each entry. Thus, one less stroke is needed as long as messages are within that environment. Examples might be a series of one-icon messages, such as OVER (icon of cup overflowing) = "Can I get a drink now?"; IDEA (icon of man scratching head) = "I don't get it"; CLOCK = "I'm almost done"; FETCH = "Could you get something for me?" Two symbol themes (e.g., HOME + MEDICAL = hospital environment; EXIT + SEMI = traveling situation) can also be used.

SUMMARY OF EXPANSION TECHNIQUES. The selection of expansion technique for an individual user will depend on needs such as the vocabulary size required (with a larger vocabulary of words, phrases, and sentences, more complex expansion techniques will likely be needed), and the ability to attach, retain, and sequence codes (e.g., performance trials on use of various codes will give information for choosing the most appropriate

a

b

think =  | Verb | games = 🎲 | Noun Pl.

disabled = ♿ | Adj. | without = ☠ | Prep.

could have been = | Pre verb | Verb + en | ?

would like to = | Pre verb | 🧑

I'm feeling great. –
[EYE represents "I"; jumping frog suggests "feeling great"]

A cold beer would hit the spot.
[cup icon denotes "drink" ice cream represents "cold"; X on map suggests "hitting the spot"]

Hey. What's up, Doc?
[SUN introduces greeting category; MEDICAL symbol suggests "Doc"]

I have an idea about that.
[VOLT used for category of quick interjections; light bulb denotes idea]

Minspeak icons courtesy of Prentke Romich Company.

Figure 9-4

Minspeak. A. Sample *Minspeak* icon set (Photo by Maggie Lauterer). B. Sample *Minspeak* icon sequences for words, phrases, and sentences.

technique). For example, an individual with limited memory may initially require use of multiple overlays, with gradual introduction of more complex expansion techniques.

RESOURCES. For more information on various processing techniques, the primary resources are: *Augmentative Communication: Assessment Resource* (Goossens' & Crain, 1985a, pp. 167–172); *Electronic Communication Aids* (Fishman, 1987, Chapter 12); "Communication systems and their components" (Vanderheiden & Lloyd, 1986); and "Features of commercially available communication devices" (Kraat & Sitver-Kogut, 1985). The Augmentative Communication Evaluation System[w] provides a computerized device simulation package for assessment of various systems processes (e.g., abbreviation expansion, word prediction, semantic compaction).

System Output

Kraat (1985b) and Goossens' and Crain (1985a) have identified a range of output forms available in electronic or computerized communication devices. Each of these output types will be briefly described in the following section.

Visual Output Forms

Several forms of visual output are possible (see Figure 9–5). With some devices, there is visual selection only, with the item indicated by a light (e.g., Zygo 16[z]) or a pointer (e.g., Clock Communicator[k] Dial Scan[d]). The selection must be visually noted and remembered by the partner.

Single line visual display is another option, in which a nonpermanent written display of 5 to 40 characters is displayed. For example, the Casio Portable Computer[c] shows a visual display of 11 letters for short messages. Some devices offer a memory buffer which allows the user to hold written material in memory (e.g., 16–1000 characters). Duplicate visual displays may be used, with one display facing the user and one facing the partner, as with the Lightwriter.[z]

Multiple line displays can allow the user and partner to read a longer message that remains visible on the display. An example is the Zygo Notebook,[z] with eight lines of 40-character display.

A video screen display is available for systems based on personal computers such as the Apple or IBM. The size of the screen may facilitate communication at a distance, and a large screen is helpful for extensive written communication. However, 120-volt current will be needed, limiting the portability of the system.

a

b

Figure 9-5
Sample of communication output with electronic devices. A. Visual selection only: Clock Communicator (Photo by Steven E. Kanor). B. Duplicate visual display: Lightwrighter. C. Multiple line display: Zygo Notebook (Photos by ZYGO Industries, Inc.). D. Single strip printer: Canon Communicator M (Photo by Canon, USA, Inc.).

c

d

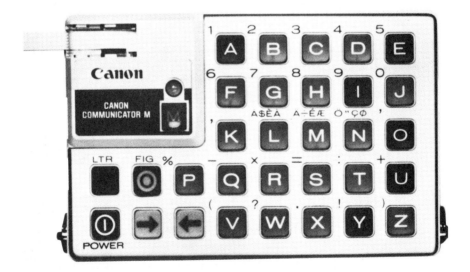

e

f

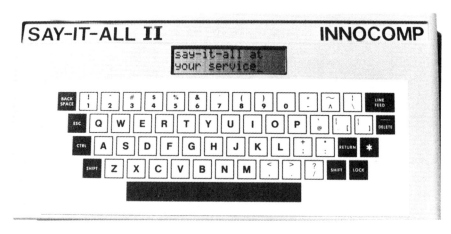

Figure 9-5 *(continued)*
E. Synthetic speech-multiple languages: Multi-Talk (Photo by Royal Institute of Technology). F. Male, female, and child voices: Say-It-All II (Photo by Innocomp).

Hard Copy

Permanent written copy can be helpful in many situations, such as preparing lengthy messages in advance of a conversation and sharing quiet messages with a partner. Forms vary from single strip printers, such as the Canon Communicator M^c to wide column printers, such as the ACS SpeechPAC,[a] to full page printers such as those available for personal computers.

Speech Output

Vocal output communication aids (VOCAs) have become increasingly popular. As Creech (1984) noted, "The difference between a VOCA and other kinds of communication aids can be compared to the difference between the car and the Conastoga wagon.... A car does in four days what took four months to do in a wagon" (p. 53). To demonstrate the recent advances in techology, it is now possible to produce speech in a variety of languages with a single device. For example, Multi-Talk[z] has programs available for speech in English (American or British), French, Spanish, German, Swedish, Italian, and Norwegian.

Speech output may be taped human speech (e.g., Form-A-Phrase), recorded digitized speech (e.g., Alltalk[a]), or synthesized speech (e.g., most VOCAs). Fishman (1987) observed that a speech synthesizer creates speech output according to programmed instructions, while digitized speech uses human speech as its basis and digitally records it. While digitized speech can be more intelligible and natural sounding, it is more expensive and limits the vocabulary to prestored words. The intelligibility of a VOCA depends on several factors, according to Fishman: (1) The intelligibility of the particular synthesizer used in the device (e.g., what are the intonation features?); (2) The skills required of the user, such as phoneme use or altered spelling, and the ability of the user to manipulate those variables; and (3) The ability of the partners to be trained to understand the particular speech output produced by the device. Devices offer variable speech characteristics. For example, Multi-Talk[z] allows the user to select from four different voice types and to change intonation and speed of talking; whispering is also possible. The VOIS 136[pe] includes 10 characteristics representing male, female, and child speech. Say-It-All[i] presents eight including male, female, and child speech.

Kraat (1985a) cautioned that some augmented speakers or partners may have positive reactions to synthetic speech (e.g., feeling more in control, creating a self-identity) while others may have negative reactions (e.g., feeling frustrated at the quality of speech, finding it difficult to identify with a synthetic voice).

Other Outputs

Communication aids may have additional outputs that are standard or optional, such as TTY, or telephone use, originally used by deaf individuals, to allow for printed communication between two parties over the telephone lines. Connection to computers and other controls are other potential output options.

Summary of Output Selection

An individual user typically has a variety of needs that mandate more than one form of output. For example, a student may need speech output (for conversations and group settings), visual display (to aid in communication repair), full-page hard copy (for homework), and computer access (for word processing and leisure activities).

RESOURCES. Primary resources for determining output include: *Augmentative Communication: Assessment Resources* (Goossens' & Crain, 1985a, pp. 161–166); Electronic Communication Aids (Fishman, 1987, Chapters 7, 8, and 9); and "Features of commercially available communication devices (Kraat & Sitver-Kogut, 1985).

Portability of Device

Kraat (1985b) has identified two basic areas of concern with regard to portability (see Figure 9-6). The first is the locations in which a user requires the device. For a person who needs to access the device from multiple locations, either a desk-top or a highly portable device will be needed, while an individual who stays in one location may be able to use a stationary aid such as the Rescue Speech System[r] on a cart. As Fishman (1987) observed, individuals not requiring portable devices will typically have degenerative diseases and/or be dependent on a nonportable respirator.

The second concern with regard to portability is the mobility of the individual, which will influence decisions concerning overall size and weight of a device. An individual in a wheelchair might find a desk-top device sufficiently portable for mobility. However, issues of size and appropriate mounting are still important, to ensure that the device will be taken from room-to-room, on outings, and so forth. Highly portable devices must be small and light enough to be carried by an ambulatory or partially ambulatory individual without interfering with mobility (Fishman, 1987). The Canon Communicator M,[c] QED Scribe,[z] or the Casio Personal Computer[c] would clearly fit this description for most individuals. Larger devices such as the Wolf[ad] or the Say-It-Simply Plus[l] may also fit portability needs when placed in a shoulder bag, due to light weight and moderate dimensions. Fishman noted that user preferences can be strong

a

b

c

Figure 9–6
Relative portability of electronic devices. A. Stationary aid: Rescue Speech System on cart (Photo by Rescue Speech System. B. Wolf (Photo by Adam Lab). C. Device with carrying handles: Say-It-Simply Plus (Photo by Innocomp).

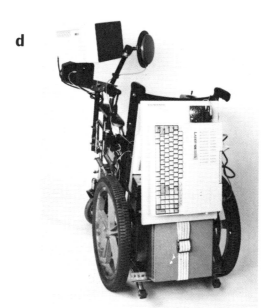

d

e

Figure 9-6 *(continued)*
D. Device powered by wheelchair battery: Rescue Speech System (Photo by Rescue Speech System). E. QED Scribe (Photo by ZYGO Industries, Inc.).

regarding this issue, and should be carefully considered. For example, a user might feel that a large device calls attention to itself and blocks his or her vision. Creative mounting of systems that might be considered stationary, such as those based on personal computers (IBM, Apple IIe/gs, Laser 128), can greatly increase portability. For example, the Rescue Speech System[r] may be mounted with the console behind an electric wheelchair on a folding shelf, with a small video monitor mounted to the wheelchair in front of the user. The system can be modified to accept power from the wheelchair battery, rather than requiring current from a wall socket.

RESOURCES. For discussion of concerns about portability, see *Electronic Communication Aids* (Fishman, 1987, Chapter 16), and "Features of commercially available devices" (Kraat & Sitver-Kogut, 1985).

Special Considerations in Device Matching

Kraat (1985b) identified numerous secondary characteristics that may make a difference in device matching. These are features that may assist in choosing between two devices when each has the primary features to meet major user needs. These features have been summarized by Goossens' and Crain (1985a, pp. 178–179). Sample features are technique features (e.g., rate and type of scan), language features (e.g., nature and content of the fixed layout), outputs (e.g., size and quality of visual display and printer), availability of repair service and reputation of company regarding repairs, and the amount and availability of the training required. These considerations should be discussed with the user, and the importance of each determined before making final selection decisions.

Intervention Issues in Technology for Aided Communication

Current intervention for augmentative communicators focuses to a great extent on training of technical aspects and symbol meanings. However, traditional training methods have often employed an artificially structured, drill-type approach. Intervention for use of a device can often be simulated using simple electronic devices (toys, tape recorders), microcomputers, or nonelectronic displays. For example, for purposes of documentation of potential for device use, or for training while securing funding, the future device user might practice skills such as (1) switch activation and release (e.g., using battery toys and adaptive switches or software such as *Catch the Cow*[j]; (2) headstick use to activate a membrane square (e.g., using a device such as the Wolf[ad] or the Power Pad[du]; (3) use of encoding by levels or abbreviation expansion (e.g., practicing logical letter encoding or semantic compaction on a nonelectronic display, with the partner providing vocal output); and (4) exploration of outputs (e.g., playing with a calculator with printed output, using tape recorders for voice output).

Specific strategies for developing a means to indicate through adaptive play have been suggested by Goossens' and Crain (1985a; 1985b) and Musselwhite (1986a; 1986b). Those same resources also include strategies and case studies for introducing various modes of output to augmented communicators. For example, Goossens' and Crain (1985b), Musselwhite (1986b), and Fried-Oken, Howard, and Prillwitz (1987) have each suggested specific procedures for establishing initial communicative control using a tape-loop system. Additional resources for training strategies were suggested in the previous sections, "System Input" and "System Output."

Strategies for teaching system process typically vary extensively according to the device. For example, different intervention strategies will be required for teaching use of levels (as for the VOIS 136^{pe} or the Wolf^{ad}), logical letter coding (as used with the ACS SpeechPAC^a), or semantic compaction (as used with the *Minspeak* software for the Light Talker^{pr} or Touch Talker^{pr}). A variety of training strategies are offered by device vendors in the form of training workshops, materials (books, booklets, seminar handouts, newsletters), or applications software. These materials also provide suggestions for intervention with input and output features distinctive to the specific devices (e.g., setting scanning patterns, how to manipulate voice output parameters such as pause, intonation, and pronunciation).

It is important that intervention on the technical aspects of device use be as interactive as possible. The potential device user should be helped to understand how skills fit together through telescoping of activities. The focus must ultimately be on functional use of a device for communicative purposes, not just on technical excellence.

Environmental Issues in Technology Intervention

Many of the environmental issues covered in Chapters 7 and 8 apply to technology intervention. This section will present additional issues that may arise in intervention with technology.

Affective Concerns

Acceptance of technology may be a concern for either the user or the partner(s). For example, a person who has lost speech due to a stroke or an accident may find introduction of an electronic device to be far more threatening than nonelectronic displays, because the electronic displays appear more permanent. This feeling should be discussed if necessary, with reassurance given as appropriate (e.g., reassuring the person that speech will continue to be a priority in intervention). Others in the environment may be hesitant to accept technology for the same resason, or due to technological anxiety. Fear of failure with the technology should be dealt with by offering hands-on experience, ensuring a high rate of success initially. Another, contrasting issue that may arise is the belief that the device will "cure" the person's problems. Education should be given in advance to ensure that all parties have reasonable expectations, and realize that training will involve both technical and interactive areas.

Support in Technical Learning

Individuals in the environment will need to have differing levels of expertise regarding device use. For example, the parent of a child using a voice output device with a printer will need to know basic device operation (e.g., how to retrieve coded messages, how to change the printer paper), how to program the device, and some problem-solving strategies (e.g., what if the voice doesn't work; where to call if the problem can't be solved locally). The child's respite care worker may need less expertise; knowing merely how to turn it on and how to recharge the batteries may be enough.

This technical learning may be accomplished in a variety of ways. Vendors typically offer training workshops for their devices. This may provide direct learning to families and users, or may offer a pyramid approach, with professionals (speech–language pathologist, special education teacher) first learning the information, then sharing it with families and users. A variety of support materials (manuals, videotapes, booklets) are also available for assisting in learning device operation. User groups are also being formed in some areas, with users, families, and professionals getting together to share information on strategies for learning about and using specific devices. More traditional support will likely be needed as well, with professionals such as speech–language pathologists or occupational therapists teaching skills such as storing and retrieving encoded messages and accessing techniques.

Training Techniques and Interaction Strategies

This area requires involving both staff and families in the training process, and training staff and families to use appropriate interchange strategies. Higgins and Mills (1986) have developed procedures for implementing communication training in real environments, using a "buddy" approach. The buddy is a facilitator who is familiar with the user and the device, and can intervene when communication breakdowns occur to ensure message completion. The process involves a series of steps, from modeling of the interaction process with the buddy, to simulations in clinical settings, to interaction in actual environments. A staff member or family member can serve as the communication buddy. Staff and family members might take responsibility for other specific types of technology training, such as switch use, learning sequence codes, or practice in modifying spelling to achieve desired vocal output. It is important that responsibility be clear to all individuals involved, and that potential trainers fully understand the procedures to be used.

Communication partners will also need to be trained to use the differing pattern of interchange needed when an individual begins using a device. For example, partners may find that the user can now be more independent; they need to allow for this independence, rather than relying on previous patterns such as guessing and twenty questions. This may be accomplished in a variety of ways, such as in-service presentations, role playing, and observation.

Summary

This chapter has presented a brief overview of the components of communication devices that must be considered in matching devices to user needs. A three-phase selection process was outlined, as proposed by Kraat (1985b); that selection process is summarized in Goossens' and Crain (1985a, pp. 174–179). One caution should be stressed regarding device selection — while an electronic deice can serve as an effective medium for communication, prescription and purchase of a device must not be viewed as an end goal. First, a single device will rarely, if ever, meet all the communication needs of a user. Second, training will generally be necessary to help the user and his or her communication partners develop effective interaction strategies using the device and other communication modes to achieve optimum communication.

References

Abkarian, G., Dworkin, J., & Brown, S. (1978). *An adventitiously non-verbal child: Signed English as a transitional step in Reye's syndrome.* A paper presented at the American Speech–Language–Hearing Association Convention, San Francisco.

Adler, D. (1980). *Fingerspelling fun.* New York: Watts.

Ahlers, J., Bortnem, P., Brady, H., & Leite, J. (1987). *Weekly communication group: Adult mediated, same-age and cross-age discourse activities. Implementation strategies for improving the use of communication aids in schools serving handicapped children* (pamphlet). Rockville, MD: American Speech–Language–Hearing Association.

Akamatsu, C. (1982). *The acquisition of fingerspelling in pre-school children.* Unpublished doctoral dissertation. University of Rochester, Rochester, NY.

Akamatsu, C. (1985). Fingerspelling formulae: A word is more or less than the sum of its letters. In W. Stokoe & V. Volterra (Eds.), *SLR '83: Sign language research.* Silver Spring, MD: Linstok Press.

Alexander, R. (1987). Prespeech and feeding development. In E. McDonald (Ed.), *Treating cerebral palsy: For clinicians by clinicians* (pp. 133–152). Austin, TX: Pro-Ed.

Alpert, C. (1980). Procedures for determining the optimal nonspeech mode with the autistic child. In R. L. Schiefelbusch (Ed.), *Nonspeech language and communication: Analysis and intervention* (pp. 389–420). Austin, TX: Pro-Ed.

American Radio Relay League. (1985). *ARRL Program for the disabled.* Newington, CT: American Radio Relay League.

Anderson, J. (1980). Spatial arrangement of stimuli and the construction of communication boards for the physically handicapped. *Mental Retardation, 18,* 41–42.

Anthony, D. (1966). *Seeing essential English.* Unpublished manuscript, Ypsilanti, MI.

Anthony, D. (1971). *Seeing Essential English* (Vols. 1 & 2). Anaheim, CA: Educational Services Division, Anaheim Union School District.

Apffel, J., Kelleher, J., Lilly, M., & Richardson, R. (1975). Developmental reading for moderately retarded children. *Education and Training of the Mentally Retarded, 10,* 229–236.

Arnold, L. (1978). *Helping parents help their children.* New York: Brunner/Mazel.

Ashcroft, S., & Henderson, F. (1963). *Programmed instruction in Braille.* Pittsburgh, PA: Stanwik House.

Azrin, N., Kaplan, S., & Foxx, R. (1973). Autism reversal: Eliminating stereotyped self-stimulation of retarded individuals. *American Journal of Mental Deficiency, 78,* 241–248.

Babbini, B. (1974a). *Manual communication: Fingerspelling and the language of signs. A course of study outlines for instructors.* Urbana, IL: University of Illinois Press.

Babbini, B. (1974b). *Manual communication: Fingerspelling and the language of signs. A course of study for students.* Urbana, IL: University of Illinois Press.

Baer, D. (1978). The behavioral analysis of trouble. In K. Allen, V. Holm, & R. Schiefelbusch (Eds.), *Early intervention — A team approach* (pp. 57–93). Baltimore: University Park Press.

Baker, B. (1985). The use of words and phrases on a *Minspeak* communication system. *Communication Outlook, 7*(1), 8–10.

Baker, B. (1986). *How to establish a core vocabulary through the dialogue method and how to write dialogue.* Unpublished manuscript, Pittsburgh, PA.

Baker, B. L. (1976). Parent involvement in programming for the developmentally disabled. In L. Lloyd (Ed.), *Communication assessment and intervention strategies* (pp. 691–733). Baltimore: University Park Press.

Baker, C., & Padden, C. (1978a). *American sign language: A look at its history, structure, and community.* Silver Spring, MD: T.J. Publishers.

Baker, C., & Padden, C. (1978b). Focusing on nonmanual components of American Sign Language. In P. Siple (Ed.), *Understanding language through sign language research* (pp. 27–57). New York: Academic Press.

Baker, M. (1984). Who knows what the future holds? In *Conversations with non-speaking people.* Toronto, Ontario: Canadian Rehabilitation Council for the Disabled.

Bannatyne, A. (1968). *Psycholinguistic color system: A reading, writing, spelling, and language program.* Urbana, IL: Learning Systems Press.

Bassin, J., & Kreeb, D. (1978). *Reaching out to parents of newly diagnosed retarded children.* St. Louis: St. Louis Association for Retarded Children.

Bates, E. (1976). *Language and context: The acquisition of pragmatics.* New York: Academic Press.

Beaupre, W. (1984). *Gaining Cued Speech proficiency: A manual for parents, teachers, and clinicians.* Washington, DC: Office of Cued Speech Programs.

Beck, R. (1977). Interdisciplinary model: Planning distribution and ancillary input to classrooms for the severely/profoundly handicapped. In E. Sontag (Ed.), *Educational programming for the severely and profoundly handicapped* (pp. 397–404). Reston, VA: Division on Mental Retardation, Council for Exceptional Children.

Bender, M., & Valletutti, P. (1976). *Teaching the moderately and severely handicapped.* Baltimore: University Park Press.

Bender, M., Valletutti, P., & Bender, R. (1985). *Teaching the moderately and severely handicapped. Volume II: Communication, socialization, safety, and leisure skills.* Austin, TX: Pro-Ed.

Bellugi, U., & Fisher, S. (1972). A comparison of sign language and spoken language: Rate and grammatical mechanisms. *Cognition, 1,* 173–200.

Bergen, A., & Colangelo, C. (1982). *Positioning the client with central nervous system deficits: The wheelchair and other adapted equipment.* Valhalla, NY: Valhalla Rehabilitation Publications, Ltd.

Beukelman, D. (1985). Interaction in augmentative communication. A seminar presented at the North Carolina Augmentative Communication Association Conference, Winston-Salem, NC.

Beukelman, D. (1986). Evaluating the effectiveness of intervention programs. In S. Blackstone (Ed.), *Augmentative communication: An introduction* (pp. 423–445). Rockville, MD: American Speech–Language–Hearing Association.

Beukelman, D., & Yorkston, K. (1977). A communication system for the severely dysarthric speaker with an intact language system. *Journal of Speech and Hearing Disorders, 42,* 265–270.

Beukelman, D., & Yorkston, K. (1980). Nonvocal communication: Performance evaluation. *Archives of Physical Medicine and Rehabilitation, 61,* 272–275.

Beukelman, D., & Yorkston, K. (1982). Communication interaction of adult communication augmentation system use. *Topics in Language Disorders, 2*(2), 39–53.

Beukelman, D., Yorkston, K., & Dowden, P. (1985). *Communication augmentation: A casebook of clinical management.* San Diego: College-Hill Press.

Bigge, J., & O'Donnell, P. (1982). *Teaching individuals with physical and multiple disabilities* (2nd ed.). Columbus, OH: Charles E. Merrill.

Blacher, J. (1984). *Severely handicapped young children and their families: Research in review.* Orlando, FL: Academic Press.

Blau, A. (1983). Vocabulary selection in augmentative communication: Where do we begin? In H. Winitz (Ed.), *Treating language disorders: For clinicians by clinicians* (pp. 205–233). Austin, TX: Pro-Ed.

Bliss, C. (1965). *Semantography — Blissymbolics.* Sydney, Australia: Semantography Publications.

Bliss, C., & McNaughton, S. (1975). *The book to the film: "Mr. Symbol Man."* Sydney, Australia: Semantography Publications.

Blissymbolics Communication International. (1984). *Picture your Blissymbols.* Toronto, Ontario: Author.

Blissymbolics Communication International. (1985a). *Blissymbol applications readings from B.C.I. Newsletters 1974–1982* (Monograph No. 2). Toronto, Ontario: Author.

Blissymbolics Communication International. (1985b). *Blissybolics: Independent study guide.* Toronto, Ontario: Author.

Blissymbolics Communication International. (1985c). *Teaching aids and ideas* (Monograph No. 9). Toronto, Ontario: Author.

Bloom, L., & Lahey, M. (1978). *Language development and language disorders.* New York: John Wiley.

Bluma, S., Shearer, M., Frohman, A., & Hillard, J. (1976). *Portage guide to early education.* Portage, WI: Cooperative Educational Services.

Bolton, S., & Dashiell, S. (1984). *Interaction Checklist for augmentative communication (INCH).* Huntington Beach, CA: INCH Associates.

Bonvillian, J., & Nelson, K. (1978). Development of sign language in autistic children and other language handicapped individuals. In P. Siple (Ed.), *Understanding language through sign language research.* New York: Academic Press.

Bornstein, H. (1973). A description of some current sign systems designed to represent English. *American Annals of the Deaf, 118,* 454–463.

Bornstein, H. (1974). Signed English: A manual approach to English language. *Journal of Speech and Hearing Disorders, 39,* 330–343.

Bornstein, H., & Jordan, K. (1984). *Functional signs: A new approach from simple to complex.* Austin, TX: Pro-Ed.

Bornstein, H., & Saulnier, K. (1984). *The Signed English Starter.* Washington, DC: Gallaudet University Press.

Bornstein, H., & Saulnier, K. (1987). *The Signed English schoolbook.* Washington, DC: Gallaudet University Press.

Bornstein, H., Saulnier, K., & Hamilton, L. (1979a). *Signed English for the classroom.* Washington, DC: Gallaudet College Press.

Bornstein, H., Saulnier, K., & Hamilton, L. (1979b). *Signed English for the residence hall.* Washington, DC: Gallaudet College Press.

Bornstein, H., Saulnier, K., & Hamilton, L. (1983). *The comprehensive Signed English dictionary.* Washington, DC: Gallaudet College Press.

Bottorf, L., & DePape, D. (1982). Initiating communication systems for severely speech-impaired persons. *Topics in Language Disorders, 2*(2), 55–72.

Bove, L. (1985). *The Sesame Street sign language ABC.* New York: Random House.

Brandenburg, S., & Vanderheiden, G. (1987a). *Communication, control, and computer access for disabled and elderly individuals. ResourceBook 1: Communication aids.* San Diego: College-Hill Press.

Brandenburg, S., & Vanderheiden, G. (1987b). *Communication, control, and computer access for disabled and elderly individuals. ResourceBook 2: Switches and environmental controls.* San Diego: College-Hill Press.

Brandenburg, S., & Vanderheiden, G. (1987c). *Communication, control, and computer access for disabled and elderly individuals. ResourceBook 3: Hardware and software.* San Diego: College-Hill Press.

Bricker, D. (1983). Early communication: Development and training. In M. Snell (Ed.), *Systematic instruction of the moderately and severely handicapped* (2nd ed., pp. 269–288). Columbus, OH: Charles E. Merrill.

Bricker, D., & Dennison, L. (1978). Training prerequisites to verbal behavior. In M. Snell (Ed.), *Systematic instruction of the moderately and severely handicapped* (pp. 157–178). Columbus, OH: Charles E. Merrill.

Bricker, D., Dennison, L., & Bricker, W. (1975). *Constructive interaction — adaptation approach to language training.* MCCD Monograph Series No. 1. Miami, FL: Mailman Center for Child Development, University of Miami.

Bristow, D., & Fristoe, M. (1984). *Systematic evaluation of the nonspeaking child.* A miniseminar presented at the American Speech–Language–Hearing Association Convention, San Francisco, CA.

Brown, L., Falvey, M., Vincent, L., Kaye, N., Johnson, F., Ferrara-Parrish, P., & Gruenewald, L. (1980). Strategies for generating comprehensive, longitudinal, and chronological age appropriate individual education programs for adolescent and young adult severely handicapped students. *Journal of Special Education, 14,* 199–215.

Brown, I., Nietupski, J., & Hamre-Nietupski, S. (1976). Criterion of ultimate functioning. In M. Thomas (Ed.), *Hey, don't forget about me* (pp. 2–15). Reston, VA: The Council for Exceptional Children.

Bruno, J. (1986). Modeling procedures for increased use of communicative functions in communication aid users. In S. Blackstone (Ed.), *Augmentative communication: An introduction* (pp. 301–306). Rockville, MD: American Speech–Language–Hearing Association.

Burkhart, L. (1987). Using computer and speech synthesis to facilitate communicative interaction with young and/or severely handicapped children. College Park, MD: Author.

Buscaglia, L. (1975). *The disabled and their parents: A counseling challenge*. Thorofare, NJ: Slack.

Buzolich, M. (1987a). *Creative funding for services. Implementation strategies for improving the use of communication aids in schools*. Rockville, MD: American Speech–Language–Hearing Association.

Buzolich, M. (1987b). *Facilitating interaction in communication groups involving individuals who use augmentative communiction aids and techniques and their speaking peers. Implementation strategies for improving the use of communication aids in schools*. Rockville, MD: American Speech–Language–Hearing Association.

Buzolich, M. (1987c). *Teaching students and their speaking peers to repair communication breakdowns caused by unintelligible speech. Implementation strategies for improving the use of communication aids in schools*. Rockville, MD: American Speech–Language–Hearing Association.

Calculator, S., & Luchko, C. (1983). The use of communication boards in a residential setting: An evaluation. *Journal of Speech and Hearing Disorders, 47,* 281–287.

Campbell, P., Green, K., & Carlson, L. (1977). Approximating the norm through environmental and child-centered prosthetics and adaptive equipment. In E. Sontag (Ed.), *Educational programming for the severely and profoundly handicapped* (pp. 300–320). Reston, VA: Division on Mental Retardation, Council for Exceptional Children.

Cansler, D., Martin, G., & Valand, M. (1975). *Working with families*. Winston-Salem, NC: Kaplan Press.

Carlson, F. (1981). A format for selecting vocabulary for the nonspeaking child. *Language, Speech, and Hearing Services in the Schools, 12,* 240–245.

Carlson, F. (1982). *Prattle and play*. Omaha, NE: Meyer Children's Rehabilitation Center, Media Resource Center.

Carlson, F. (1985). *Picsyms categorical dictionary*. Lawrence, KS: Baggeboda Press.

Carlson, F. (1987). Communication strategies for infants. In E. McDonald (Ed.), *Treating cerebral palsy: For clinicians by clinicians*. Austin, TX: Pro-Ed.

Carlson, F., Hough, S., Lippert, E., & Young, C. (1987). *Facilitating interaction during mealtime. Implementation strategies for improving the use of communication aids in schools serving handicapped children*. Rockville, MD: The American Speech–Language–Hearing Association.

Carmel, S. (1982). *International hand alphabet charts*. Rockville, MD: Author.

Carr, E. (1981). *How to teach sign language to developmentally disabled children*. Austin, TX: Pro-ED.

Carr, E., Binkoff, J., Kologinsky, E., & Eddy, M. (1978). Acquisition of sign language by autistic children: Expressive labelling. *Journal of Applied Behavioral Analysis, 11,* 489–510.

Carrier, J., Jr. (1976). Application of a nonspeech language system with the severely language handicapped. In L. Lloyd (Ed.), *Communication assessment and intervention strategies* (pp. 523–547). Baltimore: University Park Press.

Carrier, J., Jr., & Peak, T. (1975). *Non-speech language initiation program (Non-SLIP)*. Lawrence, KS: H and H Enterprises.

Carrow, E. (1973). *Test for auditory comprehension of language*. Austin, TX: Learning Concepts.

Cassatt-James, L. (1986). Establishing the use of multimodalities using the communicative interaction assessment procedure. In S. Blackstone (Ed.), *Augmentative communication: An introduction* (pp. 307–319). Rockville, MD: American Speech–Language–Hearing Association.

Catalog of federal domestic assistance. (1986). Washington, DC: Superintendent of Documents, United States Government Printing Office.

Cenoplano, S., Gustason, G., & Zawolkow, E. (1981). *Signing Exact English vocabulary development kits*. Los Alamitos, CA: Modern Signs Press.

Chapman, R. (1974). Discussion summary: Developmental relationship between Receptive and expressive language. In R. Schiefelbusch & L. Lloyd (Eds.), *Language perspectives: Acquisition, retardation, and intervention* (pp. 335–344). Baltimore: University Park Press.

Chapman, R., & Miller, J. (1975). Early two and three word utterances: Does production precede comprehension? *Journal of Speech and Hearing Research, 18*, 355–371.

Chapman, R., & Miller, J. (1980). Analyzing language and communication in the child. In R. Schiefelbusch (Ed.), *Nonspeech language and communication: Analysis and intervention* (pp. 159–196). Austin, TX: Pro-ED.

Chappell, G., & Johnson, G. (1976). Evaluation of cognitive behavior in the young child. *Language, Speech, and Hearing Services in Schools, 7*, 17–27.

Charlebois-Marois, C. (1985). *Everybody's technology: A sharing of ideas in augmentative communication*. Montreal, Quebec: Charlecoms Enr.

Chen, L. (1968). "Talking Hands" for aphasic patients. *Geriatrics, 23*, 145–148.

Chen, L. (1971). Manual communication by combined alphabet and gestures. *Archives of Physical Medicine and Rehabilitation, 52*, 381–384.

Christopher, D. (1976). *Manual communication: A basic text and workbook with practical exercises*. Austin, TX: Pro-ED.

Clark, C., Davies, C., & Woodcock, R. (1974). *Standard rebus glossary*. Circle Pines, MN: American Guidance Service.

Clark, C., & Moores, D. (1984). *Clark early language program*. Allen, TX: DLM Teaching Resources.

Clark, C., Moores, D., & Woodcock, R. (1975). *The Minnesota early language development sequence*. Minneapolis, MN: Research, Development, and Demonstration Center in Education of Handicapped Children.

Clark, C., & Woodcock, R. (1976). Graphic systems of communication. In L. Lloyd (Ed.), *Communication assessment and intervention strategies* (pp. 549–605). Baltimore: University Park Press.

Clark, R. (1980). *Guidelines for NU-VUE-CUE*. Bowling Green, IN: R.D. Clark, Inc.

Clark, R. (1984). *Verbal eyes verbalize*. A presentation at the Council for Exceptional Children Convention.

Clark, W. (1885). *Indian sign languages*. Philadelphia, PA: L.R. Hammersley and Co.

Clarke, B., & Ling, D. (1976). The effects of using Cued Speech: A follow-up study. *Volta Review, 78,* 23–34.

Cohen, C. (1986). Total habilitation and lifelong management. In S. Blackstone (Ed.), *Augmentative communication: An introduction* (pp. 447–469). Rockville, MD: American Speech–Language–Hearing Association.

Cohen, M., Gross, P., & Haring, N. (1976). Developmental pinpoints. In N. Haring & L. Brown (Eds.), *Teaching the severely handicapped* (Vol. 1, pp. 35–110). New York: Grune & Stratton.

Constable, C. (1983). Creating communicative context. In H. Winitz (Ed.), *Treating language disorders: For clinicians by clinicians.* Austin, TX: Pro-Ed.

Cook, S. (1987). *Using "topic specific" miniboards to allow individuals who use augmentative communication aids to initiate communication with school staff members. Implementation strategies for improving the use of communication aids in schools.* Rockville, MD: American Speech–Language–Hearing Association.

Cornett, O. (1975). Cued Speech and oralism: An analysis. *Audiology and Hearing Education, 1,* 26–33.

Cornett, O. (1985). Update on Cued Speech. *Cued Speech Annual, 1,* 3–8.

Costello, E. (1983). *Signing — How to speak with your hands.* New York: Bantam Press.

Craig, E. (1976). A supplement to the spoken word — The Paget-Gorman Sign System. In Royal National Institute for the Deaf (Ed.), *Methods of communication currently used in the education of deaf children.* Letchworth, England: The Garden City Press.

Creech, R. (1984). The key that releases the soul of a man. In *Conversations with non-speaking people* (pp. 51–56). Toronto, Ontario: Canadian Rehabilitation Council for the Disabled.

Cregan, A. (1982). *Sigsymbol dictionary/teaching pack.* Available from the author, 76 Wood Close, Hatfield, Herts AL10 8TX, England.

Cregan, A., & Lloyd, L. (1988). *Sigsymbol dictionary: American edition.* Wauconda, IL: Don Johnston Developmental Equipment.

Crickmay, M. (1966). *Speech therapy and the Bobath approach to cerebral palsy.* Springfield, IL: Charles C. Thomas.

Culatta, B., & Blackstone, S. (1980). A program to teach non-oral communication symbols to multiply handicapped children. *Journal of Childhood Communication Disorders, 4,* 29–55.

Cuvo, A., & Riva, M. (1980). Generalization and transfer between comprehension and production: A comparison of retarded and nonretarded persons. *Journal of Applied Behavioral Analysis, 13,* 315–331.

Daniloff, J., Lloyd, L., & Fristoe, M. (1983). Amer-Ind transparency. *Journal of Speech and Hearing Disorders, 48,* 103–110.

Daniloff, J., & Shafer, A. (1981). A gestural communication program for severely-profoundly handicapped children. *Language, Speech, and Hearing Services in Schools, 12,* 258–268.

Dawson, K. (1982). *Standard language assessment tests capable of modification and use with non-speaking persons.* Unpublished manuscript, Communication Enhancement Clinic, Children's Hospital, Boston, MA.

Deich, R., & Hodges, P. (1978). *Language without speech.* New York: Brunner/Mazel.

Dennis, R., Reichle, J., Williams, W., & Vogelsberg, R. (1982). Motoric factors influ-

Communication Programming

encing the selection of vocabulary for sign production programs. *The Journal of the Association for the Severely Handicapped, 7,* 20–32.

Devereaux, K., & Van Oosterom, J. (1984). *Learning with rebuses.* Stratford Upon Avon, England: NCSE.

Doherty, J. (1985). The effects of sign characteristics on sign acquisition and retention: An integrative review of the literature. *Augmentative and Alternative Communication, 1,* 108–121.

Doherty, J. (1987). Handling, positioning, and adaptive equipment. In E. McDonald (Ed.), *Treating cerebral palsy: For clinicians by clinicians* (pp. 153–170). Austin, TX: Pro-Ed.

Doherty, J., Daniloff, J., & Lloyd, L. (1985). The effect of categorical presentation on Amer-Ind transparency. *Augmentative and Alternative Communication, 1,* 10–16.

Doherty, J., Karlan, G., & Lloyd, L. (1982). Establishing the transparency of two gestural systems by mentally retarded adults (absract). *Asha, 24,* 834.

Dolan, E., & Burton, L. (1976). *The severely and profoundly handicapped: A practical approach to teaching.* New York: Grune & Stratton.

Duckman, R. (1987). Visual problems. In E. McDonald (Ed.), *Treating cerebral palsy: For clinicians by clinicians* (pp. 105–131). Austin, TX: Pro-Ed.

Duffy, L. (1977). *An innovative approach to the development of communication skills for severely speech handicapped cerebral palsied children.* Unpublished master's thesis, University of Nevada, Las Vegas, NV.

Duffy, R., & Duffy, J. (1984). *New England pantomime tests.* Austin, TX: Pro-Ed.

Dunn, L., & Dunn, L. (1981). *Peabody Picture Vocabulary Test — Revised.* Circle Pines, MN: American Guidance Service.

Dunn, L., Smith, J., Dunn, L., Horton, K., & Smith, D. (1981). *Peabody language development kids (Revised).* Circle Pines, MN: American Guidance Service.

Dunn, M. (1982). *Formal pre-sign language motor skills.* Tucson, AZ: Communication Skill Builders.

Dunst, C. (1981). *Infant learning.* Allen, TX: DLM/Teaching Resources.

Elder, P., & Bergman, J. (1978). Visual symbol communication instruction with non-verbal, multiply handicapped individuals. *Mental Retardation, 16,* 107–112.

Enders, S. (1983). Funding for devices. *Rehabilitation Technology Review, 2*(4), 4–5.

Eriksson, B. (1985). *Headsticks and optical headpointers.* Bromma, Sweden: Handicappinstitutet.

Fairweather, B., Haun, D., & Finkle, L. (1983). *Communication systems for severely handicapped persons.* Columbus, OH: Charles E. Merrill.

Falvey, M. (1986). Community-based curriculum: Instructional strategies for students with severe handicaps. Baltimore: Paul H. Brookes.

Fantz, R., & Nevis, S. (1967). The predictive value of changes in visual preferences in early infancy. In J. Hellmuth (Ed.), *Exceptional infant: The normal infant.* New York: Brunner/Mazel.

Farb, P. (1968). *Man's rise to civilization as shown by the Indians of North America.* New York: E.P. Dutton.

Favell, J., Favell, J., & McGimsey, J. (1978). Relative effectiveness and efficiency of group vs. individual training of severely retarded persons. *American Journal of Mental Deficiency, 83,* 104–109.

304

Favell, J., & Greene, J. (1980). *How to treat self-injurious behavior.* Austin, TX: Pro-Ed.

Fell, A., Lynn, E. & Morrison, K. (1984). *Non-oral communication assessment (NOCA).* Ann Arbor, MI: Alternatives to Speech.

Fewell, R., & Cone, J. (1983). Identification and placement of severely handicapped children. In M. Snell (Ed.), *Systematic instruction of the moderately and severely handicapped* (2nd ed., pp. 46–73). Columbus, OH: Charles E. Merrill.

Finnie, N. (1975). *Handling the young cerebral palsied child at home.* New York: E.P. Dutton.

Fiocca, G. (1981). Generally understood gestures: An approach to communication for persons with severe language impairments. Unpublished master's thesis, University of Illinois, Urbana, IL.

Fishman, I. (1987). *Electronic communication aids: Selection and use.* San Diego: College-Hill Press.

Fitzgerald, E. (1949). *Straight language for the deaf.* Washington, DC: The Volta Bureau.

Foxx, R., & Azrin, N. (1973). *Toilet training the retarded.* Champaign, IL: Research Press.

Fried-Oken, M., Howard, J., & Prillwitz, D. (1987). *Implementation strategies for improving the use of communication aids in schools serving handicapped children.* Rockville, MD: American Speech–Language–Hearing Association.

Frishberg, N. (1979). Historical change: From iconic to arbitrary. In E. Kluma & U. Bellugi (Eds.), *The signs of language* (pp. 67–83). Cambridge, MA: Harvard University Press.

Fristoe, M., & Lloyd, L. (1978). A survey of the use of non-speech communication systems with the severely communication impaired. *Mental Retardation, 16,* 99–103.

Fristoe, M., & Lloyd, L. (1979). Signs used in manual communication training with persons having severe communication impairments. *AAESPH Review, 4,* 364–373.

Fristoe, M., & Lloyd, L. (1980). Planning an initial expressive sign lexicon for persons having severe communication impairment. *Journal of Speech and Hearing Disorders, 45,* 170–190.

Frumkin, J. (1986). Enhancing interaction through role playing. In S. Blackstone (Ed.), *Augmentative communication: An introduction* (pp. 329–335). Rockville, MD: American Speech–Language–Hearing Association.

Fry, E. (1964). A diacritical marking system to aid beginning reading instruction. *Elementary Engineering, 41,* 526–529.

Fulwiler, R., & Fouts, R. (1976). Acquisition of sign language by a non-communicating, autistic child. *Journal of Autism and Child Schizophrenia, 6,* 43–51.

Gallagher, J., & Vientze, P. (1986). *Families of handicapped persons: Research, programs, and policy issues.* Baltimore: Paul H. Brookes.

Garcia, E., & DeHaven, E. (1974). Use of operant techniques in the establishment and generalization of language: A review and analysis. *American Journal of Mental Deficiency, 79,* 169–178.

Gaylord-Ross, J. (1977). The development of treatment techniques for the remediation of self-injurious behavior in the classroom and home. *Annual Reports,* New York Bureau of Education for the Handicapped, Washington, DC.

Ginsburg, H., & Opper, S. (1969). *Piaget's theory of intellectual development: An introduction.* Englewood Cliffs, NJ: Prentice-Hall, Inc.

Glennen, S., & Calculator, S. (1985). Training functional communication board use: A pragmatic approach. *Augmentative and Alternative Communication, 1,* 134–142.

Goddard, C. (1977). Application of symbols with deaf children. *Blissymbolics Communication Institute Newsletter, No. 3.* Toronto, Ontario: Blissymbolics Communication Institute.

Goetz, L., Gee, K., & Sailor, W. (1985). Using a behavior chain interruption strategy to teach communication skills to students with severe disabilities. *Journal of the Association for Persons with Severe Handicaps, 10,* 21–30.

Goldstein, H. (1985). Enhancing language generalization using matrix and stimulus equivalence training. In S. Warren & A. Rogers-Warren (Eds.), *Teaching functional language* (pp. 225–249). Austin, TX: Pro-Ed.

Golin, A., & Ducanis, A. (1981). *The interdisciplinary team.* Rockville, MD: Aspen Systems.

Goodenough-Trepagnier, C. (1978). Language development of children without articulate speech. In R. Campbell & P. Smith (Eds.), *Recent advances in the psychology of language: Part A, language and mother–child interaction* (pp. 421–426). New York: Plenum Press.

Goodenough-Trepagnier, C., & Deser, T. (1980). *Rate of output with a SPEEC nonvocal communication board.* Paper presented at the International Conference on Rehabilitation Engineering, Toronto, Canada.

Goodenough-Trepagnier, C., & Prather, P. (1981). Communication systems for the non-vocal based on frequent phoneme sequences. *Journal of Speech and Hearing Research, 24,* 322–329.

Goodenough-Trepagnier, C., & Prather, P. (1982). *Manual of teachers of SPEECH.* Biomedical Engineering Center, Tufts–New England Medical Center.

Goodenough-Trepagnier, C., Tarry, E., & Prather, P. (1982). Derivation of an efficient nonvocal communication system. *Human Factors, 24,* 163–172.

Goodman, L., Wilson, P., & Bornstein, H. (1978). Results of a national survey of sign language programs in special education. *Mental Retardation, 16,* 104–106.

Goolsby, E., & Porter, P. (1984). Augmentative communication: The team approach. *North Carolina Augmentative Communication Association Newsletter, 2*(2), 3–4.

Goossens', C., & Crain, S. (in press). *Utilizing switch interfaces with physically challenged individuals: Assessment and intervention considerations.* San Diego, CA: College-Hill Press.

Goossens', C., & Crain, S. (1985a). *Augmentative communication: Assessment resource.* Wauconda, IL: Don Johnson Developmental Equipment.

Goossens', C., & Crain, S. (1985b). *Augmentative communication: Intervention resource.* Wauconda, IL: Don Johnston Developmental Equipment.

Goossens', C., & Crain, S. (1986). Establishing multiple communication displays. In S. Blackstone (Ed.), *Augmentative communication: An introduction* (pp. 337–344). Rockville, MD: American Speech–Language–Hearing Association.

Grabowski, K., & Shane, H. (1986). *Communication profile for severe expressive impairment.* Unpublished manuscript, Communication Enhancement Clinic, Children's Hospital, Boston, MA.

Griffith, P., & Robinson, J. (1980). The influence of iconicity phonological similarity on sign learning in mentally retarded subjects. *American Journal on Mental Deficiency, 85,* 291–299.

Guess, D., & Helmstetter, E. (1986). Skill cluster instruction and the individualized curriculum sequencing model. In R. Horner, L. Meyer, & B. Fredericks (Eds.), *Education of learners with severe handicaps: Exemplary service strategies.* Baltimore: Paul H. Brookes.

Guess, D., Sailor, W., & Baer, D. (1977). A behavioral–remedial approach to language training for the severely handicapped. In E. Sontag (Ed.), *Educational programming for the severely and profoundly handicapped* (pp. 360–377). Reston, VA: Division on Mental Retardation, Council for Exceptional Children.

Guess, D., Sailor, W., & Baer, D. (1978). Children with limited language. In R. Schiefelbusch (Ed.), *Language intervention strategies.* Baltimore: University Park Press.

Guillory, L. (1966). *Expressive and receptive fingerspelling for hearing adults.* Baton Rouge, LA: Claitors.

Gunter, C., & van Kleeck, A. (1984). *The integration of social routines into language evaluation and treatment.* Poster session presented at the American Speech–Language–Hearing Association convention, San Francisco, CA.

Gustason, G. (1975). Signing Exact English *Gallaudet Today, 5,* 11–15.

Gustason, G. (1983a). *Teaching and learning Signing Exact English: An idea book.* Los Alamitos, CA: Modern Signs Press.

Gustason, G. (1983b). *Student workbook.* Los Alamitos, CA: Modern Signs Press.

Gustason, G., Pfetzing, D., & Zawolkow, E. (1980). *Signing Exact English* (3rd ed.). Los Alamitos, CA: Modern Signs Press.

Halle, J., Alpert, C., & Anderson, S. (1984). Natural environment language assessment and intervention with severely impaired preschoolers. *Topic in Early Childhood Special Education, 4*(2), 35–56.

Halle, J., Baer, D., & Spradlin, J. (1981). Teachers' generalized use of delay as a stimulus control procedure to increase language use in handicapped children. *Journal of Applied Behavioral Analysis, 14,* 389–409.

Hamre-Nietupski, S., Stoll, A., Holtz, K., Fullerton, P., Ryan-Flottum, M., & Brown, L. (1977). Curricular strategies for teaching selected nonverbal communication skills to nonverbal and verbal severely handicapped students. In L. Brown, J. Nietupski, S. Lyon, S. Hamre-Nietupski, T. Crowner, & L. Grunewald (Eds.), *Curricular strategies for teaching functional object use, nonverbal communication, problem solving and mealtime skills to severely handicapped students* (Vol. VII, Part 1, pp. 95–250). Madison, WI: Department of Specialized Educational Services, Madison Metropolitan School District.

Hanna, R., Lippert, E., & Harris, A. (1982). *Developmental communication curriculum.* Columbus, OH: Charles E. Merrill.

Hanson, M., & Harris, S. (1986). *Teaching the young child with motor delays.* Austin, TX: Pro-Ed.

Harris, D., & Vanderheiden, G. (1980). Enhancing the development of communicative interaction. In R. Schiefelbusch (Ed.), *Nonspeech language and communication: Analysis and intervention* (pp. 227–257). Austin, TX: Pro-Ed.

Harris, S. (1975). Teaching language to nonverbal children — with emphasis on problems of generalization. *Psychological Bulletin, 82,* 565–585.

Harris, S. (1976). *Managing behavior 8. Behavior modification: Teaching speech to a nonverbal child.* Lawrence, KS: H and H Enterprises.

Harris-Vanderheiden, D. (1976). Blissymbols and the mentally retarded. In G. Vanderheiden & K. Grilley (Eds.), *Non-vocal communication techniques and aids for the severely physically handicapped* (pp. 123–131). Austin, TX: Pro-Ed.

Hart, B. (1985). Naturalistic language training techniques. In S. Warren & A. Rogers-Warren (Eds.), *Teaching functional language* (pp. 63–88). Austin, TX: Pro-Ed.

Hart, B., & Risley, T. (1982). *How to use incidental teaching for elaborating language.* Austin, TX: Pro-Ed.

Hart, B., & Rogers-Warren, A. (1978). A milieu approach to teaching language. In R. Schiefelbusch (Ed.), *Language intervention strategies* (pp. 193–235). Baltimore: University Park Press.

Hart, V. (1977). The use of many disciplines with the severely and profoundly handicapped. In E. Sontag (Ed.), *Educational programming for the severely and profoundly handicapped* (pp. 391–396). Reston, VA: Division on Mental Retardation, Council for Exceptional Children.

Hayden, A., & McGinness, G. (1977). Bases for early intervention. In E. Sontag (Ed.), *Educational programming for the severely and profoundly handicapped* (pp. 153–165). Reston, VA: Division on Mental Retardation, Council for Exceptional Children.

Haynes, U. (1976). *Staff development handbook: A resource for the transdisciplinary process.* New York: United Cerebral Palsy Association.

Hehner, J. (1979). *Blissymbols for use.* Toronto, Ontario: Blissymbolics Communication International.

Henegar, M., & Cornett, O. (1971). *Cued Speech handbook for parents.* Washington, DC: Cued Speech Program, Gallaudet College.

Higgins, J., & Mills, J. (1986). Communication training in real environments. In S. Blackstone (Ed.), *Augmentative communication: An introduction* (pp. 345–352). Rockville, MD: American Speech–Language–Hearing Association.

Hill, L., Bennett, R., & Pistell, D. (1985). *Communicating Together, 3,* 23–25.

Hobson, P., & Duncan, P. (1979). Sign learning and profoundly retarded people. *Mental Retardation, 17,* 33–37.

Hofmann, A. (1984). *The many faces of funding.* Mill Valley, CA: Phonic Ear.

Hofmann, A. (1986, January). *The many faces of funding* (update). Mill Valley, CA: Phonic Ear.

Hogg, J. (1975). Normative development and educational program planning for severely educationally sub-normal children. In C. Kierman & F. Woodford (Eds.), *Behavior modification with the severely retarded.* Amsterdam, Holland: Associated Scientific Publishers.

Holland, A. (1975). Language therapy for children: Some thoughts on context and content. *Journal of Speech and Hearing Disorders, 40,* 514–523.

Holm, V., & McCartin, R. (1978). Interdisciplinary child development team: Team issues and training in interdisciplinariness. In E. Allen, V. Holm, & R. Schiefelbusch (Eds.), *Early intervention — A team approach* (pp. 97–122). Baltimore, MD: University Park Press.

Holvoet, J., Guess, D., Mulligan, M., & Brown, F. (1980). The individualized curriculum sequencing model (III): A teaching strategy for severely handicapped students. *Journal of the Association for Persons with Severe Handicaps, 5,* 352–367.

Horner, R., McDonnell, J., & Bellamy, T. (1986). Teaching generalized skills: General case instruction in simulation and community settings. In R. Horner, L. Meyer, & B. Fredericks (Eds.), *Education of learners with severe handicaps: Exemplary service strategies* (pp. 289–314). Baltimore: Paul H. Brookes.

Horner, R., Meyer, L., & Fredericks, B. (1986). *Education of learners with severe handicaps: Exemplary service strategies.* Baltimore: Paul H. Brookes.

Horstmeier, D., & MacDonald, J. (1978). *Ready, set, go: Talk to me.* Columbus, OH: Charles E. Merrill.

House, L., & Rogerson, B. (1984). *Comprehensive screening tool for determining optimal communication mode.* East Aurora, NY: United Educational Services.

Huer, M. (1983). *The nonspeech test.* Wauconda, IL: Don Johnston Developmental Equipment.

Huer, M. (1987). White's gestural system for the lower extremities. *Communicating Together, 5,* 3–4.

Humphries, T., Padden, C., & O'Rourke, T. (1980). *A basic course in American Sign Language.* Silver Spring, MD: TJ Publishers.

Hunt, P., Goetz, L., Alwell, M., & Sailor W. (1986). Using an interrupted behavior chain strategy to teach generalized communication responses. *The Journal of the Association for Persons with Severe Handicaps, 11,* 196–204.

Hutinger, P. (1986). *ACTT Curriculum.* Macomb, IL: Project ACTT.

Huttenlocher, J. (1974). The origins of language comprehension. In R. Solso (Ed.), *Theories in cognitive psychology.* New York: Halsted Press.

Jastak, J., Bijou, S., & Jastak, S. (1978). *Wide range achievement test.* Wilmington, DL: West Psychological Services.

Jensema, C. (1979). Communication methods used with deaf-blind children: Making the decision. *American Annals of the Deaf, 124,* 7–8.

Johnson, P. (1987). *Express yourself: Communication disabilities need not be handicaps.* Richfield, MN: Pegijohn.

Johnson, R. (1985). Picture communication symbols. *Communicating Together, 3*(3), 23.

Johnson-Martin, N., Jens, K., & Attermeier, S. (1985). *The Carolina curriculum for handicapped infants and infants at risk.* Baltimore: Paul H. Brookes.

Jolie, K. (1985). On peer interaction. *Communicating Together, 3*(1), 18–19.

Jones, P., & Cregan, A. (1986). *Sign and symbol communication for mentally handicapped people.* London: Croom Helm.

Jordan, I., Gustason, G., & Rosen, R. (1976). Current trends in programs for the deaf. *American Annals of the Deaf, 121,* 527–532.

Jordan, I., Gustason, G., & Rosen, R. (1979). An update on communication trends at programs for the deaf. *American Annals of the Deaf, 124,* 350–357.

Kahn, J. (1978). Acceleration of object permanence with severely and profoundly retarded children. *American Association of Education for the Severely and Profoundly Handicapped Review, 3,* 16–22.

Karlan, G., & Lloyd, L. (1983). Considerations in the planning of communication intervention: Selecting a lexicon. *Journal of the Association for the Severely Handicapped, 8,* 13–25.

Kates, B., & McNaughton, S. (1975). *The first application of Blissymbolics as a communication medium for nonspeaking children: History and development, 1971–1974.*

Toronto, Ontario: Blissymbolics Communication International.

Keeney, T., & Wolfe, J. (1972). The acquistion of agreement in English. *Journal of Verbal Learning and Verbal Behavior, 11,* 698–705.

Keogh, W., & Reichle, J. (1985). Communication intervention for the "difficult-to-teach" severely handicapped. In S. Warren & A. Rogers-Warren (Eds.), *Teaching functional language.* Austin, TX: Pro-Ed.

Kent, L. (1974). *Language acquisition program for the retarded and multiply impaired.* Champaign, IL: Research Press.

Kettrick, C. (1984). *American Sign Language: A beginning course.* Silver Spring, MD: National Association for the Deaf.

Kiernan, C. (1981). A strategy for research on the use of nonvocal systems of communication. *Journal of Autism and Developmental Disablities, 11,* 139–151.

Kiernan, C., Jordan, R., & Saunders, C. (1978). *Starting off: Establishing play and communication in the handicapped child.* London: Souvenir Press.

Kiernan, C., Reid, B., & Jones, L. (1979). Signs and symbols — Who uses what? *Special Education: Forward Trends, 6,* 32–34.

Kimble, S. (1975). *Signed English: A language teaching technique with totally nonverbal, severely mentally retarded adolescents.* Paper presented at the American Speech–Language–Hearing Association convention, Washington, DC.

Kirchner, S. (1977). *Signs for all seasons: More sign language games.* Northridge, CA: Joyce Media.

Kirk, S., McCarthy, J., & Kirk, W. (1968). *The Illinois test of psycholinguistic abilties* (Rev. ed.). Urbana, IL: University of Illinois Press.

Klima, E., & Belluggi, U. (1979). *The signs of language.* Cambridge, MA: Harvard University Press.

Kollinzas, G. (1983). The communication record: Sharing information to promote sign language generalization. *Journal of the Association for Persons with Severe Handicaps, 8,* 49–55.

Konstantareas, M., Oxman, J., & Webster, C. (1978). Iconicity: Effects on the acquisition of sign language by autistic and other dysfunctional children. In P. Siple (Ed.), *Understanding language through sign language research* (pp. 213–237). New York: Academic Press.

Kopchick, G., & Lloyd, L. (1976). Total communication for the severely language impaired: A 24-hour approach. In L. Lloyd (Ed.), *Communication assessment and intervention strategies* (pp. 501–522). Baltimore: University Park Press.

Koselka, M., Hannah, E., Gardner, J., & Reagan. (1975). *Total communication therapy for a non-deaf child and his family.* Paper presented at the American Speech and Hearing Association convention, Washington, DC.

Kraat, A. (1985a). *Communication interaction between aided and natural speakers: A state of the art report.* Toronto, Ontario: Canadian Rehabilitation Council for the Disabled.

Kraat, A. (1985b). The technical aid maze. A short course at the Southeast Augmentative Communication Conference, Birmingham, AL.

Kraat, A. (1986). Developing intervention goals. In S. Blackstone (Ed.), *Augmentative communication: An introduction* (pp. 197–266). Rockville, MD: American Speech–Language–Hearing Association.

Kraat, A., & Sitver-Kogut, M. (1985). *Features of commercially available communication devices.* Flushing, NY: Augmentative Communication Program, Speech and Hearing Center, Queens College.

Kriegsmann, E., Gallaher, J., & Meyers, A. (1982). Sign programs with nonverbal hearing children. *Exceptional Children, 48,* 436–445.

Krogman, W. (1979). The cleft palate team in action. In H. Cooper, R. Harding, W. Krogman, M. Mazaheri, & R. Millard (Eds.), *Cleft palate and cleft lip: A team approach.* Philadelphia: W.B. Saunders.

Kuhn, D. (1973). Imitation theory and research from a cognitive perspective. *Human Development, 16,* 157–180.

Kyle, J., & Woll, B. (1983). *Language in sign: An international perspective on sign language.* London: Croom Helm.

Lahey, M., & Bloom, L. (1977). Planning a first lexicon: Which words to teach first. *Journal of Speech and Hearing Disorders, 42,* 340–350.

Lane, H. (1977). *Notes for a psychohistory of American Sign Language. Deaf American, 30,* 3–7.

Langley, B. (1980). *Functional vision inventory for the multiply and severely handicapped.* Chicago, IL: Stoelting Company.

Lapidus, D., Adler, N., & Modugno, P. (1984). *The use of communication boards with the autistic population: A training workshop for educators and parents.* Paper presented at the Council for Exceptional Children convention, Washington, DC.

Larson, S., & Hammill, D. (1976). *The test of written spelling.* Austin, TX: Pro-Ed.

Leathers, D. (1986). *Successful nonverbal communication: Principles and applications.* New York: MacMillan.

Liddell, S. (1978). Nonmanual signals and relative clauses in American Sign Language. In P. Siple (Ed.), *Understanding language through sign language research* (pp. 59–90). New York: Academic Press.

Liebergott, J. (1980). Facilitating communication and linguistic abilities in preschool language impaired children. A short course presented at the Three Rivers Conference on Communicative Disorders, Pittsburgh, PA.

Liebman, R. (1977). Feeding therapy and speech: Some problems of oral motor control. In A. Golbin (Ed.), *Cerebral palsy and communication: What parents can do* (pp. 27–44). Washington, DC: George Washington University.

Light, J., McNaughton, D., & Parnes, P. (1986). *A protocol for the assessment of the communicative interaction skills of nonspeaking severely handicapped adults and their facilitators.* Toronto, Ontario: Augmentative Communication Service, Hugh MacMillan Medical Centre.

Lippman, M. (1974). Enactive imagery in paired-associate learning. *Memory and Cognition, 2,* 385–390.

Lipschultz, S., & Shane, H. (1980). *Assessment procedures for nonspeaking persons* (Experimental ed.). Unpublished manuscript, Boston, MA.

Lloyd, L. (1982). Symbol and initial lexicon selection. *Proceedings of the Second International Conference on Non-Speech Communication,* 9–15. Toronto, Ontario: Ontario Institute for Studies in Education.

Lloyd, L. (1985). Comments on terminology. *Augmentative and Alternative Communication, 1,* 95–97.

Lovaas, O. I. (1981). *Teaching developmentally disabled children: The ME book.* Austin, TX: Pro-Ed.

Love, R., Hagerman, E., & Taimi, E. (1980). Speech performance, dysphagia and oral reflexes in cerebral palsy. *Journal of Speech and Hearing Disorders, 45,* 59–75.

Luce, S., & Christian, W. (1981). *How to reduce autistic and severely maladaptive behaviors.* Austin, TX: Pro-Ed.

Luftig, R. (1984). An analysis of initial sign lexicons as a function of eight learnability variables. *Journal of the Association for Persons with Severe Handicaps, 9,* 193–200.

Luftig, R., Page, J., & Lloyd, L. (1983). Ratings of 854 ASL signs for perceived translucency. *Journal of Children with Communication Disorders, 5,* 50–70.

Lytton, R., Carlson, J., DeSilva, A., Glass, J., Lake, K., & Pensa, D. (1987). *Fostering child–child communicative interaction in the classroom. Implementation strategies for improving the use of communication aids in schools serving handicapped children.* Rockville, MD: The American Speech–Language–Hearing Association.

MacDonald, J. (1985). Language through conversation: A model for intervention with language-delayed persons. In S. Warren & A. Rogers-Warren (Eds.), *Teaching functional language: Generalization and maintenance of language skills* (pp. 89–122). Austin, TX: Pro-Ed.

MacDonald, J., & Gillette, Y. (1986). *Ecological communication system (ECO).* Columbus, OH: Nisonger Center, Ohio State University.

MacDonald, J., Gillette, Y., Bickley, M., & Rodrigues, C. (1984). *Conversation routines.* Columbus, OH: Ohio State University.

Madsen, W. (1982). *Intermediate conversational sign language.* Washington, DC: Gallaudet University Press.

Makohon, L., & Fredericks, H. (1985). *Teaching expressive and receptive language to students with moderate and severe handicaps.* Austin, TX: Pro-Ed.

Mallary, G. (1881). *Sign language among North American Indians compared with that among other peoples and deaf mutes.* In *First annual report of the Bureau of Ethnology to the Secretary of the Smithsonian Institution 1879–1880* (pp. 263–552). Washington, DC: Government Printing Office.

Manolson, A. (1984). *It takes two to talk: A Hanen early language parent guide book.* Toronto, Ontario: Hanen Early Language Resource Centre.

Markowicz, H. (1977). *American Sign Language: Fact and fancy.* Washington, DC: Gallaudet College.

Mayberry, R. (1976). If a chimp can learn sign language, surely my nonverbal client can too. *Asha, 18,* 223–228.

Mayberry, R. (1978). Manual communication. In H. Davis & S. Silverman (Eds.), *Hearing and deafness.* New York: Holt, Rinehart, and Winston.

McBride, T., & Blau, A. (1985). A letter to our nonspeaking friends. *Communicating Together, 3*(3), 4–6.

McCormack, J., & Audette, R. (1977). Developing twenty-four hour service plans for severely handicapped learners. *AAESPH Review, 2,* 209–216.

McDonald, E. (1980a). Early identification and treatment of children at risk for speech development. In R. Schiefelbusch (Ed.), *Nonspeech language and communication: Analysis and intervention* (pp. 49–79). Austin, TX: Pro-Ed.

McDonald, E. (1980b). *Teaching and using Blissymbolics.* Toronto: Blissymbolics Communication International.

McDonald, E. (1987). *Treating cerebral palsy: For clinicians by clinicians.* Austin, TX: Pro-Ed.

McLean, J., & Snyder-McLean, L. (1978). *Transactional approach to early language training.* Columbus, OH: Charles E. Merrill.

McLean, J., Snyder-McLean, L., Jacobs, P., & Rowland, C. (1981). *Process-oriented educational programs for the severely/profoundly handicapped adolescent.* Parsons, KS: Parsons Research Center, University of Kansas, Bureau of Child Research.

McNaughton, D., & Light, J. (1986). Strategies to facilitate communication. *Communicating Together 4*(1), 10–11.

McNaughton, S. (1985). *Communicating with Blissymbolics.* Toronto, Ontario: Blissymbolics Communication International.

McNaughton, S., & Kates, B. (1980). The application of Blissymbolics. In R. Schiefelbusch (Ed.), *Nonspeech language and communication: Analysis and intervention* (pp. 303–321). Austin, TX: Pro-Ed.

McNaughton, S., & Warrick, A. (1984). Picture your Blissymbols. *Canadian Journal on Mental Retardation, 34*(4), 1–9.

Meyer, L., & Evans, I. (1986). Modification of excess behavior: An adaptive and functional approach for educational and community contexts. In R. Horner, L. Meyer, & H. Fredericks (Eds.), *Education of learners with severe handicaps* (pp. 315–350). Baltimore: Paul H. Brookes.

Miller, A. (1968). *Symbol accentuation — A new approach to reading.* Santa Ana, CA: Doubleday Multimedia.

Miller, J. (1977). On specifying what to teach: The movement from structure, to structure and meaning, to structure and meaning and knowing. In E. Sontag (Ed.), *Educational programming for the severely and profoundly handicapped* (pp. 378–388). Reston, VA: Division on Mental Retardation, Council for Exceptional Children.

Miller, J., Chapman, R., Branston, M., & Reichle, J. (1980). Language comprehension in sensorimotor stages V and VI. *Journal of Speech and Hearing Research, 23,* 284–311.

Miller, J., Reichle, J., & Rettie, M. (1977). *Sensorimotor, Stage 5 — Children's responses to requests and demands in a free play task.* Unpublished manuscript, Madison, WI.

Miller, J., & Yoder, D. (1974). An ontogenetic language teaching strategy for retarded children. In R. Schiefelbusch & L. Lloyd (Eds.), *Language perspectives: Acquisition, retardation, and intervention* (pp. 505–528). Baltimore: University Park Press.

Mills v. Board of Education of the District of Columbia. (1972). 348 Federal Supplement 866, DCDC.

Mills, C., & Weldon, L. (1983). Effects of semantic and cheremic context on acquisition of manual signs. *Memory and Cognition, 11,* 93–100.

Mills, J., & Higgins, J. (1983). *Non-oral communication assessment and training guide.* Encinitas, CA: Authors.

Mirenda, P. (1985). Designing pictorial communication systems for physically able-bodied students with severe handicaps. *Augmentative and Alternative Communication, 1,* 58–64.

Montgomery, J. (1979). Potential funding sources for the purchase of non-oral communication systems. In C. Cohen, J. Montgomery, & D. Yoder (Eds.), *Phonic Mirror Handivoice Seminar Manual* (pp. 166–167). Mill Valley, CA: H.C. Electronics.

Montgomery, J. (1980a). Measuring communication aid effectiveness. *Non-oral Communication Center Newsletter, 3,* 1–3.

Montgomery, J. (1980b). *Non-oral communication: A training guide for the child without speech.* Fountain Valley, CA: The Plavan School

Moores, D. (1980). American Sign Language: Historical perspectives and current issues. In R. Schiefelbusch (Ed.), *Nonspeech language and communication: Analysis and intervention* (pp. 93–100). Austin, TX: Pro-Ed.

Morris, S. (1982a). *The normal acquisition of oral feeding skills: Implications for assessment and treatment.* New York: Therapeutic Media.

Morris, S. (1982b). *Pre-speech assessment scale.* Clifton, NJ: J.A. Preston.

Mueller, H. (1975). Feeding. In N. Finnie (Ed.), *Handling the young cerebral palsied child at home* (pp. 113–132). New York: E.P. Dutton.

Munson, J., Nordquist,C., & Thuma-Rew, S. (1987). *Communication systems for persons with severe neuromotor impairment.* Iowa City, IA: The University of Iowa.

Musselwhite, C. (1982). *A comparison of three symbolic communication systems.* Unpublished doctoral dissertation, West Virginia University, Morgantown, WV.

Musselwhite, C. (1984). Use of ideosyncratic signals by motorically impaired non-speakers. *Aug-Communique, 3*(4), 2.

Musselwhite, C. (1985). *Songbook: Signs and symbols for children.* Wauconda, IL: Don Johnston Developmental Equipment.

Musselwhite, C. (1986a). *Adaptive play for special needs children: Strategies to enhance communication and learning.* San Diego, CA: College-Hill Press.

Musselwhite, C. (1986b). Introducing augmentative communication: Interactive training strategies. *NSSLHA Journal, 14,* 68–82.

Musselwhite, C. (1987). Augmentative communication. In E. McDonald (Ed.), *Treating cerebral palsy: For clinicians by clinicians* (pp. 209–238). Austin, TX: Pro-Ed.

Musselwhite, C., & St. Louis, K. W. (1982). *Communication programming for the severely handicapped: Vocal and non-vocal strategies.* San Diego: College-Hill Press.

Musselwhite, C., & Ruscello, D. (1984). The transparency of three communication symbol systems. *Journal óf· Speech and Hearing Research, 27,* 436–443.

Nicholls, C. (1979). *Cued Speech and the reception of spoken language.* Unpublished master's thesis, McGill University, Montreal, Canada.

Nietupski, J., & Hamre-Nietupski, S. (1979). Teaching auxiliary communication skills to severely handicapped learners. *AAESPH Review, 4,* 107–124.

Nietupski, J., & Williams, W. (1974). Teaching severely handicapped students to use the telephone to initiate selected recreational activities and to respond to telephone requests to engage in selected recreational activities. In L. Brown, W. Williams, & T. Crowner (Eds.), *A collection of papers and programs related to public school services for severely handicapped students* (Vol. 4, pp. 507–560). Madison, WI: Madison Metropolitan School District.

Newell, A. (1974). Morse Code and voice control for the disabled. In K. Copeland (Ed.), *Aids for the severely handicapped* (pp. 54–58). New York: Grune & Stratton.

Norris, L. (1985). Parent involvement in augmentative communication programs. *Communicating Together, 3*(2), 13.

Norton, S., Schultz, M., Reed, C., Braida, L., Durlach, J., Rabinowitz, W., & Chomsky, C. (1977). Analytic study of the Tadoma method: Background and preliminary results. *Journal of Speech and Hearing Research, 20,* 574–595.

Oakander, S. (1980). *Language board instruction kit.* Fountain Valley, CA: Non Oral Communication Center, Plavan School.

Oliver, P., & Scott, T. (1981). Group versus individual training in establishing generalization of language skills with severely handicapped individuals. *Mental Retardation, 19,* 285–289.

Olswang, L., Kriegsmann, E., & Mastergeorge, A. (1982). Facilitating functional requesting in pragmatically impaired children. *Language, Speech, and Hearing Services in Schools, 13,* 202–222.

Orcutt, D. (1984). *The Worldsign Symbolbook.* Winlaw, British Columbia: Worldsign Communication Society.

Orcutt, D. (1985). Worldsign update. *Communicating Together, 3*(4), 24–25.

Orcutt, D. (1987). *The Worldsign exposition.* Winlaw, British Columbia: Worldsign Communication Society.

Orelove, F., & Sobsey, D. (1987). *Educating children with multiple disabilities: A transdisciplinary approach.* Baltimore: Paul H. Brookes.

Owens, R. (1982). *Program for the acquisition of language with the severely impaired (PALS).* Columbus, OH: Charles E. Merrill.

Owens, R., & House, L. (1984). Decision-making processes in augmentative communication. *Journal of Speech and Hearing Disorders, 49,* 18–25.

Paget, R. (1951). *The new sign language.* London: The Welcome Foundation.

Paget, R., Gorman, P., & Paget, G. (1976). *The Paget Gorman Sign System* (6th ed.). London: Association for Experiment in Deaf Education.

Paivio, A., Yuille, J., & Madigan, S. (1968). Concreteness, imagery, and meaningfulness values for 925 nouns. *Journal of Experimental Child Psychology Monographs, 76,* 245–263.

Piaget, J. (1954). *The construction of reality in the child.* New York: Ballentine.

Piaget, J. (1966). *The origins of intelligence in children.* New York: International University Press.

Piaget, J., & Inhelder, B. (1969). *The psychology of the child.* New York: Basic Books.

Popovich, D. (1981). *A prescriptive behavioral checklist for the severely and profoundly retarded.* Austin, TX: Pro-Ed.

Porter, P., Carter, S., Goolsby, E., Martin, N., Reed, M., Stowers, S., & Wurth, B. (1985). *Prerequisites to the use of augmentative communication.* Chapel Hill, NC: Division for Disorders of Development and Learning.

Potoki, P., Miller, B., & Canosa, D. (1980). *Hands on: A manipulative curriculum for teaching multiply handicapped hearing impaired students.* Tucson, AZ: Communication Skill Builders.

Powell, T., & Ogle, P. (1985). *Brothers and sisters — A special part of exceptional families.* Baltimore: Paul H. Brookes.

Premack, D. (1970). A functional analysis of language. *Journal of Experimental Analysis of Behavior, 14,* 107–125.

Prentke-Romich Funding Packet. (1986). Wooster, OH: The Prentke-Romich Company.

Radtka, S. (1978). Feeding reflexes and neural control. In J. Wilson (Ed.), *Oral-motor function and dysfunction in children.* Chapel Hill, NC: Division of Physical Therapy, University of North Carolina.

Rees, N. (1975). Imitation and language development: Issues and clinical implications. *Journal of Speech and Hearing Disorders, 40,* 339–350.

Reichle, J., & Karlan, G. (1985). The selection of an augmentative system in communication intervention: A critique of decision rules. *Journal of the Association for Persons with Severe Handicaps, 10*(3), 146–156.

Reichle, J., & Keogh, W. (1985). Communication intervention: A selective review of what, when, and how to teach. In S. Warren & A. Rogers-Warren (Eds.), *Teaching functional language* (pp. 25–59). Austin, TX: Pro-Ed.

Reichle, J., & Keogh, W. (1986). Communication instruction for learners with severe handicaps: Some unresolved issues. In R. Horner, L. Meyer, & H. Fredericks (Eds.), *Education of learners with severe handicaps: Exemplary service strategies*. Baltimore, Paul H. Brookes.

Reichle, J., Williams, W., & Ryan, S. (1981). Selecting signs for the formulation of an augmentative communication modality. *Journal of the Association for Persons with Severe Handicaps, 6*(1), 48–56.

Reichle, J., & Yoder, D. (1979). Assessment and early stimulation of communication in the severely and profoundly mentally retarded. In R. York & E. Edgar (Eds.), *Teaching the severely handicapped* (Vol. 4, pp. 155–179). Columbus, OH: Special Press.

Reichle, J., & Yoder, D. (1985). Communication board use in severely handicapped learners. *Language, Speech, and Hearing Services in Schools, 16,* 146–157.

Reid, D., & Favell, J. (1984). Group instruction with persons who have severe disabilities: A critical review. *Journal of the Association for Persons with Severe Handicaps, 9,* 167–177.

Rieke, J., Lynch, L., & Soltman, S. (1977). *Teaching strategies for language development.* New York: Grune & Stratton.

Rincover, A. (1981). *How to use sensory extinction.* Austin, TX: Pro-Ed.

Risley, T., Hart, B., & Doke, L. (1972). Operant language development: The outline of a therapeutic technology. In R. Schiefelbusch (Ed.), *Language of the mentally retarded* (pp. 107–123). Baltimore: University Park Press.

Robinson, C., & Robinson, J. (1978). Sensorimotor functions and cognitive development. In M. Snell (Ed.), *Systematic instruction of the moderately and severely handicapped* (pp. 102–153). Columbus, OH: Charles E. Merrill.

Robinson, C., & Robinson, J. (1983). Sensorimotor functions and cognitive development. In M. Snell (Ed.), *Systematic instruction of the moderately and severely handicapped* (2nd ed., pp. 227–266). Columbus, OH: Charles E. Merrill.

Robison, A. (1986). An open letter to my daughter's teacher. *Communicating Together, 4,* 8–9.

Robison, G., & Robison, A. (1985). Obtaining insurance funding for your handicapped dependent's needs. *Communicating Outlook, 7*(3), 7–8.

Romski, M., & Ruder, K. (1984). Effects of speech and speech and sign instruction on oral language learning and generalization of action + object combinations by Down's syndrome children. *Journal of Speech and Hearing Disorders, 49,* 293–302.

Romski, M., Sevcik, R., Pate, J., & Rumbaugh, D. (1985). Discrimination of lexigrams and traditional orthography by nonspeaking severely mentally retarded persons. *American Journal of Mental Deficiency, 90,* 185–189.

Romski, M., White, R., Millen, C., & Rumbaugh, D. (1984). Effects of computer-keyboard teaching on the symbolic communication of severely retarded persons: Five case studies. *The Psychological Record, 34,* 39–54.

Roos, P. (1977). A parent's view of what public education should accomplish. In E. Sontag (Ed.), *Educational programming for the severely and profoundly handicapped* (pp. 72–83). Reston, VA: Division on Mental Retardation, Council for Exceptional Children.

Rothschild, N. (1984). Sharing ideas with Nora. *Communicating Together, 2*(3), 15.

Rothschild, N. (1985). Sharing ideas with Nora. *Communicating Together, 3*(4), 17–18.

Rothschild, N. (1986). Partner assisted scanning. *Communicating Together, 4*(3), 22–23.

Ruder, K., & Smith, M. (1974). Issues in language training. In R. Schiefelbusch & L. Lloyd (Eds.), *Language perspectives: Acquisition, retardation, and intervention.* Baltimore: University Park Press.

Ruggles, V. (1979). *Funding of non-vocal communication aids: Current issues and strategies.* New York: Muscular Dystrophy Association.

St. Louis, K. O., & Ruscello, D. (1987). *Oral speech mechanism screening examination, revised.* Austin, TX: Pro-Ed.

St. Louis, K. W., Mattingly, S., & Esposito, A. (1986). Receptive language curriculum for the moderately, severely, and profoundly handicapped. In J. D. Cone (Ed.), *Pyramid system curriculum.* Morgantown, WV: Pyramid Press.

St. Louis, K. W., & Rejzer, R. (1986). Expressive language curriculum for the moderately, severely, and profoundly handicapped. In J. D. Cone (Ed.), *Pyramid system curriculum.* Morgantown, WV: Pyramid Press.

Sailor, W., & Guess, D. (1983). *Severely handicapped students: An instructional design.* Boston: Houghton Mifflin.

Sapon, S., Kaczmarek, L., Welber, E., Rouzer, R., & Sapon-Shevin, M. (1976). *Readings in the descriptive analysis of behavior: Teaching strategies.* Rochester, NY: University of Rochester Verbal Behavior Laboratory.

Saulnier, K. (1974). *Songs in Signed English.* Washington, DC: Gallaudet University Press.

Savage-Rumbaugh, E. (1986). *Ape language research: From conditioned response to symbol.* New York: Columbia University Press.

Saya, M. (1979). *Adult aphasics and the Bliss symbol language.* Paper presented at the American Speech and Hearing Association convention, Atlanta, GA.

Sbaiti, M. (1983). *Cued Speech instructional manual.* Raleigh, NC: Cued Speech Center.

Schaeffer, B. (1980). Spontaneous language through signed speech. In R. Schiefelbusch (Ed.), *Nonspeech language and communication: Analysis and intervention* (pp. 421–446). Austin, TX: Pro-Ed.

Schery, T., & Wilcoxen, A. (1982). *Initial communication processes.* Monterey, CA: Publishers Test Service.

Scheuerman, N., Baumgart, D., Sipsma, K., & Brown, L. (1976). Toward the development of a curriculum for teaching nonverbal communication skills to severely handicapped students: Teaching basic tracking, scanning, and selection skills. In L. Brown, N. Scheuerman, & T. Crowner (Eds.), *Madison's alternative for zero exclusion: Toward an integrated therapy model for teaching motor, tracking, and scanning skills to severely handicapped students* (Vol. 6, Pt. 3). Madison, WI: Department of Specialized Educational Services, Madison Metropolitan School District.

Schumaker, B., & Sherman, J. (1978). Parent as intervention agent: From birth onward. In R. Schiefelbusch (Ed.), *Language intervention strategies* (pp. 237–315). Baltimore: University Park Press.

Schwartz, L., & McKinley, N. (1984). *Daily communication: Strategies for the language disordered adolescent.* Eau Claire, WI: Thinking Publications.

Seery, J. (1985). *Eye gaze communication systems, games, activities, interactions.* Unpublished manuscript, Spring Valley, NY.

Shane, H. (1981). Decision making in early augmentative communication system use. In R. Schiefelbusch & D. Bricker (Eds.), *Early language intervention.* Austin, TX: Pro-Ed.

Shane, H. (1986). Goals and uses. In S. Blackstone (Ed.), *Augmentative communication: An introduction* (pp. 29–48). Rockville, MD: American Speech–Language–Hearing Association.

Shane, H., & Bashir, A. (1980). Election criteria for the adoption of an augmentative communication system: Preliminary considerations. *Journal of Speech and Hearing Disorders, 45,* 408–414.

Shane, H., & Melrose, J. (1975). *An electronic conversation board and an accompanying training program for aphonic expressive communication.* Paper presented at the American Speech and Hearing Association convention, Washington, DC.

Shane, H., & Wilbur, R. (1980). Potential for expressive signing based on motor control. *Sign Language Studies, 29,* 331–340.

Shea, V., & Mount, M. (1982). *How to arrange the environment to stimulate and teach pre-language skills in the severely handicapped.* Austin, TX: Pro-Ed.

Sheppard, J. (1964). Cranio-oropharyngeal motor patterns associated with cerebral palsy. *Journal of Speech and Hearing Research, 7,* 373–380.

Shroyer, E., & Shroyer, S. (1984). *Signs across America.* Washington, DC: Gallaudet University Press.

Siegel, G., & Spradlin, J. (1978). Programming for language and communication therapy. In R. Schiefelbusch (Ed.), *Language intervention strategies* (pp. 357–398). Baltimore: University Park Press.

Siegel-Causey, E., & Guess, D. (in press). *Enhancing interactions between service providers and individuals who are severely multiply disabled: Strategies for developing nonsymbolic communication.* Monmouth, OR: Teaching Research.

Silverman, F. (1980). *Communication for the speechless.* Englewood Cliffs, NJ: Prentice-Hall.

Silverman, H., McNaughton, S., & Kates, B. (1978). *Handbook of Blissymbolics for instructors, users, parents, and administrators.* Toronto, Ontario: Blissymbolics Communication International.

Simpson, M., & McDade, H. (1979). *A total communication approach in an interdisciplinary infant development program.* Paper presented at the American Speech–Language–Hearing Association convention, Atlanta, GA.

Siple, P. (1978). Linguistic and psychological properties of American Sign Language: An overview. In P. Siple (Ed.), *Understanding language through sign language research* (pp. 3–23). New York: Academic Press.

Skelly, M. (1979). *Amer-Ind gestural code based on universal American Indian hand talk.* New York: Elsevier-North Holland.

Small-Morris, S. (1986). *Transparency of two representational systems: Picsyms and Picture Communication Symbols.* Unpublished master's thesis, Western Carolina University, Cullowhee, NC.

Smith, L. (1972). *Comprehension performance of oral deaf and normal hearing children at three stages of language development.* Unpublished doctoral dissertation, University of Wisconsin, Madison, WI.

Snell, M. (1983). Functional reading. In M. Snell (Ed.), *Systematic instruction of the moderately and severely handicapped* (2nd ed., pp. 445–487). Columbus, OH: Charles E. Merrill.

Snell, M., & Gast, D. (1981). Applying time delay procedure to the instruction of the severely handicapped. *Journal of the Association for Persons with Severe Handicaps, 6*(3), 3–14.

Snyder-McLean, L. (1978). *Language training procedures for non-verbal severely retarded clients: Functional stimulus and response variables.* Paper presented at the American Association for the Education of the Severely/Profoundly Handicapped Convention, Baltimore, MD.

Snyder-McLean, L., Solomonson, B., McLean, J., & Sack, S. (1984). Structuring joint action routines: A strategy for facilitating communication and language development in the classroom. *Seminars in Speech and Language, 5,* 213–228.

Sobsey, D. (1983). Comparison of feeding pureed and whole food to a multihandicapped adolescent. *Mental Retardation and Learning Disabilities Bulletin, 11,* 85–91.

Sobsey, R., & Bieniek, B. (1983). A family approach to functional sign language. *Behavior Modification, 7,* 488–502.

Soltman, S., & Rieke, J. (1977). Communication management for the nonresponsive child: A team approach. In E. Sontag (Ed.), *Educational programming for the severely and profoundly handicapped* (pp. 348–359). Reston, VA: Division on Mental Retardation, Council for Exceptional Children.

Song, A. (1979). Acquisition and use of Blissymbols by severely mentally retarded adolescents. *Mental Retardation, 17,* 253–255.

Sternat, J., Messina, R., Nietupski, J., Lyon, S., & Brown, L. (1977). Occupational and physical therapy services for severely handicapped students: Toward a naturalized public school service delivery model. In E. Sontag (Ed.), *Educational programming for the severely and profoundly handicapped* (pp. 263–278). Reston, VA: Division on Mental Retardation, Council for Exceptional Children.

Sternberg, M. (1981). *American Sign Language: A comprehensive dictionary.* New York: Harper & Row.

Stokes, T., & Baer, D. (1977). An implicit technology of generalization. *Journal of Applied Behavioral Analysis, 10,* 349–367.

Stokoe, W. (1980). The study and use of sign language. In R. Schiefelbusch (Ed.), *Nonspeech language and communication: Analysis and intervention* (pp. 123–155). Austin, TX: Pro-Ed.

Stokoe, W., Casterline, D., & Croneberg, C. (1978). *Dictionary of American Sign Language on linguistic principles* (Rev. ed.). Silver Spring, MD: Linstock Press.

Storm, R., & Willis, J. (1978). Small-group training as an alternative to individual programs for profoundly retarded persons. *American Journal of Mental Deficiency, 83,* 283–288.

Streifel, S., Wetherby, B., & Karlan, G. (1976). Establishing generalized verb–noun instruction-following skills in retarded children. *Journal of Experimental Child Psychology, 22,* 247–260.

Stremel-Campbell, K., & Campbell, C. (1985). Training techniques that may facilitate generalization. In S. Warren & A. Rogers-Warren (Eds.), *Teaching functional language* (pp. 251–285). Austin, TX: Pro-Ed.

Stremel-Campbell, K., Cantrell, D., & Halle, J. (1977). Manual signing as a language system and as a speech initiator for the nonverbal severely handicapped student. In E. Sontag (Ed.), *Educational programming for the severely and profoundly handicapped* (pp. 335–347). Reston, VA: Division on Mental Retardation, Council on Exceptional Children.

Struck, R. (1977). *Behavioral characteristics progression (BCP)*. Palo Alto, CA: VORT Corporation.

Stuart, S. (1986). Expanding sequencing, turntaking, and timing skills through play acting. In S. Blackstone (Ed.), *Augmentative communicatioin: An introduction* (pp. 389–396). Rockville, MD: American Speech–Language–Hearing Association.

Stump, R., Weinberg, W., & Baker, B. (1987). *Vocabulary development for augmentative communication*. Unpublished manuscript, Pittsburgh, PA.

Supalla, T., & Newport, E. (1978). How many seats in a chair? The derivation of nouns and verbs in American Sign Language. In P. Siple (Ed.), *Understanding language through Sign Language research* (pp. 91–132). New York: Academic Press.

Switzky, H., Rotator, A., Miller, T., & Freagon, S. (1979). The developmental model and its implications for assessment and instruction for the severely/profoundly handicapped. *Mental Retardation, 17,* 167–170.

Teaching American Sign Language as a second/foreign language. (1982). Silver Spring, MD: National Association of the Deaf.

Tennell, B. (1986). Talking with Tina. *Proceedings, Minspeak Conference* (pp. 44–49). Wooster, OH: Prentke Romich Company.

Thorndike, E., & Lorge, I. (1944). *The teacher's word book of 30,000 words*. New York: Columbia University Teachers College.

Tingey-Michaelis, C. (1983). *Handicapped infants and children: A handbook for parents and professionals*. Austin, TX: Pro-Ed.

Tompkins, W. (1931). *Universal sign language*. San Diego: Author.

Tomkins, W. (1969). *Indian Sign Language*. New York: Dover Publications, Inc.

Topper-Zweiban, S. (1977). Indicators of success in learning a manual communication mode. *Mental Retardation, 15,* 47–49.

Trantham, C., & Pedersen, J. (1976). *Normal language development: The key to diagnosis and therapy for language-disordered children*. Baltimore: The Williams & Wilkins Company.

Turnbull, A. (1978). Parent–professional interactions. In M. Snell (Ed.), *Systematic instruction of the moderately and severely handicapped* (pp. 458–476). Columbus, OH: Charles E. Merrill.

Turnbull, A. (1983). Parent–professional interactions. In M. Snell (Ed.), *Systematic instruction of the moderately and severely handicapped* (Rev. ed., pp. 18–43). Columbus, OH: Charles E. Merrill.

Utley, B., Holvoet, J., & Barnes, K. (1977). Handling, positioning, and feeding the physically handicapped. In E. Sontag (Ed.), *Educational programming for the severely and profoundly handicapped* (pp. 279–299). Reston, VA: Division on Mental Retardation, Council for Exceptional Children.

Uzgiris, J., & Hunt, J. (1975). *Assessment in infancy: Ordinal scales of psychological development.* Urbana, IL: University of Illinois Press.

Vagnini, C. (1984). Critical questions to consider in selecting a communication aid. *Communicating Together, 2*(3), 16–17.

van Oosteroom, J., & Devereux, K. (1984). *Learning with rebuses glossary.* Stratford Upon Avon, England: National Council for Special Education.

Van Tatenhove, G. (1978). *Augmentative communication board development: A response training protocol.* Paper presented at the American Speech–Language–Hearing Association convention, Atlanta, GA.

Van Tatenhove, G. (1986a). Transition through graphic symbol systems. *Communication Outlook, 6*(3), 27–29.

Van Tatenhove, G. (1986b). Vocabulary versatility for the person who is nonspeaking. *Communicating Together, 4*(3), 19–20.

Van Tatenhove, G. (1986c). Development of a location, color-coded etran. In S. Blackstone (Ed.), *Augmentative communication: An introduction* (pp. 397–409). Rockville, MD: American Speech–Language–Hearing Association.

Van Tatenhove, G. (1987). *Training caregivers and facilitators to select vocabulary. Implementation strategies for improving the use of communication aids in schools.* Rockville, MD: American Speech–Language–Hearing Association.

Vanderheiden, G. (1984). A high efficiency flexible keyboard input acceleration technique: SPEEDKEY. *Proceedings of the Second International Conference on Rehabilitation Engineering* (pp. 353–354). Washington, DC: RESNA.

Vanderheiden, G. (1987). Advanced techology aids for communication, education, and employment. In E. McDonald, *Treating cerebral palsy: For clinicians by clinicians* (pp. 257–273). Austin, TX: Pro-Ed.

Vanderheiden, G., & Grilley, K. (1976). *Non-vocal communication techniques and aids for the severely physically handicapped.* Austin, TX: Pro-Ed.

Vanderheiden, G., & Lloyd, L. (1986). Communication systems and their components. In S. Blackstone (Ed.), *Augmentative communication: An introduction* (pp. 49–161). Rockville, MD: American Speech–Language–Hearing Association.

Vanderheiden, G., & Yoder, D. (1986). Overview. In S. Blackstone (Ed.), *Augmentative communication: An introduction* (pp. 1–28). Rockville, MD: American Speech–Language–Hearing Association.

Vicker, B. (1974). *Nonoral communication system project, 1964/1973.* Iowa City, IA: Campus Stores, Publishers, The University of Iowa.

Walker, M. (1976). *The revised makaton vocabulary.* Camberley, Surrey, England: Makaton Vocabulary Development Project.

Ward, D. (1986). *Positioning the handicapped child for function.* Chicago, IL: Phoenix Press.

Warren, S. (1985). Clinical strategies for the measurement of language generalization. In S. Warren & A. Rogers-Warren (Eds.), *Teaching functional language* (pp. 197–224). Austin, TX: Pro-Ed.

Warren, S., & Rogers-Warren, A. (Eds.). (1985). *Teaching functional language.* Austin, TX: Pro-Ed.

Warrick, A. (1984). Worldsign: A kinetic language. *Communicating Together, 2*(3), 17–19.

Warrick, A. (1985). Picture your Blissymbols. *Aug-Communique, 3*(1), 5–6.

Warrick, A. (1987). Can we play a game tonight? *Communicating Together, 5*(3), 15–16.

Waryas, C., & Stremmel-Campbell, K. (1978). Grammatical training for the language-delayed child: A new perspective. In R. Schiefelbusch (Ed.), *Language intervention strategies* (pp. 145–192). Baltimore: University Park Press.

Wasson, P., Tynan, T., & Gardiner, P. (1982). *Test adaptations for the handicapped.* San Antonio, TX: Education Service Center, Region 20.

Westby, C. (1980). Assessment of cognitive and language abilities through play. *Language, Speech, and Hearing Services in Schools, 11,* 154–168.

Wetherby, B., & Streifel, S. (1978). Application of miniature linguistic system of matrix-training procedures. In R. Schiefelbusch (Ed.), *Language intervention strategies* (pp. 317–356). Baltimore: University Park Press.

Whitley, K. (1985). Picture communication symbols (PCS): A review. *Aug-Communique, 3*(1), 3.

Whitman, T., Zakaras, M., & Chardos, S. (1971). Effects of reinforcement and guidance procedures on instruction-following behavior of severely retarded children. *Journal of Applied Behavioral Analysis, 4,* 283–290.

Wilbur, R. (1976). The linguistics of manual language and manual systems. In L. Lloyd (Ed.), *Communication assessment and intervention strategies* (pp. 423–500). Baltimore: University Park Press.

Wilbur, R. (1979). *American Sign Language and sign systems.* Baltimore: University Park Press.

Wilbur, R. (1987). *American Sign Language: Linguistic and applied dimensions.* San Diego: College-Hill Press.

Williams, J., Csongradi, J., & LeBlanc, M. (1982). *A guide to controls: Selection, mounting, applications.* Palo Alto, CA: Rehabilitation Engineering Center, Children's Hospital at Stanford.

Williams, W., Brown, L., & Certo, N. (1975). Basic components of instructional programs for severely handicapped students. *Theory Into Practice, 14,* 123–136.

Williams, W., & Fox, T. (1977). Communication. In W. Williams & T. Fox (Eds.), *Minimum objective system for pupils with severe handicaps: Working draft number one.* Burlington, VT: Center for Special Education, University of Vermont.

Wojcio, M., Gustason, G., & Zawolkow, E. (1983). *Music in motion.* Los Alamitos, CA: Modern Signs Press.

Woll, B., Kyle, J., & Deuchar, M. (1981). *Perspectives on British Sign Language and deafness.* London, England: Croom Helm.

Woodcock, R. (1968). *Rebuses as a medium in beginning reading instruction.* Nashville, TN: Institute on Mental Retardation and Intellectual Development.

Woodcock, R., Clark, C., & Davies, C. (1969). *The Peabody rebus reading program.* Circle Pines, MN: American Guidance Service.

Woodward, J. (1976). Signs of change: Historical variation in American Sign Language. *Sign Language Studies, 10,* 81–94.

Woodward, J. (1978). Historical bases of American Sign Language. In P. Siple (Ed.), *Understanding language through sign language research* (pp. 333–347). New York: Academic Press.

Woolman, D. (1980). A presymbolic training program. In R. Schiefelbusch (Ed.), *Nonspeech language and communication* (pp. 325–356). Austin, TX: Pro-Ed.

Wright, C., & Nomura, M. (1985). *From toys to computers: Access for the physically disabled child.* Wauconda, IL: Don Johnston Developmental Equipment.

Wulz, S., & Hollis, J. (1980). Word identification and comprehension training for exceptional children. In R. Schiefelbusch (Ed.), *Nonspeech language and communication: Analysis and intervention* (pp. 357–387). Austin, TX: Pro-Ed.

Yorkston, K., & Karlan, G. (1986). Assessment procedures. In S. Blackstone (Ed.), *Augmentative communication: An introduction* (pp. 163–196). Rockville, MD: American Speech–Language–Hearing Association.

Yorkston, K., Marriner, N., Smith, K., Dowden, P., & Honsinger, M. (1987). *Vocabulary selection.* Unpublished manuscript, Seattle, WA.

Appendix A
Glossary

SPEECH: the exposed — voiced and/or articulated — output of the communication system.[1]

LANGUAGE: a conventional set of arbitrary symbols, and a set of rules for combining these symbols, to represent ideas about the world for the purpose of communication.[1]

COMMUNICATION: the transmission of meaning from one individual to another whatever the means used (verbal, with and without speech; nonverbal, with and without vocal output). Communication implies a process of social interaction.[1]

AUGMENTATIVE COMMUNICATION: techniques that supplement speech for communication. It should be noted that everyone uses augmentative techniques, such as writing, gestures, facial expression, and so on, when communicating and interacting with others. Individuals with severe speech impairments must relay more on these standard augmentative techniques, as well as on special and more developed augmentative techniques, to better meet their communication needs.[2]

MODE OF COMMUNICATION: A different major channel or form of communication, such as speech, gesture, and writing.[2]

COMMUNICATION SYSTEM: the integrated network of techniques, aids, strategies, and skills that a person uses to communicate. For example, an individual system would be comprised of an integrated set of components, including facial and manual gestures, speech and other vocalizations, conversation and writing aids, as well as specific strategies and skills for using these various modes successfully in a variety of communication contexts. An aid is *not* a communication system, but rather one *component* of an individual's electronic communication overall system.[2]

---

[1] Adapted from Lloyd (1985).
[2] Adapted from Vanderheiden and Yoder (1986).

UNAIDED: symbols and symbol systems that do not require any aids or devices but use only the sender's face, head, arms and other parts of the body. These are sometimes referred to as "manual," "sign," or "gestural" systems. Those symbols are nonenduring, and frequently involve movement or change. Thus, they may also be termed "dynamic." Examples are natural sign language (e.g., American Sign Language), manually coded English (e.g., Signed English), and manual alphabets.[1]

AIDED: symbols and symbol systems that require some type of external assistance, or an aid or device such as paper, pencil, pictures, charts, communication boards, or electronic devices. Graphic symbols, such as pictures, symbolic systems (e.g., Blissymbols), or traditional orthography are typically used as aids, and are often termed "static," as they are relatively fixed or permanent.[1]

SYMBOLS: spoken, graphic, or manual representations of objects, actions, relationships, and so forth. While spoken symbols are temporal and are conveyed through the auditory–vocal modality, graphic and manual symbols are spatial and temporal, and are conveyed through the visual modality.[1]

GESTURES AND SIGNS: two related types of manual symbols used in non-speech communication. Signs and gestures that have been conventionalized must conform to certain rules or are constrained in their formation and usage; unconventionalized gestures have no such linguistic constraints, but do have cultural interpretations. Most signs — the linguistic elements of meaning in sign language — are relatively abstract, while gestures tend to be concrete. The meaning of most gestures, therefore, tends to be concrete; the meaning of most gestures can often be guessed, while the meaning of most signs cannot.[1]

Appendix B
An Annotated Bibliography

The following annotated bibliography is designed to acquaint the reader with recent literature in the area of communication theories, programs, and therapy techniques rather than to provide reviews of technical research studies. The entries selected for inclusion are representative of available material in the area of communication programming for severely handicapped people, and are not intended to be an exhaustive examination of the literature.

The entries are listed alphabetically by authors. To assist the reader in locating entries related to specific communication modes and related topics, the following codes are used:

VOC   =   Vocal
TECH =   Technology
AID   =   Aided communication system
UNA   =   Unaided communication system
PH   =   Physically handicapped
DD   =   Developmentally delayed
AS   =   Assessment
INT   =   Intervention
PRE   =   Preliminary Skills
GEN   =   General theoretical or background information

Babbini, B. E. (1974). *Manual communication: Fingerspelling and the language of signs. A course of study for instructors.* Order from University of Illinois Press, distributed by Harper & Row, Inc., Keystone Industrial Park, Scranton, PA 18512; 203 pages (UNA).

This manual is designed for use by instructors of manual communication courses. It is intended for use in courses focusing on American Sign Language and the

American Manual Alphabet. The manual is divided into two main sections. The first section includes chapters covering general principles, general procedures, the use of videotaping equipment, and the teaching of fingerspelling. The second section presents an outline for a course of study divided into two levels: beginning (14 lesson plans) and intermediate (11 lesson plans). The material in each lesson is designed to be covered in a 2- or 3-hour class session. Each lesson includes drill and practice materials, lists of signs to be taught, an outline format lesson plan, and tests to be administered. An annotated bibilography is provided including books, films, and teaching media relative to signs, fingerspelling, and deafness. A student manual is available.

Beaupre, W. (1984). *Gaining Cued Speech proficiency: A manual for parents, teachers, and clinicians.* Order from Dr. Walter J. Beaupre, Department of Communicative Disorders, University of Rhode Island, P.O. Box 8, Kingston, RI 02881; 149 pages (INT/UNA).

This manual is intended for those who need to gain proficiency in Cued Speech. It will thus be useful for parents, relatives, teachers, clinicians, and others working or conversing with persons needing a supplementary visual model of oral language. While this manual is primarily for American dialects, it can be adapted for other spoken English dialects. Phonemic spelling, a respelling system, is used throughout the book to clarify correct pronunciation and cueing. A copy of the Basic Cued Speech Proficiency Rating Profile is included, for analyzing skills of cuers. The lessons follow proficiency goals and error factors identified in that profile (e.g., eliminating halting or chopping phrases within utterances). Practice materials are provided throughout, plus nursery rhyme cue tips and cue practice with the 1,000 most common words.

Behrmann, M. (Ed.). (1984). *Handbook of microcomputers in special education.* Order from College-Hill Press/Little, Brown and Company, Customer Service Department, 200 West Street, Waltham, MA 02254, 290 pages (INT/PH/TECH).

The format of this book takes the reader from the basics about computers and what they can do for educators through applications for specific groups. Use of the computer as an instructional medium is described, with special emphasis on programming and instructional methodology. The second section describes current microcomputer applications with a variety of populations, including people who are physically impaired and young or cognitively low-functioning. One section concentrates on training professionals in computer use, with special emphasis on software evaluation and hardware selection. The final section addresses the future of computers in special education, with the inclusion of fascinating projections.

Bender, M., Valletutti, P. J., and Bender, R. (1985). *Teaching the moderately and severely handicapped. Vol. II: Communication, socialization, safety and leisure skills.* Order from Pro-Ed, 5341 Industrial Oaks Blvd., Austin, TX 78735; 352 pages (PRE, DD, VOC, AS, IN).

This volume contains a detailed section describing a practical method for assessing communication abilities and activities for training receptive and expressive language skills in the moderately and severely handicapped population. Although the major emphasis of this program is on eventual speech production, modification of procedures are suggested for the client who has severe motor coordination problems.

Bergen, A., and Colangelo, C. (1982). *Postitioning the client with central nervous system deficits: The wheelchair and other adapted equipment.* Order from Valhalla Rehabilitation Publications, Ltd., P.O. Box 195, Valhalla, NY 10595; 191 pages (PH).

This manual in intended to help professionals in prescribing positioning devices with the goal of yielding maximum function with minimal pathology. Guidelines are presented for evaluating, problem solving, and constructing or ordering equipment. Topics covered are the pros and cons of adapted equipment, sitting, upper extremity positioning, the wheelchair as a custom device, assessment and measuring of the lapboard, specialized wheelchairs, and other positioning devices (e.g., prone positioners). More than 400 illustrations and photographs supplement the text.

Beukelman, D., Yorkston, K., and Dowden, P. (1985). *Communication augmentation: A casebook of clinical management.* Order from College-Hill Press/Little, Brown and Company, Customer Service Department, 200 West Street, Waltham, MA 02254; 244 pages (AID/AS/INT/TECH).

The overview for this book covers a general orientation to aided communication augmentation and the strategies to be used in making selection decisions (needs assessment, assessment of user capability, and performance trials). Twelve case examples are presented, representing a variety of etiologies and approaches. For each case, the following information is provided: background, description of initial evaluation; intervention approach; and a set of questions for the clinician. Photographs and diagrams are used extensively to illustrate case management. Appendices present an assessment of needs and an augmentative communication evaluation intake form.

Bigge, J. L. and O'Donnell, P. A. (1982). *Teaching individuals with physical and multiple disabilities* (2nd ed.). Order from Charles E. Merrill Publishing Co., 1300 Alum Creek Drive, Box 508, Columbus, OH 43216; 424 pages (PH, INT).

This book provides an overview of many physically handicapping conditions and offers suggestions for developing individualized training programs to meet specific needs (e.g., self-care, communication, leisure activities, work). The general framework for the book concerns using task analysis to assess carefully the client's abilities and to plan training procedures. Each chapter includes references and "Resources," which are sources of additional program suggestions.

Blacher, J. (Ed.). (1984). *Severely handicapped young children and their families: Research in review.* Order from Academic Press, Harcourt Brace Jovanovich Building, Orlando, FL 32887; 449 pages (GEN).

This book details research conducted with families and professionals dealing with handicapped children. The issue of placement alternatives is addressed realistically. Stress factors within families are discussed. Family involvement in the educational process is explored. Several of the contributing authors comment that special educators are sometimes unrealistic about the influence the family has on the student, and about their own ability to assist the families to meet their unique needs.

Blackstone, S. (Ed.). (1986). *Augmentative communication: An introduction.* Order from American Speech-Language-Hearing Association, 10801 Rockville Pike, Rockville, MD 20852; 505 pages (AID/AS/GEN/INT/UNA).

This narrative is intended to be used as a text for augmentative communication courses. It is an edited book, with chapters by many well known professionals in the area of augmentative communication. Chapters are presented on the following topics: overview of augmentative communication; goals and uses; communication systems and their components; assessment procedures; developing intervention goals; training strategies (including 13 specific strategies); evaluating the effectiveness of intervention programs; total habilitation and life-long management; and future needs and directions in augmentative communication. Each chapter includes both objectives and study questions.

Bloom, L. and Lahey, M. (1978). *Language development and language disorders.* Order from Macmillan Publishing Co., Front and Brown Streets, Riverside, NJ 08075; 689 pages (GEN).

This book is divided into six main parts. Part 1 defines language and presents principles and procedures for describing language behavior. Part 2 contains seven chapters on the topic of normal language development from the perspective of an integration of content, form, and use. Part 3 comprises several chapters on deviant language development. Part 4 presents four chapters relating to developing goals of language learning based on normal development. Part 5 reviews the correlates of language disorders from several viewpoints. The final part covers general and specific procedures for facilitating language learning.

Bluma, S., Shearer, M., Frohman, A., and Hillard, J. (1976). *Portage guide to early education.* Order from Cooperative Educational Services Agency 12, Box 564, Portage, WI 53901; (VOC, AS, INT).

The *Portage Guide* contains a detailed checklist of behavior for assessing and training severely handicapped individuals. The system has color-coded cards containing a training objective and activities that correspond to the assessment items. Language development is only one area covered by this program. The objectives range from early awareness of sound to carrying on a conversation using complete sentences. This is a speech-oriented program and does not present alternative communication systems.

Bolton, S. O., and Dashiell, S. E. (1984). *INCH: The Interactive checklist for augmentative communication.* Order from INCH Associates, 9568 Hamilton Avenue, Suite 104, Huntington Beach, CA 92647; 48 pages (UNA, AS).

INCH is an observational tool to assess interactive behavior of nonspeakers. It was developed ". . . to describe the critical features of interaction between augmentative system users and their receivers" (p. 3). The observation form is divided into sections dealing with strategies, modes, and contexts. The strategies included are: initation, facilitation regulation, and termination of a communication interaction. The behavior of the nonspeaker as sender and receiver of a message is recorded according to the mode of response (e.g., linguistic, paralinguistic, kinesic, proxemic, or chronemic). All terms are well defined and suggestions for training in increasing the use of each strategy are offered in the manual.

Bornstein, H., and Jordan, I. (1984). *Functional signs: A new approach from simple to complex*. Order from Pro-Ed, 5341 Industrial Oaks Boulevard, Austin, TX 78735; 392 pages (UNA/INT).

This dictionary presents 330 American Sign Language signs for frequently appearing words to be used with persons having severe communication impairment. Bornstein and Jordan identified sign characteristics (movement, handshape, and location) that are not necessary for the sign to be recognized by persons familiar with the sign. The book uses this informaton to help instructors determine where and how to begin teaching a sign if the whole sign cannot be produced. Information is provided to indicate which signs may cause confusion if specified sign characteristics cannot be produced. Suggestions are also provided regarding signs that are easily recognized even if produced imperfectly. Teaching strategies are presented for promoting production of various sign characteristics.

Bornstein, H., and Saulnier, K. (1984). *The Signed English starter*. Order from Gallaudet Bookstore, Kendall Green, P. O. Box 300, Washington, DC 20002; 208 pages (INA).

This dictionary provides a basic vocabulary of Signed English signs. Signs are presented through line drawings, with explicit verbal descriptions of sign production. Signs are arranged categorically (e.g., people and pronouns, things, the body, descriptions). In each section, basic Signed English markers and principles relating to the category are presented. For example, in the section on nature and animals, examples are given for the iconic nature of signs, and markers are described for adjectives ending in -*y* or -*ly* . A glossary of terms and a sign index are provided. A comprehensive set of exercises is included with each section to allow practice in the production of Signed English.

Bornstein, H., Saulnier, K. L., and Hamilton, L. B. (Eds.). (1983). *The comprehensive Signed English dictionary*. Order from Gallaudet University Press, 800 Florida Avenue NE, Washington DC 20002; 454 pages (UNA).

The purpose, nature, and use of Signed English are discussed in the introduction. Various teaching aids for Signed English, such as story books and posters, are described. The dictionary includes over 3,100 signs that represent the meaning of English words used frequently by and with preschool children. For each sign, the English gloss, an illustration, and a short description are provided. The American Manual Alphabet, numbers, and 14 sign markers (e.g., past regular -*ed,* adjectives -*y)* are also provided.

Brandenburg, S., and Vanderheiden, G. (1987a). *Communication, control, and computer access for disabled and elderly individuals. ResourceBook 1: Communication Aids.*

Order from College-Hill Press/Little, Brown and Company, Customer Service Department, 200 West Street, Waltham MA, 02254; 264 pages (AID/TECH).

This resource book presents communication aids in six categories: speech aids, pointing and typing aids, training and communication initation aids, nonelectronic communication aids, electronic communication and writing aids, and telecommunication devices for the deaf. Each entry includes the following information: vendor, size, weight, power source, cost, and a prose description of the aid. Four indices provide a cross-listing of the products according to function (e.g., Braille, word processing), input/output feature (e.g., directed scanning, large print), switches listed by input/output feature (e.g., movement activated, joystick output), and computer system used (e.g., Apple IIe, IBM PC). Appendices present a wide range of additional sources of information, a glossary, manufacturers listed with their products, and an alphabetical listing of all products.

Brandenberg, S., and Vanderheiden, G. (1987b). *Communication, control, and computer access for disabled and elderly individuals. ResourceBook 2: Switches and environmental controls.* Order from College-Hill Press/Little, Brown and Company, Customer Service Department, 200 West Street, Waltham, MA 02254; 276 pages (AID/TECH).

This resource book includes product descriptions for items in three categories: (1) switches and controls, (2) environmental controls, and (3) calling, monitoring, and memory systems. For each entry, the following information is included: vendor, number of switches, activation pressure, connector type, and cost. Indices and appendices are identical to those described in *ResourceBook 1* (listed previously).

Brandenburg, S., and Vanderheiden, G. (1987). *Communication, control, and computer access for disabled and elderly individuals. ResourceBook 3: Hardware and Software.* Order from College-Hill Press/ Little, Brown and Company, Customer Service Department, 200 West Street, Waltham, MA 02254; 516 pages (AID/TECH).

This resource book includes two major sections. The first covers microcomputer adaptations, divided into eight categories, such as modifications for standard keyboards, input adapters for computers, and speech synthesizers. Indices and appendices are identical to those described in *ResourceBook 1* (listed previously).

Burkhart, L. (1980). *Homemade battery powered toys and educational devices for severely handicapped children.* Order from Linda J. Burkhart, 8303 Rhode Island Ave., College Park, MD, 20740; 57 pages (DD/INT/PH).

This is the first of two how-to books on constructing simple switches and toy adaptations easily and inexpensively. Switches include a pressure switch and a head control switch. Very simple adaptive toys can also be made from the illustrated instructions. The book is intended for parents, teachers, and other professionals.

Burkhart, L. (1982). *More homemade battery devices for severely handicapped children with suggested activities.* Order from Linda J. Burkhart, 8303 Rhode Island Ave., College Park, MD, 20740; 169 pages (DD/INT/PH).

This is the second book in this how-to series. Chapter 1 presents step-by-step instructions for constructing 29 switches (e.g., cookie sheet, ring pull, and penny-pincher switches), while Chapter 2 provides toy adaptations for various battery sizes. Chapter 3 describes construction of four communication training devices (e.g., pointing training switch). Chapter 4 offers specific programming instructions for developing cognitive communication, motor, and social/self-help skills. Six appendicies cover topics such as soldering and locating supplies.

Burkhart, L. (1987). *Using computers and speech synthesis to facilitate communicative interaction with young and/or severely handicapped children.* Order from Linda J. Burkhart, 8303 Rhode Island Ave., College Park, MD, 29740.

This book presents a compilation of ideas and strategies for use with children who are young or have severe handicaps. The primary focus is on use of speech synthesis for children who are non-speaking, pre-speaking, or beginning to speak. Numerous strategies and activities are presented for teaching communicative interaction using speech synthesis or recorded voice and for teaching scanning. Alternative methods of computer input and construction of adaptive devices are also covered. Specific directions are provided for using speech synthesis with five types of computers (Commodore 64, Vic 20, Apple, TRS-80, and TI-99/4A).

Canadian Rehabilitation Council for the Disabled. (1984). *Conversations with non-speaking people.* Order from University Centers for International Rehabilitation, Michigan State University for International Rehabilitation, Michigan State University, 513 Erickson Hall, East Lansing, MI, 48824; 63 pages (AID/PH/TECH).

This book is a project of the International Project on Communication Aids for the Speech-Impaired (IPCAS). It includes first-person narratives by users of communication aids, and third-person accounts by clinicians or family members. Contributions come from aid users from Canada, Sweden, the United Kingdom, and the United States. The accounts range from poignant insights, to humorous discussions, to practical tracing of steps taken to establish or reestablish communication. The selections are extremely readable and of interest to professionals, family members, and augmentative communication users.

Carlson, F. (1985). *PICSYMS categorical dictionary.* Order from Baggeboda Press, 1128 Rhode Island St., Lawrence, KS, 66044; 190 pages (AID/INT).

This manual is intended for use by parents or professionals who have already been trained in working with symbol users. The first section presents the rules for using PICSYMS, describes specific techniques for drawing the symbols, and provides suggestions for making the symbols meaningful to children. The second section presents samples of PICSYMS, arranged in categories, that may be copied for classroom or home use. These symbols are presented in various sizes and alternatives are depicted for many symbols, allowing for maturational considerations. Grids are provided for adding symbols to the system. The book is presented with a nontechnical, highly readable orientation.

Carlson, F. (1982). *Prattle and play: Equipment recipes for nonspeech communication.* Order from Media Resource Center, Meyer Children's Rehab Institute, University of Nebraska Medical Center, Omaha, NE 68131; 63 pages (AID/INT/PRE).

This book is divided into two sections. "Equipment" covers the materials and instructions needed to make each project, and "Adaptations" tells how to make changes to modify equipment to meet the needs of individuals. Examples of equipment include the looking board, playboard, and symbol blocks.

Catalog of Federal Domestic Assistance. (1986). Order from Superintendent of Documents, Government Printing Office, Washington, DC 20402; (GEN).

This document is issued yearly and describes government programs, containing such information regarding each program as its objectives, eligibility requirements, and information contacts. Several potential federal funding programs, and the agencies that they fall under, are:

1. Public Health Service I: Crippled Children's Services
2. Health Care Financing Administration: Medicaid and Medicare
3. Office of Human Development Services: Vocational Rehabilitation Services for Social Security Disability Beneficiaries.

All of these programs fall under the Department of Health and Human Services and information on them may be obtained by writing the appropriate agencies of that department.

Charlebois-Marois, C. (1985). *Everybody's technology: A sharing of ideas in augmentative communication.* Order from Charlecoms Enr., P. O. Box 419, Jean-Talon Station, Montreal, Quebec, Canada H1S 2Z3; 188 pages (AID/PH/PRE/TECH).

This book represents a sampling of ideas for augmentative communication materials. The chapters cover portable communication displays, laptrays, accessing tools such as headsticks, encoding techniques, commercial materials and products, and readiness skills. Each presentation includes a photograph or illustration, a description, the source, and the material required. Appendices present a variety of information sources. The entries are from a variety of professionals in a range of clinical settings.

Cregan, A. (1982). *Sigsymbol dictionary teaching pack.* Order from Ailsa Cregan, 76 Wood Close, Hatfield, England AL1O 8TX (UNA/INT).

The Sigsymbol Dictionary presents 240 entries. A variety of teaching materials are included in the teaching pack that accompanies the dictionary. General guidelines and specific rules for drawing Sigsymbols are included, so that additional entries can be developed. Activity cards are included for training specific entries and for teaching specific skills (e.g., answering questions).

Cregan, A., and Lloyd, L. (1988). *Sigsymbol dictionary: American edition.* Order from Don Johnson Developmental Equipment, P. O. Box 639, Wauconda, IL 60084 (UNA/INT).

This resource presents a modification of Sigsymbols to apply to American audiences. Most of the Sigsymbols in this dictionary are based on American signs, such as Signed English. A Sigsymbol overview is presented, followed by extensive Sigsymbol guidelines. More than 350 Sigsymbols are depicted, with the corresponding sign picture where appropriate. An expanded and revised version of the teaching activities from the *Sigsymbol Teaching Pack* (Cregan, 1982) is also included.

Christopher, D. A. (1976). *Manual communication.* Order from Pro-Ed, 5341 Industrial Oaks Blvd., Austin, TX 78735; 544 pages (UNA).

This is a programmed text and workbook designed to assist the beginning student professional (e.g., speech–language pathologist) learning the fundamentals of manual communication. Fingerspelling, number concepts, and Signed English using American Sign Language signs are presented. Forty-eight lessons are included. The first 44 cover the American Manual Alphabet, number concepts, and the basic vocabulary needed to communicate in sign language. Each lesson covers 20 signs; the signs are not arranged in alphabetical order or in any functional grouping or categories. An illustration, a written description, and one English translation are provided for each sign. Exercises in encoding and decoding are included at the end of the lessons. The final four chapters involve application of the material learned for conducting speech, language, and hearing evaluations.

Clark, C. R., Davies, C. O., and Woodcock, R. W., (1979). *Standard rebus glossary.* Order from American Guidance Services, P. O. Box 99, Circle Pines, MN 55014; 95 pages (AID, INT).

The *Standard Rebus Glossary* includes a listing of 2,000 words derived by combining the 818 basic rebus symbols with other symbols or letters. This system is useful for instruction with non-English speakers, as well as for nonspeaking communication for nonreaders who are developmentally delayed, hearing impaired, or severely physically handicapped. Rebuses can be put together to construct sentences providing natural language context for developing speech or augmented communication.

Clark, T. C., Morgan, E. C., and Wilson-Vlotman, A. L. (1984). *The INSITE Model. Volume III: Communication.* Order from the Utah Schools for the Deaf and the Blind, 846 20th Street, Ogdon, UT 84401; 159 pages (VOC, AID, UNA, INT).

This volume on communication is part of a four-volume program designed as a "parent centered, in-home, sensory interventive, training and educational program." Each volume is a curriculum manual for parent training. The other volumes cover the following areas. *Volume I: Manual for Parent Advisors to Accompany INSITE Curriculum. Volume II: Parent Discussions: Treatment of Sensory Disorders. Volume IV: Developmental Skills: Assessment/INSITE Checklist, Learning Activities, and Cross Reference Materials.* The *Communication* volume contains material regarding developing love and attachment, promoting sensorimotor responses, and developing communication skills. Although the focus is on speech communication, optional communication modes are addressed (signs and communication boards).

Darley, F. L. (Ed.). (1983). *Evaluation of appraisal techniques in speech and language pathology.* Order from Macmillan Publishing Co., Front and Brown Streets, Riverside, NJ 08075; (GEN, AS).

Communication Programming

Critical reviews of over 80 published tests are presented in this book. It is designed to acquaint speech–language pathologists with a variety of tests available to assess abilities such as language, speech production, and auditory discrimination. Each test critique includes the following: identifying information; purpose; administration, scoring, and interpretation; evaluation of test adequacy; a summary.

Duffy, R., and Duffy, J. (1984). *New England pantomine test.* Order from Pro-Ed, 5341 Industrial Oaks Boulevard, Austin, TX 78735; (AS/PRE/UNA).

This set of tests was developed to investigate the abilities of aphasic and other communicatively disordered adults to send and receive information nonverbally. Materials include a test manual and a booklet of picture plates. The set includes three tests. (1) Pantomime Recognition test: A nonverbal test of ability to recognize pantomimed acts associated with common objects (e.g., handkerchief, apple). (2) Pantomime Expression test: A measure of the ability to pantomime use of common objects from a picture cue. The 16-point multidimensional scoring system of the PICA is used for scoring. (3) Pantomime Referential Abilities test: A measurement of the communicative effectiveness of the individual on a simple pantomimic referential task, in which distractors have a shape or function similar to that of the target. Normative data is included. The authors suggest that these tests would be useful with children having disordered communication as well as with persons having aphasia.

Dunn, L. M., Smith, J. O., Dunn, L. M., Horton, K. B., and Smith, D. D. (1981). *Peabody language development kits.* Order from American Guidance Service, P. O. Box 99, Circle Pines, MN 55014; (VOC, INT).

The *Peabody Language Development Kits* provide a wide variety of materials and lesson plans to enrich language experiences in the classroom. There are four levels for ages ranging from 4 to 8 years old. Each kit includes from 275 to 500 colorful durable cards (8 × 9 inches). These cards are useful for stimulating associative thinking, classification, and vocabulary development. Audiocassettes are provided to teach songs and listening skills. Puppets are featured in many of the lessons and are part of each kit. Color chips for counting, sequencing, grouping, and reinforcement are contained in each kit. Large story posters encourage observation and story telling skills.

Dunn, M. (1982). *Pre-sign language motor skills.* Order from Communication Skill Builders, P.O. Box 42050-J, Tucson, AZ 85733; 105 pages (PRE/INT/UNA).

This workbook assists instructors in analyzing the motor components of signs, the motor skills an individual can use in signing, and methods for sign instruction. The perspective of occupational therapy is applied to sign training for children with cognitive delay. The workbook can be used as a self-teaching tool, with periodic probes to assess learning. Many of the worksheets for assessment and instruction may be reproduced for classroom use. The text is supported by numerous illustrations and examples.

336

Dunst, C. J. (1981). *Infant learning: A cognitive–linguistic intervention strategy.* Order from DLM/Teaching Resources, P.O. Box 4000, Allen, TX 75002; 217 pages (AS, INT, VOC).

This program is intended for use by teachers, therapists, and child-care workers. It uses a Piagetian-based model in developing cognitive, social, and language abilities for prelinguistic children. Target populations are children who are at risk, developmentally delayed, or severely handicapped. The three phases are (1) response-contingent behaviors (e.g., reaching, visual tracking), (2) sensorimotor abilities (e.g., vocal imitation, means–ends behaviors), and (3) early cognitive–linguistic abilities (e.g., symbolic play).

Elder, P. (1978). *Visual symbol communication instruction. Part I: Receptive instruction.* Order from Don Johnson Developmental Equipment, P.O. Box 639, Wauconda, IL 60084; 74 pages (AID).

This program provides an instructional protocol which specifically teaches a visual symbol system (Blissymbols, rebuses, etc.) to nonspeaking individuals, allowing a visual response by the severely physically handicapped person. The receptive instruction manual includes 25 sequential lesson plans which provide specific steps in teaching, reinforcement, and correction using the Visual Communication Display training device. Program guidelines, record keeping, scoring, and retention testing are described, and data sheets are provided for reproduction.

Eriksson, B. (1985). *Activities using headsticks and optical pointers.* Order from Handicappinstitutet, Box 303, S-161 26, Bromma, Sweden; 32 pages (AID/PRE/TECH).

This publication is intended as a follow-up to an earlier booklet entitled *Head-mounted aids.* The first section suggests ways to introduce head-mounted aids, including modifications of the work position, work surface, and the aid itself. Specific suggestions are made for adapting traditional games (hide-and-seek, doll play, board games) for use with head-mounted aids. Strategies are presented for using head-mounted aids for communication and for classroom activities, including craft, music, and cooking activities. The final section covers use of head-mounted aids in prevocational or vocational activities. Attractive and imaginative illustrations provide a helpful supplement to the text.

Evans-Morris, S. (1986). *Pre-speech assessment scale.* Order from J. A. Preston Corporation, 60 Page Road, Clifton, NJ 07012 (AS/PRE).

This tool is intended for assessing prespeech and feeding abilities of children functioning within the birth to two-year level of prespeech development. It reflects a neurodevelopmental treatment philosophy. The tool contains all information, instructions, and materials needed to complete an assessment. Assessment covers 27 prespeech performance areas within the following categories: feeding behavior, sucking, swallowing, biting and chewing, respiration–phonation, and sound play. Abnormal and normal scores can be assigned and tranferred to a graph to assist in monitoring the child's progress.

Favell, J., and Greene, J. (1980). *How to treat self-injurious behavior.* Order from Pro-Ed, 5341 Industrial Oaks Blvd., Austin, TX 78735-8898; 46 pages (PRE).

This manual is one in a how-to series for teaching autistic children. It is intended for parents, teachers, and therapists working with persons who engage in self-injurious behaviors such as head-banging and eye-poking. Topics covered include consideration of why a person might be self-injurious, pretreatment strategies (e.g., providing protection), assessment of the behavior in relation to the environment, specific treatment strategies, and techniques to promote generalization. The manual is written with carefully defined terms with numerous examples, and follows a workbook format.

Fell, A., Lynn, E., and Morrison, K. (1984). *Non-oral communication assessment (NOCA).* Order from Alice Fell, Alternatives to Speech, Inc., 1030 Duncan, Ann Arbor, MI 48103; 4 books (AS/PH).

This assessment tool is intended for speech, occupational, and physical therapists, and special educators. It offers a systematic approach to assessment of individuals experiencing severe physical and/or mental disabilities. The NOCA is divided into three parts: (1) motoric assessment for switching, (2) motoric functioning assessment for pointing, and (3) communication capacity assessment. The NOCA is packaged in four separate manuals. A 180-page instruction manual offers information relative to administration, scoring, and interpretation of the assessment, plus score forms. The other three manuals provide pictures for assessment.

Finnie, N. R. (1975). *Handling the young cerebral palsied child at home.* Order from E. P. Dutton Co., 2 Park Avenue, New York, NY 10016; 337 pages (PH/INT).

This book is intended for parents of cerebral palsied children. It may also be used by teachers or therapists working with parents or parent groups. Topics addressed include general areas, such as parents' emotional problems, and more specific areas, such as dressing, carrying, and teaching speech. Information regarding equipment, including chairs, wedges, and prone boards, is provided. The chapters on feeding and speech were written by a speech–language pathologist. They provide brief introductions to normal development, common problems, and beginning intervention.

Fiorentino, M. R. (1981). *Reflex testing methods for evaluating C.N.S. development.* Order from Charles C. Thomas Co., 2600 South First St., Springfield, IL 62717; 72 pages (AS).

This text is intended to assist in the assessment of the central nervous system of children through six years of age, and in the programming for neurophysiologically involved children. The focus for occupational, physical, and speech–language pathologists is to determine the maturational level and abnormal reflexes for planning implementation. Procedures are presented for testing reflexes at the spinal, brain stem, midbrain, and cortical levels. The test position, test stimulus, negative and positive reactions, and interpretation of findings are included for each reflex test.

Photographs are provided to illustrate negative and positive reactions for each test.

Fishman, I. (1987). *Electronic communication aids: Selection and use.* Order from College-Hill Press/Little, Brown and Company, Customer Service Department, 200 West Street, Waltham, MA 02254; 148 pages (AS/PH/TECH).

This book was written to serve as a practical guide to the selection and use of electronic communication aids. It is intended for students as well as practicing professionals in fields such as speech–language pathology, physical and occupational therapy, and special education. Families and users of electronic aids are also appropriate audiences. The book includes seven parts. Part I includes definitions of terms, roles, and realities, covering issues such as the importance of clear terminology and the need for both electronic and nonelectonic aids. Part II covers the crucial area of determining the range of communication needs for speech/writing impaired individuals, and dimensions of augmentative communication that must be considered in evaluating those needs. Part III describes the output of communication aids, divided into four chapters: attention-getters, visual selection, speech output, and visual displays and printers. In Part IV the various selection techniques for augmentative communication aids are considered, including direct selection and scanning, practical considerations in choosing and using a selection technique, encoding techniques, and control switches used with electronic aids. Part V presents a brief overview of symbols, vocabulary items, and vocabulary capabilities of communication aids. Dimensions for evaluating portability and mounting of communication aids are considered in Part VI. The final section introduces the issue of computer-based versus dedicated communication aids. The book includes numerous case examples, illustrations, and photographs to clarify and support the text. The format and the content combine to make the book extremely readable and comprehensible. Terms are clearly defined with examples provided so that the book is useful for persons unfamiliar with electronic aids.

Fredericks, H., Baldwin, V., Riggs, C., Furey, T., Grove, D., Moore, W., McDonnell, J., Jordon, E., Hanson, W., and Wadlow, M. (1976). *Teaching research motor development scale for moderately and severely retarded children.* Order from Charles C. Thomas, 2600 South First Street, Springfield, IL 62717; 345 pages (VOC/PRE).

This curriculum guide presents teaching objectives and some suggested procedures for a wide range of adaptive behaviors, including areas such as motor development, socialization, and receptive and expressive language development. The main emphasis of the language areas is on comprehension and ultimate speech production as the primary means of communication.

Gallagher, J. J., and Vietze, P. M. (Eds.). (1986). *Families of handicapped persons: Research, programs, and policy issues.* Order from Paul H. Brookes Publishing Co., P.O. Box 10624, Baltimore, MD 21285; 307 pages (GEN).

This book provides a comprehensive view of parenting practices, social interactions, counseling and intervention, family classification, and related family policy issues. The contributing authors present a multidisciplinary approach to serving families and fostering a supportive environment for growth of all family members. The special stresses and challenges faced by all people caring for the person with a handicap are presented realistically.

Gallender, D. (1979). *Eating handicaps; Illustrated techniques for feeding disorders.* Order from Charles C. Thomas, 2600 South First Street, Springfield, IL 62717; 312 pages (PH).

This book contains two major sections related to the eating problems of handicapped individuals. The first covers the basic anatomy and physiology of structures involved in the eating process, such as muscles and nerves. The second considers techniques and instructional materials for dealing with various eating problems. Over 200 techniques are suggested for decreasing abnormal behaviors, such as the bite or gag reflex, or enhancing normal behaviors such as jaw stability. Numerous pictures, diagrams, and illustrations are provided to clarify the text.

Goossens', C., and Crain, S. (1985). *Augmentative communication: Assessment resource.* Order from Don Johnston Developmental Equipment, P.O. Box 639, Wauconda, IL 60084; 200 pages (AS/GEN).

This resource book provides a variety of support materials for assessment of persons using augmentative communication. A wide range of topics are covered: candidacy for aided versus unaided technique; candidacy for input technique (direct selection, scanning); and candidacy for electronic aid/device. Materials provided include specific forms (e.g., intake forms, an initial letter/sound cueing test), guidelines (e.g., behavioral observations for cognitive assessment), information review (e.g., commercially available and homemade accessing tools), and how-to construction plans (e.g., constructing an adjustable pegboard easel). Numerous illustrations, cartoons, and examples provide support for the text.

Goossens', C., and Crain, S. (1985). *Augmentative communication: Intervention resource.* Order from Don Johnston Developmental Equipment, P.O. Box 639, Wauconda, IL 60084; 223 pages (INT/GEN).

This book provides a variety of resource materials for providing intervention services to persons needing augmentative communication. Intervention topics cover early augmentative communication, interactive play, early intervention with electronics, and aided and unaided communication. As with the companion *Assessment resource,* this book presents a range of supportive materials: guidelines (e.g., for establishing early communicative signals, for establishing interactive symbolic communication); summary information of sources (e.g., commercially available graphic symbol sets); and construction plans (e.g., constructing a multiple-display eye gaze communication vest).

Guess, D., Sailor, W., and Baer, D. (1974–1978). *Functional speech and language training for the severely handicapped.* Order from Pro-Ed, 5341 Industrial Oaks Blvd., Austin, TX 78735; each book 70 to 93 pages (VOC, INT).

This program is comprised of four books: *Part 1: Persons and Things, Part 2: Actions with Persons and Things, Part 3: Possession and Color, Part 4: Size, Relation, and Location.* The program was developed for persons with very limited language skills. The program is very specific in design so that the need for specifically trained teachers is eliminated, although some knowledge of behavior management techniques is useful. The program can be used in settings ranging from institutions to the home. Each book comes with scoring forms for recording progress in the program for each individual.

Gustason, G. (1983). *Teaching and learning Signing Exact English: An idea book.* Order from Modern Signs Press, Inc., P.O. Box 1181, Los Alamitos, CA 90720; 470 pages (UNA/INT).

This manual is intended to be used by teachers in conjunction with the Signing Exact English text (dictionary). The manual is arranged in a three ring binder format with five sections: (1) background information; (2) ideas, rules, and activities; (3) two sample curricula; (4) word groups; and (5) sign families with practice sentences. A variety of support materials is included, including charts, sample tests, and worksheets. Beginning, intermediate, and advanced levels are covered.

Gustason, G. (1983). *Student workbook.* Order from Modern Signs Press, Inc., P.O. Box 1181, Los Alamitos, CA 90720; 123 pages (UNA/INT).

This workbook includes lesson plans from Curricula A and B in the idea book by Gustason (1983). It also presents affixes for use with both the SEE text and the idea book. Curriculum A presents more than 700 words and affixes in a variety of categories (e.g., food, clothing, animal, family, house, adjectives). Fourteen lessons are included, with 30 new words included in each lesson. Curriculum B includes many of the same words, but is organized differently. Twenty-four lesson plans are included, with 30 words introduced in each. An additional 350 vocabulary words plus affixes are presented in a section on affixes.

Gustason, G., Pfetzing, D., and Zawolkow, E. (1980). *Signing Exact English* (3rd edition). Order from Modern Signs Press, Inc., P.O. Box 1181, Los Alamitos, CA 90720; 490 pages (UNA).

This sign dictionary contains manual signs representing nearly 4,000 words, as well as signs for letters, numbers, prefixes, and suffixes. Simple line drawings are accompanied by brief descriptions. For many signs, embellishments are included to indicate the origin of signs. Examples are the addition of facial expressions (e.g., smile for HAPPY) or line drawings of referents (e.g, a lei and drawing of the islands accompanying HAWAII). One chapter presents the background on SEE, suggestions for creative signing, and references for further reading.

Hagen, D. (1984). *Microcomputer resource book for special education.* Order from Don Johnson Developmental Equipment, P.O. Box 639, Wauconda, IL 60084; 205 pages (DD/INT/PH/TECH).

In this book, the author attempts to convey a dual purpose for the microcomputer in special education: (1) the special needs side, focusing on bringing equality to the special needs child through adaptations, and (2) traditional applications such as computer assisted instruction and word processing. The key focus is using microcomputer hardware and software to provide access, motivation, authoring systems, self expression, and normal function. Location of appropriate software is a major emphasis, with rules suggested for locating software. Appendices cover resources available for special education applications.

Hamre-Nietupski, S., Stoll, A., Holtz, K., Fullerton, P., Ryan-Flottum, M., and Brown, L. (1977). Curricular strategies for teaching selected nonverbal communication skills to nonverbal and verbal severely handicapped students. In *Curriculum strategies for teaching functional object use, nonverbal communiation, problem solving, and mealtime skills to severely handicapped students, Volume VII, Part 1.* Order from Department of Specialized Education Services, Madison Metropolitan School District, 545 West Dayton Street, Madison, WI; 156 pages (GEN/PRE/AID/UNA).

This curriculum covers three augmentative communication approaches: communication boards and booklets, generally understood gestures, and standardized signs. Considerations in selecting the optimum system and initial communicative content are covered. Two sets of curricular strategies are presented, one for communication boards/booklets and one for gestures/signs. Examples of instruction protocols, activities, and vocabulary lists are provided, with the bulk of the curricula consisting primarily of objectives. An appendix provides a list of more than 160 generally understood gestures.

Hanna, R. M., Lippert, E. A., and Harris, A. B. (1982). *Developmental communication curriculum.* Order from Charles E. Merrill Publishing Co., Test Division, Box 508, Columbus, OH 43216; (AS/INT/VOC/UNA).

This curriculum includes the following materials: curriculum guide, activity handbook, developmental communication inventory (package of 12), parent handout (package of 12). It is intended to help extend the prelinguistic communication skills on which language is based. The curriculum uses play as a natural context for learning, with specific objectives divided into three domains: content (64 objectives); function (51 objectives); and form (64 objectives).

Hanson, M., and Harris, S. (1986). *Teaching the young child with motor delays: A guide for parents and professionals.* Order from Pro-Ed, 5341 Industrial Oaks Boulevard, Austin, TX 78735; 228 pages (GEN/PRE).

This book has two major purposes; to answer basic questions about motor disabilities and suggest sources of additional information and assistance, and to offer basic teaching and handling strategies that can be used in daily activities to help overcome a child's motor problems. Part I provides parents with general information about delays in motor development and intervention approaches. Material covered includes personal accounts from parents, a medical perspective on motor impairment, issues encountered and case studies relative to those issues, the role of parent–infant interaction, and how to develop teaching goals and organize activities. Part II presents specific teaching and therapy activities in the following areas: positioning, handling, and adaptive equipment; specific activities for enhancing gross, fine, and oral–motor development; and activities for social, cognitive, and communication development. Appendices provide developmental milestones and resource lists.

Hart, B. M., and Risley, T. R. (1982). *How to use incidental teaching for elaborating language.* Order from Pro-Ed 5341 Industrial Oaks Blvd., Austin, TX 78735; 32 pages (VOC/INT).

This book is designed for parents and teachers concerned with improving language in children and encouraging them to use more language at home and in school. The concept of incidental teaching is explained, and detailed examples and steps are given to demonstrate its usage. Guidance in recognizing the best times to use this technique are presented.

Hoffman, A. (1986). *The many faces of funding (3rd edition).* Order from Phonic Ear Inc., 250 Camino Alto, Mill Valley, CA 94941; (AID).

This funding book in loose-leaf format begins with an overview section, reviewing major third-party funding programs. The method section outlines steps that should be taken to prepare for pursuing funding, including a funding sources checklist and strategies to consider in assembling supportive documents and building credibility. The third section presents case histories. A final section consists of short monthly newsletters providing updated information on funding. Samples are "How to appeal a denied insurance claim payment" and "Rehabilitation act reauthorized for five years."

Horner, R., Meyer, L., and Fredericks, H. (Eds.). (1986). *Education of learners with severe handicaps: Exemplary service strategies.* Order from Paul H. Brookes Publishing Company, P.O. Box 10624, Baltimore, MD 28285-0624; 371 pages (GEN).

This multi-authored text provides an excellent overview of many of the issues in educating persons having severe handicaps, including communication handicaps. The three sections are Exemplary Service Delivery Models (e.g., community-based service delivery), Curriculum Development (e.g., issues in communication instruction for learners with severe handicaps; skill cluster instruction), and Instructional Procedures and Technology (e.g., teaching generalized skills, modifying excess behavior). Chapters are written from theoretical perspectives, backed by research findings.

Horstmeier, D. S., and MacDonald, J. D. (1978). *Ready, set, go: Talk to me.* Order from Charles C. Thomas, 2600 South First Street, Springfield, IL 62717; (VOC/ PRE).

This book is intended for use by parents and professionals. It covers prelanguage and initial verbal communication skills. The content is based on a normal developmental sequence, with training being carried out continually in the child's environment. The book includes a series of prescriptive packets intended to be adapted to the needs of each child. A diagnostic screening test is provided to assist in determining which packet should be used. The authors also suggest how to adapt the program for classroom use.

This book is one component of the *Environmental Language Intervention Program,* which was designed for and tested on developmentally delayed children, and also includes the following materials: Oliver — a parent-administered communication inventory; Environmental Prelanguage Battery; and Environmental Language Inventory.

House, L., and Rogerson, B. (1984). *Comprehensive screening tool for determining optimal communication mode (CST).* Order from United Educational Services, Inc., Publishing Division, P.O. Box 357, East Aurora, NY 14052; (AS/AID/PRE/UNA).

This test was designed to systematize and objectify the decision process for determining whether to use an aided, unaided, or oral communication mode. It can also be used to document candidacy for an augmentative communication system. Three batteries are included. The Manual Skills Battery consists of three subtests (manual training, prerequisites for movement patterning, and cognitive correlates for manual communication). The goal is assessing skills needed for training of unaided communication. The Pictographic Skills Battery assesses skills that can predict successful use of an aided communication system. Three subtests are included (prerequisites for visual training, attending behaviors and accuracy of movement, and cognitive correlates). The Oral Skills Battery is intended to assess behaviors necessary for successful use of oral communication. Three subtests are included in that battery (oral reflexes, oral tactile sensitivity, respiratory and phonatory support and feeding sections). Materials include an administration manual, packages of scoresheets for individual subtests, and a scoring/summary profile.

Huer, M. (1983). *The nonspeech test (NST).* Order from Don Johnston Developmental Equipment, P.O. Box 639, Wauconda, IL 60084; (AS/PH).

This assessment tool was developed by a speech–language pathologist for use with nonspeaking physically-handicapped students. It was normed on a multi-handicapped population and a preschool population, providing an age equivalency score of birth to 48 months, given in monthly increments. Test materials include a picture book with 52 color pictures and 12 black and white drawings, a manual, tablets with 50 expressive and 50 receptive scoring forms, a set of objects, an audio tape explaining special applications for the test. Instructions are provided for observing a range of communication signals such as eye-pointing, use of communication boards, and sign language.

Hutinger, P. (1986). *ACTT Curriculum.* Order from Project ACTT, College of Education, Western Illinois University, 27 Horrabin Hall, Macomb, IL 61455; (INT/PRE/TECH).

This curriculum is based on the premise that the young disabled child must have the opportunity to be independent, a goal that can be accomplished by interacting with the environment through computers. Initial sections cover the philosophy of using the computer as a curricular tool, and teacher competencies for using the computer with disabled children. Three components cover various populations: birth to three years old, three to five years old, and severely/profoundly disabled children. Each of the components includes sections on learning environments (e.g., switch determination), curriculum activities (e.g., switching onto toys, discovering shapes), and parent involvement (e.g., switch involvement, hands-on training). Additional sections cover special issues for various populations, such as the Adaptive Firmware Card for severely/profoundly disabled people, and One Touch INSTANT LOGO for children three to five years of age. A Behavioral Interaction Tool allows the tutor to observe child–adult interaction skills (e.g., gaining attention), child–child interaction skills (e.g., cooperative behavior), and child–computer interaction skills (expressive behavior). A resource section includes adaptations for blind individuals; however, many of the resources would be helpful for working with all populations.

Johnson, P. (1987). *Express yourself: Communication disabilities need not be handicaps.* Order from Pegijohn, 6432 Fifth Avenue South, Richfield, MN 55423; 192 pages (GEN/PH/TECH).

This book is a compilation of information on selecting electronic communication devices for individuals with severe communication impairment. More than 50 portable communication devices are covered, with illustrations or photographs, text description, and ordering information provided for each device. Device selection is also considered, including assessment and evaluation considerations. Another section presents specific strategies and resources for funding of electronic communication devices. Appendices provide resource listings, with an emphasis on resources in the United States midwest.

Johnson-Martin, N., Jens, K., and Attermeier, S. (1986). *The Carolina curriculum for handicapped infants and infants at risk.* Order from Paul H. Brookes Publishing Company, P.O. Box 10624, Baltimore, MD 21285; 332 pages (AS/INT/PRE/GEN).

This curriculum is intended for providing assessment and intervention with infants and children with disabilities in 24 subdomains of development. A number of subdomains are preliminary to augmentative communication (e.g., visual pursuit and object permanence) or related directly to augmentative communication (e.g., gestural imitation, gestural communication). The curriculum is field-tested and follows a developmental model. A 20-page "Assessment Log" is included for charting the child's progress. For each objective, the following information is provided: position of child, materials needed, teaching procedure (including modifications for children with special needs), recording procedure, and criteria.

Jones, P., and Cregan, A. (1986). *Sign and symbol communication for mentally handicapped people.* Order from Croom Helm, Ltd, Provident Hosue, Burrell Row, Beckenham, Kent, England BR3 1AT; 147 pages (GEN/INT/AID/TECH/UNA).

This book covers both aided and unaided systems, with an emphasis on the status of augmentative communication in the United Kingdom. The first chapters cover background information and considerations regarding populations. The major emphasis of the book is presentation of specific unaided systems (e.g., British Sign Language) and aided systems (e.g., Sigsymbols). For each system covered, the authors consider issues through the use of "discussion points." Communication aids, and accessing, and teaching strategies are covered briefly. Appendices provide further sources of information.

Kent, L. R. (1974). *Language acquistion program for the retarded and multiply impaired.* Order from Research Press, Box 3177, Dept. D, Champaign, IL 61821; 200 pages (VOC/UNA/PRE).

This program is primarily designed to elicit oral expressive language in severely handicapped individuals. Preverbal skills are taught, including attending and motor imitation. Verbal skills are developed in two sections; receptive and expressive. Assessment inventories and criteria for passing each objective are detailed. A chapter for modifying the program procedures for manual communication as a supplemental or alternative communication system is provided.

Kraat, A. (1985). *Communication interaction between aided and natural speakers: A state of the art report.* Order from Canadian Rehabilitation Council for the Disabled, One Yonge Street, Suite 2110, Toronto, Ontario, Canada M5E 1E5; 379 pages (GEN/AID/AS/INT).

This book resulted from a study by the International Project on Communication Aids for the Speech-Impaired (IPCAS). Initial sections provide a framework for looking at communication use and interaction, including a description of factors such as natural communication and interaction, and interaction contexts (participants, communication setting). Kraat also stresses the need to use an adapted model of communication interaction. She provides an in-depth summary of our current knowledge based on interaction between aided communicators and others, and draws observations about that interaction based on existing data. Appendices cover unpublished research studies, published research studies, structured contexts for the study of augmentative communication use, transcription and coding systems, and clinical observation forms and questionnaires.

Light, J., McNaughton, D., & Parnes, P. (1986). *A protocol for the assessment of the communicative interaction skills of nonspeaking severely handicapped adults and their facilitators.* Order from Easter Seal Communication Institute, 24 Ferrand Drive, Don Mills, Ontario, Canada M3C 3N2; 159 pages (AS/PH).

Following a brief description of related literature, this protocol presents a model for communication assessment, covering six related components: (1) gathering background information; (2) observing client interaction skills in naturally occurring contexts; (3) investigating skills further to determine potential; (4) setting appropriate goals for client intervention; (5) observing and evaluating facilitator interaction strategies; (6) setting goals for facilitator training. Assessment procedures and case study examples are provided for each of the six components. Appendices include coding definitions and recording sheets.

Luce, S., and Christian, W. (1981). *How to reduce autistic and severely maladaptive behaviors.* Order from Pro-Ed, 5341 Industrial Oaks Blvd., Austin, TX 78735-8898; 39 pages (PRE).

This manual is one of several in a how-to series intended for persons living and working with children having severe behavior disorders. It presents simple but functional examples of techniques to reduce maladaptive behaviors. Following background information, specific strategies are suggested for defining, assessing, and changing the behavior, and evaluating and maintaining behavior change. Numerous examples are provided within a workbook format.

MacDonald, J. D., and Gillette, Y. (1986). *Ecological communication system (ECO).* Order from James MacDonald, Nisconger Center, Ohio State University, Columbus, OH 43210; (AS/INT/VOC).

This set of materials includes several components. The *Ecoscales and Assessment Manual* presents guidelines for conducting an assessment according to the ECO Model, examining targets, problems, and strategies of the child or significant others. A treatment manual, entitled *Communicating Partners,* provides instruction in the areas of social play, communication, language, and conversation. The *Conversation Routine Manual* presents sample training activities for many natural events. Each conversation routine includes goals, a materials list, and sample scripts. Sample topic areas include object play routines (e.g., working a puzzle); people play routines (e.g., greeting); teaching routines (e.g., book reading); and spontaneous routines (e.g., eating, traveling in the car). A video training module that illustrates the principles and procedures of the ECO model with adults and children having a variety of delays has been developed to demonstrate pre- and post-treatment contrasts of adults and children at different stages of training.

Madsen, W. (1982). *Intermediate conversational sign language.* Order from Gallaudet Bookstore, Kendall Green, 800 Florida Avenue, NE, Washington, DC 20002; 400 pages (UNA/INT).

This text offers materials to facilitate use of American Sign Language (ASL) and English in a bilingual setting. The 25 lessons present sign language conversation using the colloquialisms that are typical in everyday conversatons. Each lesson includes ASL idiomatic expressions accompanied by equivalent English expressions. For each lesson, the following is included: an introductory paragraph; glossed vocabulary review; translation exercises from ASL to English to ASL; grammatical notes; substitution drills; and suggested activities.

Makohon, L., and Fredericks, H. D. (1985). *Teaching expressive and receptive language to students with moderate and severe handicaps.* Order from Pro-Ed, 5341 Industrial Oaks Blvd., Austin, TX 78735; 224 pages (VOC/INT).

This curriculum is designed as a comprehensive instructional tool to be used by parents, teachers, or aides to teach language skills to handicapped students of any chronological age. The receptive language objectives begin with response to sounds, and progresses through the discrimination of syntactic structure. The expressive language curriculum progresses from engaging in vocal play, imitating mouth positions, and using sounds in isolation, to the ability to describe actions with appropriate verb tenses. A data system is provided to chart progress and continually assess functional language abilities.

Manolson, A. (1984). *It takes two to talk: A Hanen early language parent guide book.* Order from Hanen Early Language Resource Centre, Room 4-126, 252 Bloor Street West, Toronto, Ontario, Canada M5S 1V6; 142 pages (AS/INT/VOC).

This parent handbook was designed to accompany a Hanen Early Language Parent Program; however it may also be used alone following a professional evaluation. It is divided into two parts. The first, "Let Your Child Initiate," focuses on the child's attempt to communicate, with suggestions provided to guide parents and teachers in responding in ways that facilitate interaction. The second part, "You Initiate Opportunities for Language Learning," suggests enjoyable ways in which parents can increase opportunties for communication and learning. This includes activities in the domains of play, music, books, game playing, and art. Chapters are accompanied by observation checklists, practice opportunities, sample activities, and evaluation sheets, with numerous illustrations for demonstration purposes.

McCormack, J. E., and Chalmers, A. J. (1978). *Early cognitive instruction for the moderately and severely handicapped.* Order from Research Press, Box 3177, Dept. D., Champaign, IL; 338 pages (INT/PRE).

The program guide presents the rationale and details for implementing the entire instructional program. The program is designed for teachers, parents, or aides and has a training component (Volunteer Training Simulation) to acquaint trainers with the program objectives and procedures. The skills targeted within the program are matching, sorting, constructing, recognizing, identifying, memorizing, and sequencing. The training steps are presented in a chart format with materials, instructions, expected responses, and correction procedures specified.

McDonald, E. (1980). *Teaching and using Blissymbolics.* Order from Blissymbolics Communication International, c/o Easter Seal Communication Institute, 24 Ferrand Drive, Don Mills, Ontario M3C 3N2; 176 pages (AID/INT).

This book begins with a history of the development and use of Blissymbolics, then provides a description of the system. Chapters are presented on specific topics such as techniques for changing symbol meaning, Bliss syntax, and how to draw Blissymbols. Several chapters cover applications of Blissymbolics through assessment, developing a training program, accessing the symbols, and teaching Blissymbolics to children. Numerous examples and illustrations support the text.

McDonald, E. (Ed.). (1987). *Treating cerebral palsy: For clinicians by clinicians.* Order from Pro-Ed, 5341 Industrial Oaks Blvd., Austin, TX 78735; 302 pages (GEN/AID/AS/INT/PH).

This multi-authored text provides an in-depth approach to intervention with persons having cerebral palsy. Many of the topics are preliminary to or directly related to augmentative communication. Sample chapters are: prespeech and feeding development; handling, positioning, and adaptive equipment; communication strategies for infants; augmentative communication; educational programming; and advanced technology aids for communication, education, and employment. Each chapter includes a summary list of questions for review and consideration.

McNaughton, S. (1985). *Communicating with Blissymbolics.* Order from Blissymbolics Communication International, c/o Easter Seal Communication Institute, 24 Ferrand Drive, Don Mills, Ontario, Canada M3C 3N2; 256 pages (AID/INT).

This book provides an in-depth overview of Blissymbolics and strategies for using it communicatively. Part I covers the system, including (1) different ways of looking at the system (classes of symbols, composition of symbols), (2) factors that affect meaning (configuration, size), (3) features of the system (indicators), (4) syntax, (5) Blissymbol shape alphabet, and (6) drawing Blissymbols. Part II considers communication, including issues such as using Blissymbolics with other augmentative systems. Part III covers programming, with specific strategies suggested for initiating use of Blissymbolics, selecting vocabulary, organizing displays, and using special Blissymbols. Three sample introductory programs are also presented, as well as use of Blissymbols to enrich all areas of meaning. Special considerations are discussed relative to programming for persons with a severe disability, and using Blissymbolics with technology. A number of appendices present further information, such as the Blissymbol alphabet song, commercially available input switches, and the effect of Blissymbolics on speech and language development.

Mills, J., and Higgins, J. (1982). *The assessment for non-oral communication.* Order from Jayne Higgins, 530 Lomas Santa Fe Drive, Suite F, Solana Beach, CA 92075; 66 pages (AS/PH).

This tool is designed to develop an appropriate match of system and client through an overall assessment. Both structured observation and elicitation-based procedures are used. Chapter 1 introduces an overview (e.g., directions for scoring, description of assessment sections). Chapter 2 is a one page assessment of the variables (e.g., portability, display type) of a system. Chapter 3 covers an assessment of human variables (readiness, signal, reception, expression, mechanic, interaction). Chapter 4 presents an assessment report form, and a recommendation form is provided in Chapter 5. Appendices include: A — Communication Checklist; B — Receptive Language Sequence; C — Expressive Language Sequence; D — Vocabulary Lists (beginning, intermediate, advanced); E — Language Sample; F — Environmental Assessment.

Montgomery, J. (Ed.). (1980). *Non-oral communication: A training guide for the child without speech.* Order from Non-Oral Communication Center, Plavan School, 9675 Warner Avenue, Fountain Valley, CA 92708; 200 pages (AID/PH/INT).

This guide book, organized in a three-ring binder, presents materials for assessing, training, and applying augmentative communication systems. The curriculum was developed and field tested in a public school program with children who were physically disabled and nonspeaking. The major areas covered are assessment, test modification, vocabulary selection, educational carryover, monitoring the use of augmentative communication systems, and writing goals and objectives.

Musselwhite, C. (1986). *Adaptive play for special needs children: Strategies to enhance communication and learning.* Order from College-Hill Press/Little, Brown and Company, Customer Service Department, 200 West Street, Waltham, MA 02254; 249 pages (AS/INT/PRE).

This book presents adaptive play as a framework for learning, with an emphasis on facilitating communication development. The first part offers an overview of adaptive play, and the second part presents procedures for selecting, adapting, and constructing play materials. Part III covers adaptive play strategies for communicative goals, including symbolic play skills and early augmentative communication. Part IV suggests ways to support adaptive play, such as initiation of a toy lending library. Appendices consist of resources such as manufacturers, organizations, and annotated bibliographic entries.

Musselwhite, C. (1985). *Songbook: Signs and symbols for children.* Order from Don Johnston Developmental Equipment, P.O. Box 639, Wauconda, IL 60084; 96 pages (AID/INT/UNA/PRE).

This songbook presents more than 40 beginner-level songs, including 18 songs designed to introduce target phonemes. Songs are based on simple melodies or familiar tunes. Signs from the Signed English system, and symbols from the Blissymbolics and PICSYMS systems, are depicted to represent all key words in the songs. The 25 primary songs include specific goals in the areas of communication, motor skills, and cognitive and social skills, with training activities presented for each song. A review of the literature on music in augmentative communication is provided, with general training strategies for facilitating oral language, signing, or symbol use through signing.

Oakander, S. M. (1980). *Language board instruction kit.* Order from Exemplary/ Incentive Dissemination Project, ESEA, Title IV-C, Non-Oral Communication Center, Plavan School, 9675 Warner Avenue, Fountain Valley, CA 92708; 34 pages (AID/AS/INT).

This instruction kit is intended to serve as a step-by-step guide for determining goals, constructing a language board, and evaluating effectiveness of the board. Eight tasks are covered, with worksheets and suggestions for completing each. Examples of tasks are: What are the motor skills? Which types of symbols can be used? Appendices include category suggestions for a customized vocabulary, suggested items for language boards, and sources for symbol systems.

Orcutt, D. (1984). *Worldsign symbolbook.* Order from Worldsign Communication Society, Perry Siding, Winlaw, BC, Canada V0G 2J0; 136 pages (AID).

This book is primarily a "dictionary" of Worldsign written symbols. An introduction to Worldsign is provided in Worldsign with English translation. A brief how-to section describes use of the symbolbook. Hints are given for reading the symbols for the meaning implied in each, and rules are provided for forming Worldsign symbols (e.g., how to indicate gender). The major portion of the text includes symbols for writing and descriptions for signing. Simple illustrations and written instructions are provided.

Orcutt, D. (1987). *Worldsign exposition.* Order from Worldsign Communication Society, Perry Siding, Winlaw, BC, Canada V0G 2J0; 54 pages (AID).

This reference was intended as a proposal for financial assistance in the development of computer software related to Worldsign. The intent is to promote an interlink communication system (Worldsign) in order to facilitate intercultural and economic exchange. The text provides a description of Worldsign and suggests potential applications of the system, including applications with persons needing augmentative communication. The Worldsign research and development project is described, with budgetary information included. Numerous examples of Worldsign are provided at the end of the text.

Orelove, F. P., and Sobsey, D. (1987). *Educating children with multiple disabilities.* Order from Paul H. Brookes Publishing Co., P.O. Box 10624, Baltimore, MD 21285; 367 pages (GEN/PH/AS/INT).

This book stresses a transdisciplinary approach to the delivery of services to individuals with multiple disabilities. The authors offer many practical techniques for assessment and treatment of a variety of conditions affecting people with multiple disabilities. Specific chapters address normal motor development, atypical motor development and cerebral palsy, handling and positioning, sensory impairments, seizure disorders and medications, curriculum and instructional programming, mealtime skills, toileting and dressing skills, communication skills, and working with families.

Owens, R. E. (1982). *Program for the acquistion of language with the severely impaired.* Order from Charles E. Merrill Publishing Co., Test Division, 1300 Alum Creek Drive, Box 508, Columbus, Ohio 42126; (AS/INV/VOC/PRE).

This package of materials includes the following components: Program Manual; Caregiver Interview and Environmental Observation (package of 12); Diagnostic Intervention Survey/Developmental Assessment Tool (package of 12); and Training Level Activities Guide. The program emphasizes the communicative context of client–caregiver interaction for assessment and training. Three modes of training are included: formal training (two 5- to 10-minute sessions daily); incidental teaching strategies; and stimulation methods. The program targets presymbolic and early symbolic skills for training.

Picture Your Blissymbols. (1986). Blissymbolics Communication International, c/o Easter Seal Communication Institute, 24 Ferrand Drive, Don Mills, Ontario, Canada M3C 3N2; (AID/INT).

The entire *Picture Your Blissymbols (PYB)* kit includes a Teaching Manual, Blissymbols for Use, and PYB materials. Sample PYB materials are a vocabulary of 312 items, enhanced in a humorous and meaningful way, two sets of flashcard-size adhesive stamps, with one set embellished and the other plain, and a PYB visor, all packaged in a tote bag. Demonstration instructional modules describe specific procedures (materials, preparation, teaching ideas) for focusing on objectives such as communicative interaction, attending to meaningful elements, and fading of embellishments.

Popovich, D. (1977, 1981). *A prescriptive and behavioral checklist for the severely and profoundly retarded.* Order from Pro-Ed, 5341 Industrial Oaks Blvd., Austin, TX 78735; (three volumes) Vol. I 448 pages, Vol. II 247 pages, Vol. III 263 pages (VOC/PRE/AS/INT).

Volume I presents behavioral checklists for the following areas: motor development; eye–hand coordination; language development; and physical eating problems. It also includes task analysis steps and implementation suggestions for the language development area for the following behaviors: attending; physical imitation; auditory training; object discrimination; concept development; and sound imitation. Each implementation item describes the materials needed, necessary prerequisite skills, and procedures to follow to meet the stated objective. Volumes II and III contain objectives related to daily living activities.

Porter, P., Carter, S., Goolsby, E., Martin, N., Reed, M., Stowers, S., and Wurth, B. (1985). *Prerequisites to the use of augmentative communication systems.* Order from Augmentative Communication Team, Division for Disorders of Development and Learning, Biological Sciences Research Center 220-H, Chapel Hill, NC 27517; 32 pages (DD/INT/PRE).

This handbook is intended for use by professionals, paraprofessionals, or family members of people who are nonspeaking and have not achieved the prerequisites for initiating an aided communication system. Assessment and intervention focuses on nine steps, ranging from demonstrating preferences, to using a signal to indicate desire for an object/event, to using a signal to indicate a choice among three or more pictured objects/events. Each skill is clearly defined, with methods of elicitation described. Training procedures are presented in practical terms for each skill.

Powell, T. H., and Ogle, P. A. (1985). *Brothers & sisters — A special part of exceptional families.* Order from Paul H. Brookes Publishing Co., P.O. Box 10624, Baltimore, MD 21285; 226 pages (GEN).

The important role of siblings in the family, and the special challenges of having a sibling who has a handicap, are the focus of this book. Nonhandicapped siblings contribute substantially to the growth and happiness of their handicapped sibling. Each individual is affected uniquely by the stresses and rewards of living together. This book offers support and assistance in helping families cope with the realities of their situation. Two appendices are included listing information and service sources and literature for siblings pertinent to a wide variety of handicaps.

Riekehof, L. L. (1978). *The joy of signing.* Order from The Gospel Publishing House, 1445 Boonville Ave., Springfield, MO 65802; 324 pages (UNA).

This manual "is meant to provide the learner with knowledge of the basic traditional signs used by adult deaf persons today and with knowledge concerning the base on which new signs were developed" (p. 4). Signs are grouped into natural categories such as family relationships, location and direction, and nature. For each sign the following are provided: an illustration; potential English glosses;

brief description of sign execution; origin, if known; and usage. It is recommended that the phrases and sentences be used as practice material.

Rincover, A. (1981). *How to use sensory extinction.* Order from Pro-Ed, 5341 Industrial Oaks Blvd., Austin, TX 78735-8898; 34 pages (PRE).

As one entry in a how-to series on teaching autistic children, this manual covers nonaversive treatment for self-stimulation and other behavior problems. It is intended as a step-by-step approach to using sensory extinction procedures by parents, teachers, and therapists. The general goal of the procedure is to mask or remove naturally occurring sensory consequences of the unwanted behavior, then remove the consequence, thus taking the fun out of the behavior. Topics include assessment of when sensory extinction should be used, determination of which sensory extinction to use, specifics regarding implementation of sensory extinction, and techniques for promoting generalization of results. Numerous case examples and a workbook format are used.

Ruggles, V. (1979). *Funding of non-vocal communication aids: Current issues and strategies.* Order from Muscular Dystrophy Association, 810 Seventh Avenue, New York, NY 10019; 30 pages (TECH).

This packet describes strategies for achieving funding of augmentative communication devices. A four-step procedure is directed toward development of funding by the person needing a device. The steps are (1) self-evaluation (e.g., capitalizing on strengths, increasing knowledge of potential resources), (2) professional education; (3) client evaluation, and (4) submitting the actual funding requests. Numerous resources are outlined, including a summary of the Rehabilitation Act, extensive listing of references, and federal domestic assistance programs.

St. Louis, K. W., Mattingly, S., and Esposito, A. (1986). Receptive language curriculum for the moderately, severely, and profoundly handicapped. In J. D. Cone (Ed.), *Pyramid system curriculum.* Order from Pyramid Press, West Virginia University, P.O. Box 604, Olgebay Hall, Morgantown, WV 26506; approximately 350 pages (AS/INT).

The *Receptive Language Curriculum* binder contains the following information: (1) a discussion of language assessment; (2) procedures for developing individual educational plans; (3) detailed method cards divided into 25 areas for teaching specific receptive language behaviors; (4) a scope, sequence, and correspondence chart as a cross-reference guide to selective commercially available tests and programs. The program was originally designed to meet the communication needs of the severely and profoundly retarded. However, it can be used with the mild to moderately retarded, and adapted for use with nonspeaking, multiply handicapped people.

St. Louis, K. W., and Rejzer, R. (1986). Expressive language curriculum for the moderately, severely, and profoundly handicapped. In J. D. Cone (Ed.), *Pyramid system curriculum.* Order from Pyramid Press, West Virginia University, P.O. Box 604, Olgebay Hall, Morgantown, WV 26506; approximately 350 pages (AS/INT/VOC/AID/UNA).

The *Expressive Language Curriculum* binder contains the following information: (1) a discussion of language assessment; (2) procedures for developing individual education plans; (3) detailed method cards divided into 25 areas for teaching specific expressive language behaviors; (4) a scope, sequence, and correspondence chart as a cross-reference guide to selective commercially available tests and programs. The curriculum contains two areas with specific suggestions and methods for adapting the vocal program for use with nonspeakers, adaptation of the curriculum for communication boards, and adaptation of the curriculum for manual communication.

Sbaiti, M. (1985). *Cued Speech instructional manual* (2nd edition). Order from Cued Speech Center, P.O. Box 31345, Raleigh, NC 27612; 174 pages (INT/UNA).

This spiral-bound training manual is intended for use by expert cuers in teaching Cued Speech to adults and teens. Suggestions are given for teaching beginners, intermediate learners, and advanced cuers. Lessons increase in difficulty, beginning with teaching of flat vowels and progressing to complex practice with consonant groups (e.g., word and sentence practice, plural endings, multisyllabic words, consonant blend practice). "Funetik Speling" is used throughout to show proper pronunciation and thus the proper way to cue each word. A section on "Cuescript," or graphic representation of Cued Speech, is also included.

Schery, T. K., and Wilcoxen, A. G. (1982). *Initial communication processes*. Order from Publishers Test Service, CTB/McGraw-Hill, 2500 Garden Road, Monterey, CA 93940; (AS/INT/VOC/PRE).

This program consists of a manual (35 pages), a scales book (22 pages), and an objective bank (26 pages). It was designed to assess early communication processes for children at risk and handicapped individuals functioning below the developmental level of three years old. The observational scales are used as a screening device. The screening results indicate which objectives in the objective bank to use for instruction in communication skills. The content areas included are auditory skills, visual skills, manual fine motor skills, oral vocal motor skills, manipulative play skills, symbolic object play skills, problem-solving skills, affective development, comprehension and expressive communication skills.

Scheuerman, N., Baumgart, D., Sipsma, K., and Brown, L. (1976). Toward the development of a curriculum for teaching non-verbal communication skills to severely handicapped students: Teaching basic tracking, scanning, and selection skills. In L. Brown, N. Scheuerman, and T. Crowner (Eds.), *Madison's alternative for zero exclusion, Vol. VI, Part 3*. Order from Specialized Educational Services, Madison Metropolitan School District, 545 West Dayton Street, Madison, WI 53703; (PRE).

The tracking skills section of this task force curriculum covers tracking people or objects through various paths (e.g., horizontal path) and barriers (e.g., transparent visual barrier). The second section covers the skills of attending, scanning, and selecting. Students are taught to scan and select items that are presented concurrently or consecutively. This is a naturalized curriculum, with training taking place throughout the day in a variety of settings.

Schiefelbusch, R. L. (Ed.). (1980). *Nonspeech language and communication: Analysis and intervention.* Order from Pro-Ed, 5341 Industrial Oaks Blvd., Austin, TX 78735; 544 pages (AID/UNA/INT/AS/PRE).

This book includes 20 chapters centering on the topic of nonspeech language and communication. It presents perspectives on American Sign Language, assessment strategies for the physically handicapped, autistic and severely retarded children, and interpretive issues.

Schwartz, A. (Ed.). (1984). *Handbook of microcomputer applications in communication disorders.* Order from College-Hill Press/Little, Brown and Company, Customer Service Department, 200 West Street, Waltham, MA 02254; 354 pages (INT/PH/TECH).

This text is a detailed work covering all aspects of microcomputer applications in communication disorders. Section I covers terminology and possible microcomputer applications. Funding and software resources, plus procedures for evaluating hardware and software are described in the second section. Section III is devoted to specific applications, including research, administrative, and clinical uses. Part IV covers pertinent issues and controversies of microcomputer application, such as locating and selecting applicable software.

Seery, J. (1984). *Eye gaze communication systems: Games, activities, interactions.* Order from The Cerebral Palsy Treatment Center of Middlesex County, c/o Travis Tallman, Director, Speech and Hearing Department, Roosevelt Park, Edison, NJ 08817; 12 pages (AID/INT).

This packet provides a set of games and activities to use in developing eye-pointing and scanning abilities for use with ETRAN communication systems, and peer interaction utilizing augmentative communication systems. For each activity, the following is provided: a list of the skills involved; materials needed; procedures; and variations. Simple illustrations accompany the text.

Shane, H., and Sauer, M. (1986). *Augmentative and alternative communication.* Order from Pro-Ed, 5341 Industrial Oaks Blvd., Austin, TX 78735; 81 pages (AID/AS/INT/GEN).

This monograph is intended to provide a general overview of the field of augmentative and alternative communication. Introductory material is presented for a range of topics, including terminology, evaluation, system selection, training strategies, and case examples. Appendices offer resource information such as addresses, control interfaces, suggested readings, and selected communication software. The emphasis of this text is on aided communication systems and devices, with information presented in a clinically oriented manner, with numerous tables and figures.

Shea, V., and Mount, M. (1982). *How to arrange the environment to stimulate and teach pre-language skills in the severely handicapped.* Order from Pro-Ed, 5341 Industrial Oaks Blvd., Austin, TX 78735; 32 pages (PRE).

This book is a companion to *How to Recognize and Assess Pre-Language Skills in the Severely Handicapped* (Mount and Shea, 1982). In this book, suggestions are given for using play activities of daily living to assist in developing prerequisites for language training. Specific recommendations are provided, and numerous case examples are given. The book is arranged in a workbook format to promote practice of skills learned. This is part of a series that is highly appropriate for parents and other caregivers.

Shroyer, E., and Shroyer, S. (1984). *Signs across America.* Order from Gallaudet Bookstore, 800 Florida Avenue NE, Washington, DC 20002; 304 pages (UNA).

This book presents a look at the regional variations in American Sign Language. The authors contacted native signers in 25 states to determine the signs used for 130 target words. More than 1,200 signs were identified, and are presented in this book. This book can be used to demonstrate the geographic differences and subtleties of signing.

Silverman, F. H. (1980). *Communication for the speechless.* Order from Prentice-Hall, Englewood Cliffs, NJ 07632; 291 pages (GEN/AID/UNA/PRE).

Silverman presents a comprehensive review of nonspeech communication aids classified according to response mode: gestural, gestural-assisted, and neuro-assisted. Specific suggestions for selecting a nonspeech communication mode are detailed. Many factors regarding intervention strategies, such as gaining acceptance, assessing the impact of the system, and maintaining the device are discussed. Five appendices supplement the text with valuable information, including a comprehensive bibliography, sources of materials, sources of components for gestural and neuro-assisted modes, construction details for inexpensive displays, and an evaluation summary for selecting a nonspeech mode.

Skelly, M. (1979). *Amer-Ind gestural code based on universal American Indian Hand Talk.* Order from Elsevier-North Holland, Inc., 52 Vanderbilt Avenue, New York, NY 10017; 494 pages (AS/INT/UNA).

This text on Amer-Ind is based on the author's extensive use of the code with a wide range of persons. Part 1 presents a clinical investigation, with a review of the history of Amer-Ind and its use with persons having severe communication impairment, including results of several research projects. Part 2 covers the clinical application, including a description of Amer-Ind and a presentation of specific strategies for clinical assessment and programming, using three treatment program approaches. Part 3 presents the clinical signal repertoire, with presentation of 250 signals representing concept labels. More than 2,500 English words are represented by those concept labels.

Sternberg, M. (1981). *American Sign Language: A comprehensive dictionary.* Order from National Association for the Deaf, 814 Thayer Avenue, Silver Spring, MD 20910; 1132 pages (UNA).

This extensive sign language dictionary contains 5,430 word entries and cross references, a bibliography of nearly 1,300 items, and seven foreign langauge indexes.

Each entry is presented in a line drawing with written instructions on sign production. For each entry, notes are also provided on pronunciation, parts of speech, cross references, and explanation of how signs were developed.

Struck, R. (1977). *Santa Cruz special education management systems: Behavioral characteristics progression (BCP)*. Order from VORT Corporation, Palo Alto, CA; 550 pages (VOC/UNA/PRE).

Book Three of this curriculum, entitled *Method Cards: Communication Skills,* is divided into 11 strands. Each strand contains a series of method cards. Each method card provides a specific activity to meet a specific objective. Language comprehension, oral expression, and manual communication can be taught with this system. Prerequisite abilities, type of setting, length of session, and materials needed are listed on each card.

Tingey-Michaelis, C. (1983). *Handicapped infants and children: A handbook for parents and professionals.* Order from Pro-Ed, 5341 Industrial Oaks Blvd., Austin, TX 78735; 224 pages (INT/PRE).

This book is organized like a dictionary or an encyclopedia, with a list of problems that special needs babies and their parents may have. It is designed to offer straightforward help to parents regarding specific problems in general areas such as health, feeding, sleep, movement, social, language, self-help. Specific health problems and syndromes are also discussed. The book offers a brief description of the problem (e.g., seizures, self-stimulation, dislike of being touched), ideas for determining the extent of the problem (e.g., documenting seizures), information on possible causes of the problem, and suggestions for dealing with the problem. The format includes bold face presentation of the problem (e.g., Some babies have problems with their eyes), followed by brief statements relating to the problem, offered in extremely simple terms, with frequent examples and suggestions for when and to which professional a child should be referred. This book does not offer technical information, but rather presents practical and psychological support for parents of children with special needs. The author is the parent of a special needs person, and is an associate professor.

Vanderheiden, G. (1984). *Comparison of Apple, Epson, IBM microcomputers for applications in rehabilitation systems for persons with physical handicaps* (Revision D). Order from Trace R&D Center, Reprint Service, 314 Waisman Center, 1500 Highland Ave., Madison, WI 53705-2280; 99 pages (PH/TECH).

This report provides a framework for comparing microcomputers for rehabilitation applications, including use with nonspeaking people. Microcomputers are evaluated according to three sets of characteristics: those affecting the user's ability to operate the aid (e.g., inputs); those affecting the ability of the aid to meet the individual's needs (e.g., outputs, transportablity); and those affecting purchase, maintenance, and so forth. Comparative profiles are offered to assess various features (size, weight), benchmark tests (running a series of programs in BASIC), and cost comparison. Blank columns allow profiling of additional computers by the reader. A final section suggests eight steps to be followed in choosing a microcomputer.

Vanderheiden, G. C., and Grilley, K. (Eds.). (1976). *Non-vocal communication techniques for the severely physically handicapped.* Order from Pro-Ed, 5341 Industrial Oaks Blvd., Austin, TX 78735; 246 pages (AID/INT/PRE).

This book is based on transcriptions of the 1975 Trace Center National Workshop Series on Nonvocal Communication Techniques and Aids. The major areas considered are the problems (e.g., identification of children at risk), the tools (e.g., types of symbols), and the applications (e.g., use of Blissymbols with the mentally retarded). Due to the many advances in technology that have been made in recent years, parts of this book are out of date. However, it remains a classic introduction to the field of augmentative communication.

Vicker, B. (Ed.). (1974). *Nonoral communication system project, 1964/1973.* Order from Campus Store Publishers, University of Iowa, 17 West College, Iowa City, IA 52242; 261 pages (AID).

This monograph was prepared by speech–language pathologists and occupational therapists to describe an approach to nonoral programming: "the use of nonmechanical display materials that are designed to facilitate syntactic nonoral expression and are designed to accommodate the individual needs of children of varying ages and levels of educational skills" (p. 8–9). Appendices include sample communication display materials and communication board display frames. These appendices are contained in a separate packet and are useful as demonstration aids.

Warren, S., and Rogers-Warren, A. (Eds.). (1985). *Teaching functional language: Generalization and maintenance of language skills.* Order from Pro-Ed, 5341 Industrial Oaks Blvd., Austin, TX 78735; 351 pages (GEN/PRE).

This multi-authored text emphasizes principles and procedures of intervention. Section I covers current perspectives on language remediation, providing a general perspective. Section II presents applications of functional language training, including a chapter on communication intervention for the "difficult-to-teach" severely handicapped. The third section focuses on facilitating and measuring generalization. In the final section, the topic is utilizing significant others in the development of functional language. The chapters provide a synthesis of theoretical and research materials.

Wasson, P., Tynan, T., and Gardiner, P. (1982). *Test adaptations for the handicapped.* Order from Educational Service Center, Region 20, 1314 Hines Avenue, San Antonio, TX 78208, ATTN: Mary Black; 110 pages (AS/PH).

This book presents an approach to modifying standardized tests for presentation to persons with a variety of impairments. The first chapter presents the problem and suggests general solutions to using standardized tests, and the second chapter provides a brief literature review. Chapter 3 describes a brief research study on adapting tests to avoid underassessing individuals with physical and sensory impairments. Chapter 4 presents a protocol for analyzing tests, plus analyses of 12 standardized tests (e.g., Peabody Individualized Achievement Test). The fifth chapter, the core of the book, describes and illustrates a variety of test adaptations. Final chapters include an index of tests and devices.

Wilbur, R. (1987). *American Sign Language: Linguistic and applied dimensions* (Revised Edition). Order from College-Hill Press/Little, Brown and Company, Customer Service Department, 200 West Street, Waltham, MA 02254; 400 pages (UNA).

This is an in-depth text on American Sign Language. The first section is written from a linguistic perspective, covering topics such as traditional and current approaches to sign phonology and morphology, ASL syntax, sign language acquisition, and sociolinguistic aspects of sign language and deaf culture. The second section considers applications of sign languages and sign systems. Chapters cover sign systems used in educational settings, the education of deaf children relative to sign language, and use of signs with communicatively handicapped individuals who are not deaf.

Williams, J., Csongradi, J., and LeBlanc, M. (1982). *A guide to controls: Selection, mounting, applications.* Order from Rehabilitation Engineering Center, Children's Hospital at Stanford, 520 Willow Rd., Palo Alto, CA 94304; 144 pages (AS/PH/ TECH).

This document provides considerable information on environmental control systems, plus numerous sources of further information. The first section presents a brief review of methodology (e.g., control site selection) and evaluation tools in the selection of controls. Section II presents a variety of switches, each described according to a variety of parameters (e.g., pressure, feedback). The third section describes mounting fixtures, including a brief discussion of approaches to mounting and description of adaptive features. Section IV suggests several applications for environmental control systems. The resources section presents a wide range of information sources.

Wright, C., and Nomura, M. (1985). *From toys to computers: Access for the physically disabled child.* Order from Don Johnston Developmental Equipment, P.O. Box 639, Wauconda, IL 60084; 192 pages (DD/INT/PH/TECH).

This book offers a wealth of information regarding application of the microcomputer to children with physical disabilities. The first three chapters summarize methods for adapting battery operated toys, offer suggestions for selecting and adapting specific toys for a toy lending library, and provide an overview of interface switches. The fourth chapter presents a guide to positioning in sitting for optimal motor control. The remainder of the book covers use of the microcomputer with physically disabled children, including basic information on microcomputers, and adaptations for accessing the computer (e.g., expanded keyboards, switch input). Checklists for evaluating access, and guidelines for establishing a microcomputer center, are also presented. Appendices provide a wide variety of practical resources and support materials, such as sample proposals for a microcomputer center and a toy lending library.

Appendix C

Listing of Manufacturers and Distributors

Below is a representative sample of manufacturers whose products are listed in this book.

ADAPTIVE COMMUNICATION
SYSTEMS, INC. (a)
994 Broadhead Road, Suite 202
Coraopolis, PA 15108

AMERICAN GUIDANCE
SERVICE, INC.
Publishers' Building
Circle Pines, MN 55014

ADAMLAB (ad)
Wayne County Intermediate
School District
33500 Van Born Road
Wayne, MI 48184

BAGGEBODA PRESS
1128 Rhode Island
Lawrence, KS 66044

BOSTON CHILDREN'S HOSPITAL
MEDICAL CENTER (b)
Communication Enhancement Clinic
300 Longwood Avenue
Boston, MA 02115

CRESTWOOD COMPANY (c)
P.O. Box 04606
Milwaukee, WI 53204

DON JOHNSTON
DEVELOPMENTAL
EQUIPMENT (d)
P. O. Box 639
Wauconda, IL 60084

DUNAMIS, INC. (du)
2856 Buford Highway
Duluth, GA 30136

GALLAUDET UNIVERSITY
BOOKSTORE
Kendall Green
P. O. Box 300
Washington, DC 20002

INNOCOMP (i)
Innovative Computer Applications
33195 Wagon Wheel
Solon, OH 44139

Letters in parentheses refer to text citations of materials available from these manufacturers and distributors.

JANA BIRCH (j)
2346 Wales Drive
Cardiff, CA 92007

JOYCE MEDIA
P.O. Box 458
Northridge, CA 91328

STEVEN E. KANOR, PH.D., INC. (k)
8 Main Street
Hastings-on-Hudson, NY 10706

MAYER-JOHNSON CO.
P. O. Box AD
Solana Beach, CA 92075-0838

PHONIC EAR, INC. (pe)
250 Camino Alto
Mill Valley, CA 94941

PRENTKE ROMICH
COMPANY (pr)
1022 Heyl Road
Wooster, OH 44691

R.D. CLARK, INC.
Box 22
Bowling Green, IN 47833

READ-A-BOL GROUP
P. O. Box 3333-137
Encinitas, CA 92024

RESCUE SPEECH SYSTEM (r)
5937 Portland Avenue South
Minneapolis, MN 55417

SCHNEIER
COMMUNICATION UNIT
Cerebral Palsy Center
1603 Court Street
Syracuse, NY 13208

SENTIENT SYSTEMS
TECHNOLOGY, INC. (ss)
5001 Baum Boulevard
Pittsburgh, PA 15213

SHEA PRODUCTS, INC. (sp)
1042 West Hamlin Road
Rochester, MI 48063

SIGN UP
2590 Channing Way
Berkley, CA 94704

TEXAS INSTRUMENTS, INC. (ti)
P. O. Box 53
Lubbock, TX 79408

TUFTS-NEW ENGLAND
MEDICAL CENTER (t)
Biomedical Engineering Department
171 Harrison Avenue, Box 1009
Boston, MA 02111

WORDS+, INC. (w)
1125 Stewart Court, Suite D
Sunnyvale, CA 94086

ZYGO INDUSTRIES, INC. (z)
P. O. Box 1008
Portland, OR 97207

Appendix D

Organizations, Agencies, and Publications

This appendix covers selected sources of information on persons with severe handicaps. Since the first edition of this book, international interest has grown in the area of augmentative communication. This appendix has therefore been expanded to include representative organizations from many countries. The entries are listed alphabetically by country. Each entry includes information regarding the services provided in relationship to people with communication handicaps.

Australia

AUSTRALIAN GROUP ON SEVERE COMMUNICATION IMPAIRMENT (A.G.O.S.C.I.)
Yooralla Centre
Box Forest Road
Glenroy, Victoria
Australia 3046
(03) 359-9366

A.G.O.S.C.I. was established to provide a means for information exchange amongst all persons involved in the area of severe communication impairment. It is open to health care workers, educationalists, rehabilitation engineers, and people who use alternate systems of communication, their family, and friends.

The aims of the organization are to educate the community, professionals, and consumers about severe communication impairments. A.G.O.S.C.I. has an annual national study day, state study groups, and a biannual newsletter.

COMPIC DEVELOPMENT ASSOCIATION, INC.
P.O. Box 351
NTH. Baldwyn
Victoria
Australia 3104

This group was set up as a research and development group to standardize pictographic communication materials in use throughout the state of Victoria, and to produce software to enable electronic publishing of communication and/or teaching materials. The management committee consists of representatives from the key agencies in Victoria that provide services to people with severe communication impairments.

The group has produced software for electronic publishing of pictographs in a range of sizes and colors, a manual to accompany the software, a manual for people who wish to order customized materials without purchasing software and required equipment, and a manual of teaching cards for use with groups or clients who require a large pictograph representation. People become members of the association by purchasing a manual, which entitles them to update COMPIC information. Phase I of the research is available, and includes 580 pictographs.

MICROCOMPUTER APPLICATIONS CENTRE (N.A.C.)
52 Thistlethwaite Street
South Melbourne
Victoria
Australia 3205
(03) 690-9177

This centre provides the following services for people with disabilities, their families, advocates, and professionals: (1) an information service about microcomputer-based technology (including electronic communication aids); (2) assessment for a microcomputer-based device and access; (3) training of people with disabilities and professionals; (4) display of the range of equipment available in Australia. The M.A.C. publishes a newsletter quarterly. It is a free community service.

SPEECH PATHOLOGY ACCESS GROUP-INTELLECTUAL DISABILITY
Australian Association of Speech and Hearing
212 Clarendon Street
East Melbourne
Victoria
Australia 3002

This organization is an informal study group formed in 1981 for speech pathologists who have an interest in intellectual disability. The main aim is to provide access to resource material and a forum for discussion, sharing ideas and mutual support. Regular discussion meetings are held a metropolitan venue; however, present aims include at least one country meeting each year.

Canada

BLISSYMBOLICS COMMUNICATION INTERNATIONAL (BCI)
24 Ferrand Drive
Toronto, Ontario
CANADA M3C 3N2
(416) 421-8377

The focus of BCI efforts is threefold; (1) to continue the development of Blissymbolics as a means of augmentative communication; (2) to explore ways of improving the quality of augmentative communication; and (3) to create an awareness, through a newsletter, *Communicating Together,* and the BCI training programs, of the environmental changes which are necessary for the successful integration of nonspeaking people into society. A variety of products are available from BCI, including books, Blissymbol stamps, various teaching aids, and professional materials. A wide variety of training programs are offered, ranging from orientation presentations to special interest training sessions and internships. A lending library of videotapes, slides, and books is available.

CANADIAN REHABILITATION COUNCIL FOR THE DISABLED
One Yonge Street, Suite 2110
Toronto, Ontario M5E 1E5
Canada
(416) 862-0340

This organization serves as a clearinghouse of information for persons with disabilities. The populations served include persons needing augmentative communication. For example, this organization distributes publications related to augmentative communication, developed by the International Project on Communication Aids for the Speech-Impaired (IPCAS).

INTERNATIONAL SOCIETY FOR AUGMENTATIVE
AND ALTERNATIVE COMMUNICATION (ISAAC)
P.O. Box 1762, Station R
Toronto, Ontario M4G 4A3
Canada

ISAAC was founded by representatives of seven countries in May, 1983. Membership is international, with current members in more than 20 countries. The purposes of ISAAC include the advancement of the transdisciplinary field of augmentative and alternative communication, the facilitation of information exchange, and the focus of attention on work in the field. ISAAC has two publications: a journal, *Augmentative and Alternative Communication (ACC),* and a newsletter, *The ISAAC Bulletin.*

WORLDSIGN COMMUNICATION SOCIETY
Perry Siding
Winlaw, British Columbia V0G 2J0
Canada
(604) 355-2408

This organization develops and distributes information regarding Worldsign. Information includes pamphlets, books, articles, and videotapes. The organization also pursues research and development of the Worldsign communication system.

Denmark

CENTER FOR HJERNESKADE (CENTER FOR
REHABILITATION OF BRAIN DAMAGE)
University of Copenhagen
Njalsgade 88
DK-2300
Copenhagen 0-54 22 11
Denmark

The center is a private foundation which opened in 1985. The purpose of the center is to offer patients who have suffered brain damage, and who exhibit disturbances in social adaptation, optimal treatment and rehabilitation. The rehabilitation program normally takes 4½ months, 4 times a week, 6 hours a day. Consideration is given during assessment and rehabilitation to the use of augmentative communication systems if appropriate.

DANSK HJAELPEMIDDEL INSTITUTE
(DANISH INSTITUTE FOR TECHNICAL AIDS)
Gregersemsvej 1A
DK-2630 Tastrup
02-99 33 22
Denmark

The Institute is an independent organization established in 1980. The purpose of the Institute is to promote the development of good and suitable technial aids for the elderly and the handicapped. Informative material consisting of uniform and comparable information on each technical aid is available. D.H.I. also holds courses, mainly for technicians and therapists, at the county centers. D.H.I. takes part in national and international standardizing work to have equivalent quality requirements and methods of testing technical aids.

PROJECT H.I.T. (HANDICAP INFORMATION TECHNOLOGY)
The Royal Danish College for Educational Studies
The Department in Esbjerg
Skolebakken 171
DK-6705
Esbjerg 0 05-14 17 22
Denmark

Located at the Royal Danish College for Educational Studies, the Project H.I.T. aims at the research and development of communication software, as well as alternative input devices for the IBM computer and compatibles. In the local community the members of the interdisciplinary team are active in the development, implementation, and evaluation of communication devices, as well as in the training of the potential users, their families, and care persons.

England

ISAAC UNITED KINGDOM (UK)
Sandwell Communication Aids Centre
Boulton Road
West Bromwich
West Midlands
England B70 6NN

A chapter of ISAAC has been established within the United Kingdom to promote membership in ISAAC and to enhance the service to professionals in the field. The primary conceptual basis of establishing ISAAC UK is to provide an organization that offers local professionals and augmented speakers information and help which is of direct relevance to their "everyday needs." Secondary to this, but an essential aspect, is to promote and provide access to the international aspects of ISAAC, thereby widening and strengthening the corporate ability to provide and support augmentative and alternative communication.

ROYAL ASSOCIATION FOR DISABILITY AND REHABILITATION
25 Mortimer Street
London
England W1N 8AB
01-637-5400

This organization serves as a clearinghouse of information for persons with disabilities. The population served includes persons needing augmentative communication. For example, this organization distributes publications related to augmentative communication, developed by the International Project of Communication Aids for the Speech-Impaired (IPCAS).

India

INSTITUTE OF CEREBRAL PALSY
c/o Spastics Society of East India
15, Belvedere Court
11 & 13 Alipore Road
Calcutta
India 700 027

This organization covers areas of research, study, training, expansion, and mass communication for providing services for persons with cerebral palsy in India. Outreach service projects offer guidance and expertise to both new and established centers to upgrade services to persons with cerebral palsy. The organization is also serving as an advocate to agencies in labour and education for vocational rehabilitation training.

Israel

M.I.L.B.A.T.
THE ISRAEL CENTER FOR TECHNICAL AIDS, BUILDING
AND TRANSPORTATION FOR THE DISABLED
Tel Hashomer 52621
Isreal
(03) 711-739

M.I.L.B.A.T. is a resource center, with demonstration facilities for aids, including augmentative communication systems, for the disabled. It functions as a cost-free consultation center for both professionals and the handicapped and their families. A comprehensive reference library is available for use by all interested persons. The Center hosts the "communication group," a multi-disciplinary voluntary group which meets once a month for the purpose of providing assessment and appropriate on-going referrals to meet the communication needs of nonspeaking persons. M.I.L.B.A.T. holds workshops on the development of aids and serves as an educational facility for students in the medical and various paramedical professions.

THE SOCIETY FOR THE DEVELOPMENT OF
BLISSYMBOLICS IN ISREAL
c/o Judy Wine
Ramat Motza
Jerusalem
Isreal 95740
(02) 531-1878

This Society was formed for the purpose of developing Blissymbol materials in Hebrew and disseminating information regarding alternative and augmentative communication in general, and Blissymbolics in particular, in Israel. Blissymbol materials are sold on a nonprofit basis through the Society. An annual newsletter is published. Membership is open to all interested persons.

Italy

ASSOCIAZIONE PER IL POTENZIAMENTO DELLA COMUNICAZIONE
Via Gozzano, 4
20130 Milano
Italy
(02) 266-6874

This Association was established in 1982 by a group of professionals belonging to different disciplines, with the purpose of evaluating, researching, and spreading communication systems and devices for nonspeaking people. Information is disseminated through a quarterly newsletter. The Association supports the following: training programs in the form of workshops; development, translation, and availability of communication aids; and consultation services to other professionals and assessment of nonspeaking people.

Japan

AITOKUEN
5-21 3-chome, Imabuku
Wakayama City, 641
Japan

This organization currently has several nonverbal handicapped children, who are using Blissymbolics and other augmentative communication systems. Clients manipulate Japanese characters and augmentative communication systems to the best of their ability.

TOKYO METROPOLITAN INSTITUTE OF GERONTOLOGY
c/o Dr. Sumiko Sasanuma
35-2 Sakae-Cho, Itabashi-ku
Tokyo 173
Japan

This organization works on many different augmentative communication systems for elderly and handicapped individuals.

Scotland

CALL CENTRE (COMMUNICATION AIDS FOR
LANGUAGE AND LEARNING)
Education Department, University of Edinburgh
4 Buccleuch Place
Edinburgh, EH8 9LW
Scotland
(031) 667-1438

This action research project covers various areas of communication aids for disabled learners. CALL offers (1) a resource center with a client assessment service, a specialized reference library, distribution of literature and software, and equipment loans; (2) research and development on a "smart" wheelchair for severely disabled, for assessment and development of control, training of mobility, and as a control device for communication/learning systems; (3) intensive case study work in schools and adult centers introducing and integrating communication/learning aids, giving technical support and staff development; (4) training — CALL does workshops with professionals involved with communication-impaired learners, and takes intern trainees.

SCOTTISH CENTRE FOR AUGMENTATIVE
COMMUNICATION SYSTEMS
Victoria Infirmary
Glasgow, G42
Scotland

The aims of the Centre are to increase the general awareness of the devices available to alleviate the problems of communication for the speech impaired. The Centre provides an assessment facility for speech-impaired patients referred from throughout Scotland, makes a recommendation for suitable communication aids, and, where appropriate, arranges subsequent follow-up. The Centre offers seminars, advice, and instruction to practicing speech therapists and other professional staff which will help them in selection and use of aids. The Centre has a display of communication aids and a data bank. Research and development of aids is also a focus of the Centre.

Sweden

ICTA INFORMATION CENTRE
Box 303
S-161 26 Bromma
Sweden

The ICTA Information Centre is a nonprofit centre collecting and disseminating information in the fields of technical aids, housing, and transportation for the disabled. It is operated by the Swedish Institute for the Handicapped and Rehabilitation International. The Centre issues the newsletter *ICTA Inform,* as well as other publications.

Switzerland

SWISS FOUNDATION FOR ELECTRONIC AIDS (FST)
CH-2002 Neuchatel (Swisse)
Cret-Taconnet 32
Case Postale 1755
Switzerland
(038) 24-67-57

The Swiss Foundation for Electronic Aids (FST) was founded by the Swiss Spastic Foundation and the Swiss Paraplegic Foundation in 1982. The main activities of FST are the application of electronic aids, as well as their development and adaptation, and research when available aids do not meet user needs. FST has created an augmentative communication aid called HECTOR, a universal infrared environmental control, which allows disabled persons the access to keyboards. FST also provides information, training, consulting, and assistance to disabled persons or specialized organizations.

United States

ACTIVATING CHILDREN THROUGH TECHNOLOGY (ACTT)
27 Horrabin Hall
Western Illinois University
Macomb, IL 61455
(309) 298-1014

ACTT provides a wide range of services relative to microcomputer use with children. Software programs are developed to fill identified needs, such as early single-switch activation. Sample publications are software reviews, a curriculum, and an outreach newsletter. Numerous computer training programs are also offered by the staff.

ALEXANDER GRAHAM BELL ASSOCIATION FOR THE DEAF
3417 Volta Place, N.W.
Washington, D C 20007
(202) 337-5220 (voice or TDD)

This organization includes professionals and parents concerned with providing services to the deaf. The group conducts information collection and dissemination, including personalized information to parents, access to the Volta Bureau Library, and numerous pamphlets and reprints. Publications include a journal, *The Volta Review*, a newsletter, *Newsounds Our Kids*, and an annual, *Monograph*. Several books are published each year by the organization, and it distributes other books. Several special interest sections have been organized, such as the International Parents Organization. The Association also serves as a leading advocate of oral education of the hearing impaired and engages in advocacy activities through its Children's Rights Program. A regular active membership including all benefits is $85 per year.

AMERICAN FOUNDATION FOR THE BLIND (AFB)
15 West 16th Street
New York, NY 10011
(212) 620-2000

Through six regional and national offices, AFB maintains a direct liaison with public and private institutions and agencies serving blind and visually impaired persons in the United States. There are national consultants in areas such as education, employment, aging, and rehabilitation, AFB manufactures, researches, develops and distributes consumer products, aids, and technology. AFB also publishes monographs, manuals, texts, information brochures, and periodicals, including the monthly *Journal of Visual Impairment and Blindness,* in print and, in some cases, in large type, recorded, and braille formats. The *Journal* is available at a cost of $25 for one year and contains major articles on subjects such as rehabilitation, psychology, medicine, legislation, lifestyle, and employment.

AMERICAN RADIO RELAY LEAGUE (ARRL)
225 Main Street
Newington, CT 06111
(203) 666-1541

This organization is concerned with providing services to amateur radio operators. This a binational, nonprofit, scientific, and experimental association which consists of over 140,000 members in the U.S. and Canada who are organized for the advancement of amateur radio. One of the many membership services of the ARRL is the ARRL Program for the Disabled. This program helps handicapped persons become amateur radio operators (hams) if they have a sincere interest. Prospective hams may receive the names of ham instructors in their area.

AMERICAN SPEECH-LANGUAGE-HEARING ASSOCIATION (ASHA)
10801 Rockville Pike
Rockville, MD 20852
(301) 897-5700

ASHA is the national professional organization for speech–language pathologists and audiologists. It is an accrediting agent for programs in speech–language pathology and a certifying agency for speech–language pathologists and audiologists, ASHA publishes three quarterly and one monthly journals, plus frequent monographs and reports. Numerous pamphlets are also available through this organization. ASHA members serve a wide range of communication-handicapped clients, in addition to the severely handicapped.

CLEARINGHOUSE ON THE HANDICAPPED
Office of Special Education and Rehabilitative Services
U.S. Department of Education
330 C Street, S.W.
Room 3132, Switzer Building
Washington, DC 20202
(202) 732-1245 or (202) 732-1244

The purpose of the clearinghouse is to respond to a wide range of inquiries from disabled persons, researchers, advocacy groups, and Federal, State, and local government agencies; to refer inquirers to Federal, national, state, and local information resources and services; and to provide information on government benefits and services for the handicapped. The Clearinghouse monitors legislation and other Federal activities concerning the disabled population.

CLOSING THE GAP
P. O. Box 68
Henderson, MN 56944
(612) 248-3294

This organization offers a bimonthly newsletter relative to the use of microcomputers in rehabilitation and special education. Information includes reviews of software and hardware, user comments, and articles. A database on hardware, software, publications, organizations, and practices/procedures is available for a fee. Presentations on a range of microcomputer topics are also offered.

COMMUNICATION OUTLOOK
Artificial Language Laboratory
405 Computer Center
Michigan State University
East Lansing, MI 48824-1042

This quarterly is an affiliate publication of the International Society of Augmentative and Alternative Communication (ISAAC). It covers areas of international interest such as review of current literature, new aids, conference notices, funding, reader viewpoints, and provides general articles and features regarding nonvocal communication. Subscriptions are available for $15 (U.S.) and $18 (overseas and Canada).

THE COUNCIL FOR EXCEPTIONAL CHILDREN
1920 Association Drive
Reston, VA 22091
(703) 620-3660

This is an umbrella organization for professionals serving handicapped or gifted children. Divisions exist within the organization, including Division for Children with Communication Disorders, Division on Physically Handicapped, Division on Mental Retardation. Each division publishes a journal and/or a newsletter, CEC also publishes several periodicals (*Exceptional Children, Teaching Exceptional Children,* and *Exceptional Child Education Resources)* and a variety of books, bibliographies, and nonprint media (e.g., films). Membership varies according to state (ranging from $37 to $53), with an additional fee for division membership.

COUNTERPOINT
Editorial Office
2150 Brisbane Avenue
Reno, NV 89503
(702) 747-7751

Subscriber Service
9618 Percussion Way
Vienna, VA 22180
(703) 281-3601

Counterpoint is sponsored by the National Association of State Directors of Special Education and is distributed four times during the school year to more than 100,000 recipients across the United States. In newspaper format, *Counterpoint* prints articles on various programs and practices in the United States, including information on communication disorders and programs for students with severe handicaps. *Counterpoint* also sponsors recognition programs entitled "Discover American Educators" and "Discover Exceptional Parents." A complimentary copy may be requested; the subscription rate is $36 per year ($45 overseas and Canada).

THE DISABLED CHALLENGER
Kissick's Consultant, Inc. (K.C.I.)
1615 South Fourth, Suite M-3210
Minneapolis, MN 55454

The Disabled Challenger is a quarterly newsletter published by K.C.I., and edited by Lake Kissick, who is "physically inconvenienced" by cerebral palsy. Lake sums up the purpose of the newsletter best. "In a world full of negativity, all of us need to deliberately seek out and plug into the uplifting influences wherever possible . . . . It is precisely in order to spread the positive attitude further that K.C.I. powered up the scene with an empathically positive newsletter." The first issue is free. The yearly subscription rate is $15 for four issues.

ERIC CLEARINGHOUSE ON HANDICAPPED AND GIFTED CHILDREN
The Council for Exceptional Children
1920 Association Drive
Reston, VA 22091

ERIC, The Educational Resources Information Center, consists of a network of 16 clearinghouses that gather literature in specialized fields of education. This clearinghouse abstracts and indexes literature for inclusion in ERIC reference publications, publishes a variety of materials, such as bibilographies, monographs and newsletters, conducts individualized computer searches of the ERIC database, and distributes information such as digests.

THE EXCEPTIONAL PARENT
605 Commonwealth Avenue
Boston, MA 02215
(617) 536-8961

The Exceptional Parent is a magazine for parents and professionals concerned with the care of disabled children and young adults. The subscription cost is $16 a year for eight issues. The Exceptional Parent Bookstore sells books of interest to readers concerned with the life of disabled children and young adults.

GALLAUDET UNIVERSITY
800 Florida Avenue, NE
Washington, DC 20002
1-800-672-6720 (voice or TTD)

Gallaudet serves individuals with hearing impairment in a number of ways, in addition to providing higher education for deaf individuals. Information concerning Cued Speech can be obtained from the Cued Speech Team in the Department of Audiology. A newsletter, *Cued Speech News,* is published quarterly by that group. The Gallaudet Bookstore offers a wide range of precollege outreacn materials including informational books on deafness and sign texts, dictionaries, and storybooks.

LINC RESOURCES, INC.
3857 North High Street
Columbus, OH 43214
(614) 263-5462

This organization offers a directory of specialized microcomputer software for persons with disabilities. Twenty categorical subsets of software reviews are also available for purchase (e.g., programs using speech synthesis, programs teaching readiness skills). Customized software searches can also be generated (e.g., single-switch software).

NATIONAL ASSOCIATION OF THE DEAF (NAD)
814 Thayer Avenue
Silver Spring, MD 20910

Individual membership of $20 per year entitles the member to a subscription to the monthly *Broadcaster,* as well as to the quarterly *Deaf American.* Requests for information and referral are welcome. The NAD is one of the largest publishers of books related to deafness.

NATIONAL ASSOCIATION OF THE
PHYSICALLY HANDICAPPED (NAPH)
76 Elm Street
London, OH 43140
(614) 852-1664

This association attempts to advance the social, economic, and physical welfare of physically handicapped adults. The organization focuses on encouraging legislation to benefit the physically handicapped, and on increasing public awareness. NAPH is run by members (handicapped and nonhandicapped) and supported by dues. NAPH publishes a national newsletter which is available to members or to nonmembers by subscription.

THE NATIONAL CENTER, EDUCATIONAL MEDIA, AND
MATERIALS FOR THE HANDICAPPED (NCEMMH)
The Ohio State University
College of Education
356 Arps Hall
1945 N. High Street
Columbus, OH 43210
(614) 292-8787

This organization offers training and other inservice support sessions designed and conducted to facilitate use of their products. Products include a variety of books and programs related to intervention with exceptional individuals. *The Directive Teacher,* a yearly magazine intended for teaching personnel, is available without charge in the United States. Each issue focuses on a major theme, such as language instruction.

THE NATIONAL EASTER SEAL SOCIETY (NESS)
2023 West Ogden Avenue
Chicago, IL 60612
(312) 243-8400/voice
(312) 243-8880/TDD

This organization provides direct services to persons with a variety of disabilities through its approximately 2,000 facilities and programs. NESS offers a variety of pamphlets, reprints, and other publications on topics such as attitudes, speech-language disorders, stroke, independent living, prevention, and recreation. A free catalog is available on request. A quarterly newsletter, *Computer-Disability News,* is published through the national office.

NATIONAL INFORMATION CENTER FOR HANDICAPPED
CHILDREN AND YOUTH (NICHCY)
P.O. Box 1492
Washington, DC 20013
(703) 522-3332

The National Information Center for Handicapped Children and Youth (NICHCY) is a free information service that assists parents, educators, caregivers, and others in ensuring that all children and youth with disabilities have a better opportunity to reach their fullest potential.

NATIONAL SOCIETY FOR CHILDREN AND
ADULTS WITH AUTISM (NSAC)
1234 Massachusetts Avenue, N.W.
Suite 1017
Washington, DC 20005
(202) 783-0125

This is a national advocacy center serving people with autism and their families. The organization provides information and referral on topics such as education and treatment programs and techniques; taxes, guardianship, and estate planning; and organizing for better community services. The yearly membership of $20 for individuals and $30 for families includes a subscription to *Advocate,* the NSAC newsletter. The NSAC mailorder bookstore sells numerous publications on the subject of autism.

SIBLINGS FOR SIGNIFICANT CHANGE
Room 808
823 United National Plaza
New York, NY 10017

Siblings for Significant Change is a division of Special Citizens Futures Unlimited, Inc. One of its major goals is to promote public awareness of the needs of the disabled and their families. It is designed to unite siblings of disabled individuals for the purposes of advocacy and sharing of information regarding handicapping conditions, and the effects of these conditions on family members.

SIBLING INFORMATION NETWORK
Department of Educational Psychology
Box U-64
The University of Connecticut
Storrs, CT 06268
(203) 486-4034

This organization was formed to serve as a bridge for sharing ideas, programs, research, or needs regarding siblings and families of people with handicaps. A quarterly *Sibling Information Network Newsletter* is published by this group.

THE ASSOCIATION FOR PERSONS WITH SEVERE HANDICAPS (TASH)
7010 Roosevelt Way N.E.
Seattle, WA 98115
(206) 523-8446

TASH is a nonprofit, membership-supported international organization concerned with issues of human dignity, education, and independence for individuals with physical handicaps and profound mental retardation. TASH is an advocate for comprehensive integrated education and habilitative services. It disseminates research findings and practical applications for education and habilitation, encourages the effective use and sharing of experience and expertise, and supports services that enable people with disabilities to participate fully in integrated community settings. TASH has several publications; the *TASH Newsletter* and *DC Update* (monthly) and a journal, *JASH* (quarterly).

TELEPHONE PIONEERS OF AMERICA
22 Cortland Street
New York, NY 10017
(212) 393-2512

This is a volunteer organization of telephone people throughout the United States and Canada. It comprises 99 chapters, which develop their own programs. Many chapters have developed special devices to aid the blind, hearing, speech, motion, and mentally disabled. A manual entitled *Helping the Handicapped — A Guide to Aids Developed by the Telephone Pioneers of America* is available at this address. The address of the chapter serving a region can be obtained by writing the address provided here.

TRACE RESEARCH AND DEVELOPMENT CENTER
S-151 Waisman Center
1500 Highland Avenue
Madison, WI 53706
(608) 262-6966

This organization is a research, development, and information resource center in the area of augmentative communication systems and computer access for severely handicapped persons. The group has five major programs: (1) a communication processes research program (e.g., word frequency and vocabulary studies); (2) a development and availability program (e.g., development of a Blissymbol Printing Communication Aid); (3) an information and resource program (e.g., Trace publication and reprint series); (4) a training and inservice program (e.g., "Where to begin" workshop series); and (5) a client services program (e.g., consultative service delivery program).

UNITED CEREBRAL PALSY ASSOCIATION (UCPA)
66 East 34th Street
New York, NY 10016
(212) 481-6300

UCPA programs and services have two major goals; the prevention of cerebral palsy, and meeting the needs of those who are affected by cerebral palsy, and their families.

Subject Index

Key: (f) indicates figure; (t) indicates table.

Notes

Notes

Notes